Spanish

Cassell's Colloquial Spanish

A HANDBOOK OF IDIOMATIC USAGE

Including Latin-American Spanish

Completely revised by A. Bryson Gerrard

Formerly *Beyond the Dictionary in Spanish*

COLLIER BOOKS
MACMILLAN PUBLISHING COMPANY
New York

Library of Congress Cataloging in Publication Data

Gerrard, A. Bryson (Arthur Bryson)
Cassell's Colloquial Spanish.

Reprint. Originally published: 3rd rev. ed.
London : Cassell ; New York : Macmillan, 1980
Includes index.
1. Spanish language—Usage—Dictionaries.
2. Spanish language—Dictionaries—English.
3. English language—Dictionaries—Spanish. I. Title.
[PC4445.G4 1984]   463'.21   84-21464
ISBN 0-02-079430-4

First edition 1953
Second (revised) edition 1972
Third (revised) edition 1980

10   9   8   7   6

Printed in the United States of America

Contents

Introduction

This book is intended as a supplement to—in domestic matters even a substitute for—the dictionary. A dictionary has, inevitably, several disadvantages:

(a) It is far too big for the pocket or the handbag.

(b) It contains vastly more words than are needed for everyday purposes.

(c) It cannot give much indication of the frequency, the nuances or the limitations of any given word; it simply lists all the possible equivalents and one needs guidance as to which will be the most appropriate.

The present book offers such guidance. It is important to know how common, or uncommon, a given word may be; whether it is 'literary' or stilted or slangy, what sort of image it evokes in the native mind, what type of context it is used in. Anyone looking up the Spanish for 'hole' will find *agujero*, *horado*, *orificio*, *cavidad*, *hueco*, *boquete*, *hoyo*, and possibly a number of others, some of which may be more closely defined. What he will not discover is that there is no one 'all-purpose' word for 'hole' in Spanish and so will not appreciate that the various words given will apply to different types of hole (*v.* **agujero**). Similarly, Spanish has no generic word for 'nut'; the dictionary will give you *nuez* but in fact this means 'walnut' (in Mexico: 'pecan nut'), and other nuts have different names (*v.* **nuez**).

Equally, Spanish has a large number of common words which have no exact counterpart in English and which we may omit to use for this reason. *Caber*, *cobrar*, *sacar*, *soltar* are examples of extremely common verbs whose use does not come easily unless one makes a special effort and I have therefore expatiated on these, even at the risk of repeating what is contained in many

7

grammar books. Correspondingly, words like 'wonder', 'involve', 'accidentally' are continually on Anglo-Saxon lips but have no one easy translation into Spanish (*v.* **preguntarse, envolver, accidente**). Another very common source of confusion is:

False Cognates, usually called False or Unreliable Friends ('Unreliable' means that the word may sometimes mean the same as in English and sometimes not). English has absorbed so much Latin into its vocabulary, either direct or via Norman French, that there is a multitude of words which, because they look almost alike, are assumed to mean the same, and dictionaries, here, can lead one astray. *Ilusión, decepción, comprometer, pretender, desgracia, contestar* are examples. *Decepción* is given 'deception' as one of its meanings in almost every dictionary I have ever seen but its real meaning is 'disappointment' and 'deception' is *engaño*. How many innocents, confronted with, say, *la pieza inmediata* would wonder what could be meant by 'the immediate piece' and fail to appreciate that it probably meant 'the adjoining room'? The total list of such words is enormous and they seem to me such an important way of transcending the dictionary that I included them whenever I came across them, even a few which are not in everyday use. In the First Edition I listed them in an Appendix, but it was a very short list. The Second Edition contained so many more that I came to doubt the usefulness of such a list, especially for the Unreliables, since one cannot indicate the meanings without repeating what is already in the main text, or else misleading in the very way that dictionaries do. I like to think this aspect of the book will be useful to quite advanced students, and even many teachers of Spanish, as well as translators and others.

There is another respect in which it can, I think, be useful to advanced students: it is above all a book on the *spoken* language, concerned with what natives spontaneously say when they are at home. A large number of students, although excellent on written work, do not have the opportunity of spending much time in a Spanish-speaking country nor, when they do get there, do they easily find their way into private houses since it is not the Hispanic custom to invite outsiders to their homes. In this respect the Hispanic world differs from the Anglo-Saxon and it means that much domestic talk and vocabulary, the sort of thing normally picked up in childhood, is less easily come by. Such advanced students will undoubtedly be able to 'get by' but—to repeat what I said in the First Edition—'The gap between the written word, as acquired from grammar books, and the living speech as spoken by a native, is not necessarily a wide one but an inordinate amount of time is often spent in crossing it and perhaps even more in not realizing that it is there to be crossed. It is all too easy for a person who has reached a point in his studies where he can understand and make himself understood with ease to imagine that he is doing splendidly, but most of us have met the fluent foreign student who says: "I am in England since five months; actually I go to the university where I assist at conferences", and we understand him so readily—or we think we do—that it would hardly occur to us to point out that there are five mistakes in that one sentence.' Any reader who fancies testing his own authenticity may here think up translations for the following:

'I wonder whether the milkman's been yet.'
'I originally met her by chance.'
'They brought everything except the kitchen sink.'
'I'll try it but it probably won't work.'
'He reckons the whole thing's a racket.'
'I'm not involved,'

and, having done so, now consult *preguntarse, casualidad, faltar, mejor, salir, concepto, allá, trampa, corresponder, éxito, margen* and see how he fared. It will give him a very sizeable idea of how useful this book is likely to be to him.

Many students who are excellent on written work are less ready with the tongue and one recalls Thurber's remark about the best cracks being made on the way home. One of the difficulties in speaking a language is to remember to use the right word *in time!* This is my justification for reiterating points which may well have been attended to in grammar books but need a little rubbing in. It is also a justification for the anecdotes and jokes. What is read with interest and amusement is more likely to be remembered. This brings me to the difficult question of:

'Four-letter' words. This is the spoken language with a vengeance but I hope no one will accuse me of merely following the current fashion: it was a nettle which had to be grasped for the simple reason that one man's meat is another man's poison; a word which is everyday in one country may be unspeakable in another. *Coger* is a famous case; in Spain it is almost as common as the English 'get'; in the River Plate region it is grossly indecent and is suspect in much of Latin America. *Pico*, *polla*, *tirar* and others are in a similar case; it is essential to warn readers of their dangers in certain countries. Here again dictionaries are inadequate. Some omit the words altogether, for prudish reasons, others include them (or some of them) but without sufficient indication of their level. Two of the best dictionaries, for example, give '*mear*—to urinate', but omit the fairly vital information that it is extremely vulgar; you would certainly not use it to a doctor.

I had more doubts about unmistakably 'taboo' words such as *joder* and *coño* but there is no doubt about their everydayness, especially in Spain, and I feel sure that readers ought to be warned. Mothers who find their children coming home from school using them need to appreciate what is going on and everyone likes to be aware of the social level of the people they meet. A man invited to the house who used such words in the presence of ladies might well be considered too insensitive to be desirable company but it is difficult to make enquiries about such matters and therefore useful to have a book where they can be looked up on the quiet without asking anybody.

A thornier problem was what English equivalents to give. In the past, prudishness in such matters has reigned supreme but since the 'break-through' in the 1960's it has been allowed that in a book about language, particularly spoken language, it is out of place. Taboo words, since they exist, must be squarely confronted and it is only by giving the stark Anglo-Saxon monosyllables that one can convey the full impact of their Spanish equivalents. I have no desire to shock, only to inform.

When writing a book of this sort one is either tormented by wondering who one's readers will be or else unjustifiably contented by having a particular audience in mind at a particular moment oblivious of the fact that it will be read by somebody quite different in quite a different mood. Much of the above may suggest that I have chiefly advanced students in mind and I therefore hasten to say that, for a good deal of the time, I have half-consciously assumed the opposite, viz.: that many readers, either by their newness to the country or by their not-very-precise recollection of what they learnt in class, will feel as ignorant as I often did myself. This book is addressed just as much to that numerous class who, for adventitious reasons—business, Diplomatic Corps, Peace Corps, retirement, tourism, etc.—find themselves in the Hispanic world before they have had time to do the language justice. Their attention is particularly drawn to the:

Special Vocabularies. These word-lists give, in

compact form, most of the vocabulary likely to be needed in the given situations in the various countries. The great majority of the words will be found in dictionaries, even if less conveniently, but lexicographers are not always expert in such matters and these lists—and indeed the whole book—have been compiled out of direct experience and with an eye to female readers as well as male.

Food. One cannot take a dictionary when one goes shopping, nor into a restaurant, yet many readers will want to know what the menu means. In this department regional variation can be considerable and the list is likely to be useful to the pure tourist who has hardly any knowledge of Spanish at all. Similar considerations apply to:

Cars. Most readers will possess one and not all will be willing to leave it to the tender mercies of the local garage, unable to discuss even minor technicalities with the garage man. Here, too, regional variation can be considerable and I know of no other book which pays as much attention to it.

Telephones. Without a knowledge of the local jargon, answering the telephone can be somewhat unnerving. One may expect a voice to say *¡Aló!* and be thoroughly disconcerted when it says *¡Bueno!* or *¡Dígame!* or *¡A ver!* Telephone operators are not renowned for tempering the wind to the shorn lamb and large amounts of expensive time can be wasted by failing to 'get the message' or to give it intelligibly.

Household Words. These are aimed at housewives who, even if they do not do the shopping themselves, will probably have servants and children to cope with and must give orders, understand recipes, deal with plumbers and the like, but I have cast the net wide enough to include the commoner tools—hammer, screwdriver, pliers, etc.—so that the average husband may well find it useful.

Office matters. Since a high percentage of those suddenly thrust into the Hispanic world have to work in offices, and are often secretaries, the usefulness of this list should be obvious and much of it, though it exists in up-to-date dictionaries, is not readily accessible there.

Courtesy. This did not appear in the First Edition but I feel it should have done. The idea was happily bethought in the other books of this series which were modelled on my original Spanish Edition and I was glad to follow the example. I was obliged, for reasons of space, to omit appendices for Playing Cards and Music from the Second Edition but they are admittedly less everyday and the jargon for both is very quickly acquired in practice. Two new appendices took their place, viz.:

Lectures, Conferences and Congresses. In these days of air travel there is considerable traffic in 'specialists' on a great variety of technical and scientific subjects but their specialism does not always include much knowledge of the language and these notes are aimed at supplying some of their more immediate wants.

Latin-American usage and pronunciation. This was entirely ignored in the First Edition for the simple reason that I knew nothing about it. I was glad to repair such a serious omission but, even so, have to confess to certain limitations. Contemporary circumstances made it impossible for me to visit Cuba and an intended visit to Puerto Rico was frustrated by a strike. Caribbean usage, therefore got, I fear, much shorter shrift than it deserves, though Venezuela, northern Colombia, Central America and, in some degree, Mexico, where I spent in all a good many months, are all to some extent Caribbean countries.

The Second Edition was nearly twice the size of the First, partly due to the inclusion of Latin-American usage but also to the addition of much basic material which would have gone into the First if I had had world enough and time then. Spanish is the most widely spoken language in the world after English and since it was an exceptionally rich one, even before the discovery of America, it is only to be expected that this particular handbook should be larger than the others of the series. It has been a major problem to keep it as small as it is and this accounts for many omissions which, I fear, may strike some readers.

Such reflections make me feel a little guilty about the erratic scattering of 'slang' words which I have included, since these, to people who know anything of the matter, will make a multitude of other words conspicuous by their absence; guiltier still at having expatiated at considerable length on words which, at the strictly utilitarian level, might have been dismissed in a sentence or even omitted altogether.

At this point I cling to another criterion established in the First Edition where I expressed the hope that 'the whole book, although primarily arranged as a dictionary, will be found more profitable when browsed in as a sort of bedside book than when merely consulted as a book of reference.' Correspondence received has made it clear that many have so browsed and it seems only fair —as well as good psychology—to provide them with a little comic relief. I like to think this may be not only amusing but will illuminate the Hispanic background. It may be presumptuous for me to tell young ladies how they ought to behave in certain circumstances (e.g. the entries under *piropo* and *puta*) but they will rarely have heard, as I so often have, the kinds of conversation that go on behind their backs. The Hispanic world is not dedicated to the proposition that all men—still less all women—are created equal and to go beyond the dictionary is also to enter the vast, and fascinating, terrain of values. Any good teacher knows that his main business is not so much to impart information as to stimulate, so that the pupil acquires an appetite to do the rest for himself. Knowledge is far too big to be contained within the narrow confines of a handbook—it is far too big altogether! —and the following pages are, inevitably, a personal selection.

The selection includes many words which are well within the dictionary but seem worth drawing attention to, since otherwise they may lurk there for years unsuspected. How many readers are conscious, for example, of that curious verb *holgar*, or *idear*, or of adjectives like *imprescindible* or *sumo*? The discovery of one such word can often stimulate towards the discovery of others, though they are sometimes included to ensure that a common English idiom, not easily translated, gets a mention in the Cross-Reference index.

In previous editions I invited readers to write to me, c/o the publishers, if they felt that any word had been unjustifiably omitted or inadequately handled. This produced so many rewarding letters that I have no hesitation in repeating the invitation. I am—at present— happy to be written to about any aspect which readers feel to be interesting or important, and will do my best to reply. It is useful to know, in such cases, whether the words were read, heard or overheard, as well as the type of person who used them. It is also always interesting to know how the reader came across this book itself in the first place.

Abingdon, 1980.   A. BRYSON GERRARD.

Acknowledgements

There is so much of the First Person in these pages that the reader may be led to think that it is all my own work. This is far from the truth and I record with gratitude the names of some of the more outstanding people whose brains I have mercilessly picked in order to write it.

For Peninsular Spanish, and in any case top of the list, is Dr. José de Heras. His knowledge of English puts mine of Spanish to shame. I must also record a debt to Sr. Antonio Campos of Alicante and Sr. Angel Villanueva of Zaragoza. Also on this side of the Atlantic are Mr. Robert Pring-Mill of St. Catherine's College, Oxford, and Mr. Eric Gover of Bexhill. In the Americas: Miss Estanislada Lesser and Sr. Gerardo Fernandez of Montevideo, also Mr. G. C. Pullen; Mrs. Conchita Plume, formerly of Lima; Mr. Clive Bashleigh, lately of Caracas; Sr. Rogelio García Mendoza of Mexico City and the late Mr. George Wright of New York.

Within my gratitude are many anonymous souls who never knew that their brains were being picked but who have nevertheless contributed, and sometimes valuably, to the contents of these pages.

Miscellaneous Notes

Pronunciation is not easily dealt with in writing but there are a few points which deserve to be stressed. Any language is murdered if it is spoken as though it were some other language, however closely related. Spanish is a very beautiful tongue and to speak it well is immensely rewarding. One's approach should therefore be not merely modest but admiring and appreciative. Some have a better gift of mimicry than others but an obviously sincere attempt to attain the subtleties and avoid crudities goes a long way, even as a gesture. Obviously this requires the most attentive listening and I therefore mention a few of the subtleties to listen out for (and practise on the quiet):

Keep your vowels pure. English has a far greater variety of vowel sounds and few of them are pure. We hear a complete difference between, say, 'sin' and 'seen', 'ham' and 'hum', 'cloak' and 'clock'—a difference lost on most Hispanics—but even our 'seen' is not as pure as their *sin*; their *u*'s will be smoother than our 'moon', and so on. Having mastered these highly distilled purities one then needs to bring them out in rapid succession. It requires an effort we are not used to making: *Casi todo* involves a lightning ah-ee-aw, but the effort is well worth it if one wants to sound convincing. Care should be taken, too, with repeated vowels, as in *Federico*. We are apt to pronounce it like 'Federation', i.e. making the second 'e' an 'ə' when it should be likewise 'e'.

The consonant b/v *needs to be cultivated.* I put the two together since Hispanics really make no difference between them. To our ears it often sounds as if the other letter were being used; *Valencia* sounds like *Balencia* and *Bilbao* like *Vilvao* but the real noise is something like mv:

Vale—mvully (approximately).

Other noises are too subtle to be usefully written about but a good approach is to imitate as one would when copying a regional speech in English. Most of us occasionally tell a funny story which involves imitating, say, a Texan or a Scotsman—or indeed a Britisher or an American—and one should not be put off because the imitation is not aimed at producing a laugh. We all sound funny to outsiders. If you want to get inside—and if you did not you would hardly be reading this book—do not be inhibited by 'funniness'; the better you mimic that noise the more authentic you will sound to insiders; you will be admired and be proud of it.

Spanish is very evenly accented and, well spoken, has few heavy stresses. It would seem to have been evolved by aristocratic gentlemen who believed above all in moderation and restraint, in not going to excess. History suggests that this ideal was not always realized in the matter of behaviour but it was, and is, for the language. Heavy stresses are 'out'. You must speak it 'trippingly on the tongue . . . use all gently . . . and beget a temperance that may give it smoothness' (*Hamlet* III, ii). This very smoothness is one of the things that makes it hard to understand in one's early stages; it is difficult to navigate in such a sea of monosyllables, especially for us of Germanic speech whose poetry is measured by weight rather than by prosody. We depend very much on heavy stresses and this is one of the things we have to unlearn. Spanish does it not by weight of voice so much as by word order and by the interpolation of (usually) monosyllables which would otherwise not have been expected. Examples are *lo*, *ni*, *que*, and *ya*; often, too, the interjection of the personal pronoun (not normally employed in Spanish or its precedent Latin).

To take the last first: 'I say', is *digo*; if you mean: '*I* say', then the Spanish is *digo yo*. Bringing the important word to the end is one device for achieving emphasis, though to some extent we do this in English too. Of the monosyllables, examples are: 'But you *are*, aren't you?'—*Pero lo eres ¿No?* and there is no particular stress on *eres*. Similarly: 'Well, that's *some*thing!—*Pues, ¡ya es algo!;* 'I *know* we shall have trouble over this'—*Ya veo que vamos a tener problemas.* It is the interpolation of the *ya* which does the trick; no use trying to accent the *vé* or shouting *Sé. Ni* applies to negative sentences: 'I hadn't a *cent* on me'—*No tenía ni un céntimo;* 'Don't you have a *radio* in this house?'—*¿No tienen ni un(a) radio? Que* is used where we might say: 'I'm telling you,' but often might not because simply accenting the word would serve. A thunderous 'YES!' is not infrequently uttered in the Anglo-Saxon world but no Hispanic could content himself with an equally formidable *¡SÍ!,* he would instinctively say *¡Que sí! ¿Qué?* is also used at the end of a sentence where we say: 'What about . . .?' at the beginning: 'What about *me*?'—*Y de mi ¿qué?* but note that an *Y* is slipped in at the beginning: 'What about the *work*ers?' —*¿Y los obreros? (v.* **que**).

At a less impassioned level Hispanics will often use terminology which we associate with the written word, e.g. *en cambio*—'whereas', 'on the other hand', but often equating with a mere 'but' plus an accented word: 'The British say *pave*ment but Americans say *side*walk'—*Los ingleses dicen 'pavement' pero en cambio los Americanos . . .* . People of quite humble education do this without thinking when, as so often, emphasis arises out of contrast. Perhaps more basic for contrast are the monosyllables *Sí* and *No*: '*We* do but *they* don't'—*Nosotros sí, pero ellos no.* If you had been asked to supply a suitable, shoutable translation of: 'Make *love*, not *war!*' would it have occurred to you to say *¡Guerra no! ¡Píldora sí!* as was done in some Latin-American student riots? And it will have been the *no* and *sí* which received the emphasis, not the nouns.

Where it is not so much a matter of contrast as of surprise at something unexpected then *hasta* or *incluso* (both to be translated as 'even') are likely: 'There must have been *forty* of them there!'—*¡Han debido estar hasta cuarenta!* Our: 'Even *dogs* do it', might well emerge in practice as: *'Dogs* do.' The former would probably be *Incluso/Hasta los perros lo hacen*; the latter, *Los perros, sí.*

Another method of singling out a word for special treatment is the use of the *Diminutive*: 'But she was such a *sweetie*!'—*¡Pero era tan bonita!* but here it is the sweetness, more than anything, which calls it forth. The Diminutive is much used to denote friendliness, kindliness or a desire to seem pleasant or to put things pleasantly. If a telephonist says *Espere un momento* this is the straightforward: 'Will you hang on a moment?' but if she says *Espere un momentito* she is being rather more cordial and polite about it. I remember once being stopped by a Civil Guard whilst driving in Spain some twenty years ago. He examined my papers as a matter of routine and then said *¡Muy solo va Vd.! ¡Solito!* In so far as this is translatable it would be something like: 'You're a lonely traveller! All by yourself!', but what it chiefly indicated was a friendly sympathy at my having to travel such distances on my own. I have since wondered whether he may have been fishing for a lift. On another occasion I gave a man a lift and as we were descending a series of hairpin bends he made some reference to *las curvitas estas*. It was a form of understatement, as they were very sharp curves, but he was clearly a trifle nervous of them and was trying to suggest, as nicely as he could, that I should take them gently. In Latin America the friendly camaraderie(?) of El Dorado has carried this even further; they use the Diminutive almost to excess. I recall asking for a beer in a Chilean bar and being confused for a moment as the barman seemed to be asking whether I wanted a brand called El Aita; what he was really asking was whether I wanted it *heladita*, i.e. 'chilled' (dim. of *helada*) but I doubt whether he was being especially friendly; I suspect it was simply habit.

The Diminutive is also a useful way of dealing with such words as 'rather', 'somewhat' and the suffix '-ish': *tempranito*—'fairly early', 'earlyish'; *cerquita*—'quite near', 'not very far', and there is one very common Double Diminutive you should know, viz.: *chiquitito*, double diminutive of *chico* and meaning: 'teeny-weeny', 'minute'. In short, understatement as well as cordiality rather calls for the diminutive.

Spanish does not greatly care for double consonants, especially when one of these is 's', and where it has them it nearly always has a vowel on each side to keep them well ventilated. The Italian for 'Spain' is *Spagna* but the Spanish: *España* and when speaking English Hispanics will often say 'an especial one' rather than 'a special one'. As for three consonants together, it gives them the horrors. The clot of consonants in words like 'stretched' or 'twelfth' looks to them as some Polish or Czechoslovakian words do to us, indeed it astonishes them that a word of eight letters can possibly be a monosyllable. Ask one of them to pronounce 'crisps'; it is almost a physical impossibility; he will say 'creeps' or 'crísapas'. The sound 'ks' is almost equally repugnant to their instincts and the very letter x, though it exists in Spanish, is named *équis*. X is usually pronounced like an s; *explosión* becomes almost *esplosión*, indeed this tendency has officially transformed many former double or treble consonants; the verb *mistificar* seems a False Friend since it looks like: 'to mystify', but originally it was *mixtificar*—'to mix up (deliberately)' and so 'to adulterate', or, figuratively 'to hoodwink', 'to equivocate'; it has nothing to do with 'mystery'. Similarly *destreza* looks like 'distress' but is in fact a corruption of the Latin *dexteritas* and still means 'dexterity'. Words beginning with the prefix 'trans' are tending to lose the 'n' and many have already lost it; *transcendencia* is now more often spelt *trascendencia; transladar* has officially become *trasladar* and *transducir* is down to *traducir*.

They are also not fond of final consonants, especially in words of foreign origin, e.g. *coñac* (cognac) which they invariably pronounce *coñá*. It is true they will accept the ones directed by their own language, i.e. words ending in J, L, N, R, S and Z but a final 'd', although authoritative, tends to get ignored, e.g. *Madrid* is pronounced *Madrí, Usted as Usté*, and if a word ends in any other letter than those mentioned, so much the worse for the letter; Dry Sack (the sherry) is called *Drisa; Closet* becomes *closé*. I recall being rather pleased with myself in Lima, Peru, when I was told that a place I wanted was next to the 'Café Mosa' and managed to work out (correctly, as it proved) that this was probably the 'Café Mozart'. Readers should be on the look-out for this sort of thing. You are quite likely to hear a very slithery *nuevayor*, spoken as though you will certainly understand it, and by now you will probably have guessed that it is none other than our old friend: 'New York'.

Clearly this smoothness in turn begets its own shapes and intonations and *intonation is always one of the most important things to master*, in any language, if one is going to be easily understood; especially for sudden remarks, made before they have had time to attune their ears to your way of speaking. Get the tune, the line of phrase, dead right and you will probably be understood even if your vowels and consonants are wrong; conversely, spend no end of time getting the latter right but say them with an intonation which no Hispanic would ever use and the chances are that he will wonder what on earth you are talking about.

Here there may be differences in British and American English, e.g. an incredulous: You gave it *away*? We both accent the *way* but, whereas the British start low on it and come up higher, Americans hit it high, come down and then go up again slightly. No Hispanic is likely to go gyrating around on one vowel sound in this way (unless he were taking off an Anglo-Saxon); he keeps the pitch pure in the same way as the sound; one vowel, one note; one monosyllable, one even pitch. It is sometimes half-reminiscent of the Doppler effect. The accented syllable will be high, the next abruptly lower: *¡Oiga! ¡Oye!* The *i* in *Oiga* and the *O* in *Oye* will be high but stable; the *ga* and the *ye* will be lower (not always so very much lower) but still stable. They rarely wobble on their notes though they may sometimes drag them along the straight line, e.g. *¡E-e-e-so es!*; we are quite likely to do a bit of fluctuation on our equivalent: 'Tha-a-a-t's it!' This is particularly so in Latin America and readers are referred to the Appendix at the end of this book.

Obviously intonation, above all things, cannot be taught via the written word but these notes may guide readers in the sort of thing to listen out for. The rest must be done by the direct method.

Abbreviations

Arg	Argentina
Ch	Chile
Co	Colombia
C/A	Central America (in a rather rough sense; it may sometimes include the Caribbean islands)
C/S	*Cono Sur*—Southern Cone, i.e. that part of South America south of the Brazilian bulge. For the purposes of this book it means Argentina, Chile and Uruguay
Ec	Ecuador
Gu ·	Guatemala
Ho	Honduras
L/A	Latin America (excluding Brazil)
Me	Mexico
Pe	Peru
P/R	Puerto Rico
R/P	River Plate—in theory Argentina and Uruguay but in practice chiefly Buenos Aires and Montevideo
S/A	South America, i.e. anywhere south of the Panama Canal (except Brazil)
Sp	Spain
Ur	Uruguay
Ve	Venezuela
Z/A	*Zona Andina*—Andean Zone. This region is centred on Peru but extends northwards to Ecuador and southern Colombia and southwards to Bolivia and sometimes Chile. It approximates to the old Inca empire but the Andes are such a huge barrier that it is little wonder if some usages are peculiar to the Pacific side

Spanish-English

A

abandonar. A little Unreliable; applied to persons it is likely to mean: 'to leave for good', or, 'to one's fate', but applied to things it can often mean simply: 'to leave'. You may see a picture in the paper of some official leaving the Ministry building and the caption will describe him as *abandonando el Ministerio* though he is merely going home after work.

abarrotes (m.pl.). The usual word for a 'grocery store' in Mexico; it is short for *tienda de abarrotes* and you may therefore hear it referred to as *la abarrotes*. In Spain the sign over such shops is likely to be *Ultramarinos* or, in Catalonia, *Colmado*. In S/A *Pulpería* is common. Another possibility is *Víveres* (provisions, victuals).

abono (m). A 'payment' of money but it suggests one of a series, a payment, as it were, to-the-good-of something or other. Its everyday meanings are therefore: (a) 'a subscription'; (b) 'a down payment', 'deposit', for something paid for by instalments or one of such instalments; *en abonos*—'by instalments' (*v.* also **enganche, plazo**); (c) 'a season-ticket'; (d) 'a discount' (i.e. to-the-good-of the customer for a change).

In an agricultural context it is used more metaphorically, to-the-good-of the soil, and so means 'fertilizer', 'manure'.

aborto (m). Unreliable to the point of Falsity; its primary meaning is simply 'miscarriage', though *malparto* is also used for this. Since abortions are illegal in many Hispanic countries 'an abortion' is likely to be called *un aborto criminal*.

absoluto. The normal adjective for 'absolute', but the adverb *absolutamente* is less used than the English 'absolutely'; natives, particularly Spaniards, tend to prefer *por completo* in conversation.

A very common phrase is *en absoluto* which looks as though it means 'absolutely' but in fact means 'absolutely *not*', 'not in the slightest', 'haven't a clue', etc. A context I remember is: Q. ¿*Sabes nadar?* A. *En absoluto*—Q. 'Can you swim?' A. 'Not a stroke.' A friend of mine once got it in reply to the question ¿*Sabe Vd. dónde vive el Señor . . .?* and was led to believe that *Absoluto* was the name of a street in Madrid. The proper use of both *por completo* and *en absoluto* will make your conversation sound a good deal more authentic.

29

abuela, -o. 'Grandmother, -father.' They sound innocuous enough but, surprisingly, are words to be steered clear of in Mexico, where they are very sensitive about mothers and grandmothers (*v.* note under **madre**). A Mexican is unlikely to talk about *mi abuela*. Just as *madre* is euphemized into *mamá* so is *abuela* into *abuelita* since a common, if vulgar, exclamation is *¡Tu abuela!* which is the equivalent of 'Balls!' 'Boloney!' (Readers are strongly discouraged from using this expression; they may give serious offence.) By extension *abuelo* becomes *abuelito* (and *padre—papá*) though they are not really sensitive about him.

aburrido. Means 'bored', but the illogical part is that it also means 'boring': *¡Qué película más aburrida!* 'What a boring film!'; *¡Qué aburrido!*—'How boring!' 'What a bore!' Similar considerations also apply to *divertido* and *entretenido* (*q.v.*).

abusar. Unreliable; it goes a long way with 'to abuse', in the sense of abusing somebody's kindness or confidence, or of going too far: *No abuses el tabaco*, 'Don't smoke too much'; *Espero que no esté abusando de su tiempo*, 'I hope I'm not taking too much of your time', and is much commoner than 'to abuse' in English, but it will not extend to pitching into somebody, using strong language, etc. For this you would have to use some such expression as *poner verde*: *Me puso verde*, 'He abused me roundly', 'he gave me a fearful talking to'. If it were a matter of using bad or insulting language then *insultar* or *injuriar* (*q.v.*).

In Mexico they have a curious adjective *abusado* to describe a very clever person, a fearful 'swot'/'grind'. I suppose the concept is of somebody who has gone too far in pursuing his studies.

a. de J. C. Those who read Spanish will no doubt be well aware that this stands for *antes de Jesucristo* and equates with our 'B.C.'. They may not know that, when speaking, or reading aloud, one simply says *antes de Cristo*. The same applies to *d. de J.C.* (i.e. 'A.D.') which is spoken *después de Cristo*.

acá, aquí. Both words mean 'here', as you know, and are almost interchangeable, but it seemed to me that *acá* was commoner in L/A and *aquí* in Spain. Perhaps worth reminding readers, too, that *acá* is always used when it follows *más, muy* or *tan*: e.g. when calling out instructions to someone who cannot see what he is doing: *¡Más acá!* 'More this way'; *No tan acá*, 'Not so far this way', are likely to be said to someone hanging a picture. *Muy acá* is uncommon but might occur, a little facetiously, in such a context; in L/A *acacito* is a more probable alternative for it.

acabar. Basically (and cognately) 'to achieve', and, as you probably know, the usual verb for handling our 'just': *Acabo de hacerlo*, 'I've just done it'. In Spain it is the normal verb for 'to finish': *está acabado*, 'the job's done'. In L/A they mostly seem to prefer *terminar*, perhaps because *acabar* is the usual word, in many countries, for to 'come' in the sexual sense. In Spain this is usually *correrse* (*q.v.*).

acaso. On the face of it 'in case', but often used as a substitute for 'perhaps', 'maybe': *Acaso venga,* 'Maybe he'll come.' The full phrase *por si acaso,* however, does mean: 'just in case', 'if by any chance', etc.: *Los guardaré por si acaso,* 'I'll keep them just in case.' Normally it would not take the subjunctive: *Por si acaso viene el Señor Fulano,* 'If by any chance Mr. So-&-So comes', but if the chances are more doubtful then the use of the subjunctive enhances the doubt: *Por si acaso viniera,* 'Just in case he might come'. You may also use the *por si* by itself: *Por si viene* (or *viniera*), 'In case he comes' (or 'should happen to come').

accesorio (m). 'Accessory', yes, but the English word has a much wider range, even extending to people, i.e. 'aiders and abettors', for which the Spanish would be *fautor* or *cómplice*. In a car context we tend to think of accessories almost as spare parts but in Spanish *accesorios* are strictly the optional 'extras'—radios, electric fans, etc.—which one may have added to one's car. 'Spare parts' are *repuestos* or, in Mexico, *refacciones.*

accidentado, accidental, accidentarse, accidente (m). All this is very unreliable terrain, geographically as well as linguistically, and perhaps the best concept is 'up-and-down', in a not-too-precise sense.

Accidentado, applied to a road, may mean either that the road is 'bumpy' in itself or that the land over which it runs goes 'up and down' (and the road therefore in-and-out, so that it will make a wiggly line on the map). Only the context can make clear which is intended. Applied to a person *accidentado* means that the person has 'suffered injury' in an accident and it is therefore the word for a 'casualty' in a hospital context. Applied to a car, in Venezuela, it means simply that the car has 'broken down' and *not* that it has been involved in an accident. In Mexico to break down is *estar descompuesto* and in Spain *tener una avería.* In the Z/A often *tener un pane* or *una pana.*

Accidente may be used of accidents in a general sense but the moment a particular crash, i.e. 'a collision', is involved, then the universal word which will occur to a Hispanic is *choque* (*q.v.*).

'Accidental' and 'accidentally' are words which we use a great deal in English where Spanish has other ways of handling the matter. One can readily perceive different shades of meaning between: 'by mistake', 'by chance', and 'involuntarily', but we tend to use 'accidentally' or 'by accident' to cover the lot. Spanish is more precise: 'I accidentally put salt in my coffee', *Me equivoqué y eché sal en el café*; 'I met him by accident', *Me lo encontré por casualidad*; 'I did it by accident', *Lo hice sin querer* (*v.* also **caer(se)**).

aceite (m). It is surprising to discover that so very Latin a language as Spanish does not use some cognate of the Latin *oleum* for 'oil' but the fact remains that this is an Arabic word. Strictly speaking it means 'olive oil' and it will be assumed that this is meant unless the context suggests some other sort when it can mean any kind of oil you please. In a car context it means 'lubricating oil'; in an artist's studio it could mean 'linseed oil' though, for 'oil painting', Latin is resorted to: *pintura al óleo.*

Aceitunas is the all-but-universal word for 'olives', though olive-trees are *olivos.* Rather disconcertingly, *olivas* is sometimes used for 'olives' in Andalusia (the most Arabic part of Spain!) and, conversely, in other parts of Spain, it is used for 'olive-trees' instead of *olivos.*

acepción (f). This word should be carefully distinguished from *aceptación*, otherwise you might be tempted to think it means 'acceptance'. In fact it means 'meaning', 'recognized usage': *Esta palabra tiene otra acepción,* 'This word has another meaning/can be used for another purpose.'

acera (f). The most usual word for 'sidewalk'/'pavement'. In the R/P they mostly say *vereda,* in Mexico *banqueta* (*q.v.*).

acholar(se). 'To blush', mostly used in the Z/A. The usual expression is *ponerse colorado* though in L/A one may hear *ruborizarse. Acholar* can be used actively for 'to embarrass'.

acostar(se). False; it does not mean 'to accost' but: 'to put to bed', or, reflexively; 'to go to bed', and is the usual word for this: *Está acostado,* 'He's gone to bed'. There is a subtle distinction between this and *está en cama; acostado* implies that he has 'gone to bed' in the normal way; *en cama* suggests unexpected circumstances, e.g. because he is ill, or very tired, 'in bed' at an unusual time of day.

'To accost' does not have a very precise equivalent in Spanish but *abordar* more or less conveys the meaning. *Dirigirse (a alguien)* is another possibility, provided the context is clear.

actual, -mente. False; it means 'present', 'current', 'going on at the moment': *Las circunstancias actuales,* 'The present circumstances'; *actualmente,* 'at the present time'; *actualidades,* 'current events', and will often mean a newsreel.

In so far as 'actually' can be translated it is something like *realmente, en realidad* or *efectivamente,* but you will often find you can do without it altogether. If you mean more precisely: 'in actual fact', then include the Article: *en la realidad, en la verdad,* or use *concretamente.*

acuerdo. *v.* **conforme.**

acusar. A little Unreliable; its commonest everyday use is in business letters where *acusamos recibo de . . .* is still a recognized way of saying 'we acknowledge receipt of . . .' though it is tending to be replaced by the simpler *hemos recibido . . .*

In legal contexts its Unreliability stems perhaps more from differences in legal procedure than in its basic meaning; *acusar a alguien de algo* would be understood throughout the Hispanic world as 'to charge somebody with something' but *denunciar* or *hacer/poner una denuncia* are more likely when one private individual makes an official accusation against another. In L/A newspapers I have seen *acusarse culpable de* for 'to plead guilty to' (it may have been a bit of journalese) and in Uruguay, for example, where they do not have public trials and judgement is passed on the strength of written documents, *acusar* has almost acquired the meaning of 'to summon', which elsewhere would be *citar*.

adecuado. False, in its way, since 'adequate' usually means 'sufficient' *but no more* and in some contexts and tones of voice can be very faint praise. *Adecuado* does not carry this stigma; it means: 'suitable', 'fitting', 'appropriate', 'satisfactory': *Lo más adecuado*, 'the most appropriate'; *muy adecuado*, 'very satisfactory'. 'Adequate' is probably best handled by *suficiente*, with its converse *deficiente* for 'inadequate'. A piece of L/A journalese coinage for the latter is *deficitario*.

adelantar(se), adelante. The basic concept is 'forward' and the commonest everyday meaning of *adelantar* is probably 'to overtake/pass' (in a car) though some countries use other words for this: *rebasar* (Mexico, Guatemala); *adelantarse* (Argentina); *ventajar* (Nicaragua). It is used a good deal meaning 'to promote', 'to advance', 'to make progress'. Care should be taken over the prepositions used: *adelantar a alguien*, 'to overtake somebody'; *adelantar en los estudios*, 'to make progress with one's studies'; *adelantar el proyecto* (no preposition), 'to push the project forward'. *Adelantar los acontecimientos* is a useful expression for, 'to anticipate', 'to take action in advance', and *No adelante los acontecimientos* would do quite well for 'Don't cross your bridges before you come to them'.

¡Adelante! means 'Go ahead!' and is the word needed for giving the green light in almost any kind of context; in a studio, for example, it would be the signal to start recording. It is the proper word for 'Come in!' when anyone knocks at your door and perhaps to be preferred to *¡Pase!* though you will often hear this. If you get it when asking directions it will mean 'Straight ahead', 'straight on'.

adicto(m). On the face of it 'addict', but in normal circumstances it is likely to mean simply a 'supporter' of a political party. In L/A it can extend to the supporter of, say, a football team: *Es adicto del Céltico*, 'He's a Celtic supporter', 'He's for Celtic'. In Spain they would say *Es del Céltico* or else use the rather slangy *hincha* for a supporter in this sense, i.e. 'a rooter'. Neither word is quite the same as 'fan' which suggests enthusiasm for the game as such rather than for a particular team or person and would be *un aficionado*: *Es aficionado al golf*, 'He's crazy about golf'. *Fan* is occasionally heard, usually in connection with 'pop' singers, but there is no saying how long it will last (*v.* also **partidario**).

A 'drug addict' usually has to be translated *toxicómano* or *morfinómano* (with no suggestion that the drug is necessarily morphine) but in these days you will find *drogadicto* creeping in, in places. I noticed *tóxico* in a Bogotá newspaper.

Afición hardly seems to warrant a separate entry so it may be worth remarking here that it may mean 'enthusiasm' or 'hobby' or else the (sporting) 'fraternity', i.e. those who are crazy about a given sport: *No está muy bien considerado por la afición*, 'He's not thought much of by the experts'.

adiós. Everyone knows that this is the Spanish for 'good-bye', but the word is used a great deal for *greeting* a person *in passing* when there is no question of stopping to exchange a word and when we should say 'Hello!' or 'Morning!' Your hall porter may well say it to you as you pass him in the *portal*. For a consideration of 'good-bye' problems, *v*. **hasta.**

advertir. False; it does not mean 'to advert', nor 'to avert', nor even 'to advertise'; it means 'to give notice or warning', to advise in the sense of 'to inform' (not 'to give advice', which is *aconsejar*). It is therefore common in business letters: *Les advertimos que . . .* 'We would advise you that', but it can often contain a note of warning: *Me advirtió que iban a cortar el teléfono*, 'He warned me that they were going to cut the telephone off'.

The warning may not necessarily be a very serious one. A common expression is: *Te/Le advierto que . . .* which is something like: 'Mind you . . .' or 'Do you realize that . . .'; it can be the introduction to a sentence that may warrant incredulity and so equate with 'Believe it or not but . . .'.

Advertencia is the noun and means more decidedly 'warning', since it is nearly always used to announce something unpleasant: *Le doy advertencia que . . .*, 'Mark my words . . .'. If you seriously want to warn then *dar advertencia* is more unmistakable (*v*. also **prevenir**).

aeromoza (f). An 'air-hostess', 'stewardess' in L/A. (*v*. also **azafata**).

aerobus (m). You might imagine that this is the 'bus' that takes you to the airport but in Venezuela it means a 'long-distance bus' of the more comfortable sort (*v*. **bus**).

afección (f). Unreliable; it equates with 'affection' only in the medical sense: *Una afección cardiaca*, 'a heart affection'. 'Affection' in the usual sense is *afecto*, 'feeling'; or, perhaps commoner, *cariño*: *Le tengo mucho afecto/cariño*, 'I'm very fond of him'.

afición, aficionado. *v*. **adicto.**

afilador (m), **afilar.** Afilar is 'to sharpen', and *un afilador is* 'a knife grinder'. This solitary traveller, in these days usually bicycle-borne, ranges the roads from Spain to some of the remotest parts of the Hispanic world and, by a most ancient tradition, announces his advent on Pan-pipes. When you hear this delirious skirl of wood-notes wild, it is the signal to hurry out into the street with anything that needs sharpening. The *afilador* usually makes an excellent job of it. He sets up business by the kerb and children cluster round to watch the sparks flying. My penknife is still satisfyingly sharp from the attentions of an Aztec *afilador* in Mexico City over a year ago (though his pipes were less Pan-like).

I regret to report that the verb *afilar* has suffered debasement in the C/S, above all in Chile where it has become the equivalent of *joder* in Spain. In the Argentine it means nothing worse than 'to flirt' but if they mean 'sharpen' in those parts they mostly use *aguzar*.

aftosa. Most dictionaries give 'aphthous'. Does that leave you any further on? Yet *fiebre aftosa* is a fairly everyday pair of words and in fact means 'foot-and-mouth disease'. The *fiebre* is often omitted so that *aftosa* becomes a feminine noun. *Glosopeda* is also used.

afueras (f.pl.). 'Outskirts', i.e. of a town or city. It is a useful word to bear in mind since it means no more than it says (*v.* **suburbio**).

agarrar. 'To grasp', 'seize', 'get hold of', 'catch', 'obtain', etc., in short most of the meanings that in Spain would be handled by that indispensable word *coger*. I did not often hear *agarrar* in Spain but it is very much an everyday word in the R/P since *coger* (*q.v.*) has gone into disrepute there and they must needs find something else. *Agarrar* covers the commonest meanings though *conseguir* will fit some of them. Visitors to Argentina and Uruguay are advised to make themselves familiar with it (*v.* also **atender**).

agonía (f). False; the Spanish does not mean 'great pain' but that last ultimate act 'which ends this strange, eventful history': the act of expiry and so: 'dying breath', 'last gasp', etc. *En su agonía*, 'on his death-bed'. There is no one Spanish word for 'agony'; you would have to say *un dolor horrible* or something of the sort. *Angustia* is not strong enough.

agradar. A perfectly proper verb for 'to please', and an alternative to *gustar*, but I confess I was barely aware of it until I went to Mexico where it is used a great deal: *¿Le agradó?* 'Did you like it?' 'Was it all right?' *Me agrada*, 'I like it'.

aguantar. 'To tolerate', 'support', 'put up with', 'stand'. It is a very useful verb but will probably not come easily unless you make yourself aware of it: *No lo puedo aguantar*, 'I can't stand it'; *Yo no voy a aguantar todas sus manías*, 'I'm not going to put up with all her fads and fancies' (*v.* also **soportar**).

aguamala, aguaviva (f). Both words mean 'jellyfish', *aguamala* being used in Mexico and the Caribbean and *aguaviva* in the R/P; in Spain they say *medusa*. It may not seem an everyday word but sea-bathing is a popular sport and jellyfish can occasionally be a most unpleasant hazard and the word for it most painfully impressed upon your consciousness, to say nothing of some part of your anatomy.

agujero (m). One of the words for 'hole'. Spanish does not have one general, all-purpose word for 'hole' and it is therefore important to distinguish between the various types and ensure that each has the right image in your mind. *Agujero* is essentially a 'roundish hole' and usually goes through something, e.g. the holes punched in a piece of paper, the holes of a colander, the hole in my bucket, but the word derives from *aguja* 'a needle', and so is basically the *type* of hole made by a needle, i.e. tubular, and so can apply to a hole bored into anything.

A 'hole in the ground', whether natural or deliberately dug, is normally *un hoyo* but if it were a carefully dug 'round hole', say for a telegraph pole, then it might be referred to as *un agujero*. The same applies to a hole in a putting green; it might be either. A hole in the road, a 'pot-hole', might be termed *un hoyo* if it did not have a special word of its own, viz. *un bache*. Readers who are car-borne might be wise to make a note of this (*v.* also **calamina**).

A 'hole in a garment', or other textile, is normally *un roto*, whether due to wear or tear, but if it had been cut or burnt, say, with a cigarette, then it would be *un agujero*. The 'eye' of a needle itself has a special name, viz. *ojo*, as in English.

Other words for hole, e.g. *orificio, cavidad, perforación* are fairly reliable cognates. *Hueco* would sometimes equate with 'hole' but it is really a 'hollow'. It would describe, say, a wood-pecker's nest, but would apply to the cavity, not to the orifice (*v.* **hueco**). The 'holes' of animals that burrow in the ground are usually *madrigueras* but a 'mouse-hole' is *una ratonera*. Anything that is 'eaten away inside', 'shot full of holes', is likely to be *horadado* or *agujereado*.

ahí. This is useful for an indeterminate 'here/there' when the exact location is not known or is unimportant: ¡*Ahí va*!, 'There it/he goes!'; ¡*Ahí viene*!, 'Here it/he comes!'. It has a slightly stronger sense of 'there': *Tiene que estar por ahí*, 'It must be somewhere around (there, where you are).' Metaphorically it can be useful for 'hence': *El clima es seco, de ahí se deduce que no haya prados naturales*, 'The climate is dry, hence the absence of natural pasture'.

ahorita. Obviously the Diminutive of *ahora* but it is so common in L/A that it seems to deserve a special entry. The best equation is probably 'right now', but within very narrow limits it can range through past, present and future according to context and the tense used with it and so can mean 'a moment ago', 'at the moment', or 'in a moment'. Waiters are rather fond of saying it when you enquire how much longer the meal is going to be in arriving.

ajuste (m). 'Adjustment', yes, but it can have some particular meanings. In Mexico, in a car context, it means a complete 'over-haul' of the engine and involves removing all the pistons for decarbonization, so beware of thinking it is a small matter. A mere 'tuning-up', or a delicate piece of 'phasing', would be *una afinación*.

al . . . (Infinitive). This is such a common, and idiomatic, way of expressing 'when' in Spanish that I feel it deserves a mention: *Al llegar Pepe*, 'When Pepe comes'. It will not, of course, do for 'when' meaning 'at what time', which has to be *cuándo* (or *a qué hora*): *Al comprar el billete/boleto no se olvide de preguntar cuándo sale el autobus*, 'When you buy the ticket don't forget to ask when the bus leaves'. It will often serve as a translation of our 'whenever' (*v.* **cualquier**).

alberca (f). The usual word for a 'swimming-pool' in *Mexico*, though *piscina*, the more universal word, will be understood there (*v.* also **pileta**).

alcance (m), **alcanzar.** Perfectly proper and universal words for 'reach', 'stretch', 'get as far as', but it is worth making yourself conscious of them as they are used a great deal, metaphorically as well as literally. *No está a mi alcance* means 'It's beyond my reach', in both senses and *No me alcanza la plata*, 'My funds won't stretch to it'. English-speakers often cast around for an equivalent for 'I can't afford it', and *No está a mi alcance* is as good as any. *¿A cuánto alcanza?* is often used in L/A for 'How much does it all come to?'

In a physical sense *alcanzar* can also mean 'to catch up with' (e.g. the person in front): *Me alcanzó en la Plaza de Armas*, 'He caught up with me in the Central Square'. *Alcanzar* is also useful for 'to manage to', 'to succeed in', or, negatively, 'to fail to': *No alcanzo a ver*, 'I can't quite see' (*v.* also **comprensivo, medias, lograr**).

alcoba (f). A minor False Friend; it does not mean 'alcove' but 'bedroom', but it implies a very humble, simple one and is rather associated with convents and monasteries or, in L/A, a 'roomette' in a sleeper. As you might guess, it comes from the Arabic, as it was the Moorish practice to set their beds in little alcoves in the wall.

algo. *v.* **poco.**

allá, allí. Means 'there', as you well know, but there are one or two rather idiomatic phrases which you ought to be aware of:
Más allá, 'further on'. You are likely to get this when asking the way. Counterparts of it are *No tan allá*, 'Not so far'; *Muy allá*, 'much further on', 'miles away' (*v.* also **adelante**). *Más allá de*, 'beyond'.

Hispanics have a way of slipping in an *allá* when indicating a place which in the context is felt as distant, as it were 'over there', e.g. *Allá en América/Europa* where we should simply say: 'In America/Europe', so that the trick does not come easily. Conversely there are moments when we instinctively want to say 'there' and Hispanics do not, notably on the telephone when enquiring whether a given person is 'there': Q. *¿Está Fulano?* A. *No. No está.* Q. 'Is So-&-So there?' A. 'No, he isn't here'. The habit of refraining from saying *¿Está Fulano allá?* also takes a little acquiring (*v.* **estar**).

A universal, and highly idiomatic, use of *allá* is when it is followed by a pronoun and means 'that's up to' . . . (him/her/them, etc.): *Allá ella*, 'that's up to her'; *allá ellos*, 'that's their headache'. You cannot, however, say *allá yo*, nor even *allí yo* for 'that's my business'; you would probably say *Eso me corresponde a mí* (v.**corresponder**).

almacén (m). A universal word for 'store', in the widest sense, i.e. not only a 'shop' but a 'storeroom', 'storehouse', 'warehouse' (*v.* also **depósito**). In some countries, e.g. Guatemala, *almacén* is particularly applied to shops selling textiles; in Spain, and some other countries (and usually in the plural), it means a 'department store'; in the R/P it implies a 'food-store/shop', but for any room or building where anything is stored *almacén* is universally understood.

almirez (m). 'Mortar', of the type which goes with a pestle (which is *la mano de almirez*). The whole thing is often called *el mortero*. They are quite common in Hispanic kitchens—and of course laboratories.

alquilar, -er (m). *Alquilar* is the proper, and universal, verb for 'to rent', whether a car, a TV set, an apartment or a house. *El alquiler* is the 'rent' you pay for it though *renta* is used colloquially. *Alquiler sin chófer*, 'drive yourself hire' (*v.* **renta**).

alrededor de . . . 'Around/about', 'round about' . . . *alrededor de las ocho*, 'around eight o'clock'; *Le espero alrededor del quince de julio*, 'I expect him round about the 15th of July' (*v.* also **así**). Anglo-Saxon readers should be aware that *alrededor de las ocho* means, in practice, 'not before nine' and they are unlikely to cause dismay if they arrive about ten. If you 'come most carefully upon your hour' you may cause acute embarrassment since nothing and nobody is ready for you. This is particularly true of invitations to drinks. Business appointments may be rather better timed but if you are in any doubt you should ask *¿Hora inglesa u hora mexicana/chilena?* etc. or else, if you are the hostess and want your guests to be punctual (more or less) assert *¡Hora inglesa!* Hispanics are fully conscious of this difference in practice and it not infrequently happens that they assume it will be *hora inglesa* while the Anglo-Saxons assume it will be *mexicana* so that it is the Mexicans who are punctual and the Anglo-Saxons embarrassed.

alterar. Unreliable to the point of Falsity; in so far as it means 'to alter' it implies a change for the worse, an interference with the ordinary course of things, hence 'to upset, disturb': *Le altera cualquier ruido*, 'The least little noise upsets him'; *Tiene la cara muy alterada*, 'He looks very upset/distraught'. *Alterarse*, 'to get upset/excited': *No te alteres*, 'Don't get excited', 'Take it easy'; *Siguió sin alterarse*, 'He went on unabashed/unmoved'. *Una alteración*, 'a disturbance'; . . . *del orden público*, 'a breach of the peace'; . . . *del pulso*, 'an irregularity of the pulse'.

'To alter', a more formal word for 'to change', is normally

cambiar: 'He's altered a lot', *Ha cambiado mucho*; 'I altered "bought" to "brought" ', *Corregí 'bought' y puse 'brought'*. 'An alteration', *una modificación/corrección*; 'Closed for alterations', *Cerrado por reformas*.

alto. 'High', or 'tall', yes, but in connection with the speaking voice it means 'loud', or 'aloud'. The usual expression for 'to read aloud' is *leer en alta voz. Leer en voz alta*, by bringing the *alta* to the end of the phrase, gives a slightly stronger suggestion of 'loud' but if you want to be sure about it say *en una voz muy alta*. Equally there does not seem to be an expression for 'reading to oneself'; the context normally makes it clear but if forced to describe it in some way you would probably say *leer para sí mismo* though this is not a stock phrase.

In connection with the singing voice *alto* does mean 'high', and not 'loud', which in such a context would be *fuerte*. Note, too, that it cannot be used to mean contralto. In my early days in Spain, interviewing ladies with a view to their singing in a choir, I innocently asked one *¿Puede cantar alto?* and was somewhat disconcerted when she replied *No muy alto*. (*Contralto*, incidentally, remains unchanged so that you talk about *las contraltos*, unless you are dealing with choirboys.)

Dar de alta is a curious phrase for 'to discharge from hospital'. Its origin is military; *dar de baja* is the military term for 'to report (some soldier) as a casualty', and *estar de alta* is 'to be back on duty'. *Bajas*, 'casualties' (dead or wounded). The phrases are freely used in conversation; *está de alta* might be said of someone who was 'up and about again' when he (or she) had merely recovered from a love affair. *¡Alto!* is also the military word for 'Halt!' and again may be borrowed for facetious civilian purposes.

altura (f). Strictly, 'height', but much used metaphorically, e.g. by taxi-drivers who will ask you *¿A qué altura quiere?* in connection with a given street, meaning 'What number?', i.e. 'How far along?' a phrase not readily translatable into Spanish. *¿Cómo de lejos?* will not do (*v.* **tan**).

amable. Not really 'amiable' so much as 'kind', even 'lovable': *Ha sido Vd. muy amable*—'You've been awfully kind' (v. COURTESY). 'Amiable' is better handled by *afable* or *de disposición amistosa*.

amarrar. 'To tie up', usually with string or rope. It implies both tying firmly and tying *to* something, the nautical 'lash'. The ordinary word for 'to tie up', without regard to special hazards, is *atar*.

In the C/S *amarrar* is used rather more freely, e.g. for tying shoe-laces or ties. I believe this originated from immigrants showing off sailors' vocabulary picked up on the long voyage over.

ambiente (m). 'Atmosphere', 'surroundings', and a very common word: *Este café tiene un ambiente muy agradable*, 'This café has a very nice atmosphere'; *El ambiente no es muy apropiado para el* *estudio*, 'The surroundings are (or climate of opinion is) not very conducive to study'. 'Atmosphere', in a meteorological sense, is *atmósfera*.

In the Z/A *ambiente* has come to mean a 'room', usually in advertisements for houses, apartments, etc., perhaps because it is usefully imprecise about the purpose of the room (*dormitorio*, *living*, *comedor*, etc.) and covers them all in a word (*v.* also **pieza**).

Ambientarse, 'to find one's way around', 'to acclimatize oneself' (*v.* also **ubicar(se)**).

amoroso. Bordering on the False since its Spanish meaning is far less particularized than the English 'amorous' which immediately suggests sex. In Spanish it simply means 'affectionate', 'kindly', very close to *cariñoso* (*q.v.*), though less common. For 'amorous', you would probably have to say *amativo* though this is even less common.

amplio. 'Ample' in a metaphorical sense, perhaps, but its main use is for 'wide, spacious, broad, roomy'. 'Ample' is better handled by *abundante*: 'They have ample funds', *Tienen fondos abundantes*; 'He's had ample time in which to do it', *Ha tenido tiempo de sobra para hacerlo*.

añadir. 'To add', and beware of thinking that it means 'to add up'; the two processes are remarkably different: to add something means to increase the quantity of what is already there, 'to add up' means to calculate the total of what is already there and Spanish uses quite a different word for this, viz. *sumar* (*q.v.*).

andar, ¡anda! *Andar* means, basically, 'to walk', 'to go on foot', and in Spain is the normal word for this: *Andaba por la calle*, 'He was walking down the street'; *Vino andando*, 'He came on foot'. In most of L/A *caminar* tends to be preferred for physical walking, though *andar* will always be understood if the context makes it clear. Everywhere, however, *andar* is used for metaphorical 'going': *¿Cómo le anda?* 'How are you getting on?' 'How's it going?' It provides several exclamatory phrases, ranging from the encouraging to the sarcastic or impatient, which are highly characteristic and can only be conveyed by describing the sort of occasion on which they would spontaneously be used.

¡Anda! is one very common exclamation, similar to *¡Vaya!* (*q.v.*) but whereas *¡Vaya!* contains a notion of disbelief or irritation *¡Anda!* has more the feeling of encouragement or admiration. If, for example, someone is being persuaded to sing, or tell a funny story or perform some other act of heroism then the ejaculation *¡Anda!* has the force of 'Come on!' 'Let's hear it!' 'Let's see you!' If, however, you are serving at ping-pong and fluff the service, particularly if you fluff it twice in succession, then the onlookers will exclaim *¡Anda!* as conveying 'Come on!' 'Get on with it!' (You yourself are likely to exclaim *¡Vaya!* indicating impatient disgust with yourself. Our own equivalents for this would probably be a muttered oath or else a tight-lipped nothing

at all. Hispanics are very articulate and their less formal games are usually well orchestrated with noisy comments from all concerned.)

¡Andale! belongs more to L/A and is seldom heard in Spain but it can be used a little like *¡Anda!* for animated encouragement. Both in Mexico and the R/P, however, one of its commonest uses is for a rather familiar 'Good-bye', similar to *Chao* (*q.v.*). In Mexico, in a different context and tone of voice, it can mean: 'Hurry up!', 'Get a move on!', 'Get cracking!' Yet another use in Mexico is 'That's it!', 'That's the one!' i.e. when you have been casting round for the right one and finally light on it. More universal for this is *¡Eso es!*

This by no means exhausts the list of the uses of *andar* but it will give you some idea of their nature and of the importance of tones of voice.

anexo. *v.* **extenso.**

anfitrión, -a. A curious, but universal, word for 'host', or 'hostess', on a social occasion. It derives from the Classical king of Thebes who gave splendid banquets. Amphitryon's chief claim to fame was in entertaining Jove unawares and having Hercules sired on his wife in consequence so perhaps it is worth adding that *anfitrión* does not contain any notion of cuckoldry.

angosto. The usual word for 'narrow' in L/A; in Spain they prefer *estrecho*. If you drive in the Andes you will occasionally come across a sign warning you of *Puente Angosto* and associations with the German *Angst* might well lead you to equate it in your mind with 'anxious bridge'. You may care to know that, if the bridge is on an incline—as it frequently is—the car going uphill has the right of way so that if you are going downhill it is for you to *ceder* (or *conceder*). If it is on a level then priority goes to the one that blinks its lights first.

anoche. Merely to remind you that this means 'last night', and not 'tonight', as one may all too readily feel. 'Tonight' is *esta noche*.

anteojos (m.pl.). 'Spectacles', 'eye-glasses'. This unsophisticated word is used throughout L/A. In Spain they say *gafas*.

antes. 'Before', or 'beforehand', as you know, but *de antes* is used a great deal adjectivally where we should say 'previous': *lo de antes*, 'the previous one'. In the Z/A you will hear *en antes*, 'in the past' (it will often sound like *enante*) and a not-too-recent past is implied (the recent past will probably be *antecito*); also, adjectivally, *de en antes* (sounding *denante*) (*v.* also **antualito**).

anticipación (f), **anticipar, anticipo** (m). *Anticipar* is a Good Friend provided you know what 'to anticipate' really means in English, viz. 'to take action beforehand,' 'to get in first': 'He anticipated my call by telephoning me first', *Se anticipó a mi llamada llamándome primero*. Journalists and others in recent decades, casting around for more high-falutin words, have fancied 'to anticipate' as an improvement on 'to expect' and have perverted it accordingly so that it is not uncommon to hear somebody say 'I don't anticipate', when they really mean 'I don't expect'. The Spanish has not been so perverted.

Anticipación is the noun which follows logically from this but it has to be regarded as False since 'anticipation' has already come to mean 'expectancy'. In Spanish it describes the interval between the action taken and the thing anticipated: *Hay que reservarlas con unos días de anticipación*, 'you have to reserve them several days in advance'. *Lo hice con mucha anticipación*, 'I did it well beforehand'. If you want 'I got it in anticipation of his visit', you would say *Lo conseguí en previsión de su visita*.

Anticipo means an 'advance payment' of almost any sort, whether on your salary or as a down payment for some major work to be undertaken.

antualito. A curious expression used in Colombia, and deriving, I suppose, from *antes*, meaning 'right now', 'at once', sometimes 'just now'.

anunciar, anuncio (m). Unreliable; both can mean 'announce' but in everyday contexts are likely to mean something else. The likeliest, for *anunciar*, is 'to advertise' and *los anuncios* means 'the ads', 'the commercials', on a TV programme, rather a different matter from the 'announcements' which suggests news.

Apart from such latter-day phenomena *un anuncio* may well be what we should call an 'announcement', but the essence of the Spanish is something broadcast to the great, wide world; you cannot, except perhaps facetiously, *anunciar* to a restricted audience. An 'announcement' to a limited group would be *un informe* and 'to announce', *informar* (*v*. also **denunciar, participar, divulgación**).

aparecer. *v*. **parecer.**

apartamento (m). A fairly universal word for 'apartment/flat' but in Mexico and Chile they say *departamento* and in Spain, colloquially, *piso*. The abbreviation for it is *Apto.*, which should be distinguished from *Aptdo.*, short for *Apartado*, 'P.O. Box'.

aparte, apartar. 'Apart', yes, but does greater service in Spanish than 'apart' in English. If, in a shop, you were asking for something to be wrapped separately, would it occur to you to say *¿Puede darme esto aparte?* 'Separate(ly)' is probably the best equivalent; *separadamente* rather suggests 'one by one', of a number of objects. *Tirada aparte*, 'offprint'.

In office circumstances, when dictating a letter, *punto y aparte* is the phrase you need for 'paragraph', though the 'paragraphs' themselves are called *párrafos*.

The verb *apartar* is an all-purpose one with a wide range of uses, both literal and metaphorical, viz. 'to separate, detach, put/set/take aside, push away, head off; segregate', etc.: *¡Apártate!*,

'Move over!', 'get away/off!' *Un apartado* (*de correos*), as you know, is a 'P.O. Box'; and *apartado*, applied to a person, is 'with-drawn', 'detached'. In short a verb worth making oneself aware of.

apellido (m). 'Surname'. *Nombre* rather implies a Christian name though it can be used as a general word for 'name'. In the normal way a Hispanic name is divided, like Gaul, into three parts: (a) *Nombre*, 'Christian name'; (b) *Primer apellido*, 'Surname'; (c) *Segundo apellido*, 'Mother's maiden name', and if you are indexing them you should do so under (b), e.g. *José Marqués Sainz* will normally be known as José Marqués and indexed under M. The Sainz may have to be added when you write to him; an eldest son often has the same Christian name as his father and it is important to indicate which is meant. In L/A (c) is often abbreviated to a mere initial. Universally, however, if (b) is a very common name, such as Jiménez or González, (c) is often added, even when speaking, to make clear which is meant. The poet Federico García Lorca is usually known as García Lorca, or even as Lorca, because García is so common. On the envelope the address will read: *Sr./Dr. D. José Marqués Sainz*; the *D.* is short for *Don*, an honorific title similar to 'Esq(uire)'.

Hispanic women will sometimes retain their maiden name, especially if they are rather proud of it. A woman named, say, Isabel López who marries a man named Campos will let herself be known as Isabel López de Campos.

As it is quite a common practice in the Anglo-Saxon world for surnames—often the mother's maiden name—to be given as 'Christian' names readers should be alert about their middle names. President Franklin Roosevelt might well have found himself indexed under Delano and President Truman—is the legend true?—as Harry S.! I have myself had trouble once or twice over Bryson (*v.* also **apodo**).

aperitivos (m.pl.). Something of a False Friend since to us it spells drinks while to a Spaniard—in the plural—it spells eats, i.e. the little 'snacks' that usually accompany drinks. You may well be asked, when you have just ordered *una combinación* (gin and vermouth) *¿Quiere aperitivos?* or *¿Algo de aperitivo?* and be rather disconcerted in consequence but the question really means: 'Do you want something to eat with it?'—almonds, olives, chips/crisps, shrimps/prawns, etc. Quite often you will be given *aperitivos* without being asked. Another, more colloquial, word for them is *tapas*. In the R/P the equivalent is often called *una preparación* though this implies rather more made-up little snacks. Other words are: *bocaditos* (*Pe*), *pasapalos* (*Ve*), *pasabocas* (*Co*), *bocas* (*C/A*), *botanas* (*Me*). The Hispanic tradition is well-entrenched.

apodo (m). 'Nick-name', and it would certainly apply to such light-hearted designations as Fatty, Sparks, Dusty, and the *Che* in Che Guevara, but dictionaries do not usually make clear that it is a perfectly proper word for a substitute name and so can be used in a law court for a false name, an alias. *Alias* is used adverbially, as in English, e.g. Mark Twain, alias Samuel Langhorne Clemens, but less often as a noun. *Mote* is another word for *apodo*.

apología (f). A Good Friend provided you equate it with 'apologia' and not 'apology', for which the Spanish is *una disculpa*, sometimes *una excusa*. 'To apologize', *disculparse*. *Apología* is not a common word in Spanish. They are more likely to use *defensa* or *justificación*.

apreciar, apreciable. *Apreciar* borders on the False; 'appreciate' can be used in different senses in English: 'to realize', 'to assess', 'to be grateful for'. *Apreciar* is nearest to the last of these but goes beyond it and means 'to like', 'to be fond of': *Aprecia mucho a los niños*, 'She's very fond of children'. It suggests a deep, though undemonstrative, enjoyment; more open and immediate enjoyment would call for *gustar*. Negatively, *No aprecia la vida*, 'He gets little pleasure out of life'.

The adjective *apreciable* is a little more Reliable: *Hay una diferencia apreciable*, 'There's an appreciable difference', but used more positively it can mean 'valuable': *Esto es una contribución apreciable*, 'This is a valuable contribution'.

Inapreciable is distinctly Unreliable as it can mean either too small or too great to be measured and in the latter case will then equate with 'invaluable', 'inestimable': *Esta información es inapreciable*, 'This information is invaluable'. Context usually makes the meaning clear.

Apreciable Señor and *Apreciado Señor* are common openings to letters (*v*. **querer**).

In L/A *apreciar* is sometimes used transitively to mean 'to add value to', 'to enhance', e.g. an advertisement: . . . *aprecia el hogar*, ' . . . adds lustre to the home'.

apretar. Perhaps you already know this verb for 'to compress', 'tighten', 'bear down on', 'hem in', etc., with metaphorical extensions to 'harass', 'breathe down one's neck', but if suddenly confronted with the necessity of saying 'Tie it up tight', would you remember to say *Apriételo*—? If not, then a mental note is indicated. 'Fasten your seat-belt', *Apriétese el cinturón* or *Ajuste el cinturón* (*v*. also **amarrar**).

aprobar, aprobación (f). Quite valid for 'approve' or 'approve of' but *aprobar* has the additional meaning of 'to pass' (an examination) and can be used either of the setters or the sitters: *Aprobé el examen*, 'I passed the exam'; *Me aprobaron*, 'They passed me'.

Failing an exam is *reprobar* in many parts of L/A but *suspender* in Spain. Even with this, however, you can say *suspendí* or *me suspendieron* for 'I failed'. *Sacar calabaza* is a slangy expression for 'to fail'. In the University of Mexico the official terms are *acreditado* and *no acreditado*.

aprovechar. Not necessarily a colloquial word but it is tremendously common and well worth bearing in mind as we have no one word which covers it. It means 'to avail oneself of', 'to take advantage of', 'to make the most of', 'to exploit': *Aproveche bien la oportunidad*, 'Make the most of the chance'. Quite often our equivalent would be simply 'to use': *Pues ya que lo hemos comprado hay que aprovecharlo*, 'Well, now that we've bought it we shall have to use it'. It can even mean 'to use up': *Podemos aprovechar el pollo haciendo croquetas*, 'We can use up the (rest of the) chicken by making croquettes'. 'To exploit', in the sense of taking advantage of, say, somebody's kindness, would be *aprovecharse de* (or *explotar*, *q. v.*) and *un aprovechado* is a person who always takes care to get the best of everything, pinches the best seat, the largest helping, etc.

For the conventional politenesses use *Buen provecho* or *Que le aproveche*, *v.* COURTESY.

apto. You may consider this False if you are thinking of 'apt to' but it is fairly Reliable for the strict adjective 'apt': *Fue una respuesta muy apta*, 'It was a very apt reply', though the best equation is probably 'suitable': *Esta película es apta para menores*, 'This film is suitable for children'. 'Fitting' or 'appropriate' are other equations. 'Apt to' is literally *con tendencia a*, but in practice another handling is likely to be needed: 'Only children are apt to be spoilt', *A los hijos únicos casi siempre se les miman*.

apuntar. False; it does not mean 'appoint' though it has quite a range of other meanings, including 'to aim at' (with a gun) and 'to prompt' (in a theatre) but its commonest everyday meaning is 'to jot down', 'to make a note of': *Voy a apuntar los números*, 'I'll just jot down the numbers'; *¿Quiere apuntar sus señas?*, 'Do you want to make a note of his address?' 'To appoint' is usually *nombrar* or *designar*.

apurar(se). *Apurar* is given in many dictionaries as 'to purify' but I have never met this in practice; 'to purify' is always *purificar* and *apurar*, applied to things, means 'to finish off' or 'to finish up': *Apuró hasta la última gota de su bebida*, 'He finished up his drink to the last drop'. Applied to persons it takes on the force of 'to pester', 'to worry', 'to hustle': *No me apures*, 'Don't hustle me'. In L/A *apurarse* is the commonest verb for 'to hurry' (Intrans.): *Tenemos que apurarnos*, 'We shall have to hurry'; *No te apures*, 'Don't hurry'. In Spain they normally use *darse prisa* for 'to hurry' (*v.* **prisa**), and *No te apures* is there more likely to mean 'Don't worry', but they do sometimes say *¡Apúrate!* having the force of 'Hurry up!' 'Get busy!' *Apresurarse* is another verb for 'to hurry'.

árbitro (m). 'Arbiter', yes, but in these days its commonest meaning is 'umpire', or 'referee'.

ardiente. Literally 'burning', 'ardent', but undertakers will advertise that they have *capillas ardientes* available (at a price). You might imagine that this means 'cremation chapels' but in fact it refers to candles and *capillas ardientes* are chapels where the coffin is surrounded by stately candlesticks burning sorrowfully until the final ceremony. They are normally reserved for people important enough to warrant a lying-in-state but money can buy them. People have written books on the 'American Way of Death' but Hispanic customs in these matters seem to me every bit as worthy of attention. In Uruguay I saw sumptuous black, rococo hearses which put many a gilded state coach to shame, yet Uruguay has been one of the most liberal and intellectually advanced countries in Latin America.

argumento (m). Unreliable; it means 'argument' only in the sense of 'plot' e.g. of a play or a novel. For us this is a little archaic but *argumento* is not archaic in Spanish: 'What was the film about?' *¿Cuál era el argumento de la película?* 'An argument' of the sort we usually mean is *una discusión* (*q.v.*). A more general word for the 'subject' of a book, play, etc. is *el tema*, i.e. 'the theme'.

armar. 'To arm' is certainly its traditional meaning but its every-day meaning is 'to put together', 'to assemble', 'to set up','to create' (one imagines that the mediaeval knight needed quite a bit of piecing together, with much help from his Sancho Panza, when arraying himself for battle). *Armar una exposición*, 'to hang an exhibition' (in Spain they prefer *montar* for this); *armar un rompecabezas*, 'to do a jigsaw puzzle'.

It is used a good deal metaphorically in such expressions as *armar un lío* (or *un jaleo*), 'to kick up a row', 'to make a fuss'. *Armar un escándalo* strictly means 'to create a scandal', but it is often lightly used to mean much the same thing (*v.* **escándalo**). *Una armaduría* is sometimes used in L/A for a 'car assembly works'.

Desarmar is equally worth remembering; it does not mean 'to demolish' but to take carefully to pieces with a view to putting together again, 'to dismantle'. Both words are candidates for your copy-book; neither comes easily unless you make yourself aware of them. The word for 'screwdriver', in L/A, is *desarmador*, i.e. literally, 'an un-doer'.

armario (m). 'Cupboard/closet'. It implies a separate piece of furniture, especially in L/A where a 'built-in cupboard' is usually *un closet* (pronounced *closé*) or, in the R/P, *un placard*. In Spain they have no special word for this; you would have to say *un armario empotrado*.

arrabal (m). *v.* **suburbio.**

arrancar, arranque (m). 'To start up' (a car) and 'self-starter', respectively. *Puesta en marcha* is another possibility for the latter; in Mexico simply *marcha*. In a racing context *arrancar* is the usual word for 'to start': *Arrancaron juntos*, 'They (all) got away together'.

arreglar, arreglo (m). *Arreglar* is an extremely common verb meaning 'to arrange', 'to put right', 'to settle', 'to fix': *está arreglado*, 'It's O.K.', 'I've fixed it', 'It's all arranged'; *¿Puede* *arreglarme esto?* 'Can you put this right for me?'

Un arreglo is the noun for 'an arrangement', whether a business one, a private one or a musical one. It is a very useful word.

arrendar, arrendatario, etc. *Arrendar* is a fairly universal verb for 'to rent', 'hire', 'lease', though less used in everyday speech than in documents. If you rent an apartment or house you are likely to find the word in your lease, in which case you will be the *arrendatario*, your 'landlord' the *arrendador* and the 'rent' *la arrienda* (or *renta*). In the R/P it is only used for large premises and suggests a house with grounds. In Chile it can be used for anything rented—cars, apartments, TV sets. For more everyday words, *v.* **alquiler, renta, dueño.**

arrojar. 'To throw', etc., but I discovered two meanings for it which are not given in most dictionaries, viz. 'to vomit', and 'to throw away'. The latter meaning is particularly likely to be found in L/A, perhaps because *tirar*, which is the usual word in Spain, has too many indecent connotations (*v.* **tirar**).

Arrojado, 'reckless'.

arroparse. Literally 'to add clothes to oneself', and therefore 'to wrap up warm': *Arrópese bien*, 'Mind you wrap up warm'. It can be applied to putting more clothes on the bed. *Abrigarse* is another word for 'to put warm clothes on', but it would only be used for going out in the cold, not at the bedside.

arrugar. 'To crease', but it implies unintentional creases. 'Creaseless', *inarrugable*. Spanish quite rightly distinguishes them from the 'crease' which is made deliberately, e.g. in trousers/pants and which is *una raya* (*q.v.*).

asado. *Asar* means 'to roast', and *asado*, on a menu, 'roasted', but in the beef-producing countries of the R/P it has become a noun, not only for 'a steak' but for a ceremony connected with house-building. In many countries putting the roof on a house calls for a celebration and in the Hispanic world it is usual to fix the branch of a tree to the top of the topmost ladder. In the R/P the *dueño* must then give *un asado* for his workmen. Passing a building under construction you may be surprised to see, among the débris on the ground floor, a fire of embers with several enormous steaks roasting thereon. This is *el asado* and as soon as the steaks are *à point* work ceases and the men assemble for the roast offering. *Un asado* can therefore mean 'a barbecue' and *un asado con cuero* is one where the unskinned beast is roasted whole; a special delicacy because of the additional flavour of singed hide.

así. 'Thus', yes, but 'thus' is not a common word in Anglo-Saxon conversation whereas *así* is tremendously common in Spanish, so other equivalents must be sought. One is 'like': *Así*, 'like this/that'; *algo así*, 'something like that'. 'How', or 'the way' are other possibilities: *así era*, 'That's the way it was'. 'That's what it was like'; *¿No es así?*, 'Isn't that right?', 'Isn't that how it is?' *Así* *de largo* (indicating how long with the hands), 'As long as that', '*So* long'. *Aun así* could equate with 'even then' provided the *así* referred to how something was done: *Intenté con el alicate pero aun así no me salió*, 'I tried with the pliers but even then I couldn't get it out'.

'So' is yet another possibility: *Así se lo dije*, 'I told him so', 'That's what I told him'. 'So' in the rough sense of 'therefore', a kind of summing-up, is usually *así que*: *Así que has dejado de fumar*, 'So you've given up smoking'; *Así que no queda nada*, 'So there's nothing left. (For weightier equivalents of this *v.* **modo, resultar, total**).

O así is a useful, colloquial way of saying 'approximately', 'thereabouts': *A las seis o así*, 'around six o'clock'; *tres kilómetros o así*, 'three kilometres or thereabouts' (*v.* also **alrededor**). *Así, así* (probably with some appropriate gesture such as a pursing of the lips) means 'So-so', 'not up to much', 'fair to middling'. (For *así como, v.* **como.**)

asistir, asistencia (f), **asistente,—a.** Unreliable terrain and *asistir*, in particular, may be regarded as False; it does not mean 'to assist' but: 'to be present at', 'to attend' (not attend *to, v.* **atender**): *Asistí a la ceremonia*, 'I was present at the ceremony' (and with no suggestion that I was taking part); *La Reina, asistida por su dama de compañía . . .* , 'The Queen, accompanied by her lady-in-waiting . . .' .

La asistencia usually means 'those attending', and is another word for 'audience': *¿Hubo mucha asistencia?*, 'Were there many people there? In a school or college context *la asistencia* means 'attendance' at classes but at the public level *Asistencia Pública*, perhaps owing partly to Anglo-Saxon influence, means 'Public Assistance'.

Asistente basically means 'attendant', but can be used of anyone present on a given occasion: *El Señor Fulano fue uno de los asistentes*, 'Mr. So-&-So was among those present'. It may, however, have more specialized meanings; in Spain *una asistenta* means a 'charwoman', a 'daily help' (perhaps calling her an 'attendant' spares her dignity), and in the army *un asistente* is a 'batman/orderly'.

aspiración (f). Unreliable; it may mean 'aspiration' but in a mechanical context 'suction': *una bomba aspiradora*, 'a suction pump'; *una aspiradora* within the home is 'a vacuum cleaner'. In a medical context *aspiración* is 'breathing in, inhalation'. Better words for 'aspiration, aspire' are *anhelo,-ar, ambición,-ar, ilusión,-ar* (*v.* **ilusión**).

asqueroso, asco. *Asco* is a noun meaning 'repugnance', 'disgust', but the exclamation *¡Qué asco!* is a common one and equates with 'How revolting!' *Asqueroso* is the adjective. Both are strong words (though not at all vulgar) but there are undoubtedly moments when one wants to describe something as 'filthy', 'vile', 'disgusting'. A more moderate word is *repugnante*.

astuto. Almost deserves to be called False since in English it mostly has a good image and in Spanish a bad one; *astuto* equates with 'crafty', 'cunning', 'sly'; 'astute' with *listo, inteligente*.

atender. Beware of thinking it means 'to attend'; it means 'to attend *to*', i.e. 'to pay attention', 'to look after', 'to see to'. In a shop or bank you are likely to be asked ¿*Le atienden a Vd.?* 'Are you being attended to?' 'To mind', in the sense of 'look after', is often quite a good equivalent, e.g. 'to mind the telephone', *atender el teléfono*. In the R/P *atender* extends to picking up the receiver, which in Spain would be *coger (q.v.)*. In Spain it would be quite normal to say *Sonó el teléfono y Concha lo cogió*, 'The telephone rang and Concha answered it'. It is entertaining to imagine the giggles and blushes which such a statement would provoke in the R/P; they would say *Sonó el teléfono y Concepción* (an unlikely name, however, in those parts) *lo atendió* (*v.* **concha**). *Atiende a lo tuyo* is almost a set phrase for 'Mind your own business'.

For 'to attend', in the sense of 'be present at', *v.* **asistir**.

atento. On the face of it, 'attentive', but it equates better with 'kind', 'thoughtful' 'helpful': *Él fue muy atento*, 'He was awfully kind'. In the past a common ending to business letters has been: *Su atto. afmo. y S.S.*, i.e. *Su atento, afectísimo y seguro servidor*, equating perhaps with 'Your most humble and obedient servant'. Readers may be glad to know *Atentamente* has virtually replaced this (*v.* **q.e.s.m.**).

atenuar,-uante. Usually the best equivalent of 'extenuate,-ing' (*v.* **extenuar**) but in a physical context it means 'to reduce, lessen, minimize': *Una pantalla para atenuar la luz*, 'A screen to lessen the glare'; or 'tone down': *Refirió lo sucedido, pero atenuándolo*, 'He reported the occurrence but toned it down'. Given a clear enough context it might serve for 'to understate'; *atenuación*, 'understatement', but this should not be regarded as a recognized equation.

atreverse. 'To venture', 'to dare'. Not, on the face of it, an everyday word but you may have moments when you are roused enough to want to exclaim 'How dare you?' and the Spanish is ¡*Cómo se atreve!*; ¡*No te atrevas!*, 'Don't you dare!'; ¡*Atrévete!*, 'You dare!' You should embark on these with caution, however. The language required when losing one's temper effectively has to be learnt in childhood and once you venture on it you are likely to be quickly outdone by a native, with serious risk of making a fool of yourself.

auspiciar. A verb much used in L/A for 'to sponsor', 'to invite under one's auspices': *Auspiciado por . . .* , 'Sponsored by . . .'. In Spain they use *patrocinar*.

auto (m). As a noun, 'car' (short for *automóvil, q.v.*), but it is also a likely solution of our prefix 'self-': *autoservicio*, 'self-service'; *autoprivación*, 'self-denial'; *autodisciplina*, 'self-discipline', etc. *Automóvil* is the adjective for 'self-propelled'.

autobus. *v.* **bus.**

automóvil (m). The universal official word for 'car', and the colloquial *auto* (*q.v.*) is also fairly widespread, indeed usual in the C/S. In Spain the usual word is *coche* and this is often used in Mexico and the R/P. In the remaining countries, from Peru round to the Caribbean, and to some extent in Mexico, the colloquial word is *carro*. Originally this meant a 'cart' or 'waggon' so if they really mean a 'waggon' they use *carreta* (*v.* also **coche**).

As an adjective *automóvil* means 'self-propelled'.

autopista (f). 'Motorway/turnpike/freeway' (*v.* also **cuota**).

autostop (m). 'Hitch-hike'. *Viajar en autostop*, 'To hitch one's way'. There is no particular expression for 'to thumb a lift' but *hacer el autostop* would no doubt be understood (*v.* also **aventón**).

aventón (m). Generally speaking there is no official Spanish word for a 'lift' of the sort you get in a car and 'Can I give you a lift?' has to be *¿Quiere que le lleve?* In Mexico, however, they do have *aventón* so there you could say *¿Quiere un aventón?* In Venezuela the Diminutive *colita* is a colloquial word for a 'lift'. I am told that this originated from requests to hang on to the tail of a mule in the Andes.

avería. *v.* **accidente.**

avisar, aviso(m). Unreliable; they only mean 'to advise', and 'advice', in the sense of 'to inform', and even then imply warning. *Avisar* is the normal verb for 'to warn', and *aviso* is the word for an official notice which lays down the law; no question of giving advice. In Spain *una conferencia con aviso* is a 'long-distance telephone call' where the correspondent is warned that the call will be coming through at a particular time.

'To advise', in the sense of give advice, is *aconsejar* ('advice', *consejo*). The normal verbs in business letters for 'to inform' are *informar* or *poner en conocimiento*, not *avisar*, unless you expressly want to imply a warning or lay down the law.

¡ay!. *v.* **¡oh!**

ayunas. If you do not know the expression *en ayunas*, or *en ayuno*, then you may be much mystified if you hit it unawares, though you do know that 'breakfast' is *desayuno*. It is the normal medical phrase for: 'with an empty stomach/fasting'. You may have to attend a clinic early in the morning 'without having eaten anything', *en ayunas*.

azafata (f). This curious Arabic word originally meant a 'lady-in-waiting' but it has been resurrected in modern Spanish for a hostess/stewardess, e.g. on a plane. In L/A she is usually called *una aeromoza*.

-azo,-aza. Having expatiated on the diminutive (*see p. 22*) I feel I should draw attention to its augmentative opposite, a suffix which has the force of 'great' or some similar extreme: *ojazos*, 'great big eyes'; *un cuchillazo*, 'a slash/gash with a knife'; *una melenaza*, 'a great mop of untidy hair'; a Great Dane would probably be referred to as *un perrazo*. Genders are more important than word-endings; *una manaza* is 'a dirty great hand/paw' despite the fact that *mano* ends in *o*. *Un manazas* is 'a ham-fisted fellow, a butter-fingers, a clumsy clot', etc.; *un bocazas*, 'a big-mouth'. A milder form of the augmentative is the suffix *-ón*: *montón*, *bombona*, etc.; *-azo* is more melodramatic: *un plumazo*, 'a stroke of the pen'. I hesitate to suggest private coinage, which is always a risky procedure, but if the occasion warrants a 'sensational' word it may be a solution of your problems.

B

b. In Spain called simply *bé* but in Mexico *bé grande* and in S/A *bé larga* (*v.* also **v** and **w**).

balda. *v.* **estante.**

balde (m). 'Bin', 'bucket', 'pail', and, as likely as not, 'dustbin/trash-can'. In Spain it half-suggests a bucket made of plastic, in L/A more likely of metal, but nowhere is the distinction hard and fast. *Cubo* means much the same but it is perhaps more likely to be made of metal. In so far as Spanish has a precise word for trash-can it is *basurero* or *balde de basura* but in this department people are not always precise; I have heard *caneca*, *tarro* and *totoma* (Colombia) all used for it though all these, basically, mean 'pot'. If the reader uses *cubo de basura* he/she is unlikely to go far wrong.

ballesta. *v.* **muelle.**

balón (m). By way of being False since it does not mean 'balloon', which is normally *globo*. Its commonest everyday meaning is 'football', though it can apply to any large ball of this type (*v.* **bola**). In snob circles, particularly in Buenos Aires, you may hear *balón* being used, following the French, for the all-but-spherical 'brandy glasses', though the normal word for these is *copas de coñac*.

banana (f). 'Banana', yes, but not in Spain, where bananas are *plátanos*. In L/A *plátanos* are the large, greener ones used in cooking (plantains).

In an electrical context *una banana* is a 'wander-plug'.

banda. *v.* **pista.**

baño (m). Strictly 'bath', and *el cuarto de baño* is the 'bathroom' but owing to the widespread practice in the Americas of putting all the items of bathroom furniture into the one room it has come to be a euphemism there for that item which is most often urgently needed. The British practice of segregating this article into a separate 'little room' and calling it a 'water-closet' has, it is true, resulted in the word 'closet' falling into disrepute in England (though not in Scotland) but it means that the word 'bathroom' has suffered much less there in this respect. *Baño* has, I fear, gone similarly downhill and the impatient reader, unable to wait for an answer, may be relieved to know that, yes, it means 'restroom/powder room/lav/loo/can/john', etc. and *¿Dónde está el baño?* is a question not likely to be misunderstood, at events in L/A. For ladies *el tocador (de señoras)*, *los aseos* or *el excusado* are possible euphemisms; in the R/P *la toilette* (pronouned *la tualé*).

Context, however, can cleanse the word and in a hotel *Dormitorio con baño* does mean with bath, or at all events shower, and 'I'm going to have a bath' is *Voy a tomar un baño*. If you wish to refer specifically to the 'bath-tub' in which you have it then the proper word is *bañera*, though *tina* is often used in L/A.

As to the titles used to designate the 'toilet' premises, the commonest are *Caballeros* and *Damas*. In Spain *servicios* is used to cover both and it is as well to know that this does not refer to the 'kitchen'. *Ellos* and *Ellas* are another possibility so be sure of your genders; the same applies to *Señores and Señoras*. Sometimes profile figures, representing a man and a woman respectively (or a pipe and a high-heeled shoe), will be fixed to the appropriate doors but modern fashions are such that these may occasionally need a little scrutiny first. In Mexico I struck a new one: *mingitorios*, and ladies had better be warned that these are usually for gentlemen only; L/A countries are sometimes wonderfully unfussed about the segregation of the sexes. In some of the cruder bars you will simply see *Baño*, even though this refers to some stinking jakes, at the back of the bar, àfter using which you feel you could almost do with a bath. If you get really far out, e.g. in some of the wilder parts of Colombia, then ladies are simply not catered for and the 'Gents' needs no title since it is in the corner for all to see. In such a desperate contingency ladies should try to have a word with the lady of the house; she may well be serving behind the bar, though a female friend who tried this was told *No hay baño, hay campo*. In Ecuador the word *baño* has suffered less degradation and really means a bath. There they usually designate the toilet premises as *el water* or *vater* and this is widely understood beyond Ecuador. *Urinarios* is also widespread, but will not usually apply to the Ladies.

It should be added that the above was valid for the 1970's. There is, however, a universal tendency for these euphemisms to become too clearly identified with what they stand for, e.g. 'closet', 'W.C.', 'lavatory', or *retrete*, which was acceptable in Spain a few decades ago but now sounds gross. Readers are therefore advised to keep their ears open.

banqueta (f), **banquete** (m). You should distinguish between these two words since it is only the second which is Reliable and means a 'banquet'. *Banqueta* is therefore False and normally means a rectangular stool (a three-legged circular stool, or a low stool, is likely to be *un taburete*), though it applies to any chair or bench which has no back. In the R/P I heard it used for the French '*banquette*', i.e. the ornamental 'side-table' or 'half-table' of which the straight half is flush with the wall. In Mexico and C/A *banqueta* means 'sidewalk/pavement' (*v.***acera**).

barba (f), **barbudo.** *Barba* means 'beard', of course, but a common, if slangy, expression in Mexico is *hacer la barba* (*a alguien*) which means 'to suck up (to somebody)', 'to toady', and *un barbero* is therefore 'a toady', 'an ingratiator'. *Barbudos*, 'bearded', has of recent years been applied to *guerrilleros* of the Che Guevara type.

barbaridad (f), **bárbaro.** Literally: 'barbarity' and 'barbarous' respectively but widely used colloquially where we should use such words as 'awful', 'frightful', 'terrible'. *Bárbaro* can mean both 'awful' and 'awfully good': *¡Qué bárbaro!* usually means 'How awful!', 'How maddening!' but *¡Bárbaro!* in an enthusiastic tone of voice, could well be said of a particularly good shot at, say, football: *Es un tío bárbaro*, 'He's a helluva fellow'.

About *barbaridad* there is less uncertainty; it is not used in a favourable sense and *¡Qué barbaridad!* means 'How frightful!', 'How infuriating!' Very common is *una barbaridad de* for 'an awful lot of': *Había una barbaridad de gente*, 'There was a fearful crowd'; *Tuve una barbaridad de cosas que hacer*, 'I had a terrible lot of things to do'. (*Montón* can also be used as a milder term for this.)

These expressions are perhaps commoner in Spain than in L/A but readers are referred to the entry under **brutal**.

barra (f). 'Bar', in almost every sense except the sort you have drinks *in* and even there it can apply to the bar you drink them *at*. Hardly any dictionary, however, gives one meaning which is everyday in Spain, viz. a 'loaf' of bread, of the type shaped something like a bar, e.g. French bread. Less everyday, perhaps, but common is 'stroke':/, on a typewriter. In the R/P *una barra* may mean a 'coterie' of friends, a 'clique', a 'gang'. In music it means 'bar-*line*', not the space between two bar lines, which is *compás*; 'double-bar' is *las barras*.

barraca (f). False; it does not mean 'barracks', but 'hut', 'cabin'. 'Barracks' is *cuartel* (Spain) or *caserna* (L/A) (*v.* also **suburbios**). The 'cabin' on a ship is *un camarote*.

barrio (m). It seems to suggest 'barrier' but this is *barrera*; *barrio* is universally a 'quarter' of a city, e.g. *el barrio latino*, 'the Latin quarter', but its image varies and in L/A it has a bad image (*v.* **suburbios**).

bastar. 'To suffice.' This is well attended to in most dictionaries but *¡Basta!*, 'That's enough!' and *bastante* for 'fairly', 'rather', 'pretty', etc. should certainly be at your tongue's tip: *bastante caro*, 'pretty dear'.

bazar (m). A curious False Friend with a variety of images; in Spain it means a 'toy-shop'; in the R/P a 'store' for household equipment (pots, pans, cutlery, glass, etc.); in Mexico a 'shop' for both buying and selling second-hand goods.

bestia (f). 'Beast', but Reliable only at the animal level when you mean no more than the beasts of the field. In the field of metaphor, and applied to humans, it involves contempt and equates with 'idiot', 'fool', 'twirp'. It is a favourite word for stigmatizing the driver of some other car.

bien. Strictly an adverb but there is an idiomatic use of it as an adjective: *de casa bien* is a stock phrase meaning 'of good family', 'from a well-to-do home'. It is often used where we might say 'well brought up', but it implies a certain amount of wealth in the background. *Bien* can also be a noun meaning 'property': *Con todos sus bienes*, 'with all his worldly goods'.

bife (m). Literally a 'beef' but in practice a boneless 'cutlet' or 'fillet', and not necessarily of beef; you can have *bifes de cerdo*, or any other animal. It is primarily an R/P word and you can also have *un bebi bife* but do not expect it to be particularly small. In Mexico a common misspelling is *bibsteak*.

billete (m). In all countries this means a 'banknote'. In Spain it also means a 'ticket' for a journey which, in L/A, is *un boleto*. Seldom does it mean a 'ticket' for some kind of performance (bullfights, theatres, concerts, etc.) for which the usual word is *entrada* (*q.v.*) though *boleto* is often used in the C/S (*v.* also **local**).

bizcocho (m). False, in its quiet way; it does not mean 'biscuit' but 'sponge-cake', or some similar kind of cake or bun: 'Biscuit' ('cookie', 'cracker') is *galleta*. In Mexico it is vulgarly used, usually in the Diminutive, for the female organ.

blanquillo (m). Diminutive of *blanco* and so 'white' but widely used as a noun for 'white' of egg. In Mexico and Guatemala it is often used as a euphemism for the eggs themselves since *huevos* (*q.v.*) may raise giggles. In the Z/A it means a 'white' peach, as opposed to a golden one.

bloque (m). A cylinder block in a car, but *v.* also **cuadra.**

boca (f). 'Mouth', as you know, but slangily used in Venezuela (possibly elsewhere) to mean 'face' (i.e. *cara*). In El Salvador I found it used for the snacks that automatically go with drinks (perhaps short for *bocadillos*) which were taken seriously enough to be listed on the wall and you were asked to specify (*v.* **bocadillo, aperitivos**).

bocacalle (f). Literally 'street-mouth', but used in Spain where we should say 'turning', 'intersection', especially in telling you the way. *La tercera bocacalle a la izquierda*, 'The third turning on the left'. In L/A this would be *Tres cuadras, a la izquierda* (*v*. also **esquina**).

bocadillo (m). Literally 'little bite', or 'mouthful', but it can mean different things in different countries and in Spain, for example, it usually requires quite a big bite since it there means the kind of 'sandwich' made with a roll, or French bread. In many countries this will be called *un sandwich* but where tourists are common and Northern tastes better known and catered for, e.g. Mexico, Peru and indeed Spain itself, *sandwich* tends to mean one of sliced bread, often toasted (*v*. **sandwich**).

In Peru, *bocaditos* means the little 'snacks' served at cocktail parties. In Venezuela *bocadillo* is a rich 'fruit-cake' made from crystallized fruits and their rinds, sold in packets wrapped in banana leaves.

bola (f). 'Ball', of the type which rolls (billiards, bowls, etc.) as opposed to *pelota* which is usually hit in the air and may bounce (baseball, fives, tennis, etc.). Another case for quick thinking (*v*. also **balón, huevos**).

bolero (m). No doubt many readers will think of Ravel's celebrated concert piece and certainly *bolero* is an old Spanish dance but in Mexico it is the usual word for a 'shoe-shine boy' and *bolear* is 'to polish'. The official description is *aseador* but *bolero* is far commoner in practice (*v*. **limpiabotas**). *Bolera* is a 'bowling-alley' in Spain.

boleto (m). The all-but-universal word for 'ticket', in L/A, though you will occasionally hear *tique* when they know they are dealing with a Gringo. It applies only to tickets for journeys (*v*. **billete**).

Boletaría, for 'ticket-office', I only came across in the C/S but I suppose it might occur elsewhere; more usual are *taquilla*, *ventanilla*.

boliche (m). Has a variety of meanings, mostly associated with ball games. In Mexico it means a 'bowling-alley'. In the R/P it is commonly used of 'the bar on the corner', the 'local', as it were. Since their cities are usually constructed rather on the French model there are bars on a high percentage of corners.

bolsa (f), **-o** (m). Both are universal words for 'bag', and suggest bags of some pliable material. *Bolsa* is fairly universal for a 'paper bag' and 'a packet of chips/crisps' would be *una bolsa de papas/patatas fritas*. It can also be a 'purse', but a lady's 'handbag', in which the purse goes, is usually *bolso*, as is a two-handled 'grip', usually made of textile or leather. Usage may vary in different countries as to gender. *Una bolsa de agua caliente*, 'a hot water bottle' (*guatero* in Chile). *La Bolsa* (capital B) is the 'Stock Exchange'.

bomba (f). Not only 'bomb' but 'pump', of any sort; *bombear*, 'to pump', especially in L/A (in Spain usually *dar aire*). In the R/P the diminutive *bombilla* is a 'drinking straw'. *Bombona*, in Spain, means a 'drum' of butane gas (*butano*), one of the commonest forms of heating.

bonito. A very common adjective, especially in Spain where it equates with 'nice' when applied to things and 'pretty' when applied to a woman. In L/A *lindo* is more likely for 'pretty'. As a noun *bonito* means the fish, a favourite for canning in *escabeche*.

boquilla (f). Diminutive of *boca* and in practice 'mouthpiece', usually the filter of a cigarette. If you ask for cigarettes *con* or *sin filtro* you will be universally understood but if a Mexican shoots at you the question *¿Quiere con boquillas?* (and they love shooting such questions at Gringos) you may be glad to know that he's asking 'Do you want them with filters?'

borracho. The universal word for 'drunk'; *un borracho*, 'a drunkard'; *una borrachera*, 'a boozing session/a binge'. As in English, there are innumerable other words to describe varying degrees of the state and some readers may be glad of a little guidance: *Ebrio* and *bebido* are somewhat formal words such as might be used in a court of law and so equating with 'intoxicated'. *Mareado*, literally 'sick', dizzy', is a polite euphemism such as a lady might use, since *borracho* might be resented by some, in the same way as 'drunk', as being too strong. *Tomado* is a similar euphemism and common in L/A. Slangy and facetious words are, of course, legion; I mention a few for entertainment: *curado* (*Ch*), *rascado* (*Ve*), *embriagado*, *copetón* (*Co*), *pluto* (*Ec*). Verbal phrases are also highly characteristic, e.g. *estar en una bomba* (*Pe*), *tener una merluza*, *coger una borrachera* (*Sp*). After which readers will be glad to know that 'sober' is *sereno*. For 'hangover' *v.* **resaca.**

borrar, borrador (m). *Borrar* is really 'to erase', 'to rub out', but it is often loosely used for 'to cross out', and even, by extension, 'to scribble'. The proper verb for to cross out is *tachar*, though I often heard *rayar* in L/A. *Borrador* is usually the 'draft' of a letter, i.e. that can be crossed out and altered but, again by extension, is often used for a 'scribbling-pad'.

botar. *v.* **tirar.**

bote (m). 'Can/tin', i.e. of preserved food. Another word for this is *lata* (*q.v.*). Generally speaking *lata* suggests a larger can than a *bote* but on the other hand *un bote* suggests a round can and *lata* a square one. You need not bother much about the difference; either will do. *Tarro* is sometimes used in Chile. In Mexico an 'empty', i.e. a bottle that is returnable, is called *un bote* (elsewhere *un casco* or *un envase*, *q.v.*).

botones (m). A 'buttons', i.e. 'messenger boy', 'bell hop'. It has a delightfully Victorian sound to our ears but the word survives in Hispanic hotels and business firms where the boy wears a uniform.

It is less likely to be used for the messenger boy in a shop.

bragas (f. pl.), **bragueta** (f). Perhaps it borders on the improper to take these words together but the second is in fact a diminutive of the first. *Bragas*, in everyday circumstances, means 'panties'; *bragueta* means 'flies', i.e. of pants/trousers. *Bragas* is also used of very small children's 'underpants'.

brincar. A perfectly good Castilian word for 'to jump', 'to leap', but I confess I was hardly conscious of it until I went to Mexico where it seems to be commoner than the usual *saltar*.

brindar, brindis (m). Probably the commonest meaning of this verb is 'to toast', in the sense of 'to drink the health of'; *Brindo por los amigos ausentes*, 'I drink the health of absent friends' (and note that the prepositon used is *por*). *Un brindis* is a 'toast' in this sense and readers who know about bullfights will be aware of *el brindis*—the dedication of the bull—after the *banderilleros* have withdrawn at the third trumpet. *Brindar* basically means 'to offer', 'to invite', but tends to be used when the invitation can hardly be declined, otherwise *convidar* or *invitar* are more likely: *Voy a brindarte un whisky* (no preposition) in L/A means 'Let me stand you a whisky', or 'Have a whisky on me', i.e. brooking no refusal. Journalists are rather fond of *brindar* as a more grandiose substitute for *invitar*. *Brindarse* is, however, quite common for 'to offer one's services': *Manolo se ha brindado a llevar a los niños con él*, 'Manolo has offered to take the children with him'.

brocha (f). 'Brush', yet another word for which there is no one Spanish equivalent; it depends on what sort of brush you mean. *Brocha* is the type of brush used daubingly, i.e. with a backwards and forwards pasting action, hence 'shaving brush', 'white-wash brush', 'paint brush'. Not, however, an artist's paint brush which is far too delicate an affair to be accused of daubing and has a special name, viz. *pincel*. Context is usually sufficient to indicate what sort of brush is intended but if you have to make it clear then *brocha de pintar, de afeitar*, etc. *Brocha gorda* suggests a 'brush' for house-painting and *pintor de brocha gorda* is almost a cliché for a deprecatory description of an artist who daubs.

The kind of brush that has stiff bristles, and is used scrubbingly, is *cepillo*, hence 'toothbrush', 'nailbrush', 'clothes brush', etc.; precise specification involves adding *de dientes, de uñas, de ropa*, etc. In a carpentry context, however, *un cepillo* is a small 'plane' usually of metal (the large, wooden type is *garlopa*). In an electrical context a 'dynamo brush' is regarded differently in different places; in much of L/A it is called *un cepillo* (sometimes *cepillo carbón*) but elsewhere, including Spain, it is seen as the third type of brush, viz. the type used sweepingly. This is *escoba* and in domestic contexts it means a '(long-handled) broom', but in electrical contexts, *escobilla* is a 'dynamo brush'. By and large *escoba* suggests softer bristles and action in one direction only.

A diminutive of *brocha*, viz. *brocheta*, is used for a 'skewer' or 'spit', and in the R/P *brocha* itself may be used for this.

broma (f). 'A joke', but more of the practical sort; a 'funny story' is *un chiste*. *En broma*, 'for fun'. *¿En serio o en broma?*, 'Seriously, or are you joking?' Common phrases are: *Una broma pesada*, 'a poor sort of joke'; *No estoy para bromas*, 'I'm not in a joking mood'.

bronce (m). Strictly: 'bronze', but used a good deal about the house for 'brass'. The proper word for brass is *latón* but this is less often heard and even in an orchestra 'the brass' is usually *el bronce*.

brusco. It equates well enough with 'brusque', but is used rather more, particularly, perhaps, as an equivalent of our 'rude': *¡Esa mujer fue tan brusca!*, 'That woman was so rude!' (*v.* also **ordinario**). In a car context, too, when it is a matter of stopping 'suddenly' or 'abruptly', *bruscamente* is the word most likely to occur to a Hispanic. 'Abrupt' is perhaps the best equivalent to bear in mind. *Abrupto* applied to places means 'rough', 'rugged', 'steep'.

brutal. 'Brutal', yes, but much used, particularly in L/A, for: 'terrific', 'smashing', or other extremes of lavish praise: *Una comida brutal*, 'A smashing meal'. *Salvaje* is also used in the same way. If you saw the words *LIQUIDACIÓN BRUTAL* or *LIQUIDACIÓN SALVAJE* as a newspaper headline, you might be forgiven for thinking that it referred to some brutal murder by Communists but it is much more likely to refer to a 'Sale' at the local store where the prices—one is invited to think—have been savagely slashed. In Guayaquil (Ecuador) I noticed *LIQUIDA-CIÓN INCENDIO* (*v.* also **liquidación**).

budín (m). A Hispanic attempt at 'pudding' but it is not much like a pudding; it is usually some sort of cake, or trifle.

buffet (m). Not only 'buffet' but also 'diner/restaurant car' on a train and a separate class on Peruvian railways. Elsewhere this is *comedor*, *coche comedor* or *coche restaurante*.

bulla (f). Another word I only became concious of when I went to L/A where it is probably a commoner word for 'noise' than *ruido*, the usual word in Spain. *Bullangueros* can mean, not only 'rioters', but 'a rowdy lot', 'noisy boys' in general.

bus (m). It would be nice if this were the universal word for 'bus', but it is not; terminology varies from country to country. Better, for overall purposes, is *autobús* but in several countries this means specifically 'long-distance', and then implies a more comfortable bus on which all seats are bookable (and more expensive, but buses generally are absurdly cheap and the impecunious young will certainly not disdain them). Since readers cannot be in more than one country at a time it may be worth giving a brief list, country-wise, for the words for 'bus' or 'coach':
Mexico: Usually *camión*, though *Pullmán* or *camión de primera clase* may be used for the more comfortable, air-conditioned ones.
Venezuela: Mostly *autobús* but the first-class ones are *aerobuses*.

Colombia: Mostly *bus* but *flota* is often used for 'long-distance'. 'A minibus' is *una buseta*. *Un micro* may be used of any bus.

Peru: *Ómnibus* for 'municipal'; *interprovincial* for 'long-distance'. *Un micro* (m) for 'a minibus'.

Chile: *Autobús* for 'long-distance'; municipal buses have various names of which the commonest are *una góndola* or *un(a) micro*. A minibus is often called *una liebre* (literally: 'a hare').

Bolivia: In the past public buses were called *colectivos* but now the usual word is *un micro* and *un colectivo* is more likely to mean 'a collective taxi' within city limits.

Argentina: 'Municipal buses' in Buenos Aires are usually *colectivos;* 'long-distance', *autobús.*

Uruguay: 'Municipal', *ómnibus;* 'long-distance', *autobús.*

Spain: *Autobús* may serve for all sorts but *autocar* is more usual for 'long-distance'.

Guatemala: *Camioneta.*

I apologize for lack of direct knowledge of other countries but I am reliably informed that in Cuba and in the Canaries a municipal bus is *una guagua* which, in the Z/A, means 'a baby' (*v.* also **colectivo**).

buscar. 'To look for', 'to seek', as you know, but it is used a great deal in contexts where we should use other words than these. Many of our equations involve the word 'find', particularly double-action verbs: 'go-(and)-find', 'try-and-find', and the treble-action: 'to fetch': *Voy a buscar algo para leer*, 'I'm going to find something to read'; *Voy a buscar un vaso de agua*, 'I'll just fetch a glass of water'; *Tenemos que buscar un suplente*, 'We must try and find a replacement'. (Obviously 'to try-and-find' is another way of putting 'to seek'.) Needless to say, our all-purpose 'get' will sometimes be the equation: *Voy a buscar algo de comer*, 'I'm going to get (or see if I can get) something to eat'. Yet another aspect of 'to seek', in modern circumstances, is 'to pick up (in a car)': *Fue a buscar a su mujer a la peluquería*, 'He's gone to pick his wife up at the hairdresser's'; *Le buscaremos a las ocho*, 'We'll come and get you at eight o'clock'.

C

caber. This curious verb is extremely common and idiomatic but hard to remember to use since we have no one equivalent verb, except 'to accommodate', which can hardly be called everyday. 'To have room for', is certainly one of the commonest equations for it: *No caben más que cuatro*. 'There's only room for four', and you should be clear in your mind that it does not really mean 'to fit', which is *convenir*. *Caber* implies less exact fitting. It can also be used metaphorically and *No cabe duda*, 'There's no doubt about it/Undoubtedly', should be learnt off pat. Having acquired such expressions you then have to remember that it can be used in the positive as well. A man trying to fit a last piece of luggage into an already full car and finding, to his satisfaction, that it will go in will probably say *¡Sí, cabe! Cabe la posibilidad*, 'There's always the chance'.

It is also a slightly irregular verb. You might hear a man, hoping to enter an already full car, say *¿Quepo yo?*, 'Is there room for me?', without immediately realizing that *quepo* is the First Person Singular Present Indicative.

cabrón (m). Included chiefly as a warning; literally 'he-goat' but it has extended from there to 'cuckold' and thence to 'bastard'. It is one of the strongest and rudest words in the Spanish vocabulary; to call a person *un cabrón* is the equivalent of calling him a bastard or worse. Say it to a man's face, in anger, and you are likely to have a fight on your hands; in some circumstances even a knife in your back.

This gives me the opportunity of warning readers who visit Mexico by car that they should refrain from uttering, on their car horns, that famous little musical phrase which perhaps can be represented in Morse – · · · – –/– –, as in Mexico it is indelibly associated with this word. Do it in the presence of a policeman and you risk the maximum fine which can be demanded on a summary basis. Passing a traffic light at red is far less of an offence. Since Mexicans are a lively race it is not uncommon for one car to start the phrase and for another, well tucked away in the jam, to complete it for him, both no doubt counting on the lights turning green before the cop has time to do anything about it. Gringos would be wiser to take no risks (*v*. also **madre**).

Una cabronada is the kind of dirty trick that might be played by a *cabrón* but it can be used of any particularly unpleasant circumstances, much as we (some of us) might use the word 'bastard' to describe the weather, but readers are earnestly recommended not to try. There is no easier way of making oneself sound ridiculous.

In Chile the word *cabro* (without the *n*) is a slangy but otherwise harmless word for 'guy', 'chap', 'fellow'.

cacharro (m), **cachilla** (f). *Cacharro* was originally a piece of coarse crockery but it has become a useful word for any old bit of junk: *¿Qué voy a hacer con el cacharro este?*, 'What am I going to do with this (ghastly) old thing?' It is often used of an 'ancient car', a 'jalopy'.

Cachilla also means an 'old car' in the R/P (and if any reader is interested in vintage T-model Fords, Chevrolets, Studebakers, etc. he is likely to find up-country Uruguay a happy hunting ground).

Una cacharrería, 'a crockery or hardware shop'. *Estar cachondo*, 'to feel randy'.

caer(se). 'To fall', yes, but its uses are so idiomatic, and therefore difficult to remember in time that I emphasize one or two points, even at the risk of repeating what is already in the better grammar books.

Apart from things like rain and snow, which fall naturally, *caer* tends to draw attention to the end result so that if you say *cayó* or *ha caído* you ought instinctively to add some indication of where the thing fell to; *caerse* is more concerned with the act of falling and where the thing fell from so that you can say *se cayó* without indicating what happened to it thereafter.

Caer is often used where we employ the verb 'to be': *Esta calle cae en las afueras*, 'That street's in the suburbs'; *Este pueblo cae muy lejos*, 'That village is a long way away'.

Caer en is much used metaphorically for 'to tumble to': *No caigo en lo que quieres decir*, 'I don't quite see what you mean'; *¡Ah, caigo!*, 'I get it!'

Dejar caer, literally, 'to let fall', is often assumed to be the Spanish for 'to drop', but in practice it usually means 'to drop deliberately'. 'To drop accidentally', is *caérsele* (*-me, -te, -nos*, etc.): *Se me cayó*, 'I dropped it'; *Se le ha caído el pañuelo*, 'You've dropped your handkerchief'. This is highly idiomatic and strong mental notes are indicated.

café (m). 'Coffee', obviously, but the word means different things to different people and Hispanics drink such a lot of it that they have quite a large vocabulary to cover the different types. Merely to ask for *un café* will leave the waiter confused as to which sort you want. In the more touristy places he may have learnt that most Anglo-Saxons like it with a little milk but a native, asking for this, will probably ask for *un cortado* (*capuchino* (*Me*), *marrón* (*Ve*)). *Café con leche* means coffee with a *lot* of milk but it is so much associated with breakfast that in some countries (Mexico, Colombia) it will often bring a bun with it. 'Black coffee' (the most popular with natives) is *un café solo* in Spain, *un exprés* in Mexico and *un cafecito* in most of L/A (though *un negro, -ito* (*Ve*), *tinto* (*Ec, Co*)). By and large coffee is much stronger in the Hispanic world than in the U.S. There is also a large vocabulary in the field of *cortados*; those 'stained' with milk, e.g. *manchado* (Andalusia), *quemado* (Santo Domingo), *pintado* (*Co, Ec*).

cagar. Many dictionaries face up to this but their desire to spare blushes makes them use such euphemisms as 'to go to stool', as if it were a word which might be used to a doctor. It most emphatically is not; it equates with 'to shit'. Vis-à-vis the doctor the appropriate euphemism is *hacer de vientre*.

A contemptuous expression, more or less equating with 'Bugger the . . .!'; is *¡Me cago en . . .!* for which a euphemism is *¡Mecachis!*

cajetilla (f). A widespread word for a 'pack(et)' of cigarettes. In Mexico it is *the* word. In most countries one asks for *un paquete de cigarros* but if you do so in Mexico they think you mean a 'carton' (elsewhere *cartón*). In the R/P you should avoid the word as it means a 'queer'.

calamina (f). 'Corrugated iron' in the Z/A. A road whose surface is 'corrugated' is there called *calaminada*. In most countries 'corrugated iron' is *hierro ondulado* or *chapa ondulada* (*v.* **chapa**), but *hojalata* is another word for 'tin' in a not-too-precise sense.

caldera (f). Strictly 'a boiler', but Spanish does not really have a word for 'kettle' and *caldera* is often used to denote one which has been imported (sometimes *caldero*). *Pava* may also be used, especially in Spain and Argentina; occasionally even *tetera* —strictly a 'tea-pot' (likewise an imported phenomenon) since this is similar in shape and devoted to the making of tea. In Mexico 'a kettle' is often called *una marmita*. A basic, self-explanatory word is *calienta-aguas*.

calentura (f). A widespread word for '(high) temperature', when you are ill, though it is perhaps more a layman's word; the doctor himself will probably say *fiebre*: ¿ *Tiene fiebre?*, 'Have you got a temperature?'; *Tengo una fiebre de . . . grados*, 'I've got a temperature of . . . degrees'.

Since most readers will have been brought up on Fahrenheit they may find it useful, even important, to know that 'normal', in Centigrade, is 37°. It is a great advantage to be able to tell the doctor how ill the baby really is, and indeed—if you have had to buy a Centigrade thermometer—to know yourself, so: $39°C = 102°F; 40°C = 104°F$ (near enough).

Calentura should be avoided in Chile since there *tener calentura* means 'to be on heat', rather a different matter. They say *temperatura*, but *fiebre* would be understood.

calificaciones (f. pl.), **calificar**. Best regarded as False; the commonest meaning of *calificar* is probably 'to mark' (exam papers etc.) and in an educational context *calificaciones* means simply 'marks'. (*Notas* may also be used.) When it is a matter of applying for a job 'qualifications' are usually *curriculum vitae*; 'What are his qualifications?', ¿ *Qué títulos tiene?* or for humbler jobs ¿ *Qué formación tiene?* (*v.* **formación, título**).

Calificar (*de*) is probably the commonest equivalent of 'to describe (as)': *Los críticos calificaron la obra de atrevida*, 'The critics described the work as daring'; *Sus amigos le calificaban de loco*, 'His friends called him crazy'. 'To qualify for a post', *tener los requisitos/títulos para un puesto*. 'To qualify' in the sense of 'to modify' is *modificar*, or 'to tone down', *suavizar*, *atenuar* (*q.v.*).

callarse. 'To keep silent', yes, but it is too strong for politeness; *Cálle(n)se, por favor*, 'Will you kindly keep quiet', would serve for a schoolmaster addressing children but the children themselves will say *¡Cállate!* 'Shut up!', to each other. If you want to pray silence in a polite way, say: *Se ruega (guardar) silencio.*

calma (f), **calmar, calmo.** The verb *calmar* is fairly Reliable for 'to calm'; it is the adjective *calmo* which is suspect since it rarely means 'calm'; in L/A it is applied to the land, not the sea, and means 'sterile', 'uncultivated' or 'lying fallow'. *Tierras calmas*, 'barren land'. (In Spain this would be *yermo*.) 'A calm sea' is *un mar en calma, calma* being a noun, but the expression has rather a nautical ring and, for a layman, the usual word for 'calm', whether of the sea or anything else, is *tranquilo* or *sereno*. 'Keep calm', *No te excites.*

cámara (f). By way of being False; it means 'chamber' in a very general sense but its commonest everyday meaning is probably 'inner-tube', i.e. of a tyre/tire. 'A camera' is usually referred to as *una máquina (q.v.)* though shops aimed at the tourist trade are tending to use *cámara* and Spanish may slowly capitulate to international usage. The legal expression 'heard in camera', is usually *(juicio) a puerta cerrada* or even *en secreto*. 'A chamber' as short for 'chamber pot' is *un orinal*.

camarero,-a. Originally a 'room-servant' but now the usual word for 'waiter' or 'waitress' in Spain. Countries vary in the word they use for this and a list, country-wise, may be of assistance:
Mexico, Colombia: *Mesero, -a* (*v.* also **copera**).
Venezuela : *Mesonero, -a.*
Z/A: *Mozo, -a. Mozo* means 'lad' and *buen mozo* is a common expression for 'good-looking'. *Moza* seemed to me less common for 'waitress' but perhaps this was because waitresses are less common than waiters.
R/P: *Garzón* (following the French, as so often). *Joven* is almost as common. 'Waitress' was usually *Señorita*, indeed this is common everywhere for a waitress when one is addressing her personally; the other words are more likely to be used in referring to her.
In most countries it is still possible to attract the waiter's attention with a sibilant *¡Pss!*; alternatively with a couple of resonant claps of the hands.

cambiar, cambio (m). 'Change', 'exchange', as you know, but one or two points deserve attention: *Cambiar opiniones* means not 'to change one's opinions', which is *cambiar de opinión*, but 'to exchange opinions', hence 'to discuss', 'to converse' (*v.* **discutir**).
En cambio—'whereas', 'while', 'on the other hand', etc. is very common and certainly warrants a mental note: *Los ingleses dicen 'Sorry' y en cambio los norteamericanos dicen 'Excuse me'*, 'The British say "Sorry" while Americans say "Excuse me".' Natives, at all levels of education, will slip in this sort of *en cambio* without thinking (*v.* page 21, Miscellaneous Notes).
Cambiarse can mean 'to change one's clothes', provided the

context makes it clear; otherwise you would add *de vestido*, *de traje*, etc. (*v.* also **mudarse**).

caminar. The usual L/A word for 'to walk', 'to go on foot': *Vine caminando*, 'I came on foot'. In Spain they use *andar* (*q.v*).

campana (f). 'Bell', but of the sort that has a clapper, e.g. church bell, as against an electric one which is *un timbre*. *Campanilla*, 'handbell'. It may not seem very everyday but in Mexico City you are likely to hear the wild ringing of a handbell almost daily. When I first heard it it seemed much too exigent for any sort of 'muffin-man' and in fact turned out to be the signal that the dust-cart/garbage-truck was approaching and meant, in effect, 'Bring out your dead!' Shortly afterwards you heard gossiping among the servant girls, on the corner of the street, as they waited by their dustbins/trash-cans for the *camión de la basura* to appear.

campo (m). If you imagine this means 'camp' then regard it as False; it usually means 'country', or 'countryside', and implies open country. *Una casa de campo*, 'A country house'. It also means 'field', both literally and metaphorically: *En el campo de la medicina*, 'In the field of medicine'. In Spain it applies to a 'sportsfield', e.g. *campo de futbol, de golf*, but in most of L/A this would be *una cancha* (*q.v*.). The Spanish for 'camp' is *campamento* and 'to go camping' (less common than in the north) *hacer camping, acampar* or, in L/A, sometimes *campear* (*v.* **carpa**).

caña (f). L/A its commonest meaning is probably 'sugar-cane', or else the rather rough rum made therefrom. In Spain it traditionally meant a small, tube-like 'glass' used for sherry but has since come to apply to a small glass of beer in cafés where beer is *de barril*, i.e. 'draught'.

canal (m). Yes, 'canal', or 'channel' (including a TV channel) but can also be used for the 'lane' of a highway and the 'track' on a tape, though *pista* is another possibility (*v.* **pista**).

canasta (f). It may mean the card game (I believe the original full name of this was *Canasta Uruguaya*) but basically it is a 'basket' made of wicker-work. I have remarked elsewhere that bags, bins, buckets and baskets are apt to be named by what they are made of rather than by what they are about to receive so that *una canasta* may be 'a shopping-bag' in Chile and 'a waste-paper basket' in Mexico (where a 'shopping bag' may be *canasto*). *Cesto, -a* is in much the same case. It is probably not worth bothering much about these little differences. Equate it with 'basket', bearing in mind that the 'wicker-work' may be quite pliable, and you should not go far wrong.

cancelar. Strictly 'to cancel', but also 'to write off', hence quite often simply 'to pay': *Quiero cancelar esta factura*, 'I want to pay this bill'. 'To cancel' is normally *anular*.

cancha (f). A 'field' or 'court' where games are played. In Spain it is mostly confined to a *pelota* 'court' but in L/A it extends to almost any sort of game: tennis, football, even golf. There is a slangy extension of it to mean 'expertise': *Tiene mucha cancha*, 'He's had lots of experience'.

cándido. Borders on the False; it means 'simple', 'innocent', 'guileless', and refers to a person's disposition. 'Candid' refers more to words and would usually be *franco* or *sincero*.

cantegriles. *v.* **suburbios.**

cantidad (f). 'Quantity', yes, but it is harder to remember that it also means 'amount', or 'sum', and usually suggests figures. It is, however, much used domestically where we should say 'lot': *¡Qué cantidad!* 'What a lot!' In short, an all-purpose, all-class word for Hispanics; 'quantity' is slightly more educated for us (*v.* also **suma**).

cara (f). Another fairly all-purpose word which has therefore far more applications than 'face' in English. Dictionaries mention most of them and I shall only duplicate their work by mentioning that the English equivalent is often 'side': *La otra cara de . . .* would be 'The other side of . . .' anything with two sides, e.g. coins, records, the moon: *Pon la otra cara*, 'Put the other side on'. Also the 'dial' of a clock is *cara* (in Spain more often *esfera*).

    Tener cara de is also very useful for 'to look as if': *Tiene cara de haberse pasado la noche de juerga*, 'He looks as if he'd spent a night on the tiles/town'.

carácter (m), **caracteres** (pl.). 'Character' (and note that it is accented on the second syllable in the Singular and the third in the Plural) but the phrase *de mucho carácter* is very commonly applied to persons and it does not contain the notion of anything comic or eccentric; it implies strong and good character: *Es una mujer de mucho carácter*, 'She's a very fine/brave/intelligent/strong-minded woman'. An amusing, or curious, character rather calls for *tío*, *caso* or *sujeto* (*q.v.*). 'Character' in the general sense of 'type', 'nature' is *índole* or *naturaleza*.

caradura (m or f). Literally 'hard-face', and meaning a brazenly unscrupulous person, a 'tough egg' who knows what he wants and is not over-fussy about the means of getting it. 'Brazen' is perhaps the best concept but bear in mind that it may also mean 'brazenness', and as a noun it is Feminine: *Este tío tiene una caradura imponente*, 'That fellow's got the cheek of the devil'; *¡Qué cara más dura!*, 'What a nerve!'

caramelo(s) (m). In the Singular it may be 'caramel' but in the Plural the chances are it will mean 'sweets/candies'.

cardenal (m). To be distinguished from *cardinal* which is an adjective and applies only to numbers. *Cardenal* is a noun and, in addition to the ecclesiastical dignitary, has the remarkably different meaning of 'bruise'. I believe the connecting link is 'purple'.

cariño (m), **cariñoso.** 'Affection', and 'affectionate', respectively but both very common and so likely to be needed when you want equivalents for 'to like/be fond of' (persons): *Le tengo mucho cariño*, 'I'm very fond of him/like him very much' (it can be used of someone of the same sex). *Ser cariñoso con*, is quite a good equivalent of 'to be nice to'. Both are equally valid for someone of the opposite sex. For fondness for things, *v.* **partidario, apreciar.**

carpa (f). In most of S/A it means 'a tent', which in Spain would be *una tienda* (*de campaña*). In Mexico it implies a 'marquee/big top' and an ordinary 'camping tent' is usually *una casa de campaña*, though *toldo* may also be used. Camping is less common in the Hispanic world, no doubt largely because so much of the terrain does not lend itself, being either too arid or too tropical (risk of snakes, etc.).

carpeta (f). A Friend of unusual Falsity since not only does it *not* mean 'carpet' but has very diverse meanings within the Hispanic world. In Spain and Mexico it means a 'file', of the sort used in offices. In Peru it means a 'desk' of the sort used in schools (elsewhere usually *pupitre*) and in Colombia it means a 'table-cloth' (ornamental; not for meals). I have also heard it used for a 'brief-case'.

A carpet, as you know, is *una alfombra*. 'Wall-to-wall carpet' is *hecha a medida*, 'made to measure', but is often referred to as *moqueta*, 'moquette' (carpet material).

carrera (f). Basically 'career', which is certainly one of its meanings but it has a wide scope in Spanish and you may perhaps identify it, in your mind, with things which, in some sense or other, go careering along. One meaning is 'race'; another is the 'ladder/run' in a stocking. In some (more or less) rectangular cities, such as Bogotá, it is used as Avenue is in New York, i.e. in contradistinction to *Calle*; *Carrera séptima con calle 75*, 'Seventh Avenue at 75th Street' (but I warn visitors to Bogotá not to put too implicit a faith in rectangularity; *Carrera Trece* starts life legitimately enough between 12 and 14 but it graduates to *Avenida Trece* and before it has finished its career is between *Calles* 20 and 21).

Carrera is not the universal word for 'avenue' nor is the numerical system always adhered to, even when official. A businessman's card, in Nicaragua, gave not only '*4 Av. No. 304*' (using *Avenida*) but added '*De la Hormiga de Oro 1/2 c. (media cuadra) a la Montaña*' in case the new system might cause confusion. Without the system addresses can sometimes be wonderfully descriptive, e.g. this from Costa Rica: '*De la primera entrada de los Dioses* (a new housing estate), *400 varas al sur y 60 al Oeste*'.

carretera (f). 'Highway', 'main road'. It suggests a main road across country; within city limits it would apply strictly to the 'roadway' as opposed to the sidewalk/pavement. Note that 'the road *to* (say) Valencia' is *La carretera de Valencia*; one is tempted to say *a Valencia*. Obviously the road from a place is the same as the road to it but the *de* should be understood adjectivally, i.e. the Valencia road.

carril. *v.* **pista.**

carro. *v.* **automóvil.**

carta (f). A false Friend whose acquaintance you usually make pretty early on. It means 'letter', and the usual word for a 'card', or 'postcard', is *tarjeta*. 'Card' in general is usually *cartón*, 'cardboard'. Formerly the word for 'playing cards' in Spain was *naipes* but this, though it survives, is tending to be replaced by *cartas*.
　　Cartilla, in Mexico, has acquired the particular meaning of 'identity card'.

cartel (m). A minor False Friend; to the Hispanic mind it has no connection with big business but means simply a 'poster', or any 'bill-board' put up for public display. *No figura en el cartel*, 'Doesn't appear in the credits/billing'.

cartera (f). Literally 'letter-case', but it has acquired more particularized meanings of which are commonest are 'wallet' (for money), and 'brief-case/attaché case'. In L./A it is often used for a lady's 'handbag'.

casco. *v.* **envase.**

caso (m). 'Case', obviously, but much used where we have other equivalents: *El caso es* (*que*), 'The fact is', 'The position is', 'The thing is'.
　　When, as so often happens, you want to say 'In *that* case', do not forget *En aquel caso* for a famous case that really happened.
　　Caso often means not so much 'case' as 'point' especially when used in the negative: *Ése no es el caso*, 'That's not the point'. We frequently say 'That's not the case', as a sort of polite euphemism for 'That's not true', and for this the Spanish is *Eso no es exacto/cierto/así* (*v.* **cierto**). If you mean 'That's not the point', a more unmistakable alternative is *No se trata de eso* (*v.* **tratar**). *No es el caso* should be distinguished from *no hace al caso* which means 'That doesn't help', 'That's beside the point'.
　　Hacer caso, 'to take notice', 'to pay attention', is very common and idiomatic: *Se lo dije pero no hizo caso*, 'I told him so but he didn't take any notice/didn't pay attention'. If the non-taking of notice is deliberate then you need *hacer caso omiso*, *desconocer* or *desoír* (*v.* also **ignorar**). If it means failure to realize, *v.* **cuenta.**
　　Un caso, applied to a human being, is a surprisingly Good little Friend; it means, rather facetiously, 'a case' for the doctor, the law or the psychiatrist: *Eres un caso*, 'You're a (proper) case'.

castellano (m). 'Castilian', obviously, but it is the all-but-universal word for the Spanish language. You are much more likely to be asked: *¿Habla Vd. castellano?* than *¿Habla Vd. español?* even in countries where their version of the language is far from good Castilian.

castigar. Our use of the verb 'castigate' is almost confined to lashing with the tongue or pen and for this *censurar* or *atacar* are perhaps more likely in Spanish. *Castigar* is the everyday word for 'to punish', and some sort of physical action is usually implied (though rarely lashes) but I have heard it used metaphorically (in L/A) in such phrases as: *¿Pues por qué nos castigan a nosotros?* 'Well, what are they taking it out of *us* for?'

castizo. This curious adjective derives from *casta*, 'caste' (in the Indian sense), and means, literally, 'castey', much as we derive 'classy' from class. I believe it was originally applied to the language spoken at Court and it has come to mean something like 'from the Royal Mint', 'authentic', 'pukka', 'the genuine article', particularly in connection with language, i.e. what a native really would say in given circumstances.

In particular connection with Madrid *castizo* has applied in the past to a way of speaking which, Madrid-wise, is supposed to represent the real McCoy, though it is far from being the kind of speech spoken at Court; it is rather in the same category as the original Cockney spoken in London, but now rapidly disappearing.

In Latin America they, too, have their words for what is uniquely theirs and they are fully conscious of what authentically belongs to the place. In the R/P the word is likely to be *criollo* (*q.v.*), sometimes *autóctono*; in Mexico perhaps more often *lugareño* (*q.v.*) or *típico* but these words are not confined to the use of language; in this matter they, too, are likely to say *castizo*.

casual, casualidad (f). *Casualidad* may be regarded as False as it simply means 'chance', or a 'chance happening', with no sense of an unfortunate accident: *Le encontré por casualidad*, 'I met him by chance'; *¡Qué casualidad!*, 'What a coincidence!', 'How extraordinary!' 'Casualties', in a war context, are likely to be referred to as *bajas* or *heridos* (wounded) and in a hospital as *accidentados* (*v.* **accidente**), the Casualty/Emergency Department being labelled *Emergencias* or *Urgencias*.

Casual is more Reliable for 'casual' provided this means strictly 'chance', e.g. 'a casual encounter', *un encuentro casual*, but it cannot be extended to mean negligent, off-hand, unconcerned, etc., which would have to be handled by *informal, vago* or *despreocupado* (*v.* preocuparse).

categoría (f). 'Category', certainly, but the adjectival phrase: *de categoría* is extremely common and is the usual way of saying 'high-ranking', 'high-class': *Es una persona de mucha categoría*, 'He's a V.I.P.', 'a Very-Important-Person', a 'big shot'.

catire. *v.* **rubio.**

católico. In the Hispanic world this almost invariably means 'Roman Catholic', and they do not use it with a small *c* to mean universal, e.g. a man of 'catholic' tastes. They do, however, have a slightly facetious use of it, negatively, to mean 'not very good': *El tiempo no fue muy católico*, 'The weather wasn't up to much', the inference presumably being that what isn't Catholic can't be good.

catre (m). 'Cot', yes, but it can be applied informally to any sort of 'bed' if you happen to feel somewhat deprecatory, much as we might say 'pad'. In nautical circumstances it is likely to mean a 'hammock'. In the R/P they are fond of *catrera*, used in the same way.

caucho (m). Strictly means: 'rubber', in the general sense, but is widely used in L/A for a 'tyre/tire'. It refers to the outer case/shoe. In the Z/A a word used for 'rubber' or 'elastic' is *jebe*.

caución (f). Almost deserves to be called False since, if a Hispanic means 'caution' he will almost always say *precaución*. *Caución* is a much more physical object; it means 'pledge', 'security', something deposited as a guarantee (*v.* also **enganche**). *Fianza* is another possibility.

cebarse, cebador (m). *Cebarse* is a common verb in *Mexico* for 'to go wrong', 'to turn out badly': *Se me cebó*, 'It didn't work', 'I didn't succeed'. *El cebador* in the R/P is a car 'choke'. A word for 'to turn out badly', much used in S/A, is *malograr(se)*.

cebiche (m). This, which you will often see on menus, particularly in the Z/A, is not a dish but a way of preparing it. A great many fish and *mariscos* are sprinkled with the juice of a lemon (sometimes orange) so that the flesh turns white and is then ready to eat. According to the locals the juice 'cooks' the fish. The exact recipe varies from country to country and each considers its own superior.

cédula (f). The Spanish spelling of 'schedule' but although it has a variety of meanings, e.g. 'warrant', its commonest everyday meaning is 'identity card', particularly in Colombia and Venezuela. Foreigners do not usually need them since their passports serve the same purpose. In Mexico an 'identity card' is usually *una cartilla*, in Spain *una carta de identidad*, in Chile *un carnet*.

celebrar. 'To celebrate', certainly, but one can celebrate something within the quietness of one's mind: *Celebro esta noticia*, 'I welcome this news'; *celebro su conducta*, 'I applaud his conduct': *Celebraba las ventajas de vivir en el campo*, 'He was singing the praises of country life'.

celeste. 'Celestial', yes, but it usually means 'light blue'. The musical instrument is *una celesta*.

cemento (m). Strictly 'cement', but roughly applied in L/A both to concrete and to glue. 'Glue' is properly *cola*.

cena, cenar. *v.* **comida.**

central. As an adjective: 'central', but it is also a noun (N.B. Feminine) for any 'central administrative building', including both a power station and a telephone exchange (*v.* also **conmutador**).

cepillo. *v.* **brocha.**

cerilla (f), **-o** (m). *Cerillas* is the usual word for 'matches', in Spain, and *cerillos* in Mexico, both so called as they are made of *cera*—wax. The technique of striking them without mishaps takes a little acquiring. Elsewhere matches are called *fósforos*, a word which will always be understood.

césped (m). The proper word for 'lawn', but other words are used in the various countries: *pasto* (*Me*, R/P), *prado* (Z/A), *grama* (*Ve*).

cesto. *v.* **canasta.**

chance (m or f). Taken from the English and means 'chance', in the sense of an 'opportunity', a 'break': *Dale un chance*, 'Give him a break'. Its use is at present confined to L/A; in Spain they would say *oportunidad*. It would seem to have been picked up in different countries independently as it is usually Masculine in the Caribbean and Feminine in the C/S.

chao. An importation from Italian (*Ciao*) but it has become a very general familiar word for 'Good-bye'. It is less common in Mexico and Spain but not unknown there.

chapa (f). The best basic concept is a 'metal plate' but one needs to cast one's net remarkably wide to catch some of its more particularized meanings. In the R/P *una chapa* may mean the 'number/licence plate' of a car but *chapas* may mean 'small change', the metal plates, in this case, being coins. In the R/P, too, they have the expression *poner la chapa* meaning 'to be best at everything' (presumably the image is that he will shortly be putting up a brass plate on his door). In Spain a common meaning is 'bottle-top', but *un chapista*, 'tinsmith', is the man who knocks out dents in car bodies. In the Z/A *una chapa* means one of those metal door-handles which have their key-hole in the middle so that the knob is simultaneously a handle and a lock. In Mexico it simply means a 'lock', without any implication of handle, though *cerradura* is a universally understood word for 'lock'.

Chapa ondulada is fairly widespread for 'corrugated iron', but *un techo de chapa*, 'a tin roof', is clear enough colloquially (*v.* **calamina**).

charla (f), **charlar.** Both these words, plus our own 'charlatan', come from an Italian word meaning 'to babble', 'to talk too much' (the quacks of the past were evidently notorious for their sales talk). *Charlar* is therefore a slightly derogatory word for 'to talk', hence 'to gas', 'gossip', 'chatter', 'natter', etc. but bear in mind that, when one speaks of one's own activities one may often use a self-deprecatory word out of modesty. *Una charla* therefore means 'a talk'; in private circumstances 'chat' or 'gossip', but in a university, simply an 'informal talk', something less august than a *conferencia* (*q.v.*) and on the radio it is becoming so identified with a 'short talk' that this may even be announced as *una charla* in advance. In the past it would have seemed a little insulting to the speaker to have introduced him with such a term.

chaval, -a. A common colloquial word in L/A for 'child,' perhaps 'kid'. There are many other such words: *chamaco, -a* (*Me*), *pibe* (*R/P*), *patojo, -a* (*Gu*), *nene* (*R/P*, Spain), *guambito* (*Co*) (*v.* also **guagua**).

chévere. A common word for 'smashing', 'terrific', 'fabulous', etc. in the Caribbean region. I am told that it originated in a Cuban song title.

chavija. *v.* **enchufe.**

chicha (f). Originally an Amerindian drink made from the fermentation of maize chewed in the mouth and still so made in really up-country Andean places but although the name survives, the recipe is different in more populous places. In Chile it is usually grape-juice at one of the earlier stages of fermentation (but still pretty alcoholic); in Costa Rica it is not even alcoholic, it is simply *un jugo*—'a soft drink'. Readers are advised to make enquiries locally before embarking on a session. Quite often it is a name given to some sort of 'claret cup' brewed by one's hostess shortly before the party, not unlike the Spanish *sangría* and usually pretty innocuous, but one can never be sure.

chico, -a. the usual word for 'small', 'little', in L/A. In Spain they use *pequeño* but even there *chiquitito*, the double diminutive, is normal for 'teeny-weeny', 'minute'.

As a noun, 'boy/girl', but mostly rather older boys and girls; a kindly old lady could say *Es un chico muy simpático*, 'He's a very nice boy', of a man of 50. In Spain it is used a great deal for 'guy', 'chap', 'fellow', and much used in exclamations: *¡Pero chico!* 'But my dear chap!' *¡Chico!* by itself often indicates simply surprise, in the same way as *¡Hombre!* (*q.v.*)

En chico is often the equivalent for 'small size': e.g. in a record shop where *¿Tiene en chico?* is likely to mean 'Do you have it in 45 (r.p.m.)?'

chifa (f). A 'Chinese restaurant' in Peru.

chile. *v.* **pimiento.**

chimenea (f). Bordering on the False since, although it does mean a 'chimney', it suggests to a native an 'open fire' or 'hearth'. These are not usual in Hispanic countries but something that looks like a fireplace is often installed, even in hot countries, for what might be called snob reasons; it looks good, and lends 'cachet', but if you tried to light a fire there you would probably set the house on fire. On the other hand genuine hearths are often installed, say, in Bogotá, not four degrees from the equator, since the altitude can make a fire very welcome in the evening. In the R/P a genuine 'fireplace' is often called *una estufa de leña* as the fuel is nearly always wood.

chinche,chincheta (f). *Una chinche* is strictly a 'bed-bug' but both these words now mean 'thumb-tack/drawing pin'.

chingar. A very rude, but very common, word in Mexico and thereabouts; you should avoid using it though you can hardly escape hearing it. One is obliged to equate it with 'to fuck', but I fancy it is rather commoner and, as usual with such words, is most used in senses other than its basic one, mainly revolving around frustation, molestation and booze. Those interested in pursuing its subtleties may read *The Labyrinth of Solitude* by Octavio Paz, or *The Death of Artemio Cruz* by Carlos Fuentes.

chino, -a. In Spain it would mean 'Chinese', and might mean this anywhere, but it is evidently a Quechua word as well and in L/A some other meaning is more likely though this will vary from place to place. Most often it has implied some sort of *mestizo* (what with black, white and bronze, and male or female parents of any of these colours, the range of permutations and combinations is considerable) but it can also mean 'young', a 'servant', a 'low-class person', a 'concubine' and various colours (no doubt following colour of skin). In Mexico it usually means 'curly-haired'. My *muchacha* in Bogotá told me her husband had gone off with *una china* and I understood this as meaning a 'young girl' but feel no certainty about it; in the R/P it would probably have meant simply 'a woman'.

chisme (m). A 'piece of gossip', and much used in the plural: *Cuéntame los chismes*, 'Tell me all the gossip'. In the singular it is used for something you cannot remember the name of, hence 'thingummy-bob', 'what-you-may-call-it': *¿Tienes el chisme ese?*, 'Have you got that what's-its-name?'

chiste (m). 'Joke'. but of the sort that is told, a 'funny story'. A 'low story' is *un chiste verde* or, in Mexico, *un chiste colorado* (v. also **broma**).

chocar, choque (m). False; *chocar* does not mean 'to shock', but 'to collide', and *un choque*, 'a collision': *choqué contra un camión*, 'I ran into a truck'. In L/A you will often hear *Me choqué* for 'I had a crash'. Both imply collision with a solid object; if it is with a pedestrian the words needed are *atropellar* ('to knock down') and *atropello*.

   Our verb 'to shock' is usually metaphorical and the Spanish for this is *escandalizar*. For the milder 'to startle', *v.* **susto,** also **impresión.** We handle physical shock via the noun but even here

'The shock of the collision' would be *El golpe del choque* and for 'shock' in the medical sense Spanish uses the English word: 'He was suffering from shock', *Estaba en shock*.

Chok is quite a different matter; it is the English word 'choke', in a car context, which they have adopted in the Z/A round to Venezuela.

chófer (m). The Spanish form of 'chauffeur'; it denotes a 'driver' who wears a uniform, whether private or a 'bus-driver'. *Conductor* is a more usual word for 'driver' but you will often see *Alquiler sin chófer* as an advertisement for 'self-drive' cars. In L/A it is accented on the second syllable and so carries no written accent.

chomba, chompa (f). 'Jumper', i.e. the garment. One might imagine that the Spanish word is an imitation of the English but there is a strong case for thinking that it may be the other way round, i.e. a Quechua word picked up by sailors about 100 years ago and passed to us by them. It usually means one with an open neck and buttons or zipper.

chop, schop (m). Taken from the German *Schop* but usually pronounced *chop*. It normally means 'stein/mug' of beer but in countries where they specialize in wine, such as Chile, you can have a *chop* of wine. I fancy it is Cognate with the old English 'stoup': 'Get thee to Yaughan. Fetch me a stoup of liquor' (*Hamlet*, V. I.66). In the R/P they call it *una manija*, because it has a handle.

choque. *v*. **chocar.**

chorizo (m). A characteristic Hispanic salami-type 'sausage' made of pork and usually a deep orange-red in colour.

chota (f). A vulgar word for the 'police' in Mexico.

christmas (m). Not quite what you might think; it means a 'Christmas card'. *Tengo que enviarle un christmas*, 'I must send her/him a Christmas card'. It is sometimes spelt *cristmas* or *crismas*.

chucha (f). Another Amerindian word with a great variety of meanings in different countries, some of them quite respectable, e.g. in Guatemala, where *chucho*, *-a* means 'dog/bitch'. It should be avoided in most of the Z/A, particularly in Chile, since there it is the coarse word for the female organ. Any word beginning *chu . . .* is likely to be a little suspect in the Andean region; *chumbo*, in Colombia, means the male organ.

chupar. 'To suck', yes, but also used metaphorically, and a little slangily, for 'to accept (something unwelcome)' or surprising; e.g. *¡Chúpate esa!*, 'How d'you like that!', 'Wince *that* off!', 'Put *that* in your pipe and smoke it!'

churro (m). Roughly speaking 'doughnut', but there are differences. In Spain *churro* is sold virtually by the yard, though in the better *cafés* you will be given short lengths of it. Perhaps this is why, in Mexico, it is a slang word for a 'bad film' but in much of L/A they have conformed to the U.S. pattern and now produce them ring-shaped, sometimes even calling them *doughnuts* or *donuts* (usually pronounced *dona*). The more or less spherical doughnuts usual in Europe, where they exist in L/A, are usually called *berlinas*; in Spain *rosquillas*.

cierto. On the face of it 'certain', but there are traps; it has become almost synonymous with 'true' so that, if you use it in the negative, imagining that you are saying 'that's not certain', you may find yourself accusing somebody of lying. You might say *Eso es incierto*, and if you added *todavía* your meaning would be understood but the adjective which Hispanics spontaneously use is *seguro*: 'It's not (yet) certain', *(Todavía) no es seguro (q.v.)* (*v.* **caso** for an English euphemism for 'true').

¿No es cierto? is a useful phrase for 'Isn't that so?' and will equate with any of that infinite set of question tags ('haven't we'; 'aren't you'; 'don't they'; etc.) which English so cruelly demands of foreigners, but mostly when the tag really is a question demanding an answer. Alternatives for this are *¿No es así?* or *¿No es verdad?* We tend, however, to slip in such tags without thinking and largely to indicate that we are being (or trying to seem) reasonable; in these cases, if a Hispanic says anything at all, he will probably say simply *¿No?*

cigarro (m). By now one may reasonably call it False since in these days it almost invariably means 'cigarette', not 'cigar', which is *puro*. *Una cajetilla de cigarros*, 'a pack(et) of cigarettes'.

cimiento (m). It looks like 'cement' but the Spanish for this is *cemento* and *cimiento* means 'foundation'; *los cimientos* are 'the foundations' of a building. *Cimentar*, 'to lay the foundations', whether literally or metaphorically.

cinta (f). 'Ribbon', 'tape', 'band', as you no doubt know. Here it is the turn of Spanish to have an all-purpose word where English subdivides according to type. If you have to specify, then *cinta de máquina*, 'typewriter-ribbon'; *cinta magnetofónica*, 'recording tape', even *cinta adhesiva* for 'adhesive tape', though this is usually just *(e)scotch* in L/A.

In Buenos Aires, amongst the top people, it is the O.K. word for a 'film', i.e. a movie, and in those circles *película* is considered rather low class.

circulación (f). Would normally mean 'circulation' but is often used to mean 'traffic', though *tráfico* is tending to supersede this.

clandestinos. *v.* **suburbios.**

claro. Strictly speaking 'clear', but you will hear it used twenty times a day as an adverb equating with 'of course', or 'obviously'. According to tone of voice it can mean anything from 'Why, you poor lamb! Of course you were right!' to 'Obviously not! You great twirp!' (*Obviamente*, though it exists, is never heard in conversation.) Between these two extremes it can often be muttered as an occasional, confirmatory response to something one is being told. In Chile and Peru it is used so much as almost to have replaced *Sí*.

If you want to say 'Obviously', initially, as opposed to responsively, then the device is *Claro está que* . . : *Claro está que no quise que me viese*, 'Obviously I didn't want him to see me'. (For other possibilities for 'obviously', *v.* **luego, supuesto, naturalmente.**)

cliché (m). Spanish shares with English the metaphorical use of this word for a time-worn idea or group of words but is more conscious of its original (French) typographical meaning 'to stereotype', 'to print off', so that *cliché* most often denotes something physical, the most everyday being a 'wax stencil', and a 'film negative'. I have heard it used of a glass lantern-slide but the usual word for this is *una diapositiva*.

closet (m). The final *t* is rarely pronounced so you may not immediately recognize it, but it does mean 'cupboard', of the built-in variety, in most L/A countries (*v.* also **placard** and **armario**).

coba (f). Dictionaries mostly give this as 'small talk' but in practice it usually means 'flattery', and *dar coba a alguien*, 'to toady', 'to suck up to', 'to ingratiate oneself with'. *Un cobista*, 'a toady'.

cobija (f). Basically an 'outer covering' but it is one of the commonest words in L/A for a 'blanket', though *frazada* is also widespread. In Spain 'blanket' is *manta* (*q.v.*).

cobrar. A curious, but very common, verb for which we do not have an exact equivalent so that its use takes a good deal of acquiring. Basically it means 'to recover' (something owed) but in an everyday context it means 'to be paid', 'to get paid', 'to take the money', 'to collect what is due'. If, on pay-day, someone says *Voy a cobrar*, it will mean 'I'm going to draw my pay', and any day *Voy a cobrar este cheque*, 'I'm going to cash this cheque', but it can be used negatively and interrogatively as well: *No ha cobrado todavía*, 'He hasn't come for the money yet', could be said of the milkman. In a *colectivo* taxi it is a daily occurrence to hear somebody say *¿Quiere cobrar?* to the driver, while holding out the money, and here it is hard to think of an English equivalent; I suppose we should simply say 'Here you are!' if we said anything at all. It can even be used imperatively; in my early days I once saw a young woman being goaded, a little teasingly, by a male acquaintance into paying him some money she apparently owed him until finally, in exasperation, she seized her handbag, took out some money, thrust it at him and hissed *¡Cobra!* For a moment I thought she was calling him a snake but she was merely saying 'Take your (blessed) money!'

Another common use of *cobrar* equates it with 'to charge': *Le cobran veinte dólares por el pasaje*, 'They charge you twenty dollars for the journey'. As with all words for which we have no equivalent, its use is best learnt by the direct method but mental notes are certainly indicated.

El cobrador is, in a general sense, the man who collects the money and, in a London bus, would be what we call the 'conductor'. There is a wonderful source of confusion here, partly because *conductor (q.v.)* means 'driver' and partly because, in most of the Americas, the driver and the 'conductor' are the same person. 'The ticket-collector' on a train or the (occasional) inspector who hops on a bus to make sure you've bought a ticket is likely to be called *el revisor* or, in L/A, *el controlador*, since it is not (normally) his business to collect money.

Una cobranza, literally 'a recovery' (seen from the point of view of the payee) is the usual commercial word in L/A for 'payment'. In Spain they say *cobra*. It is the obverse of *pago*. What is paying-in for one party is paying-out for the other.

cocer, cocinar. Dictionaries are bound to give you both 'to cook' and 'to boil' for *cocer* and cannot readily make clear that *cocer* means 'to cook (something) by boiling'. 'To cook', in a general sense, and by any other means than simply boiling, is *cocinar* or *guisar*. 'To boil', in a general sense, though particularly in the sense of 'to bring to the boil', is *hervir*. (*Hiérvase* is a common imperative in recipes for 'Bring to the boil', and *Está hirviendo*, 'It's boiling'.) The Spanish for 'on the boil', or 'boiling-point' is *ebullición* (and in recipes, again *Llévese a ebullición, revolviendo de vez en cuando*, 'Bring to the boil, stirring from time to time'). Not many things in the Hispanic cuisine are cooked simply by boiling so that the word *cocidos* usually occurs in connection with eggs.

cocina (f), cocción (f). *La cocina* is 'the kitchen' but may sometimes mean 'the kitchen stove' (originally short for *cocina económica*). It is also the word for 'cookery' in general and for 'cuisine'. The cooking of a particular meal or dish is *la cocción* (given by one well-known dictionary as 'coction'!) which may sometimes be found in recipes in the sense of 'cooking-time', e.g. *Cocción—dos horas*.

coche (m). Originally a 'coach', or 'carriage', but now the normal word for 'car', in Spain and the R/P, to some extent also in Mexico, though the last also shares *carro (q.v.)* with the rest of the Caribbean region. A 'coach', in the sense of a long-distance bus, is usually *autobús (v. bus)*.

In Guatemala, where a car is usually *un carro*, *coche* has come to be the usual word for 'pork', no doubt short for *cochino*.

Cochera (f), traditionally a 'coach-house', is the usual word for a domestic 'garage' in Mexico, though in Mexico City itself they mostly prefer the more universal *garaje (v. also **automóvil**)*.

coctel (m). Less often a 'cocktail' than a 'cocktail party'.

coger. In *Spain* this is such all-purpose verb that it almost rivals the English 'get' which is, in fact, one of its meanings: *Cogí un taxi*, 'I got a taxi'; *cogí frío*, 'I got cold'; *¿Cogiste otra botella de ginebra?*, 'Did you get another bottle of gin?' 'To catch' is another and would fit the first two examples, though it also applies to catching a ball, *Coger una pelota*.

Other very common meanings are 'to get hold of', 'to take hold of', 'to grab', 'to seize', or simply 'to pick up', the context making clear which English equivalent is the most likely: *Cogió el teléfono*, 'He/she picked up the phone', but in some circumstances could mean 'She seized the phone'. Equally *¡Cógelo!* could mean 'Catch!' with reference to something about to be thrown; 'Pick up!' with reference to something lying on the floor, and even 'Dive down and get it!' to something at the bottom of the swimming-pool. It extends to more metaphorical uses, e.g. *coger velocidad*, 'to pick up speed'; *coger fuerza*, 'to gather strength'.

It seems remarkable that so common and useful a verb should have fallen into disgrace in the R/P and be slightly suspect in much of L/A but it nevertheless remains a fact and visitors to Argentina and Uruguay are earnestly entreated not to use it since to their ears it equates with 'to fuck' (v. also **concha**). There they have to resort to other words. *Agarrar* is perhaps the commonest equivalent for senses involving 'to get hold of', 'to seize', 'to grab', etc.; *captar* for 'to catch', e.g. a ball, but *tomar* for catching trains, buses, etc.; *conseguir* for 'to obtain'; *atender* for 'to answer/pick up' the telephone. They mind less about *recoger* which is their normal word for picking flowers, nor does the adjective *cojo*, 'lame', seem to worry them unduly though they tend to prefer *quilla* for 'cushion', elsewhere *cojín*.

In Mexico the word has suffered less contamination but is nevertheless not so everyday as in Spain.

cojín (m). 'Cushion', but in L/A often used for 'pillow', though this is strictly *almohada*. To some extent it depends on the shape; *cojín* suggests a square one and *almohada* oblong and these considerations are often stronger than the use to which the pillow will be put. *Cojín* seemed to me commoner in Mexico, however, even when the pillow was not square. In the R/P 'a cushion' is usually *una quilla*.

cojones (m. pl.). Thanks largely to Hemingway, many Anglo-Saxon readers will be confident that this is the Spanish for 'guts' (basically testicles) and had therefore better be warned that it is distinctly vulgar and not a word for scattering lightly about one's conversation especially in mixed company. *Cojonudo*, equally vulgar, means approximately 'terrific', 'bloody marvellous', etc. but again is much too strong for the average foreigner to risk making a fool of himself with.

cola (f). 'Tail', yes, but also: 'line/queue'. Within the dictionary but too everyday to be omitted.

colectivo (m). As an adjective 'collective' but as a noun, in L/A, it means a 'collective taxi', i.e. which anyone may enter, provided there is room, and pay a fixed fare for a given stage. They are quite respectable, vastly cheaper than ordinary taxis and very nearly as quick. In some countries, however, e.g. Argentina, *un colectivo* simply means an ordinary 'municipal bus'.

In Mexico 'collective taxis' are usually referred to as *peseros*, since a *peso* used to be the fare for a stage.

In Venezuela the official title is *por puesto* but within Caracas people mostly talk of going by *carro* or *carrito*; in P/R they are called *carros públicos*.

In Colombia *colectivos* are not usual in the big cities but they are very usual for long-distance so the word has a slightly different image there. *Flota* is also used for this (*v.* **bus**).

NOTE:Since the doors are opened and shut so much, most drivers of *colectivos* are very sensitive about having them banged and will often upbraid you severely if you do so.

colegiado. *Colegio*, especially in L/A, has much the same force as 'college' in the U.S., i.e. a school of higher learning, and the adjective *colegiado* has therefore been coined for application to people who have pursued higher studies, e.g. *Oftalmólogos colegiados*, 'Qualified opticians' (*Gu*). In Spain it means 'belonging to a professional association'.

collar (m). Almost False; its normal meaning is 'necklace', though it can also mean a 'dog-collar'. An ordinary 'collar' is *un cuello*.

colocar. One of the verbs which it is difficult to remember to use. You no doubt know that it means 'to put in (its) place', and if the maid said to you *La ropa está colocada* you would understand easily enough what she meant, but would you have remembered to say *Tiene que colocar esta ropa* (*en su sitio*) when asking her to put it away? The essence of the meaning is 'to put something where it belongs', 'to find the appropriate niche for'; in an office context you might well say *Está colocando las fichas* (*en el archivo*) of a secretary who is putting the cards into the card-index.

A metaphorical extension is in the matter of jobs; *colocar* can mean 'to find (somebody) a job'; 'to get a job', and *la colocación* is the 'job' itself.

Colocar is also common in recipes: *Coloque al fuego una cacerola con un litro de agua*, 'Put a saucepan containing a litre of water on the stove'.

colonia (f). 'Colony', yes, but often used of the 'higher-class suburbs' (*v.* **suburbios**). It has a further meaning which is not immediately apparent. If, in a shop, you saw the notice, *colonia a granel*, what would you understand it to mean? Answer: ' "Loose" Eau de Cologne', *Colonia* being short for *Agua de Colonia* which is so popular in Spain that you can even buy it by the pint; bring your own bottle (*v.* **granel**).

colorado. Literally 'colo(u)red', but unless some other colo(u)r is specified it means 'red'. *Una camisa colorada*, 'a red shirt'. 'A colo(u)red shirt' is *una camisa de color* if it is all of one colour and *de colores* if it is multi-coloured. *Ponerse colorado*, 'to blush';

poner colorado, 'to make (somebody) blush'. In Mexico 'a bawdy story' is *un chiste colorado;* elsewhere it is usually *verde.*

coma (m & f). A Good Friend only if you watch the gender; when Masculine it means 'coma', and Feminine 'comma'. *Comillas* are 'inverted commas/quotation marks', and *entre comillas* is a common expression for 'in quotes' (*v.* OFFICE MATTERS). *Coma* (f) also means 'decimal point': *Dos coma seis,* 'Two point six'.

comida (f). 'Meal', certainly, but in all Hispanic minds it tends to be associated with the main meal of the day and since this can be at different times in different countries it can equate with 'lunch', 'dinner' or 'supper'. The offical names for the meals, *desayuno, almuerzo* and *cena,* are universal but there is variation as to which is regarded as the most important. In Spain, Mexico and the C/S *la comida* normally means 'the mid-day meal'; in the Z/A—perhaps because the climate is hotter—it means 'the evening meal'. 'Mid-day' is, however, a somewhat relative term; in practice it is usually about 3 p.m.

For the evening meal *cena* is a shade more august and in many countries will suggest a meal in a restaurant, though *cenar* is pretty general for 'to have the evening meal' (*v.* also **merienda**).

comisaría (f). For us the word 'commissariat' has no very precise meaning, except perhaps as a facetious term for the catering department; for a Hispanic it has a very clear meaning indeed: it means the 'police station'. On board ship it spells the 'Purser's Office', and the 'Purser' himself is usually *el Comisario.*

como. Fairly well attended to in dictionaries and grammar books but I mention a few points which they, or the reader, may have overlooked:

¿Cómo . . .de . . .? is a common way of rendering: 'How . . . (adj)?': *¿Cómo es de largo?,* 'How long is it?' (*v.* also **tan**). This can lead to such telescoped sentences as: *¿A cómo está de Madrid?,* 'How far is it to Madrid?'

Así como is given in many dictionaries as 'as soon as', but in my experience a far commoner meaning is 'as well as', 'in addition to', and, particularly in business letters, 'together with': *. . . así como una copia de nuestra respuesta,* 'together with a copy of our reply'.

¿Cómo? is the commonest way of asking somebody to repeat something just said. *¿Qué?,* 'What?', is very blunt and *¿Cómo?* a great deal gentler as well as more *castizo,* though it does imply an easy equality of status (and takes an accent!). Used with *ser* it is the equivalent of 'What . . . like?' *¿Cómo son los mangos?,* 'What are mangoes like?' *Como siempre* is the stock phrase for 'As usual' (*v.* also **mandar**).

For more precise querying or challenging what someone has said the device is *¿Cómo que . . .?* and again it is gentler; *¿Cómo que no?* is far less abrupt than 'What d'you mean, no?' more like 'I don't see why not'. If the Mad Hatter's tea-party had taken place in Hispanic circumstances, Alice, when she appeared, would probably have been greeted with *¡No cabe! ¡No cabe!* for 'No room! No room!' and I feel sure that a Hispanic Alice would instinctively have replied *¿Cómo que no quepo?* whereas Lewis Carroll made her say 'There's plenty of room!' and would probably have felt it rather unbecoming for her to have said 'What do you mean, no room?'

Without question marks *Como que* is useful for 'seeing that': *¡Ya lo creo que le conozco, como que he estudiado con él!'*, 'Certainly I know him, seeing that I was a student with him!' and it is often used to introduce a sentence as a sort of equivalent of, 'It looks as though . . .': *Como que van a legalizar el divorcio*, 'It looks as though they're going to make divorce legal'. The latter is the sort of remark likely to be made when the speaker is assuming (if only for politeness) that his hearer will have read the news too. It is perhaps commoner in L/A but even in Spain quite a usual form of sentence employs *como* with the Subjunctive when envisaging a possibility: *como vengas tarde te quedas sin cenar*, 'If you're late you won't get any dinner'.

¡Cómo no! is a very common expression, especially in L/A. It seems to mean 'Why not?' but in practice is usually a politeness equating with 'Certainly', 'Of course', 'Please do', etc. It can, however, be used as a sarcastic 'Of course', and then equates with: 'Typical!' 'Just what you'd expect!' 'He *would*!' etc. (*v.* COURTESY).

cómodo, comodidades (f.pl.). False; the Spanish image is quite different. *Cómodo* means not 'commodious', but 'comfortable', and *comodidades* therefore means '(creature) comforts'. The Spanish for 'commodities' is *géneros* or *mercancías*. A house or hotel will advertise itself as having *muchas comodidades*, not merely 'comforts' but 'facilities', e.g. constant hot water, under-floor heating, air-conditioning, a swimming-pool, etc. In earth-quake zones one *comodidad* is *construcción asísmica*, 'anti-earth-quake construction'.

completo. It may mean 'complete' but another likely meaning is 'full-up', or 'full-house'. A long-distance bus in which all seats are bookable and no standing allowed will be *completo* as soon as all the seats are sold, and establishments which are 'full-up', e.g. a parking garage, are likely to put up a notice saying *COMPLETO*.

Por completo is a very common adverbial phrase and probably the best equivalent of our 'absolutely'. You may say *completa-mente* but *por completo* is rather stronger as well as being more *castizo*: *Se arruinó por completo*, 'He was absolutely ruined'. It is, however, strictly adverbial; if the 'absolutely' is merely an inten-sifier then *completamente* is needed, e.g. 'absolutely useless', *completamente inútil* (*v.* also **absoluto**).

complexión (f). False; the English applies only to the face and the Spanish equivalent of this is *el cutis* or *la tez*. *Complexión* applies to the whole person in a physical sense and so equates better with 'build': *Un hombre de complexión fuerte*, 'A man of powerful build'.

composturas (f. pl.). The usual word in Mexico for 'car repairs' (though they do also say *reparaciones*). In this they are consistent since their word for 'to break down' is *descomponerse* and 'a breakdown' is *una descompostura*.

compras (f. pl.). 'Purchases', but the usual word for 'shopping': *Tengo que hacer unas compras*, 'I've got some shopping to do'. *Ir de compras*, 'to go shopping'; *Fue de compras*, 'She's out shopping'.

comprensivo. Unreliable to the point of Falsity; it means 'understanding', 'comprehending', not 'comprehensive': *El jefe fue muy comprensivo*, 'The boss was very understanding (about it)'. 'Comprehensive' would have to be *de gran alcance* or *del máximo alcance* according to the extent of the comprehensiveness (*v.* also **envergadura**). A 'comprehensive' policy is *A todo riesgo*.

comprometer, compromiso (m), Unreliable; the Spanish is chiefly a stronger form of 'promise'. *Un compromiso* is a standard word for a 'promise', 'engagement', 'commitment', even an 'appointment': *Tengo un compromiso para las once*, 'I've an appointment at 11 o'clock' (though *cita* may also be used).

Equally *comprometer* means 'to promise' in a rather formal and weighty sense, hence 'to engage (to)', 'to undertake (to)'. In my early days I once read a magazine article which offered a good example of False Friendship; it concerned a young man who was anxious to get married and therefore went to see a lady who had several marriageable daughters and pleaded his suit. The following rather arresting (as it seemed to me) exchange then took place:
Lady: *Mis hijas están todas comprometidas*.
Young man: *¡Qué desgracia!* (*v.***desgracia**).

Comprometerse is useful for 'to commit oneself', 'to undertake (to)': *Me he comprometido a pagar cien dólares*, 'I've undertaken to pay 100 dollars', and there is nothing sinister about it. If you wanted to say 'The minister was (seriously) compromised', you could say *seriamente comprometido* but it would only be the *serio* which implied the sinister.

'To compromise', in the sense of coming to an arrangement which will work, though it involves some sacrifice, is probably best handled by *transigir*, though *arreglar* will often do for less formal and more personal arrangements.

concepto (m). 'Concept', yes, but also 'idea', 'notion', even 'opinion'. I mention it chiefly for its commonness. 'Concept', for us, is rather an educated word whereas *concepto* is frequently on the lips of the most ordinary Hispanic workman: *Tiene el concepto de que es todo una trampa*, 'He reckons the whole thing's a racket'. I feel sure it is commoner than *idea* which is the word most likely to occur to us.

concertar. A common verb meaning 'to make arrangements', 'to come to an agreement', 'to make an appointment', and much used by secretaries who have to make an appointment for the boss in his absence. In L/A I have heard it used for less serious appointments: *Hemos concertado ir al cine con Luis*, 'We've arranged to go to the movies with Luis'.

concha (f). 'Shell', i.e. of a crustacean, but also a girl's name, when it is short for *Concepción*. Most irritatingly for the ladies concerned it has, in the C/S, become the vulgar word for the female organ and is suspect in much of L/A for this reason. If you know a girl of this name in these countries it is safer to call her *Conchita* as this is somehow less blatant. In the R/P, which is where it matters most, when they find themselves obliged to talk about shells they use such words as *coquilla* or even *caracol* (snail) though people seriously concerned with natural history will use *concha* just as people seriously concerned with dogs will freely refer to bitches.

concretar. In English we have the adjective 'concrete' for metaphorical uses, e.g. concrete proposals, but we do not extend to a verb. If we did we should find it very useful and *concretar* is very useful in Spanish though it is not necessarily colloquial: *Yo quería concretar este asunto*, 'I wanted to get this matter fixed up'. It can also mean 'to summarize', e.g. at the end of a lecture: *Vamos a concretar los puntos principales*, 'Let us summarize the main points'.

Concretamente is a useful adverb for 'in short', 'in a word', 'in fact', 'more precisely', 'to cut a long story short', etc., and is used a good deal in conversation. After a long discussion someone is likely to say *Pues concretamente . . .*, 'Well, the long and short of it is . . .'. In the negative: *Pues no sé concretamente*, 'Well I don't exactly know'.

concurrencia (f), **concurso** (m). Both these words border on the False and juxtaposition may help to point them up:

Concurrencia is literally a 'running-together', but of quite a different sort from our 'concurrence'; it means a 'gathering', of people, and in practice is often another word for 'audience', i.e. the people who have 'run' together to hear you speak: *¿Hubo mucha concurrencia?*, 'Were there many people there?' 'Concurrence' would have to be *conformidad* or *acuerdo* (*v.* also **asistencia**).

Concurso also a type of running-together and sounds as though it ought to mean concourse but in fact has quite a different image; it means 'contest', or 'competition', e.g. a beauty contest. Quizzes on the TV are called *concursos*. 'A concourse' is *una concurrencia*.

condescender. False; it means: 'to acquiesce', 'to be obliging', 'to submit', and *condescendiente*, 'obliging', 'submissive', 'complaisant'. It is not a very common word; I include it because of its Falsity. 'To condescend' is *dignarse*, 'to deign to': *No se digna venir a visitarnos*, 'She doesn't condescend to come and see us', but there is no corresponding adjective; you have to manage with the verb.

condición (f), **condicionar.** *Condición* is the singular equates fairly well with 'condition' but in the plural can take on some more particularized meanings. One is 'ability': on a school report you may see *Tiene condiciones pero no trabaja*, 'Has ability but doesn't use it'. *En condiciones* means 'in working order', and *poner en condiciones*, 'to make (to) work', hence 'to mend', 'to repair', 'to set right'.

Condicionar means 'to determine the nature' (of something), hence 'to govern' (in a metaphorical sense): *La calidad del material condiciona el precio*, 'The quality of the goods governs/determines the price'. 'To dictate', is another possibility. For 'to condition', in the sense of 'to put into condition', *acondicionar* is indicated: 'air-conditioned'— *con aire acondicionado* (*clima artificial* is also used in L/A).

conducir. Distinctly Unreliable if you think it means 'conduct', though it would serve for 'conduce', should you happen to need that word. By far its commonest meaning in practice is 'to drive' (a car). 'To conduct' in the musical sense is *dirigir*.

Conductor is equally Unreliable; the only context in which it equates with 'conductor' is an electrical one and its normal meaning is 'driver'. For the British bus 'conductor' *v*. **cobrar,** also **guarda.** 'The conductor' of an orchestra is *el director* or *el maestro*.

confección (f). By and large may be regarded as False since it does not spell 'sweets' and 'candies' but 'textiles', especially in dress- or suit-making establishments, usually for ladies but also for gentlemen. *Una confección* is 'a dress or suit' (ladies' fashion magazines sometimes refer to a particularly choice one as a confection). It can, however, be used of almost anything that needs to be 'made up'; in a Spanish tourist office I saw *Confección de kilométricos*, 'Kilometric/mileage tickets made up'.

conferencia (f). Unreliable to the point of Falsity; its commonest meaning is 'lecture', of the sort given in lecture-halls, though in Spain it is also used for a 'long-distance telephone call'. In L/A it may be used to mean 'interview'; *Tuve una conferencia con el jefe*, 'I had an interview with the boss', but it is not the usual word for 'a meeting' which is *reunión* or *junta* (*q.v.*). 'A conference' of the large-scale sort would be *un congreso* (*v*. LECTURES, CONFERENCES, CONGRESSES).

confianza (f). 'Confidence', yes, but readers should be conscious of the useful adjectival phrase *de confianza* meaning 'trustworthy', 'honest'. *Es una muchacha de confianza*, 'She's an honest girl/woman', usually said of servants though it can be said of anyone who is to be trusted in given circumstances: *Él/Ella es de confianza* (indicating somebody present), 'You can speak freely in front of him/her'.

conforme. Strictly an adjective meaning 'in agreement', but used a great deal by itself to mean 'I agree', or, interrogatively 'Do you agree?' *Estar conforme*, 'to be in agreement'. *De acuerdo* is used in much the same way.

congelador (m). Literally, 'freezer'; usually the 'ice-compartment' within a refrigerator. A 'deep-freeze' unit for long-term storage is *una congeladora* (v. **-dora**).

conmoción (f). A little Unreliable since although it can be applied to a public disturbance its basic meaning is an 'emotion held in common', and it can therefore be used of quite orderly events. A line culled from a Montevideo daily describing, sympathetically, public reactions to the funeral of a 'martyr' who had been shot in some student riots offers a nice little array of False Cognates (allowing for some journalese); it reported that the people *se volcaron por la calle para exteriorizar la honda conmoción del suceso*, i.e. 'poured out into the street to manifest their deep sympathy with the event'. A better word for what we understand by 'commotion' would be *jaleo* and 'riot' is *motín*. In a medical context *conmoción* means 'concussion'.

conmutador (m). The usual word in L/A for a 'private telephone exchange'. In Spain they say *centralita*.

coño (m). This is unmistakably a 'four-letter' word and not merely a harmless one which has been downgraded, but it is so common, especially in Spain, that it must clearly be mentioned. Basically it means 'cunt' but it is rarely used for this, nor does it detonate to the same extent. It is less a noun than an exclamation, a stronger form of *¡Hombre!* (q.v.), so that its nearest equivalent is a surprised or impatient 'Christ!' There are still many respectable Anglo-Saxons who would be diffident, to say the least, about exclaiming 'Christ!' but it seems to me that Spaniards are less diffident about exclaiming *¡Coño!* Respectable women are unlikely to use it—certainly not in mixed company—but they will often hear their menfolk do so and raise no objection.

Outside Spain the word is less used and sometimes, e.g. in Chile, hardly known except as a slang word for a 'Spaniard' because the latter uses it so often. In the R/P (and the surrounding countries are contaminated) they have succeeded in transferring the odium to the word *concha* (q.v.). In Venezuela and Mexico, however, I have noticed it used as an exclamation of impatience, much as in Spain.

conocer. I shall not belabour the differences between *conocer* and *saber* but one use of the former is so easily overlooked that it deserves a little rubbing-in, viz. 'to get to know', 'to first meet': *Conocí a mi mujer en una fiesta*, 'I first met my wife at a party'; *He conocido al Presidente*, 'I've met the President'. The danger shows most in the reverse direction; how would you say 'I originally met him . . .'? Answer: *Lo conocí . . .* simply; the 'originally' is already contained in the *conocí*.

Conocer also means 'to know' in the Biblical sense, i.e. 'to have carnal knowledge of'. A friend of mine was taken by a *granadino* to see the cave in Sacro Monte, in Granada, and asked him how well he knew the dancers. The *granadino* replied: *¿ Yo? ¡ Pues en el sentido bíblico de la palabra las conozco a todas!*

conseguir. A very common verb, which you should certainly have at your command. It means 'to get', in the sense of 'to obtain', but it implies mild difficulty in the getting: *¿Has conseguido entradas?*, 'Did you manage to get tickets?' When used with a verb, instead of a noun, the sense of managing to, or succeeding in, is rather stronger: *¿Has conseguido entrar?*, 'Did you manage to get in?'; *He conseguido convencerle de que . . .* , 'I've succeeded in persuading him that . . .' (*v.* also **coger**).

Also common for 'to succeed in', 'to manage to' is *lograr*: *No logro acostumbrarme a este trabajo*, 'I've never succeeded in getting used to this job'. For *malograr v.* **cebarse**.

conserje (m). In a wide sense 'keeper', 'warden', 'concierge', 'custodian', 'caretaker', but more particularized in the different countries. In Mexico he is the man who guards the entrance to a school, hence 'porter', 'beadle', etc.; in Venezuela the man who guards the entrance to an apartment block/house, hence 'porter', 'janitor', 'superintendent'; in Spain usually the 'head-porter/bell captain' in a hotel.

conservar. 'To keep.' Easy to understand but not always to remember to use: *Voy a conservar sus cartas*, 'I'm going to keep his letters'. We tend to associate it with fruit and the like. *Guardar* may also be used, though it has a stronger sense of 'putting away'.

consideración (f). Quite a Good Friend but there is a curious use of it in the R/P for starting business letters. One does not begin with *Muy señor mío* but with *De mi consideración* or *De nuestra consideración* and then plunges straight into the text (*v.* **querer**).

constipado. A classic Falso Amigo; the noun *una constipación* refers to a blockage of the nostrils, hence 'a cold', and the adjective *constipado*, 'having a cold': *Estoy un poco constipado hoy*, 'I've got a bit of a cold today'. In L/A they tend to prefer *un resfrío* for 'a cold', with *resfriado* for the adjective. The Spanish for 'constipated' is *estreñido*.

contabilidad (f). You might imagine that this means 'accountability' but this is more likely to be handled by *responsabilidad*. *Contabilidad* (sometimes *contaduría*) simply means 'Accounts', in general, and is likely to be the sign over the door of the Accounting Department.

contador (m). Literally 'counter', but probably not of the sort you think; it is the domestic 'meter' which 'counts' gas, electricity, etc. In much of L/A it may also mean 'accountant', though the formal word for this is *contable*. A 'counter' of the sort one buys goods across is usually *mostrador* or *mesón*.

contraproducente. 'Counter-productive', 'self-defeating'. The former is not a common word in our daily conversation; it is more associated with business and economic contexts. *Contra-producente*, however, is quite common and is rather the equivalent for our 'it's no good . . . , it only . . .', e.g. 'It's no good shouting at them, it only makes them noisier', *Es contraproducente gritarles ya que sólo se ponen más nerviosos*; 'It's a mistake to . . .' 'It doesn't pay to . . .', 'It's worse than useless' are other possibilities. *Es contraproducente darle medicina sin consultar a un médico*, 'It's unwise to give him medicine before seeing the doctor'.

contestar, contestación (f). False; they mean 'reply', 'answer': *Hay que contestar a esta carta*, 'This letter will have to be replied to'. *Contestación* is the usual noun for an 'answer' in Spain; in L/A they mostly say *respuesta* and often *responder* for 'to answer'.
    'To contest' is usually *disputar* or *impugnar*.

controlar. My dictionary gives this as a 'neologism' and it is certainly of recent date. I doubt, however, whether it is taken from the English; more probably from the French *contrôler* since it bears the same meaning, viz. 'to check up': *Hay que controlar esta carta*, 'This letter will have to be checked'. 'The inspector' who checks tickets on a train or bus is *el controlador* (Fr. *contrôleur*). Its use is rather frowned on in Spain where they say *revisar*. The frown deepens when they hear Latin Americans say *chequear* for the same thing and this is certainly taken from the English.

convenir, conveniente. I am tempted to damn these as False and they are certainly Unreliable; *convenir* seems to mean 'to be convenient', but in practice it means 'to be to one's advantage', 'in one's interest', and financial advantage is rather suggested. *Venir (q.v.)* already exists for 'to suit': *Eso me viene bien*, 'That suits me very well'. To intensify *convenir* you use not *bien* but *mucho* and *Eso me conviene mucho* means 'That's very much in my interest', and suggests you hope to make a million out of it. 'Would that be convenient for you?' *¿Eso le viene bien?* The difference shows up most clearly in the negative: *No me conviene* is tantamount to saying 'It's not in my interest', 'It's not worth my while'—a very different matter from 'It's not convenient'. It would be passable in, say, a shop, but in response to an invitation it would be intolerably rude. *Convenir* can, however, mean 'to fit', in physical sense, e.g. clothing.
    Conveniente could equate with 'convenient', e.g. in describing an apartment which was handy for one's work, but its commonest equivalents are 'appropriate', 'salutary', a 'good thing': *Dados los problemas actuales sería conveniente que todos lean este documento*, 'In the light of present difficulties it would be a good thing/desirable/just as well/an advantage for everyone to

read this document'.

Inconveniente may serve for 'inconvenient' but is probably used more often as a noun meaning 'disadvantage', 'drawback', even 'nuisance': *El inconveniente es que está tan lejos*, 'The snag is that it's such a long way away'. *Si no tiene inconveniente* is a stock phrase for 'If you have no objection'. 'Difficulty' would often be the equation: *No habrá inconveniente en pagar en dólares*, 'There'll be no difficulty about paying in dollars'. Since Anglo-Saxons tend to leap on the word *dificultad* for 'difficulty', *es conveniente* to remind oneself that there is another word for it. *Contratiempo* is another (*v.* also **problema**.)

convertirse. One of the words for 'to become', in the sense of 'to turn into': *¡Te estas convirtiendo en un verdadero borracho!*, 'You're becoming a proper drunkard!'

convidar. 'To invite' but it implies a more limited and immediate type of inviting than *invitar* and most often applies to treating or standing a drink: *Voy a convidarte a una copita de vino*, 'Let me stand you a glass of wine' (*v.* also **brindar**).

copa (f). Somewhat False in its image; it is the kind of 'cup' which *has a stem* and its commonest meaning is probably 'wineglass', but it is, of course, the word for the type of cup won in athletics, etc.: *Copa Mundial*, 'World Cup'. The domestic cup, as you know, is *taza*.

In Colombia *copa* is used for the 'hub-cap' of a car wheel. One or two minor derivatives are perhaps worth putting on record: *copetín* (m) is a R/P word for a 'drink' in the sense of a small cocktail party. *Copetón* is a slang word for 'drunk' in Colombia.

copera (f). Literally a 'female cup bearer', and redolent of old colonial days in Colombia where it means, shall we say, a 'waitress'. One would not expect to find waitresses in up-country Colombia, which is very much a man's country and a *copera* does not necessarily limit her activities to bearing (and perhaps sharing) a cup (*v.* **copa**). Do not, however, address her as *¡Copera!*, say *¡Señorita!*

copia(f). 'Copy', yes, but there is a snag: in Spanish the word is more strictly applied to something that has been copied, e.g. a letter, and it is therefore incorrect for a 'copy' of a book, which is *ejemplar*. *Copia* is most likely to be used in office circumstances: *Saque una copia más para . . .*, 'Take an extra copy for . . .'; but: 'Have we got a copy of the Bible?', *¿Tenemos un ejemplar de la Biblia?*

corchete. *v.* **paréntesis.**

correr, recorrer, corredero, corredor (m). *Correr* means literally 'to run', but is probably used more metaphorically than literally: *¡Corre!¡Corre!*, 'Hurry up!' and the cliché 'How times flies!' is *¡Cómo corre el tiempo!* In a car context *No corras tanto*, 'Don't go so fast'. It can also be used transitively: *Correr las cortinas*, 'to draw the curtains'. *Córrete* is likely to mean 'Move over a bit', say, on a crowded sofa.

In the R/P *correr* can be used of the wind blowing: *¡Cómo corre!'* 'What a wind!'. In Spain this would be *¡Comó sopla!* A woman there might also say *Se me corrió* for 'I got a ladder/run in my stocking', a remark that might greatly mislead in Spain (see below).

Recorrer is even more metaphorical: *Recorrí todo el pueblo buscando una tienda abierta*, 'I scoured the whole town trying to find a shop that was open', and note that no preposition is used; you could say *Corrí por todo el pueblo . . .* but it would then suggest that you really were running. *Ha recorrido medio mundo*, 'He's travelled half round the world'. It is often useful for the figurative 'to cover': *Hemos recorrido mucho terreno*, 'We've covered a lot of ground'. *Recorrido* can also be used as a noun for 'driving time', 'a run', as well as an 'overhaul' (usually of a car).

Corredera, literally 'a slider', can have a number of technical applications to parts of machinery that slide but the adjectival expression *de corredera* is a common way of handling 'sliding', e.g. *puertas de corredera*, 'sliding doors', though in L/A *corredero* is perhaps commoner.

Corredor may mean 'corridor' but implies a spacious one in a palace or some equally august building. In domestic circumstances 'a corridor', or 'passage', is more likely to be *un pasillo*.

Correrse is the usual verb in Spain for 'to come' in the sexual sense.

correspondencia (f), **corresponder, correspondiente, corresponsal** (m). Fraught with Unreliability and mainly False; *corresponder con* can mean 'to correspond to', in the sense of 'to match up with', e.g. *Tu versión no corresponde con la suya*, 'Your version doesn't correspond to his', but it will not do for the exchange of letters which would be *estar en correspondencia con*.

The root meaning of *corresponder* is 'to respond with': *correspondió a sus atenciones enviándole un ramo de flores*, 'He repaid her kindness by sending her a bunch of flowers', but it has extended from this to meaning 'to be fitting', 'to belong', 'to behove', 'to be (one's) business', even 'one's turn': *No me corresponde a mí juzgar por qué lo hicieron*, 'It's not for me to judge why they did it'; *No le corresponde* could mean 'It's not his business', or 'It doesn't belong to him'. *A quien corresponda* is the cliché for 'To whom it may concern'. *Me dieron menos de lo que me correspondía*, 'They gave me less than was due to me'; *Te corresponde a ti*, 'Over to you'. The basic concept is of a fitting counterpart, though sometimes it may be deliberately unfitting, e.g. 'He responded with blows', *Correspondió con golpes*. You will probably need mental notes to remind yourself to use it. How about: 'I can't find a nut to fit this bolt'? Would you have remembered in time to use *corresponder*?

Correspondiente is an adjective and means 'corresponding'. The noun 'correspondent' is *corresponsal*: 'Foreign correspondent', *Corresponsal en el extranjero*.

It is something of a relief to know that *correspondencia* does mean 'correspondence' in the sense of an exchange of letters, but one should bear in mind that it is also the general noun to cover all the types of fitting and counterparting outlined above. It also has the more particular meaning of 'connection' on railroads, buses, etc. On the *Metro* for example, *Correspondencia* (*con*) . . . means 'Change . . . (for the . . . line)'.

corriente. A fairly Good Friend, for a change; it means 'current', in most senses, including electric current, though natives have a way of referring to this last as *la luz*: *Han cortado la luz*, 'They've cut the current off'. Some readers may also find it useful to know that 'A.C.' and 'D.C.' are *corriente alterna* and *corriente contínua* respectively.

As an adjective *corriente* is much used in conversation to mean 'ordinary', 'usual', 'routine', and *vino corriente* is what the French call 'vin ordinaire', i.e. the wine of the house/region (*v.* also **regular** and **ordinario**). It is, however, not the word for 'current' in the sense of going-on-at-the-time which is *actual* (*q.v.*).

cortado. 'Cut', or 'shortened', yes, but *v.* also **café.**

costa (f), **costo** (m), **cuesta, costar.** None of these is really difficult but a little disentangling is perhaps desirable. The commonest meaning of *costa* is 'coast', e.g. *Costa Brava*, *Costa Azul*, etc. Dictionaries will tell you that it also means 'cost' but its use in this sense is far from everyday and chiefly confined to the Law: 'Legal costs' are *Las costas del juicio*. *Costo* also exists and 'the cost of living' is officially *el costo de la vida* but in practice natives mostly say simply *La vida*. We use the noun 'cost' rather more than any cognate noun in Spanish; 'to pay the cost of the journey' is *pagar los gastos del viaje* but again, in practice, they will probably say simply *pagar el viaje* and 'costs' are likely to be *gastos*, i.e. expenses. If 'cost' means more strictly 'price' they will probably say *precio*. *A costa de* is a set phrase for 'at the cost of', but it is probably used more metaphorically than literally.

Cuesta, though cognate with *costa*, has a much more physical connotation and means 'slope', 'incline'; on a road we should probably say 'hill': *Cuesta arriba*, 'uphill'; *cuesta abajo*, 'downhill'. *La cuesta de enero* is a humorous, and not very important, expression for the 'uphill grind' one is faced with in January after spending all one's money over Christmas and the New Year.

Costar means 'to cost', right enough, but again is much used metaphorically where we are likely to say 'give' or 'to cause': *Me costó mucho trabajo*, 'It gave me a lot of work'.

costeño. *v.* **porteño.**

cremallera (f). In a context of mountain railways this would probably mean a 'rack-and-pinion' but a more everyday meaning is 'zipper'. In Venezuela they call 'a zipper' *un rache*, taken from the English 'ratchet'. You may sometimes hear *un cierre zip* (with the *p* scarcely audible) or *cierre relámpago*.

criatura (f). It can serve as an equivalent of 'creature' but to Hispanic ears it immediately suggests a small child: *¡Qué criatura más adorable!*, 'What an adorable little thing!' One may quite properly refer to some unfortunate grown-up as *la pobre criatura* but *el/la pobrecito*, *-a* is more likely in practice.

crimen (m). In theory 'crime'; in practice nearly always 'murder'. If you mean 'crime' in the strict sense, use *delito*.

criollo. Historically it applied to people of pure Spanish descent born in Latin America but it has come to be used of anything that belongs authentically to the (L/A) country in question. It is much used in Argentina and Venezuela. *Indígena* (m or f) ought to mean approximately the same thing but it can sometimes sound pejorative; *criollo* is said with pride (*v.* also **lugareño, típico, castizo**).

crisis (f). 'Crisis', certainly, but *crisis nerviosa* is the universal expression for a 'nervous breakdown'.

crudo, -a. Equates well enough with 'crude', or 'rough', but can also mean 'raw', in connection with fruit or vegetables. In Mexico *una cruda* means a 'hangover'.

cuadra (f). The usual word for 'block', i.e. of buildings, in L/A. In Spain and Mexico *manzana* has been the official word for this in the past but is tending to be replaced by *bloque*. You are likely to get *cuadra* when asking the way: *Tres cuadras más allá*, 'Three blocks further on'. In Peru *cuadrar* is the usual verb for 'to park' a car (*v.* also **bocacalle**).

cuadro (m). 'Square', but in domestic circumstances its likeliest meaning is 'picture' (on the wall). For the 'frame' *v.* **marco**.

cualquier,-a. *Cualquiera* means 'anybody', and you may call it common in gender since the final *a* is invariable, though it may be dropped before a noun, e.g. *cualquier persona que*, 'anybody who'; *una persona cualquiera*, 'any person whatsoever'. *Cualquiera que*, 'whichever', 'whatever'. 'Whoever' is usually simply *quien* (probably with the subjunctive), though *quienquiera* exists (*v.* **quien**).

I mention these, perhaps rather elementary, facts as they point to the whole problem of 'ever', whether by itself or as a suffix, and offer the opportunity to examine ways of handling it.

'Ever', by itself, often needs no translation: *Lo mejor que he visto en mi vida* already implies 'The best I ever saw in my life'. The question 'Have you ever . . .?' implies 'at any time' and here the device is *¿Has (visto) alguna vez . . .?* The negative is no problem since Spanish does have *nunca*, though you need to keep awake about hidden negatives, e.g. 'I haven't ever' = 'I have never'.

Where the suffix is concerned there is a category which may be termed rhetorical, e.g. 'Whoever can that be?' or 'Whatever did you do that for?' In these cases the 'ever' is implied by the use of the future tense, and perhaps by a preliminary *Pero*: *¿Pero quién será?* or, since our 'ever' often implies exasperation: *¿Pero ¡por Dios! por qué has hecho eso?*' (Extreme exasperation can lead to even stronger expletives being employed at this point.)

When it comes to the suffixes which are really operative, 'whenever', 'however', 'wherever', etc., there are, admittedly, official versions to cover them all: *cuandoquiera que, comoquiera que, dondequiera que* but these are too literary and, therefore pedantic-sounding, for everyday purposes. Unfortunately there is no one cut-and-dried method of reducing them to everyday size—though the subjunctive is likely to figure largely—so they had better be taken in turn.

'Whenever' is fairly straightforward, viz. *siempre que*: *Siempre que salgo*, 'Whenever I go out'. If the time is uncertain use the subjunctive: *Siempre que vengas*, 'Whenever you (happen to) come'. Other possibilities are *Cada vez que . . .* and *Al . . .* (infinitive): *Al comprar melones . . .*, 'Whenever you buy melons . . .' (*v.* **vez**).

'Whoever' is likely to be simply *quien sea*, especially when it is unemphatic, e.g. 'I'll talk to whoever-it-is and tell him . . .', *Hablaré con quien sea y le diré . . .* but if it is a matter of 'I'll talk to him, who*ever* he is' (implying even if it's the President himself) then: *Le hablaré, sea quien sea*.

'Wherever' will have more variation as it contains possibilities of both state and motion and might mean 'whithersoever': 'He follows me wherever I go', implies the latter and would be *Me sigue por donde vaya*. 'Wherever I am', is static and so *Donde esté* or again, *Esté donde esté* if I am being more emphatic.

'However' offers an even greater range of possibilities. In English it is likely to be followed by an adjective—long, far, big, much, etc.—and in Spanish these are mostly handled by the addition of *muy*: *por muy grande que sea*, 'however big it is'; *por muy lejos que sea*, 'however far away', but one needs to watch the verb; however long it *takes*, would be *el tiempo que sea*. 'Much', too, may need different treatment: 'I'll pay whatever-it-is tomorrow', *Pagaré lo que sea mañana*, but: 'I'll pay it, however much it is', *Lo pagaré, sea lo que sea*. 'However' can also mean: 'in whatever manner', and will then probably be *de cualquier forma*: 'However you do it you get the same result', *De cualquier forma que lo hagas sale lo mismo*. (*Cualquier(a)* is quite common and not pedantic in the way that *quienquiera, dondequiera*, etc., are.)

Finally, there is the strongly accented 'ever', e.g. 'I wonder whether he has *ever* done a kind action in his life'. Here the solution is *jamás*. Technically it means 'never', but in a case of this sort it comes to the same thing: *Dudo que jamás habrá/haya hecho una buena acción en su vida*. *Nunca* is similarly used: 'Better than ever', *Mejor que nunca*.

A long entry for a small word! If it is any consolation, Hispanics have great difficulty in acquiring the use of 'ever' (*v.* also **quien**).

cuarto (m). A universal word for 'room', but in the R/P it implies a 'bedroom' and in Chile a small room (*v.* also **habitación, pieza**).

cuate. A native Mexican word for 'twin', but colloquially used to mean 'buddy', 'pal', 'mate', 'chum', etc.: *Salgo con los cuates*, 'I'm going out with the boys'. A girl may also be called *una cuate*. Triplets, in Mexico, are *triates*, elsewhere normally *trillizos*.

cubierta, -o. In addition to being the past participle of *cubrir* both of these are nouns in their own right. *Una cubierta* is the word used in Spain for a 'tyre/tire' (*v.* CARS). The commonest everyday use of *cubierto* is in restaurants where it usually means the same as *menú del día*, i.e. the 'set meal' for the day with a fixed price on its head. Those anxious to economize will be well advised to look out for it, by whichever name, as it is nearly always vastly cheaper. In Mexico it is likely to apply only to lunch, not to an evening meal. In restaurant jargon it really means 'a place' at the table (we ourselves often talk about a 'cover' charge) and *los cubiertos* is a general term for 'cutlery'.

cubo. *v.* **balde.**

cuco. A word with rather diverse meanings, and chiefly used around the Caribbean, including Mexico. As an adjective it can mean 'cute', 'dainty'; as a noun 'cuckoo' or 'glow-worm'. Perhaps as a combination of these it has come to be a common word for 'smart guy', a crafty one who looks after his own interests (not, however, in Venezuela where it is the commonest vulgar word for the female organ). In Mexico it is the popular nickname for anyone named *Refugio* (*La Virgen del Refugio* is a famous Mexican Virgin) in the same way as *Paco* is short for *Francisco* and *Pepe* for *José*. (I understand that this curious diminution stems from the initials P.P., standing for *Padre Putativo*, since Joseph was the putative father of Jesus.) Girls named *Refugio* are nicknamed *Cuca*.

cuenta (f). 'Account', 'bill', 'check', of course, but much used metaphorically and, at the risk of repeating what is in most dictionaries, I draw attention to one or two of the commoner uses:

Darse cuenta is the normal way of conveying 'to realize' (*v.* **realizar** which is largely False): *No me había dado cuenta de eso*, 'I hadn't realized that' (and note that this is not the same as 'I didn't take it into account'); *Hay que darse cuenta de que* . . ., 'One mustn't forget that . . . '

Tener cuenta should be distinguished from *tener en cuenta*. *Tener cuenta* is always used in the Third Person; used negatively *No tiene cuenta* means 'There's no point in it'; used positively it means that there is very much point in it and so equates with such expressions as 'It would be a good thing if', 'It would be just as well if', etc.; *Te tiene cuenta dejar de fumar*, 'It wouldn't be a bad thing if you gave up smoking'.

Tener en cuenta (or *tomar en cuenta*) means 'to take into account', 'to bear in mind', and can be used by any person: *Debe tener en cuenta* . . . , 'You have to remember that . . . ' Used negatively it is useful for 'to forget', 'to overlook': *No tuve en cuenta que habían cambiado de dirección*, 'I'd forgotten that they'd changed their address'.

None of these uses is at all difficult; it is chiefly a matter of appreciating how common and idiomatic they are.

cuerda (f). 'Cord', but it is a general word covering 'string', 'rope', etc. though a thicker type of rope is called *soga*, a word formerly used for the hangman's rope (*v.* also **mecate, reata**). *Dar cuerda* is the normal expression for 'to wind up' a clock or watch (dating from the days when weights hung on 'strings').

cuesta. *v.* **costa.**

cuestión (f). Surprising as it may seem, this is an Unreliable Friend; it only means 'question' in the sense of subject or problem: *Es una cuestión muy importante*, 'It's a very important matter'. If you mean 'question' in the sense of enquiry then you need *pregunta* (*v.* also **caso**). The verb 'to question (a person)' is *interrogar*; 'to question a thing' is *dudar de*.

culo (m). In the 'four-letter' category; in most countries it equates with 'arse' and is distinctly vulgar. In Spain, however, it does not detonate quite so strongly and is more comparable to 'bottom', 'bum', 'ass', 'rump'; it is even used of the 'bottom' of, say, a jar or bottle. Even so it is not a word for foreigners to make free with and some readers may be glad to know that *el trasero*, 'the behind', is a more acceptable substitute.

A very rude word derived from it, used chiefly in the Z/A, is *culear*, which means 'to have sexual intercourse'—of any sort.

culpa (f). 'Blame', 'fault', of course, and you should warn yourself off *falta* which means 'default'. Dictionaries do not usually give all the verbs needed in the allotment of blame, viz.:

   tener la culpa, 'to be to blame';
   llevarse la culpa, 'to get the blame' (not necessarily to take it);
   tomar/aceptar la culpa, 'to take the blame';
   echar la culpa, 'to push the blame on to somebody else'.

culto (m). As a noun 'cult', yes, but also 'religious service', in a church; perhaps particularly associated with Protestant services since by far the commonest Catholic one is *la Misa* ('Mass').

As an adjective *culto* is the commonest equivalent for 'educated', 'cultivated', 'learned', and is widely used: *Es un hombre muy culto*, 'He's a highly educated man', and is distinctly complimentary, having no overtones of stuffiness or 'artiness', even when used—as it often is—by people of little education themselves.

Cultura is the noun for 'education' in this sense but is often used for 'manners': *No tiene cultura*, 'He's got no manners', 'He doesn't know how to behave' (*v.* also **educación**).

cumplir. If you think it means 'to comply', regard it as False; it means 'to fulfil', and 'to comply' is *condescender* or *conformarse*. There are one or two everyday uses of it which merit attention:

For a period of time, or applied to somebody's age, *cumplir* has the sense of 'to complete': *Pedro cumplió ayer seis años*, 'Pedro was six yesterday'; *El plazo se cumplirá a medianoche*, 'The term expires at midnight'. 'A birthday', as you know, is *un cumpleaños* (*v.* **santo**).

Cumplir, in a social context, means 'to do the right thing', e.g. in sending flowers to one's hostess, or presents to one's godchildren on their Saint's day. I once heard two Uruguayan girls discussing a funeral they had attended, not from grief but because convention required it; rather a depressing occasion, apparently, but the conversation ended with one of them saying *Pues, hemos cumplido*, 'Well, we did our duty', 'We fulfilled our obligations'. *No tienes que cumplir*, 'There's no obligation for you to go/do it', etc. There is a saying: *Se obedece pero no se cumple*, which is used of rules which are quietly ignored, and might sometimes serve as a Spanish equivalent of 'more honoured in the breach than the observance'.

The adjective *cumplido* is applied to the kind of person who never forgets to telephone and felicitate on birthdays, anniversaries, etc., or, of course, condole when it is the anniversary of the death of a parent or grandparent. Hispanic mores, in these matters, are rather more exigent than ours (*v.* **velatorio**).

In L/A *cumplido* is often used to mean simply 'punctual', and *No hagas cumplidos* can mean 'Don't stand on ceremony'. In Spain they are more likely to say *Déjate de cumplidos* for this.

cundir. A common verb which you may not be aware of; it means 'to spread', 'to go a long way' (in the sense that a little can): *Es un poco caro pero cunde más*, 'It's a bit dear but it goes further'. When the 1968 student riots in France spread to L/A a headline read EL EJEMPLO CUNDE. Other meanings are 'to make progress', 'to get on well' (with something): *¿Le cunde, el trabajo?*, 'How's the work going?'; *No me cunde*, 'I'm not making any progress with it'. Note that it is always used in the Third Person.

cuota (f). 'Quota', yes, but at the entrances to Mexican turnpikes you are likely to see signposts giving you the option of two alternative roads, e.g. *Querétaro—Cuota* and *Querétaro—Libre*, each with an arrow, and *Cuota* here means that you pay a toll and will find a toll-gate some little distance ahead. The 'free' road will be the old road to *Querétaro* and not a motorway.

cura (m or f). The feminine noun means 'cure'; the masculine 'priest' (of the Roman church). *Sacerdote* exists but is a more general word and could apply to a priest of Baal. A Protestant 'priest' or 'minister' is likely to be called *un pastor*.

cursi. A colloquial but widely used adjective meaning something like 'socially pretentious'; it describes people who give themselves the airs of a higher social class, non-U pretending to be U. When applied to things, e.g. furniture or clothes, it contains the idea of nouveau-riche. High-class houses in the best Spanish tradition are furnished with an aristocratic simplicity and restraint, and the gaudy, ornate, Empire-style furniture which you sometimes find in city apartments would be described as *cursi*. I once heard a Spaniard say of a friend's tie *¡Qué corbata más cursi!* He was being facetious but I wondered what an Anglo-Saxon might have said . . . 'What a fancy tie!' . . . 'What a pansy tie!' . . . perhaps 'What a ghastly tie!' since it was not a compliment. Affectation, pretentiousness, excessive ornamentation are all involved (*v.* also **guachafo**).

curso (m), **cursar.** Unreliable; it is valid for the 'course' of a river, of an illness, of the stars, and of a period of time: *En el curso de la semana siguiente*, 'In the course of the following week' (*v.* also **discurso**); *dejar que las cosas sigan su curso*, 'to let matters take their course', but *un curso* in connection with studies implies an academic year, and it will not do for the 'course' of a meal, which has to be *plato*: 'The first course was soup', *El primer plato fue sopa*.

As a rough guide it is likely to equate with 'course' when preceded by the article; without this other equations are probable: *en curso*, 'in progress'; *el año en curso*, 'the current/present year'; *Está en curso al momento actual*, 'It's going on at the moment'. *Dar curso a*, 'to deal with' as a matter of routine; it may also mean 'to give vent to': *Dió curso franco a sus sentimientos*, 'He gave free rein to his feelings'. Conversely 'in due course' is *a su debido tiempo*; 'to change course', *cambiar de rumbo*.

The verb *cursar* may mean 'to attend a course' (usually for an academic year), but also simply 'to study', as well as 'to deal with' in a routine manner, i.e. 'to send on its course'; *cursar un sitio* is 'to frequent a place'. Its subject is always a person; things which 'go coursing down/through', etc. usually require *correr*.

D

dar. Not only 'to give', but: 'give up', 'give out', 'give off', and so 'yield', 'produce', etc. *Dar* is even more all-purpose than 'give' in English. Hardly my business, perhaps, but a few verbal phrases involving *dar* should certainly be in the reader's repertory:

¿Qué más da?, 'What does it matter?', 'What difference does it make?' 'What's the odds?', 'Why worry?'

(Me) da lo mismo, 'It's all the same (to me)', '(I) don't mind'.

Da gusto . . . (Infinitive), 'It's nice to . . .': *Da gusto estar aquí*, 'It's nice to be here'; 'It's nice to get up in the morning but it's nicer to lie in bed', *Da gusto madrugar pero quedarse en cama da más todavía*.

Dar de sí is the phrase for to 'give' in the elastic sense: *Esta lana no da de sí*, 'This wool doesn't "give" ' (i.e. won't stretch).

A very common and idiomatic use of *dar* with a noun equates it with our 'make': *Me da vergüenza*, 'It makes me ashamed'; *Me da ganas de gritar*, 'It makes me want to scream'. *Dar la lata* is a somewhat slangy expression for 'to make a nuisance of oneself' (*v.* **lata**). *Dar la vuelta* is one of the commonest ways of saying 'to turn round' (e.g. in a car), i.e. to make a turn.

dato, data. *Dato* and *datos* are 'datum' and 'data' respectively but are used rather more freely than these words in English: *No faltan datos para juzgar*, 'There's no lack of evidence to judge by'; *Los datos obtenidos hablan por sí mismos*, 'The information obtained speaks for itself'. The Latin *data* survives in the Spanish equivalent of 'P.S.' (*Post Scriptum*) which is *P.D.* (*Post Data* or *Post Datum*).

deber. *v.* **tener.**

decencia (f), **decente.** 'Decency, decent' in the sense of 'proper, respectable': *La decencia exige que . . .*, 'Decency requires that . . .' but it does not extend to our colloquial uses; *un muchacho decente* is more 'an honest chap' than 'a decent chap' which would be *simpático* or *amable*; 'a very decent meal', *una comida muy adecuada*.

decepción (f), **decepcionar.** Classic False Friends, though the average dictionary will gaily lead you astray; *decepción* does not mean 'deception' but 'disappointment', and *decepcionar*, 'to disappoint': *¡Qué decepción!*, 'What a disappointment!' *Esta película me ha decepcionado mucho*, 'I was horribly disappointed in that film' (*v.* also **defraudar**). 'Deception' is *engaño* and 'to deceive', *engañar*: 'You can't fool all of the people all of the time', *No se puede engañar a todo el mundo todo el tiempo*.

decir. 'To say'; a nice easy verb on the whole but a few uses warrant a little attention:

Digo is the word for 'I mean . . .' when you have made a verbal slip and want to correct it: *Los chilenos . . . ¡digo! los peruanos*, 'Chileans . . . I mean, Peruvians'.

Digo yo obviously brings a strong emphasis on to the 'I' and is the equation for '(so) *I* think', 'in *my* opinion'.

Dígame, literally 'Say to me', or 'Say on', is something like 'Yes, Sir?' and is certainly what a waiter or taxi-driver or shop assistant is likely to say to you when asking what you want but it is also used quite commonly in conversation, e.g. in reply to somebody who calls your name, wanting to say something to you but not sure whether you are listening. The reply *Dígame*, at such a point, means that you are listening and equates with 'Yes?' It is often reduced to *Diga* or, between intimates, *Dime*. In Spain, *Dígame* is the conventional thing to say when you answer the telephone and so equates with 'Hello?' (*v.* TELEPHONES).

¡No me diga(s)! is the response to an astonishing piece of information and therefore equates with 'You don't say!', 'What do you know!', or simply an incredulous 'No!' (*v.* also **fijar**).

. . .*que digamos* is sometimes facetiously added to a negative statement to cancel it out (rather in the style of the British 'I *don't* think'), e.g. *¡No llueve, que digamos!*, literally 'It's not raining, shall we say!' but in fact meaning that it's raining hard.

dedicar(se). A common verb, used far more than 'to dedicate' in English and meaning 'to get down to', 'to pursue', even 'to earn a living': *¿A qué se dedica?*, 'What does he do for a living?' Followed by a noun denoting a period of time the equation will often be to 'spend': *Dedicó la tarde a tocar discos*, 'He spent the afternoon playing records'; *Dedícate a lo tuyo*, 'Mind your own business!'; *Apagó la radio y se dedicó a hacer su tarea*, 'He switched off the radio and got down to his homework'. For real dedication *consagrar* is probably a better word: *Consagró su vida al cuidado de los pobres*, 'She devoted her life to the care of the poor'.

defraudar. Unreliable and much will depend on context. Used for actions which get reported in the newspapers it may well mean 'to defraud', but in a merely domestic context it can simply mean 'to let down', 'to disappoint': *Me has defraudado*, 'You've let me down'. *El fraude*, however, is the official name for the crime of 'fraud' though verbs for defrauding are likely to be *desfalcar*—'to embezzle' or *estafar*—'to swindle'. There is no very good equivalent of our slightly facetious 'old fraud'; perhaps *impostor*?

dejar. Barely my business but it is such a common verb that a few mental notes are indicated. It is much used colloquially for 'to lend': *Déjame tu peine*, 'Lend me your comb', and it contains no suggestion that the loan may not be returned. For such minor purposes it is probably commoner then *prestar*.

Dejar de, literally 'to desist from', is the normal equivalent of 'to stop (doing)', 'to leave off': *Debería dejar de fumar*, 'You ought to give up smoking'; *Déjate de tonterías*, 'Stop fooling around'.

Dejar de ser, literally 'to cease to be', is the likeliest equivalent for 'to be not as . . . (adj.) . . . as formerly': *Ha dejado de ser tan animado como antes*, 'He's not as lively as he used to be'. One might imagine that, used negatively, it would mean 'to be just as . . .', but in practice it implies something on the other side of the medal and a better equivalent is 'all the same': *No deja de ser atractiva*, 'She's a pretty girl all the same', i.e. in spite of her faults; a previous 'but' is implicit in the phrase.

delicioso. Yes, 'delicious', but we tend to associate it with food while Hispanics do not, so that a better equation is 'delightful'. The normal word used in connection with nice food is *rico* and *¡Qué rico!* is a common exclamation at the meal-table. (In Mexico

¡Qué sabroso!) If you are anxious to give your hostess's food particularly high praise then a better word is *exquisito*, or of course *riquísimo*.

demandar. It seems fair to call it False since nowadays its meaning is practically always 'to sue' (in a court of law). For 'to demand', *v.***exigir.**

demás (preceded by *lo, la, los, las*). A very common expression which is useful enough to warrant a mental note. Its commonest form is probably *los demás* which, in a general sense, means 'other people', and. within a limited group of people, 'the others', 'everybody else', 'the rest of them', etc.: *Hay que respetar las opiniones de los demás*, 'One must respect other people's opinions'; *Se quedó con una y tiró/botó las demás*, 'He kept one and threw the rest away'. *Lo demás* will apply to things uncountable: *Lo demás es sencillo*, 'The rest is easy'. It can be used adjectivally: *La demás gente*, 'The rest of the people'.

demasiado. 'Too . . . (adj)', 'too much', but when I was in Colombia a man said to me, 'Is it too cold in London?' to which I unthinkingly replied, 'Too cold for what?' He meant excessively cold. Incorrect, no doubt, but since most of us are capable of saying 'I don't know too much about it', perhaps it is not for us to criticize. I did not, in any case, hear this use of *demasiado* for 'very, very', anywhere else.

demorar. An old Spanish word which has survived more robustly in S/A than it has in Spain and Mexico. It means 'to delay', 'to hold up'. *Demorarse*, 'to get held up', 'to dawdle', 'to dilly-dally' on the way. In Spain and Mexico they mostly say *tardar* (*v.* also **entretener**).

demostración. *v.* **manifestación.**

denante. *v.* **antes.**

denunciar. Unreliable; it might mean 'to denounce' but its basic meaning is simply 'to announce' in the sense of 'to denote', 'to point to': *Su escritorio bien ordenado denunciaba un hombre de hábitos metódicos*, 'His tidy desk betokened a man of methodical habits'.

departamento (m). The universal word for 'department', in an office or a large store, but in Chile and Mexico it is also the word for an 'apartment/flat', elsewhere called *apartamento* (*v.* also **piso**).

departir. No, *not* 'to depart' but, surprisingly, 'to chat', 'to talk'. Mentioned solely because of its Falsity. You will never hear it in ordinary conversation.

dependiente (m or f). Unlikely to mean a 'dependant'; in Spain it will probably mean a 'shop assistant/sales clerk'; in L/A a 'clerk' in an office. The normal way of indicating 'dependants' in a general sense is *Las personas que de Vd.* (*él, ellos,* etc.) *dependen.*

depósito (m), **depositar.** The verb is fairly Reliable for 'to deposit', but the noun has quite a different image (or images). Basically it is a place where something is stored, particularly liquids, but, failing some more precise indication (e.g. *de agua*, *de equipajes*, etc.), it will suggest, in the R/P, a 'store-room', in Spain the 'petrol/gas tank' of a car, in much of L/A a 'water cistern', and in the newspaper probably 'the morgue'.

For deposits of money, *v.* **abono, anticipo, enganche, caución.**

derecho, -a. As you know, means both 'right', and 'straight' (and, as a noun, 'law') but keep awake about the gender when you are asking directions: *vaya por la derecha*, 'Keep to the right'; *Todo derecho*, 'straight on' (*v.* also **adelante** and **allá**).

derramar. Most dictionaries start by telling you that this means 'to pour out', and fail to make clear that it refers to an accidental pouring out, e.g. blood gushing from a wound. Its most likely meaning is 'to spill', though in Spain domestic spilling is usually *tirar*. To pour out, e.g. a drink, deliberately is *echar*.

desagüe (m). The place where the water goes out, hence 'drain', or, as often as not, the 'drain pipe/plug hole' of a wash basin or sink: *El desagüe está atrancado*, 'The drain-pipe's blocked up'. I have heard it used of the 'overflow' of a cistern, which is quite logical even if not usual.

desarmar. *v.* **armar.**

descansar, descanso (m). Both very common though not always given much attention in study books; *descansar* means 'to rest', 'to relax'; *cansado* is the universal adjective for 'tired'; *descanso* the universal noun for a 'break', i.e. a period of relaxation. It is often used where we might say 'relief', e.g. when things have been tense and at last a 'break' occurs: *¡Qué descanso!*, 'What a relief!' In such a context it is more likely than *alivio*, the official word for 'relief'.

descomponer(se). Rather Unreliable; *descomponerse* does mean 'to decompose', of dead bodies, but *descomponer* means simply 'to break down', 'to go wrong' and *una descompostura* is the usual word in *Mexico* for 'a breakdown' (e.g. in a car). Elsewhere the more usual word for 'to break down'—of any kind of machinery— is *estropear* and 'a breakdown' is *una avería* (*v.* also **accidente**).

desear. 'To desire', yes, but Spanish has no one, easy verb for 'to wish' and *desear* is used for the transitive wishing of the Merry Christmas type: *Le deseo un feliz viaje*, 'I wish you a good trip' (*v.* **ojalá** for another type of wishing).

desgracia (f), **-damente.** False; *desgracia* is not 'disgrace' but 'misfortune'; *¡Qué desgracia!*, 'How unfortunate!', 'What bad luck!' *Desgraciadamente* is the normal adverb for 'unfortunately' (in L/A often *lamentablemente*), though 'fortunately' has to be *afortunadamente*. 'Disgrace' is *vergüenza* (*q.v.*).

deshacer. 'To undo', in the widest senses, both literally and metaphorically and it can therefore mean 'to open' (e.g. a parcel). *Deshacerse de* is quite a good equivalent of 'to get rid of': *Voy a deshacerme de todos estos papeles*, 'I'm going to get rid of all those papers'. *Eliminar* is another possibility for this.

desmayarse, desmayo (m). False; *un desmayo* is 'a faint', 'a swoon', and *desmayarse*, 'to faint'. *Se ha desmayado*, 'He/she's fainted'. 'Dismay' is not easy to translate and there is no stock phrase which equates with 'to my dismay'; you would probably have to say *con sorpresa*, and use *quedarse sorprendido* for 'to be dismayed', leaving it to the context to show the surprise was disagreeable or else inserting *triste*.

In L/A *un vahido*, 'a fainting fit', is often used; also for 'a black-out', of the type suffered by airmen, parachutists, etc.

desorden (m). 'Disorder', certainly, but sometimes a useful equivalent for that all-too-common word 'mess'. *¡Qué desorden!* is quite a likely exclamation when you are confronted with, say, an untidy room or desk, but it implies physical untidiness. 'His affairs were in an awful mess' would probably have to be *Sus asuntos estaban muy embrollados*. For other words for 'mess' *v.* **embrollo, follón, lío**.

despacho. *v.* **oficina.**

despegar, despegue (m). Since *pegar* means 'to stick', it is not difficult to work out that *despegar* means 'to unstick', but you may not have realized that *despegue*, on your air-ticket, means 'take-off time', i.e. the moment when the plane comes unstuck from Mother Earth. Beware of thinking, however, that *pegar* therefore means 'to land'; this is *aterrizar* (*v.* **pegar**).

desperdiciar, desperdicios (m. pl.). 'Waste' and worth a mental note. The first word that springs to mind for 'to waste' is *gastar* but this strictly means 'to expend', 'to use up'. *Desperdiciar* means unequivocally 'to waste': *Espero que no vaya a desperdiciarlo*, 'I hope you're not going to waste it'. *Desperdicios* is a likely sign on a waste-basket or litter-bin in, say, a public park, and again means any kind of 'waste', uncontaminated by notions of muck or garbage, which would be *basura* (*v.* also **gastar, perder**).

despistar, despiste (m). *Pista*, as you no doubt know, means 'track', and *despistar* therefore means 'to push off the track', 'to side-track', 'to mislead', in both literal and metaphorical senses. *Eso me despistó por completo*, 'That put me completely off the scent/ track'. The adjective *despistado* is extremely common and can mean either 'bewildered' or 'absent-minded', i.e. the side-tracking may be temporary or habitual: *Estoy despistado*, 'I'm all at sea'; *Es un hombre despistado*, 'He's an absent-minded fellow'.

The noun *despiste* can refer to going off the rails in most senses and *tener un despiste* is a common verbal phrase for 'to be wide of the mark'. In a car context it can mean a 'skid', though more general for this is *un patinazo* and *patinar*, 'to skid'. Both noun and verb are extremely common.

destacar, destacado. *Destacar* seems as though it ought to mean 'to detach', but in fact does so chiefly in the military sense so that its usual, metaphorical meaning is 'to single out' (for some special purpose). *Destacado* has therefore become the normal adjective for 'distinguished', 'outstanding': *El químico más destacado de su generación*, 'The most outstanding chemist of his generation'. If you are looking for the equivalent 'detached' then *separado* is probably best for physical senses and *apartado* for metaphorical: *Llevaba una vida muy apartada*, 'He led a very detached existence'. 'To detach', *separar*.

destino (m). 'Destiny', certainly; also 'destination', but it is also a useful word for 'Fate'. From its derivation *suerte* ought to mean 'fate' but it has come to mean simply 'luck'. If you want to say 'What a fate!' or 'a fate worse than death' then *destino* is the most indicated, though *hado* is another possiblity.

destituir, destitución (f). False; *destitución* means 'dismissal from office'; it implies high office and is associated with politics. *Destituir*, 'to dismiss from office'. 'Destitute' is *indigente*.

destreza (f). Not only a False Friend but a False Cognate; it does not mean 'distress' but 'dexterity', 'skill', 'nimbleness', 'agility', being derived from the Latin *dexteritas*. Remember this and you should have no difficulty. 'Distress', having several different meanings and applications, has several possible translations: *angustia*—'anguish', *apuro*—'embarrassment', *miseria*—'poverty' . . . *v.* also **desgracia, disgusto.**

determinar. Distinctly Unreliable; it is mostly used in the sense of 'to ascertain', usually in some sense of 'to delimit', 'to find out the extent of': *Podemos determinar las razones cuando sepamos todas las circunstancias*, 'We can decide on the reasons when we know all the circumstances'. Our equivalent would often be 'to tell' in this sense. It is not quite an everyday word but it is rather commoner in Spanish than 'to determine' (in this sense) in English. We more often use the word in the sense of 'to resolve (to)', and here *decidirse a* or *resolverse a* are more likely. For 'to determine' in the sense of 'govern', *v.* **condicionar.**

Determinado is much used where we should say 'particular', e.g. *en un caso determinado*, 'in a particular case', or a 'given' case. 'Determined', meaning 'resolute', is likely to be *decidido* or *resuelto*.

devolver, devolución (f). False. 'Devolve' and 'devolution' are not common words in English but these two are very common in Spanish and the basic concept is paying or giving back, both literally and metaphorically, in domestic or business circumstances: *La devolución del préstamo*, 'The repayment of the loan'; *Tendrás que devolvérmelo*, 'You'll have to give it me back'. *Devueltos* might apply to the books returned to the library.

In so far as Spanish has an equivalent for 'to devolve on', it would be *recaer en* or *pasar a*; perhaps *incumbir a*.

diario. Basically the adjective for 'daily', but, as in English, it has become a noun for a 'newspaper'. (It was one of the first words I ever learnt in Spanish; on my first visit to Spain, before the Civil War, there was a *Gran Diario de la Noche*, a 'Great Daily of the Night'—you might say: 'The Nightly Daily'.) It is also the noun for 'diary', when this means a record of past doings; those yet to come are more likely to be written in *una agenda*. The little pocket books in which you scribble memoranda and which people give at Christmas when all else fails you are likely to call *mi libreta*, rather than *mi diario*. If you want an adjective for 'daily' in the sense of humdrum, everyday, e.g. the daily round, then *cuotidiano* is indicated, and the adverb 'daily' is *cada día*.

dictar. 'To dictate', yes, but in L/A it is often extended to other verbal forms of 'dishing it out': *dictar una conferencia*, 'to give a lecture'; *dictar una clase*, 'to take a class'; *dictar las noticias*, 'to read the news' (i.e. on the radio).

difícil, dificultad (f), **dificultar.** On the face of it hardly worth a mention but one or two points may be noted: *Difícil* is often used of a person where we should say 'fussy', a word not easy to translate. *Dificultad* certainly means 'difficulty' but natives are more likely to use *problema* or *inconveniente (q.v.)* and readers are advised to keep aware of these two alternatives.

   Dificultar is a verb which English does not possess in such cognate form; it means 'to make more difficult', and although it does not contain any sense of deliberate obstruction it is often used where we might say 'interfere': 'His father's death interfered with his studies', *La muerte de su padre dificultó sus estudios*. If you said *interrumpió sus estudios* it would suggest that it stopped them altogether whereas *dificultó* merely suggests that it upset them temporarily. 'Interfere' is not always an easy verb to translate and, as usual in such cases, one has to consider what form of interference is intended. *Interferir* exists for purely technical and scientific contexts. For others *v.* **estorbar, meter(se).**

dije. A somewhat colloquial adjective used in Chile for 'good-looking'. It may be used of either sex.

dínamo (m & f). Obviously 'dynamo/generator', but in Spain they regard it as feminine and in S/A masculine. Where the accent comes will also vary, not so much country-wise as expert-wise; technicians tend to say *dínamo* and the man in the street *dinámo*. The latter, being in the majority, will probably win in the long run. In Mexico, where cars are concerned, they usually say *generador*.

Dios. In Spanish, as in English, the name of the Almighty is fairly liberally scattered about the average person's conversation but it does not always have the same force and readers should be aware of differences. *¡Por Dios!* for example, though often used where we might say 'For Heaven's sake!', is less strong than 'For God's sake!' and in Spain is often used as a politeness, e.g. you ask your hostess if you may smoke and she replies *¡Pero, por Dios! ¡No faltaba más!*, 'Please do! Go right ahead!' and you should not interpret this as meaning 'For God's sake do!—it is not in the least exasperated. In L/A this use is less common (*v.* COURTESY).

¡Dios mío! is likewise less strong than 'My God!' and ladies may use it with impunity. If a woman finds a ladder/run in her stocking she will quite likely exclaim *¡Ay, Dios mío!* and if she said it with a piercing shriek it would serve to receive the news that her child had been run over but muttered quietly by a typist it could simply mean that she had put in the carbons the wrong way round.

Other common phrases equate rather more exactly, e.g. *¡Gracias a Dios!*, 'Thank God!'; *Si Dios quiere*, 'God willing/ "D.V. and W.P."'.' Nuns, and sometimes beggars, will often thank you for a small offering with *Dios se lo pague*, 'May God repay you for it'.

dirección (f). Unreliable; its commonest meaning is probably 'address': *Le daré su dirección*, 'I'll give you his address.' In a car *la dirección* is likely to mean 'the steering'; in an office: 'the management'. It does, of course, also mean 'direction', but is much used in connection with 'one-way traffic', *dirección única*. Countries vary in the term they use for 'one-way': *Una mano* (*Arg*) (with its counterpart of *Contramano* for 'No entry'; 'one-way street'); *Tránsito* (*Ch*); *Una vía* (*Co*). In others *sentido único* is about as common as *dirección única*.

directa (f). *Directo* is the normal adjective for 'direct'. Used here as a noun it is short for *velocidad directa* and means 'top/high gear': *Iba en directa*, 'He was in top/high'. In some countries, e.g. Mexico, they are more likely to refer to the gears by number: *Iba en cuarta/tercera*, etc. but whichever form you use, remember that it requires a verb of motion—*ir, subir, venir*, etc. If you mean 'I'm in top', you cannot say *Estoy en directa*, you must say *Voy en directa*; 'I came up in high', *Subí en directa*, etc.

disco (m), **discar**. *Disco* has a number of everyday applications of which the most obvious is 'gramophone record'; rather less obvious is 'dial of a telephone'. As a result of the latter *discar* has crept in, in places, for 'to dial' a number, though the offical word is *marcar* (*un número*). *Disco* is also used where disc-parking has been introduced.

Una discoteca may be used for 'a discotheque' but strictly speaking it means 'a record library'. It is also sometimes used of 'a jukebox' though the proper word for this is *un tocadiscos*, 'a record-player'. *Un tocacintas*—'a cassette-player'.

discreción (f), **discreto**. Unreliable; *discreto* might mean 'discreet', and did so in the past, but now usually means 'average', 'middling', 'undistinguished'. In college reports *un alumno discreto* means 'an average student', neither dull nor brilliant. I imagine this may originally have been a euphemism on the part of the teacher to describe a pupil who never opened his mouth. If so, he has succeeded in debasing the word and it is now not easy to find a satisfactory equivalent of 'discreet'; you have to use such words as *circunspecto, prudente* or perhaps *de confianza* though none of these quite meets the suggestion of knowing when to keep one's mouth shut.

Discreción is a little better for 'discretion', but it is much used to indicate merely personal choice. In some restaurants you will find, say, *Vino a discreción* which means that you may have as much or as little wine as you have a mind for. Similarly recipes may say *Pimienta y sal a discreción*, 'Pepper and salt to taste'.

discurso (m). 'Discourse', perhaps, but it is the normal word for 'speech'; *pronunciar* (*dictar* in L/A) *un discurso*, 'to make a speech'. In the past it could mean 'course': *en el discurso del tiempo*, 'in the course of time' but nowadays this would be *transcurso*.

discusión (f), **discutir.** Unreliable to the point of Falsity since both words suggest 'argument', not merely 'discussion'; *una discusión* is much more likely to be 'an argument' with some heat than the quiet exchange of opinions evoked by the word 'discussion' which, in Spanish, would probably be simply *una conversación* or *un intercambio de opiniones. Cambiar opiniones* is a common verbal phrase for 'to have a discussion'. ('To change one's opinion' is *cambiar de opinión*.)

disgustar, disgusto (m). Very Unreliable Friends; the word 'disgust', in English, rarely carries the Article whereas in Spanish one speaks of *un disgusto* and this means, not disgust, but 'displeasure'. It is normally part of a verbal phrase, e.g. *dar un disgusto*, 'to displease (someone)', or *llevarse un disgusto*, 'to be upset': *Les dio un disgusto a sus padres casándose con esa mujer*, 'His parents were very upset when he married that woman'.

Disgustar means approximately the same as *dar un disgusto* but is far less commonly used. *Disgustado*, however, is a common adjective and *estoy disgustado con*, 'I'm upset about', 'I'm fed up about', indeed it may imply a certain amount of anger and in Chile *disgustado* equates with 'annoyed'. Where an Anglo-Saxon might say, 'What a disgusting sight!' a Hispanic would probably exclaim *¡Qué asco!* or, in the case of moral digust, *¡Qué vergüenza!* 'Disgust' is not easy to translate into Spanish; you have to choose from such words as *asco, desprecio, repulsión*, etc., according to context.

disparar, disparate (m). *Disparar*, as you probably know, means 'to shoot' (with a firearm) or, intransitively (and reflexively) 'to go off', but it is used a good deal metaphorically for 'to go charging off' (in response to some stimulus): *Salió disparado*, 'He was off like a shot'. It can even extend to 'shooting off one's mouth': *No te dispares*, 'Take it easy', 'Don't go shooting off your mouth'. If you tend to think it means to disappear then by all means regard it as False; 'to disappear', *desaparecer*.

Disparate might also be classed as False; the Spanish for our 'disparate', i.e. 'incompatible', is *dispar* or perhaps *desigual. Un disparate* is a noun for anything grossly incongruous or out of place, hence 'enormity', 'atrocity', 'monstrosity', all in a rather exaggerated, colloquial sense. A schoolboy 'howler', a 'goof', or a particularly ghastly 'folly' of a building would be *un disparate* but it can be used of lesser things; a housewife who has been asked an outrageous price for something may exclaim *¡Qué disparate!*, 'What a monstrous price!' It can even equate with 'nonsense': *No digas disparates*, 'Don't talk nonsense', 'Don't be absurd'.

disponer. False, in its way, since *disponer de* means 'to have at one's disposal', 'to have available', 'to make use of': *El sindicato dispone de fondos considerables*, 'The trade union has considerable funds at its disposal'—and this is quite different from 'disposing of' the funds which would be *deshacerse de* or *desembarazarse de*. The nearest *disponer* comes to Reliability is in the past participle: *dispuesto a* equates fairly well with 'disposed to'.

distinto. False; it does not mean 'distinct' but 'different', and is the usual word for this though *diferente* is also used. 'Distinct' has to be *visible* or *claro* or—say for the profile of mountains against the sky—perhaps *destacado* (*q.v.*).

divertido. It may mean 'amused', but is more likely to mean 'amusing': *Fue una película muy divertida*, 'It was a very amusing film'. Illogical, but there it is! (*v.* also **aburrido**).

divulgación (f). False; it means simply 'dissemination', 'broadcasting', 'making widely known', and contains no sense of divulging secrets. *Divulgar* is the verb; news agencies, radio stations, etc. *divulgan su material*. Among academics it may have a slightly disparaging ring, viz. 'pop' science, writing for the masses, not really serious work, etc. (*v.* also **vulgarización**). 'To divulge' would usually be *revelar*.

doler, dolor (m). *Dolor* means both 'grief' and 'pain' but chiefly the latter, and is the usual word for our '-ache': *dolor de cabeza*, 'headache'; *Tengo un dolor de espalda*, 'I've got a back-ache'.

When some part of the body is concerned where a pain would be less usual you use the verb *doler*: *Me duele el brazo*, 'I've got a sore arm', 'My arm hurts'. To say, e.g. *dolor de ombligo* would mean 'navel-ache', and would suggest that this was a recognized malady. *Me duele*, 'It hurts' and *¿Te duele?* 'Does it hurt?' are worth learning off pat (*v.* also **pena**).

-dora (f). Not a word but a suffix. I mention it because readers may find it useful to appreciate that it usually implies some sort of machine, apparatus or mechanical device. *-dor* is the ending corresponding to our '-er': *portador*, 'porter'; *contador*, 'counter' etc., but this often implies a human being. *Un grabador* means 'an engraver', i.e. the man who does the engraving, whereas *una grabadora* means 'a tape-recorder' (but note that, applied to a person, it means 'a woman engraver', just as *una visitadora* means 'a lady visitor'). Similarly, *grapadora*, 'stapling-machine'; *enceradora*, 'wax-polisher', and so on. The words are basically adjectival and no doubt *máquina* is understood. This general principle enables words to be coined. In the (perhaps rather unlikely) event of your inventing a device for, say, switching off other people's radios, you could say *He inventado una apagadora* and although you would certainly be plied with questions you would have got the general message across every bit as neatly as if you said 'a switcher-offer'.

dueño, -a. Normally 'owner', 'proprietor', or the 'master of the house'. For the reader its most likely meaning is probably: 'landlord, -lady'.

E

ebullición, *v.* **cocer.**

echar. This is a Spanish 'all-purpose' verb with a multitude of very diverse applications, most of which are best learnt by the 'direct' method. Since we are confined to the written word the reader should appreciate that it is cognate with 'eject' and means to 'out' in all kinds of senses: *¿Le/lo echo?* would mean, 'Shall I throw him out?' in reference to some undesirable person but *¿Lo echo?*, 'Shall I pour it out?' if the tea had just been brought in. *¿Qué echan?* literally: 'What are they emitting?' is likely to mean 'What's on?' in connection with radio, TV or movies. *Echar la culpa*, 'to push the blame (on to somebody)'; *echar un vistazo a*, 'to have a look at'; *echar empleados*, 'to lay off employees'. *Echar* is particularly likely to be used for the transference of liquids: *¿Le echo gasolina?* 'Shall I fill her up?' *¿Le echo más leche?* 'Will you have a little more milk in it?' (tea or coffee); *echar agua*, 'to quench'.

Echar a with an infinitive suggests a sudden breaking into a particular activity: *echó a correr*, 'he broke into a run'; *echaron a reír*, 'they burst out laughing'. Rather an idiomatic one is *echar a perder*, 'to spoil' (in all senses, including children).

Other everyday idiomatic uses are:
Echar una carta, 'to post/mail a letter'.
Echar una mano, 'to lend a hand'.
Echar la llave, 'to turn the key', i.e. 'to lock'; *cerrar*, though it often implies locking, really means simply 'to shut'.
Echar el freno, 'to put the brake on'; it implies the handbrake; for the footbrake one would simply say *frenar*.
Echar a cara o cruz, 'to toss up', *cara o cruz* being the equivalent of heads or tails.
Echar cuentas, 'to settle accounts', whether literally or metaphorically.

Echar un trago/cigarro, ' to have a drink/smoke'.

Echar chispas literally 'to emit sparks', i.e. 'to be furious'.

Another fairly common one is *echar una siesta*, 'to have a nap/siesta'. *Echarse* is normal for 'to lie down'.

A curious idiomatic phrase is *echar de menos*, 'to miss', in the sense of feeling the loss of: *Se le echaba mucho de menos*, 'He was sorely missed' (*v.***extrañar**, also **sacar**).

editar, editor (m). Unreliable; they might mean 'edit' and 'editor' but are much more likely to mean 'to publish', and 'publisher'. If you have to distinguish then *publicar* may be used for 'to publish'. *Una editorial* is apt to be misleading since it is usually short for *una casa editorial* and means 'a publishing house'. In a newspaper context 'the editor' is mostly called *el redactor* and 'the editing' *la redacción*. For the more scholarly type of editing there is no very satisfactory word; you would have to say *preparar para la prensa* or something of the sort.

educación (f). Unreliable; the first thing it suggests in Spanish is 'up-bringing', and *falta de educación* will usually mean 'bad manners', 'lack of breeding'. Education of the sort received at school or college is usually *enseñanza* or *instrucción*, sometimes *formación* (*q.v.*). At the governmental level, however, a Ministry of Education is quite likely to be called *Ministerio de Educación* and in some contexts *bien/mal educado* might mean 'well/badly edu-cated' but in everyday circumstances is far more likely to mean 'well/ill-bred'.

efectivamente. False; it does not mean 'effectively' but 'in effect', and can sometimes be a solidified form of 'yes': *Pues efectivamente sí*, 'Well, yes, it is, really', 'That's what it amounts to'. 'What-it-amounts-to' is the meaning, near enough; it is not a bad equiva-lent of our 'actually'. 'Effective' is *eficaz* and 'effectively', *eficazmente*.

efectivo (m). As a noun it means 'cash', in contrast to, say, cheque or other form of payment: *¿Lo quiere en efectivo?* 'Do you want it in cash?' Another expression for 'to pay cash', is *pagar al contado*, usually in contradistinction to getting (something) on credit.

egresar, egreso (m). 'Egress', and so 'to go out', and a 'going-out', and much used in L/A. In Spain they use *salir*. Exit, *egreso* (L/A), *salida* (Spain). Much the same applies to *regresar* and *regreso* for which the Peninsular usage is *volver* and *vuelta*. A 'return/round trip' ticket is *ida y vuelta* in Spain and *ida y regreso* in L/A.

ejemplar *v*. **copia**.

elección (f), **elegir**. Unreliable; the root meaning is 'choice', and *elegir* is the normal verb for 'to choose'. *Elección* certainly applies to a political 'election' but it is also the everyday word for 'choice': *Eso lo dejo a su elección*, 'I leave the choice to you' (*v*. also **discreción**). *Escoger*, 'to select', is often used for 'to choose' in L/A.

elevador (m). Yes, 'elevator/lift', but only in countries under strong North American influence, e.g. Mexico. Elsewhere the usual word is *ascensor*. *Elevador* may also apply to a grain elevator (*v.* also **PA, PB, and PC**).

embarazada. I put it in the feminine form as this is by far the commonest. It is a classic False Friend and of particular danger to ladies; beware, ladies, of saying, when you feel embarrassed, *Estoy muy embarazada*; say *Estoy muy confusa*. *Embarazada* means 'pregnant'. Originally it meant 'heavily burdened' but the word has become particularized (*v.* also **violento**).

embrollar, embrollo (m). 'Imbroglio', 'tangle'. Perfectly proper words but ones you may not be very conscious of and which can be useful when casting round for an equivalent of 'mess': *Sus asuntos estaban muy embrollados,* 'His affairs were in an awful mess'. *¡Qué embrollo!* 'What a mess!' Bear in mind, however, that it is a mess of the 'tangle' type with consequent need for disentangling. It would not apply to mere untidiness (*v.* **desorden**).

emocionar(se), emoción (f). *Emoción* is certainly the general word for 'emotion', and *emocionarse,* 'to be filled with emotion', but, given the universal human tendency to exaggerate, these are often used where we should say 'excitement', and 'to get excited'. Equally *emocionante* often means simply 'exciting', 'thrilling', and *emocionado* 'excited', 'worked up'. It should not be used too recklessly; in some contexts it could suggest sexual excitement but in connection with, say, football it is safe enough. If you mean 'moved' then a better word is *conmovido.*

'Excited' is not really an easy word to convey in Spanish and the whole field of the emotions is highly Unreliable terrain, thickly populated by Doubtful Friends (*v.* **excitar, inquieto, nervioso**).

empacar, empaquetar, empaque (m). *Empacar* may be described as the Mexican verb for 'to pack', and indicates North American influence. A more universal expression for 'to pack' (one's suitcases) is *hacer las maletas. Empaquetar* usually means 'to make a parcel (of something)' (*v.* also **envolver**).

In Mexico *un empaque* can mean 'a washer', or 'gasket'.

empalmar, empalme (m). This is such a curious word, and so common, that it is worth a mental note. *Un empalme* in connection with roads rather implies a 'T-junction'; in connection with tape-recorders 'splice'; *empalmar* (*con*), 'to join up' (something with something), physical objects being implied.

empleado, -a. Strictly 'employee', but much used in S/A for 'servant', being one of the contemporary euphemisms to cover the odium of domestic service.

enchiladas (f. pl.). A Mexican dish consisting of a few *tacos (q.v.)* covered with sauce plus a few vegetables (usually spinach). The name gives you reason to expect something pretty hot but it is not always so.

Enchilarse is a Mexican verb for 'to go red in the face' (through eating chilis) and, metaphorically, 'to get into a rage'.

enchufar, enchufe (m). *Enchufar* means 'to plug in' (an electrical appliance) and *un enchufe* is 'an electric plug'. In Spain they have extended both to metaphorical uses; there *un enchufe* can mean 'a nice, cushy job', 'a sinecure', of the sort you get through being *bien enchufado*, i.e. 'having the right contacts' on the Old Boy network. In Mexico they say *bien colocado* for this and there *enchufado* is a slang world for 'drunk', 'an electric plug' being *una chavija*.

encima. Not really 'above', as the dictionaries tell you; it means literally 'on the summit', and the best equation is 'on top': *Puso la maleta en el suelo y luego la máquina encima,* 'He put the suitcase on the floor and then the typewriter (or camera!) on top (of it)'. Until we become aware of the word we are apt to say *arriba* which merely means 'above'. 'Put it on top', *Ponlo encima.* It extends to metaphorical uses and a common idiom is . . . *y encima* . . .,'. . . and on top of all that . . .': *Llegó a casa tarde y sucio y encima borracho,* 'He got home late, and dirty, and drunk into the bargain'. 'For good measure' and 'to crown it all' are other possibilities.

encontrar, encuentro (m). Most grammar books guide one into thinking, at an early stage, that the Spanish for 'to find' is *hallar* and I therefore feel obliged to record that I can only recall two or three times hearing this word used in ordincary conversation. The commonest spoken word is undoubtedly *encontrar:* ¿*Has encontrado las llaves?,* 'Have you found the keys?' *No lo encuentro,* 'I can't find it' (though *v.* also **buscar**). *Encontrar* is, of course, cognate with our 'encounter' and so is appropriate for 'to meet' (somebody by chance): *Le encontré por la calle,* 'I ran into him in the street'. For less accidental encounters *v.* **esperar** and **conocer.**

Encontrarse is quite a good equivalent for 'to find oneself', and is used a good deal more, as a stronger form of 'being in a particular place: *Pedro se encuentra actualmente en el dentista,* 'Pedro's at the dentist's at the moment', but it can be used metaphorically, as in English. I recall an old Crazy Gang joke of some years ago: Q. 'How did you find yourself in the morning?' A. 'Oh, I just looked under the table and there I was'. For once it will translate: Q. ¿*Cómo te encontraste por la mañana?* A. *Pues, miré debajo de la mesa y allí estaba.*

Un encuentro is, of course, 'a meeting', in the sense of a chance encounter, but it does not extend to metaphorical uses. 'An unexpected find', a 'trouvaille', brings the verb *hallar* into its own since this would be *un hallazgo.*

enganche (m). Literally a 'hooking-up' or '-on' (*gancho* = 'hook') and a proper word where some sort of hook-up is implied. In Mexico, however, it is much used to mean 'initial payment', a 'first instalment', i.e. which commits you to the remaining payments, and for which a more general word is *fianza* or *caución*. In Venezuela it means a 'job', 'work', an 'engagement' as it were.

engreír, engreído. *Engreído* is a useful word for 'conceited' though *presumido* is equally common. In Peru it is used for 'spoilt' in reference to children, elsewhere usually *mimado*. The un-reflexive verb *engreír* means 'to butter (someone) up', 'to flatter'; reflexively, 'to get conceited.'

enhorabuena (f). Included because one tends to find oneself needing the word without warning so I alert the reader that *¡Enhorabuena!* is 'Congratulations!' *Tengo que darle la enhorabuena,* 'I must congratulate you'.

enseñar. 'To teach', yes, but it is not always appreciated that it is the usual verb for 'to show': *¿Quiere enseñarme sus fotografías?* 'Would you like to show me your photographs?' *¿Quieres que te enseñe mis aguafuertes?,* 'Would you like me to show you my etchings?' One learns that 'to show' is *mostrar* but in conversation this is more often used reflexively for revealing aspects of oneself: *Se mostró muy solícito,* 'He showed great kindness', 'He showed himself very attentive'.

In the R/P, where Italian influence has been very strong, *mostrar* is used more often and *enseñar* more likely to be confined to teaching.

enterarse. Literally 'to make oneself entire', and much used in Spain in the metaphorical sense of 'to inform oneself', 'to find out about': *Voy a enterarme,* 'I'm going to find out'; *Está muy bien enterado,* 'He's very well informed'. It is often a good equivalent of 'to realize', 'to appreciate': *Lo son, pero no se han enterado,* 'They are, but they haven't appreciated the fact'; *Ya me voy enterando,* 'I'm beginning to understand'.

In L/A it is perhaps more often used in the physical sense of 'to recover' (from an illness) and 'to find out', there, is usually *informarse* or *cerciorarse*. In the R/P 'well-informed' usually seemed to be *preparado*.

entonces. *v.* **luego.**

entrada (f). 'Entry', 'entrance', in nearly all senses, but you should be aware that where concerts, theatres, bull-fights, etc. are concerned it is the word for 'ticket': *¿Has conseguido entradas?,* 'Did you manage to get tickets?' *Boletos/billetes* apply to bus, plane or railroad 'tickets'.

In culinary matters *entrada* is supposed to mean 'entrée' but in the Z/A it is usually applied to the 'first course'—usually something cold and salad-like—which in Spain would be called *entremeses*.

entretener(se). Unreliable; it means 'entertain' only in the sense of 'to amuse', *not* of having guests to your house: *Este libro me entretuvo mucho,* 'I found this book very entertaining'. The adjective 'entertaining', too, is another catch as it is *entretenido,* i.e. it is in the same class as *divertido* and *aburrido. Entretenido* is very similiar in meaning to *divertido* but is perhaps more likely to be used of books or plays; *divertido* is more often applied to persons.

For entertaining guests the verb is nearly always *invitar:* 'She entertained several friends to dinner', *Invitó a unos amigos a cenar,* but Hispanics do far less entertaining in their private houses than we do; if they wish to feast somebody they mostly do it in a restaurant.

Entretenerse means 'to waste time', in a frittering sort of way, 'to potter'. A mother, despatching her child on some errand, might say: *No te entretengas por el camino,* 'Don't dilly-dally on the way'.

envase (m). 'Container' but in practice most often meaning an 'empty' (bottle). In the Hispanic world at large they have not yet become waste-makers; bottles of beer, wine, minerals, soft drinks, etc., usually require the payment of a deposit which means that when you go back for more you take your *envases* with you (and the drinks are surprisingly cheaper in consequence); not, however, spirit and liquor bottles which do have to be thrown away. One wonders how long this good husbandry will last.

In Spain and Mexico empty beer- and soft-drink 'bottles' are usually referred to as *los cascos.*

envergadura (f). 'Wing-span', but much used metaphorically and so a useful word for 'scope', 'range': *de mucha envergadura,* 'far-reading', 'wide-ranging', 'comprehensive'.

envolver. On the face of it 'to involve', but in practice its use is almost confined to meaning 'to wrap up' (and Hispanics are great wrappers-up; the most trifling purchases are likely to be clothed in paper and often tied with string as well). Sometimes you may be asked *¿Se lo envuelvo?,* 'Shall I wrap it up for you?' but more often they will do it without asking.

'To involve' is not an easy verb to translate. We use it a lot, in a variety of contexts, and since there is no one Spanish verb to equate it with this means that the translation will vary according to context. 'To be involved' in, say, a scandal, would rather call for *implicar* but 'to be involved in a car accident' would probably be simple *tener un accidente* (*v.* **accidente**). 'I'm not involved', in the sense of it not being my concern, would be *Esto no tiene nada que ver con migo, No me corresponde a mí, No es cuenta mía,* or even *Estoy al margen* (*v.* **margen**). The adjective 'involved' would be *complicado* and if things *become* very involved then the verb *complicarse* is likely. For 'I don't want to be involved', *No quiero intervenir* is probably best (*v.* **intervenir**).

epidérmico. 'Epidermic', certainly, but also used metaphorically— perhaps particularly by journalists—to mean 'skin-deep'.

equivocar(se). False; *equivocar* means 'to mistake', and *equivocarse* is the commonest way of saying 'to make a mistake': *Me equivoqué de número*, 'I mistook the number'. *Una equivocación*, 'a mistake'; *Tiene que haber una equivocación*, 'There must be some mistake'. 'To equivocate' is not a very common verb but there is no really satisfactory translation for it; *mentir* is too strong. *Palabras equívocas* half suggests it but you might need to emphasize that they were deliberately mistaken (*v.* also **vacilar**) (*evasión* might do for 'equivocation').

escándalo (m). 'Scandal', yes, and used a good deal, so much so, in fact, that it has lost some of its force and is often used where we should say 'fuss': *Armó un gran escándalo*, 'He kicked up a great fuss', 'He made a scene'.

escape (m). A singularly Good Friend, on the whole; it can be an 'escape' from prison, or of gas, or an escape mechanism in clockwork. In a car context it means 'exhaust'.

escoba. *v.* **brocha.**

escoger. *v.* **elegir.**

escolar. Both a noun and an adjective and, either way, very Unreliable; as a noun it implies a young 'scholar'; indeed, in Spain it simply means a 'schoolboy'; in L/A it may extend to students. Nowhere can it mean the older, more august type of scholar, e.g. 'a great classical scholar' for which the Spanish would be *un erudito*. As an adjective it means: 'scholastic', or 'academic', e.g. *año escolar*, 'academic year'; or simply 'school' used adjectivally: *libros escolares*, 'school books'.

ese. *v.* **este.**

esperar. One learns at an early stage that this means 'to hope', 'to expect', and 'to wait for'. You may be less aware that it often serves for 'to meet': *Voy a esperarle al aeropuerto*, 'I'm going to meet him at the airport'—when the meeting is planned in advance. *Encontrar* (*q.v.*) applies to chance meetings. Moreover, it is not automatically, perhaps not even usually, the verb for 'expect' which is frequently *suponer*: *Supongo que sí/no*, 'I expect so/not'. 'Is he expecting you?' on, say, arrival at an office, would probably be *¿Está Vd. citado?* i.e. 'Have you an appointment?' and if, in such a context, you got instead *Le está esperando* it would not mean 'He's expecting you', but 'He's waiting for you'. In other contexts waiting and expecting can be virtually the same thing: *Le/la esperaba en el café;* if he was waiting he was obviously expecting (no doubt hoping too). We might say 'I'm waiting for her but I don't really expect her', but are perhaps more likely to say: '. . . I don't suppose she'll turn up', and a Hispanic would probably say, . . . *no creo que venga*.

Esperanza is more definitely 'hope', 'something to look forward to', and 'expectation' is hard to find an equivalent for. The film 'Great Expectations' was perforce translated *Grandes Esperanzas* but to a native will have sounded like Great Hopes, which is not quite the same thing. *Grandes perspectivas* might serve but opens out rather bigger prospects than 'expectations' which, in the matter of wills, has become particularized. *Esperanza*, however, does not always imply pleasant prospects; in the R/P *¡Qué esperanza!* is a common expression meaning 'What a prospect!' rather than 'What a hope!' In Spain this would be *¡Qué perspectiva! Expectación* exists but means rather 'expectancy', and in any case is not common.

espina (f). 'Spine', perhaps, but only in the sense of 'thorn' ('vertebra', *columna*). It is, however, the word for 'fish-bone' when these are encountered on your plate, so beware of saying *hueso*. When the fish is being prepared in the kitchen the bone structure is likely to be referred to as *la raspa*; it is what is left over at the end of the meal—or what you may sometimes have to extract from your mouth—which will be called *las espinas*.

esposo, -a. 'Spouse'. The word is commonly heard, especially in L/A, but it can sometimes sound a bit *cursi* and readers may be interested to know that, when speaking of one's own husband or wife, or to other people of theirs, it is better to use *marido* and *mujer*.

esquina (f). It means 'corner', but the *outside* of a corner, e.g. of a street; the inside type, e.g. of a room, is *rincón* and you will need to make yourself conscious of the difference which does not exist in English. *La esquina* is the usual word for a 'street-corner' and if you spoke of *el rincón de las dos calles* it would be assumed that you must mean the corner of a square. Generally speaking *rincón* suggests indoors and *esquina* outdoors, though Hispanics, like ourselves, may refer to *un rincón pintoresco de Madrid* as 'a picturesque corner of Madrid'.

estampa (f), **estampilla** (f). *Estampa* only means 'stamp' in the metaphorical sense, e.g. a man of this stamp; in the normal way it means 'print', or 'engraving', though it can be used, say, of a Bible 'text'. The official title of a 'Christmas card' is *estampa de Navidad* but by now everyone calls this *un christmas. Estampilla* is a 'postage stamp' throughout L/A. In Spain they say *sello* for this (*v.* **sello**).

estancia (f). Basically 'stay', or 'station': *Una estancia de tres días*, 'A stay of three days'—but it has come to have some more particularized meanings. In much of S/A, particularly the deep south, it originally meant a 'cattle station' but now rather suggests a 'country estate' which, further north, would be called *una hacienda, una finca*, or *un rancho* (*Me*) (*v.* **rancho**). Much the same has happened to *hacienda*; it usually meant a 'farm' (in the R/P often a 'herd of cattle') but now mostly suggests a 'country estate'. In Mexico *una estancia* is most likely to mean 'a living room', especially in humbler houses where eating, sitting and nearly everything else is done in one room.

estante (m), **estantería** (f). *Estante* is literally 'stand', and may be used either for 'shelf', within, say, a bookcase, or for the 'bookcase' itself. *Estantería* is more descriptive for a 'set of shelves' and again can be used of a 'bookcase' but this is tantamount to saying 'book-stand'. A proper 'bookcase', especially if it has glass doors, is likely to be *una librería*.

In so far as there is a general word for 'shelf' it is probably *anaquel*, though *baldo/balda* and *entrepaño* apply to shelves within a piece of furniture; a projecting shelf, such as a 'mantel-piece', is *una repisa*. A shelf which pulls in and out might be *una bandeja* (tray) or *gaveta* which is a 'drawer' of the flatter type. (The deeper type would be *un cajón*.) If you are not being too precise, however, *estante* will often serve.

estar. Most dictionaries cover this verb fairly well and if I presume to draw attention to some of the commoner and more idiomatic uses it is rather in the nature of: Do not forget:

Estar, unadorned with prepositions or verbal phrases, has the force of 'to be present', and there are therefore moments when you must take care to leave it unadorned. I have mentioned elsewhere such cases as *¿Está Fernando?* 'Is Fernando there?'; *No está*, 'He/she/it isn't here'. Similarly, *No estoy para nadie*, 'I'm not at home to anyone'.

One very common use which we fail to remember in time is *estar de . . .* with a noun. There are hosts of these: *Está de paseo*, 'He's gone for a walk'; *está de compras*, 'she's out shopping'; *está de viaje*, 'he's away'; *está de exámenes*, 'he's in the middle of his exams', and more can be coined.

Estar de más, 'to be "de trop" ', 'not to be needed': *Ya veo que estoy de más*, 'I see I'm not needed'. Used negatively: 'to be not a bad idea', 'to be no harm in': *No estará de más preguntar*, 'There's no harm in asking'.

Estar en todo seems to suggest being everywhere at once but in fact means 'to be very alert': *Tu mujer está en todo*, 'Your wife doesn't miss a trick'; *Está en todo*, 'He's right on the ball'. If you mean 'to have a finger in every pie' then *meterse en todo* is indicated.

Estar por will vary in meaning according to its subject; used impersonally, with an infinitive, it means 'is yet to be': *Está por ver*, 'That remains to be seen'. If the subject is a person then it means 'to be in a mood for', 'to have a good mind to': *Estoy por dejarlo todo*, 'I've a good mind to chuck the whole thing'.

Finally, do not forget that when *estar* is followed by a reflexive verb the pronoun is often put first: *Se está poniendo insoportable*, 'He's becoming intolerable'; *Ya me estoy cansando*, 'I'm getting fed up with this'.

este, ese, eso, esto. Readers will no doubt have learnt that *este* normally relates to things near the person talking, *ese* to those near the person he is talking to, and *aquel* to things more remote from both of them. As a general rule this is quite serviceable; the main thing to bear in mind is the existence of *aquel*. Also worth making oneself aware of is the practice of putting *este* or *ese* after the noun when the sense is somewhat deprecatory: *El señor ese* means 'that man', but in a much less complimentary sense than *aquel hombre*. *Pues, ¿cuándo va a llegar el avión este?*, 'Well, when is this (blessed) plane coming?' 'This' and 'that' can also be used adverbially in English but not in Spanish, e.g. 'This long' (indicating how long with the hands) which would be *Así de largo*. 'As long as *that*?' *¿Tan largo?*; 'Not as long as that', *No tanto* (simply).

A stock phrase is *¡Eso es!*, 'That's it!', 'That's right!' You guess and guess and at last get it right and then they tell you *¡Eso es!*, often with a very long first *E*. Another is *por eso*, 'that's why': *Por eso lo ha hecho*, 'That's why he did it'. *El miércoles fue fiesta pero no viniste*. A. *Pues, por eso;* 'Wednesday was a holiday but you didn't come'. A. 'That's the very reason why I didn't'. Another colloquial use is *a eso de* meaning 'round about': *A eso de las cinco*, 'Somewhere around five o'clock'.

Esto. . . (in L/A *este*) is the Hispanic equivalent of our 'Er . . .' when we are thinking what we are going to say. They mouth the word quite distinctly, however vague their thoughts. Hispanics are articulate, even in the matter of and-er-and-um, though they often drag out the final vowel.

estrellar(se). Literally 'to star (oneself)', but in practice it usually means 'to have a crash' and suggests a serious one, a real write-off, but through a collision with a fixed object, *not* another vehicle. A more normal crash would be *un choque (q.v.)*.

estribo (m). 'Stirrup'. Hardly an everyday word in the modern world (though stirrup cup survives) but *la del estribo* is the phrase for 'one for the road', i.e. the final drink. Note that Spanish uses the article so that the literal translation is 'the one for the road' (definitely the last!). *La última ronda*—'the last round'—is another possibility (*v.* also **ñapa**).

estropear. The commonest, and most universal, verb for 'to spoil', in a general sense. 'To spoil' children is usually *mimar* (*v.* also **echar).**

estupendo. 'Stupendous'. In both languages the word invites excess and, in both cases, finds the invitation accepted; it therefore equates with 'fabulous', 'marvellous', 'terrific', 'smashing', or any other 'excess' word which happens to be fashionable when high praise is intended.

eventual, -mente. False; our understanding of 'eventually' is 'ultimately' whereas *eventualmente* means 'possibly'. The essence of the Spanish is dependence on chance events; *un trabajador eventual*, 'a casual labourer'; *en el caso eventual de que . . .*, 'in the (possible) event of . . .'.

exagerar. 'To exaggerate', certainly, but much used where we should say 'to go too far': *Creo que eso sería exagerar*, 'I think that would be going a bit far'. We do talk about 'having an exaggerated respect for' but most often 'to exaggerate' means to overstate in words whereas *exagerar* extends to actions: *Me parece que está exagerando*, 'It seems to me he's overdoing it'—and this could apply to working too hard, getting too worked up, asking too high a price, almost any aspect of *going* to excess as opposed to merely overstating the case.

excitar(se). 'To excite', or 'get excited', yes, but it is rather stronger than our word and so means 'to get highly excited', almost to the point of trembling with fear, fury or anticipation. It also has a slightly stronger sense of reacting to some purely physical/mechanical stimulus. 'Stimulants' are known as *drogas excitantes*.

'Exciting', and 'excited', are used a great deal in English and since there is no one Spanish word which fits, different types of excitement have to be considered. *Emocionante, -ado (q.v.)* clearly indicates a greater involvement of the emotions but when it is a matter of pleasurable anticipation—one of our commonest uses of it—Hispanics do not usually employ the word. If you announced that you were going on a world trip the response 'How exciting!' would probably be *¡Qué suerte tienes!* and 'I'm so excited¡', *¡Estoy tan contenta!* (I assume a woman to be speaking). Where children get (too) excited the favourite word is *nervioso*, even though this normally means 'nervous' (*v.* **nervioso**).

excusado (m). A euphemism for 'loo', 'bathroom', 'toilet' (*v.* **baño**).

exigir. 'To exact', 'demand', 'require' (transitive). It is quite a common verb, much commoner than our 'exact', and will often equate with 'to ask for', provided the person asking has a right to do so: *El policía nos exigió la documentación*, 'The policeman asked to see our papers'. Given the right, however, it may mean 'to insist on': *Exija un recibo*, 'Insist on getting a receipt', *Una exigencia*, though basically 'a requirement', is sometimes used simply for 'a need'.

éxito (m). Rather a chestnut in the way of False Friends; you must be aware that it means 'success', and has nothing to do with the 'way out'. 'Exit', *salida*. *Tener éxito* is the normal way of saying 'to be successful', 'to come off': *En el colegio tenía mucho éxito*, 'He got on extremely well at college'; *Lo intenté pero no tuve éxito*, 'I tried it but it didn't work' (*v. also* **salir**).

expediente (m). As an adjective it used to mean 'expedient' but it has chiefly come to be a noun meaning 'file' in the sense of dossier, i.e. it refers to the contents, not to the outer cover. In L/A it may be used of an ordinary office file and *el expedienteo* is a noun they have coined to describe the process of passing a file back and forth, with long sojourns in in-trays, until the whole case is nearly lost in limbo. It is fairly close to our 'red tape'.

expedir. False, in its way; it does not mean 'expedite' but simply 'to send off', 'to despatch': *Ya han sido expedidos*, 'They've been sent off already'. 'To expedite' is *meter prisa* (Spain) or *expeditar* (L/A).

explicar(se). *Explicar* is the normal verb for 'to explain', and requires no special comment. *Explicarse*, literally 'to explain to oneself', is much used for 'to understand', perhaps particularly in the negative; *No me explico cómo/por qué . . .*, 'I can't fail to understand how/why . . .' is worth learning off pat as a stock phrase.

explotar. Rather surprisingly it means both 'to explode' and 'to exploit'. Context usually makes the meaning clear but for exploiting in the sense of making the most of, do not forget that valuable little word *aprovechar* (*q.v.*), which is far more likely in ordinary conversation. For our somewhat figurative use of 'explode', e.g. with wrath, a better word than *explotar* is *estallar*.

exponer, exposición (f). Unreliable; in a context of photography *exponer* does mean 'to expose' but in the normal way it means 'to exhibit', 'to display', 'to put on show': *una exposición de fotografía*, 'a photographic exhibition'. It is also used for 'to expound', 'to set forth' (arguments, etc): *Las razones se exponen abajo*, 'The reasons are set out below'.

extender, extenso, extensión (f). Unreliable; if not in basic meaning at least in their equivalents: *Extendió el mapa*, 'He spread out the map'; *Extendía mantequilla sobre el pan*, 'He was spreading butter on his bread'. *Extendió la mano*, according to context, could mean 'He held out his hand' or 'He laid down his hand (of cards)'. It is particularly used of 'drawing up' documents: *extender un recibo*, 'to make out a receipt' and a mental note should be made of *extender un cheque*, 'to write out a cheque/check'.

Extenso is the proper adjective for 'extensive', 'vast'. *Extensivo* exists but its use is mostly confined to the verbal phrase *hacerse extensivo a*, which means 'to be applicable to'. Nor is *extenso* the noun for 'extent', a word which we use a great deal and for which a variety of equivalents are needed in Spanish: 'to its maximum extent', *a su máximo alcance*; 'not to that extent', *no hasta este punto*, sometimes simply *no tanto*; 'to some extent', *hasta cierto punto*; 'to a great extent', *por la mayor parte*. *Extensión* is a little Unreliable; in most countries it is the word for a telephone 'extension', though in the Z/A this is *anexo* and in the R/P *interno*. It is not the word for the 'extension' of your passport which would be *renovación* or *prórroga*. There may also be *una extensión de terreno* which simply means 'a stretch of land,' without any sense of extension.

extenuar. False; it means 'to weaken', 'to emaciate'; *extenuarse*, 'to waste away', 'to get exhausted': *Le han extenuado la caminata y el calor* , 'He's worn out with the heat and the long walk'. The equivalent of 'extenuate' is *atenuar*: 'extenuating circumstances', *circunstancias atenuantes* (*v.* also **atenuar**).

extraño, extrañar(se). *Extraño* is basically 'extraneous', i.e. that does
not belong; rather an educated word for us whereas *extraño* is
decidedly everyday and equates with 'strange', 'odd', 'unusual',
'funny' (in the sense of peculiar): *Es un señor muy extraño*, 'He's a
very odd sort of man'; *¡Qué extraño!*, What a funny thing!' It
should, of course, be distinguished from *extranjero*, 'foreign', i.e.
does not belong in the national sense.

    Extrañar originally meant 'to banish', 'to exile', but its
commonest everyday use is simply 'to surprise': *Me extraña
mucho*, 'I'm very surprised', and note that, in this sense, it is
always used in the Third Person. Used in the First Person it is likely
to mean 'I miss', in the sense of regret the absence of: *Le/Lo
extraño mucho*, 'I miss him very much'. In much of L/A this is the
normal way of saying 'to miss'; in Spain and the R/P *echar de
menos* is more likely (*v.* **echar**).

extravagante. Basically 'wandering away from the normal', in both
languages, but we associate it with spending unnecessary amounts
of money whereas in Spanish it means 'eccentric', 'freakish',
'odd', particularly in the matter of clothes. 'Extravagant' in the
matter of money is *pródigo* or *derrochador*.

F

fábrica (f). False; not 'fabric' but 'factory'. 'Fabric' usually suggests a
'textile' and the Spanish for this is *tejido* or *tela*. 'The fabric' of a
building is *la estructura*.

facción (f). Unreliable; it may mean 'faction' but in the plural is likely
to mean 'features': *de facciones duras*, 'rough-featured', though
the most usual word for this is *rasgos*.

facilitar. 'To facilitate', 'to make easy', yes, but it extends beyond this
to 'obtaining' (something for somebody): *Nos ha facilitado un
auto*, 'He got hold of a car for us', 'He let us have a car', and in
commercial contexts it is probably the commonest verb for 'to
supply', 'to let (somebody) have': *Mucho le agradecería nos
facilitara. . .*, 'We should be most grateful if you would let us have
. . .'

faltar, falta (f). *Falta* is best regarded as False since it seldom equates
with 'fault'. Even in the case of e.g.: *una falta de ortografía* we are
more likely to say 'a spelling mistake'. The basic concept, both for
noun and verb, is certainly 'lack', even if this word borders on the
archaic. Nowadays we mostly say 'want': *Todo por falta de unos
dólares*, 'All for want of a few dollars'. 'Default' is another

possibility: *por falta de*, 'in default of'; *sin falta*, 'without fail'.

Hacer falta is one of the commonest ways of expressing necessity and *hace falta/no hace falta* should be learnt off pat. The pronoun is, of course, often introduced especially in the negative: *No me/le/nos hace falta*, 'I/you/we don't need (one)'. (*Necesitar* is also common.)

The verb *faltar*, 'to need', 'to lack', 'to want', 'to be missing', is always used in the Third Person and it is common, idiomatic and hard to remember to use in time so strong mental notes are indicated. How would you translate: 'They brought everything except the kitchen sink'? The chances are that a Hispanic would say *Sólo les faltaba traer la pila de la cocina* and *Sólo falta(ba) (que)* . . . (subj.) is a common expression for occasions when a whole series of things have gone wrong and: 'It only needs . . .' (some final mishap) to supply the last straw. *Poco* and *mucho* are also much used in conjunction with *falta* and English requires a different formula. *Falta poco* often equates with 'nearly'. If you had to say, 'It's nearly finished', the chances are, perhaps, that you would say *Está casi terminado* but a native is quite likely to say *Falta poco para terminar*. Similarly: *Falta mucho para terminar*, 'You still have a lot to do/a long way to go'. If you were expecting some friends and all of them, except one named Federico, had arrived, would it occur to you to say *Aún falta Federico*, for 'Federico still hasn't turned up'?

In Spain there are two very common courtesy phrases: *No faltaba más* and *No faltaría más* (*v.* COURTESY).

familiar. In both languages it indicates something well-known and understood but in Spanish it is also the adjective relating to 'family' for which our equivalent is simply 'family': *Tiene que resolver unos asuntos familiares*, 'He has some family business to attend to' (*v.* relación).

fastidiar, fastidio (m). The basic notion of *fastidiar* is 'to sicken', and it can be seriously applied to someone who is ill though *Está fastidiado* suggests 'He's got worse', 'He's in a bad way'. It is, however, most used metaphorically in the same way as our 'sick' and *estoy fastidiado*, 'I'm sick (of it)', 'I'm fed up (about it)'. In some countries, e.g. Chile, it can mean 'annoyed', and even in Spain *¡Fastídiate!*, literally: 'Get annoyed about that!', is the equivalent of the childish 'So *there*!' The noun *fastidio* usually means: 'nuisance', 'annoyance': *¡Qué fastidio!*, 'What a nuisance!', 'How sickening!' 'How annoying!'

feo. 'Ugly', when applied to persons, but much used metaphorically, particularly in connection with (a) the weather, and (b) social behaviour: *Hace un tiempo muy feo*, 'It's horrible weather'. In social matters it equates with 'ill-mannered'; a little boy who wiped his nose on his sleeve would probably be told by his mama: *¡Eso es muy feo!*, 'That's not at all a nice thing to do!' 'Nasty' would often be the equivalent: *una palabra fea*, 'a bad/nasty word'. As a noun *un feo* is 'a rebuff', 'a slight'; *hacer un feo a alguien*, 'to offend somebody'.

feria (f). Generally speaking, a 'fair', e.g. *Feria Industrial*, an 'industrial fair', but can have other meanings; in the C/S it is applied to an open-air 'market'; in Spain it is more likely to apply to a village fair. In much of L/A public holidays are called *días feriados* (in Spain more probably *días de fiesta* (*q.v.*)). In Mexico *feria* can have the rather surprising meaning of 'small change' (*v.* also **sencillo**) and *feriar* means to change a larger sum into smaller denominations: *¿Puede feriar cien pesos?*, 'Can you change/break 100 pesos?'

festejar. 'To celebrate', usually in rather an unofficial sense: *Festejaba su nueva colocación*, 'He was celebrating his new job'. *Celebrar* may be used instead. *Festejar a alguien*, 'To throw a party for someone'. *Hacer festejos* is what a dog does when he is glad to see you home.

ficha (f), **fichar, fichero** (m). Dictionaries will tell you that *ficha* means 'chip', 'counter', 'domino', etc.; quite correct, but the commonest everyday meaning is 'card' of a card index (*fichero*, 'card index'). Another common meaning is the 'dummy coin' whch you obtain at the counter of a bar or café for putting in the slot of the telephone (the price of calls can thus be raised without difficulty). *Fichar* means 'to index' (card-wise), but is used colloquially as 'to have on one's list' so that *fichado* is an adjective that might have been used by the Mikado (Gilbertian style): *Le tengo bien fichado*, 'I've got him figured'. In connection with work *fichar* means 'to clock on/in'; with a club or a sports team 'to sign on'.

fiebre. *v.* **calentura.**

fiesta (f). Traditionally 'feast', in the religious sense, e.g. 'the feast of Stephen', and still the word for official 'bank' holidays. Christmas and Easter, however, are so specially celebrated that they are usually called *las Pascuas* (Easter more often in the singular) and *fiesta*, on the other hand, has become so identified with festivity and celebration that it is increasingly becoming the word for 'party'. A 'party' in a private house is something of an Anglo-Saxon phenomenon but the idea is catching on and *fiesta* seems the most appropriate word for it. *Un guateque* is another (somewhat slangy) possibility (*v.* also **feria**).

fijar(se). *Fijar* will equate with 'to fix', in a surprising number of contexts, including the fixing of photographs, and *fijar la hora*, 'to fix the time' (for some appointment), but it is wiser not to be too reckless; 'I've fixed it', meaning 'I've arranged it', would be *Lo he arreglado*.

Fijarse is not quite so simple; it means 'to fix one's mind', 'to pay special attention', 'to concentrate', and is much used exclamatorily: *¡Fíjese!* or *¡Fíjate!*, 'Just think!', 'Just imagine!'. In some circumstances its force could be: 'Get a load of that!'. 'To mind' in the sense of 'be careful about' will often be a good equivalent: *La gente debería fijarse en lo que dice*, 'People ought to mind what they say' (*v.* also **procurar**).

For 'not to mind' *v.* **dar**.

firma (f). Both 'firm', and 'signature'. Context usually leaves no doubt, but the proper word for a 'firm' is *empresa*. *Firmar*, 'to sign'.

flaco. A somewhat derogatory adjective for 'thin', and so equating with 'skinny'. *El Flaco*, 'Skinny', is the kind of nickname schoolboys will give a thin boy, just as 'Fatty' would be *El Gordo*. The proper word for 'thin', in all senses, is *delgado*.

flamante. A slightly facetious word for 'superb', 'luxurious', 'brand-new', and popular with those advertising apartments, houses, etc. trying to suggest that these are bang-up-to-date. Anything that was really 'in flames' would probably be described as *en llamas*.

flojo. 'Weak', in most contexts, whether of a person's character or of tea and coffee. In connection with clothes it will mean 'loose', as also with screws and nuts: *una tuerca floja*, 'a loose nut'. *Aflojar*, 'to loosen'. Oddly enough the Spanish for 'tight-rope' is *cuerda floja*, presumably because the loose rope is even harder to walk than the tight one.

follón (m). Rather a slangy word used in Spain for 'mess', 'fuss', and almost interchangeable with *jaleo* (*q.v.*). It suggests activities not quite under control and is mostly used with *tener*: *Tengo un follón* or *tengo mucho follón*, 'My affairs are in an awful mess'. It is also possible to *armar un follón*, i.e. 'to kick up an awful row', 'to raise hell' (*v.* also **jaleo, escándalo, liarse**).

forma (f). 'Form', 'shape', certainly, but used a great deal where we use 'way': *Me gusta de esta forma*, 'I like it that way'; *Hazlo de la forma que quieras*, 'Do it any way you like'. *De todas formas*, 'anyway', may be learnt off pat. In all these contexts it is interchangeable with *manera*. A case where it is not, but for once is Reliable, is *estar en forma*, 'to be in (good) form'. *De forma/ manera que . . .* is a common way of starting a sentence where we might say 'So . . .' (*v.* **así**). The usual expression for 'good manners' is *buenos modales* (*v.* also **formal**).

formación (f). Unreliable; it serves as a general word for 'formation', but applied to individuals it usually means 'training', 'education': *Este joven ha recibido una buena formación*, 'This young man has had a good training'. It suggests training in a particular subject, probably a technical one, and will not normally serve as an alternative to *educación* (*q.v.*). The youth might be a first-class technician and yet ill-educated in other respects. The reflexive *formarse* means not only 'to take shape', 'to form up' but also 'to get (oneself) educated', 'to receive training'.

formal. Very Unreliable; it may mean 'formal', e.g. *Hacer una* *petición formal*, 'to make a formal application', but applied to persons it signifies 'reliable': *Es un joven muy formal*, 'He's a very reliable fellow' (*de mucha formalidad* is an alternative) and it also suggests that he knows how to behave. Conversely *informal*, applied to persons, means 'unreliable', 'ill-behaved'; applied to things . . . but the fact is that in Spanish it is unlikely to be applied to things. I have been told that a group of Spanish officials visited Britain some years ago and were much mystified on receiving an invitation to 'an informal lunch'; what could be intended by an 'unreliable' lunch? In so far as it could mean anything it seemed to suggest that the host might not be there when they arrived, that the food would be half-cooked or that they might run out of drink half-way through.

How, then, would a Hispanic describe 'an informal party' to which guests might come in shirt-sleeves if they wished? Here again, the fact is that they are unlikely to give such a party—at all events by written invitation. The young, it is true, are quite capable of organizing one among themselves but invitations to it would get around by word of mouth and even then it would not be called *una fiesta informal*; more probably *una reunión entre amigos*.

fósforos. *v.* **cerilla.**

fracaso (m), **fracasar.** Not really beyond the dictionary but a useful word to have handy; it means 'failure': *La fiesta fue un fracaso*, 'The party was a wash-out'; *Fracasar*, 'to fail': *La obra fracasó*, 'The play was a flop'. *Un fracasado* is 'a human failure', a man who has made a mess of things. In L/A *fracasar* is sometimes used transitively for 'to make a mess (of something)'.

francesa. Short for *a la francesa* and, on a bill of fare, likely to mean: 'French-fried potatoes' (Britain, 'chips'). *Papas fritas*, in L/A, usually means 'chips' (Britain, 'crisps'). In Spain 'chips/crisps' are *patatas fritas* (*a la inglesa*).

franqueo (m). In Spain simply 'postage'. In much of L/A, it has become identified with the act of obliteration (*matasellos*) and in some of the larger post-offices you will see a separate *ventanilla* marked *franqueo*. You first go to the stamp counter to buy your stamps and then to the *franqueo* to get them postmarked before putting the letters in the box. In some of the more sophisticated post-offices there will be franking-machines/postage meters on the main counter so that, unless you specially ask for stamps, no *franqueo/matasellos* will be necessary.

frazada. *v.* **cobija.**

frecuencia (f). 'Frequency', yes, but *con frecuencia* is extremely common, largely, no doubt, because Spanish does not have one word for 'often' (*v.* **vez**, also **soler**). *Con mucha frecuencia* is particularly useful for 'very often'.

fregar. Basically 'to rub', 'scrub', and in the northern parts of the Hispanic world the domestic word for 'to wash up' (dishes) or 'to scrub' (floors). It is much used metaphorically and slangily to mean 'to pester', 'to muck (something or somebody) about', 'to "screw" (something) up' and in the more southern parts, notably the C/S, it has even gone beyond this, too far even to be called a euphemism; it almost equates with 'fuck', so should be avoided there. In those parts they are more likely to say *lavar los platos* for 'to wash up'.

frente (f). The usual word for 'front' (as well as 'forehead') and you might expect *en frente de* to mean 'in front of', but if it is used with precision it means 'opposite'; 'in front of' is *delante de*. Unfortunately natives are not always precise and *en frente de* (sometimes *frente a*) can mean, in practice, 'somewhere in the vicinity but, with any luck, in sight'. These descriptions obviously concern whereabouts, usually of stationary things such as buildings and parked cars. (For the whereabouts of people *v*. **paradero**.) *Al lado*, literally 'at the side', is another such description which is rather inaccurately used and may well mean 'in front', though probably not outside the front door.

When it comes to vehicles on the move there is less imprecision; 'the car in front (of me)' is *el coche/carro de delante* (*de mí*) and 'behind', *de detrás*.

Note that *frente*, meaning 'front' in the military sense, is masculine.

fresco, frescura (f). *Fresco* means 'fresh' but also does service for 'cool', both in the literal and metaphorical senses. White wine has to be served *fresco* but impertinent or presumptuous behaviour is similarly described. It is not necessarily 'getting fresh'; 'cheeky' is a better equivalent and *frescura*, 'cheek'.

fuego (m). 'Fire', in a general sense, but Hispanics use it, rather more logically, where we say 'light', i.e. for a cigarette. It is fatally easy to say *¿Tienes luz?* when we ought to say *¿Tienes fuego?* for 'Got a light?' For a 'fire', in the sense of 'conflagration', *incendio* is needed.

fuera. 'Out', 'outside', as you know, but if you go, say, to somebody's office asking for him and are told *Está fuera* it usually means 'He's away', 'He's out of town'. 'He's out' is more likely to be *Ha salido* or *No está*. In connection with sports *un partido de fuera* is 'an "away" match'. *Fuera de* is also used metaphorically as 'beyond', 'apart from': *fuera de todo eso*, 'apart/aside from all that'.

fuerte. 'Strong', of course, but do not forget that it has to do service for 'loud'. *Habla muy fuerte*, 'He talks very loud(ly)'; *Pon la radio más fuerte*, 'Turn the radio up a bit'. It is also the noun for 'forte': *La música no es mi fuerte*, 'Music's not my strong point'.

Fulano. A fictitious name, equating with 'So-&-So'. It suggests a Christian name so that if you want to say 'Mr. So-&-So', you use *El Señor Fulano de Tal*. When referring to a lady it is always better to say *La Señora/La Señorita Fulana de Tal* since *una fulana* is a common euphemism for 'a whore'. In cases where a series of names is needed, such as 'Tom, Dick and Harry', or 'Smith, Jones and Robinson', the Spanish names are *Fulano*, *Mengano*, *Zutano* and *Perengano*, in that order.

fundir, fusible (m). *Fundir* is the proper word for 'to melt' (usually of metals; in cooking *derretir* is more normal) and extends logically to the melting of filaments so that, in a domestic context, it is the verb for 'to fuse/burn out': *La bombilla se ha fundido*, 'The bulb's blown/fused'. In L/A it is often used metaphorically for 'gone phut', 'ruined'.

Fusible started life as the adjective 'fusable' but has come to be the official noun for 'fuse', of the sort contained in a box on the wall (somewhere!), though these are often referred to as *los plomos*—in Mexico *los tapones* (*q.v.*). It is a good idea to find out in advance just where *la caja de los plomos/fusibles/tapones* is located since it is proverbially difficult to do so in the dark; perhaps, too, to warn yourself off *fusa* which means 'demi-semi-quaver/thirty-second note' in music.

funesto, -a. Dictionaries have a tiresome habit of giving you 'sad', 'doleful', 'dismal', etc. for this word, perhaps because it suggests funerals. All these are understatements; the real force of the word is much stronger and a better equation is 'disastrous': *La guerra tuvo consecuencias funestas*, 'The war had disastrous consequences'. Like so many 'strong' words it is much exploited in conversation and will then equate with 'appalling', 'deplorable', 'ghastly', 'fatal', etc., the *e* taking a heavy emphasis: *¡Pero eso sería funEsto!*, 'But that would be fAtal!' *Fatal* is also used and is very similar in meaning to *funesto*, i.e. 'ill-fated'.

fusible. *v.* **fundir.**

G

gachupín. *v.* **gringo.**

gafas. *v.* **anteojos.**

gajes (m.pl.). In the R/P this means 'wages', 'salary', 'pay', but there is a universal expression: *Los gajes del oficio*, which dictionaries usually give as 'the cares of office'. This is not quite the whole story; it is more like 'occupational hazards', 'the risks of the profession'.

'Wages' are simultaneously both given and received, so that *los gajes del oficio* can also imply the perquisites of office, as well as the hardships; you take the smooth with the rough.

gallego. *v.* **gringo.**

ganar, gana (f). *Ganar*, 'to gain', yes, but also 'to win', 'to earn', and 'to make money'; context indicates which: *¿Cuánto ganas?*, 'How much do you earn?'; *Está ganando mucho*, 'He's making lots of money'.

In a betting context *¿Cuánto has ganado?*, 'How much did you win?' In sport *¿Quién ganó?*, 'Who won?' In L/A *vencer* is often used in connection with games.

Gana, 'desire', 'inclination': *de buena gana*, 'willingly', 'gladly'. Its commonest use is probably in the plural and *tener ganas de* is a good equation for 'to feel like': *No tengo ganas*, 'I don't feel like it'.

garzón, -a. I have only heard this word used in the C/S where it means 'waiter' or 'waitress'. When hailed, I rarely heard him called *¡Garzón!*: it was usually *¡Joven!* and a waitress *¡Señorita! Garzón, -a* seem to be used more in reference to them than in addressing them.

gasa (f). 'Muslin', 'gauze', but *gasa higiénica* is a common euphemism for a 'tampon' or 'sanitary towel/napkin' and you may see it marked on the appropriate bins.

gaseosa (f). One of my very first recollections of Spain, more than forty years ago, in those prehistoric days before the Civil War, was the cry *¡Hay gaseosa!* uttered in the middle of the night when the train stopped at some remote station. I knew hardly any Spanish but enough to work out that this was literally 'There is gaseous!' and to be intrigued both by the wording and what the drink might be. Dictionaries tell you 'soda water' but in fact it is sweetish, though it is often used for diluting other stronger drinks. In the plural it implies most fizzy soft drinks sold by the bottle. A more general word for 'soft drinks' is *refrescos*.

gasfitero (m). This quaint word means 'plumber', in the Z/A, and clearly derives from the British gas-fitter who installed gas in their houses in the 19th century. His premises are entitled *Gasfitería*. In the rest of L/A the usual word for 'plumber' is *plomero*, sometimes *cañero;* in Spain *fontanero*.

gasolina (f). A universally understood word for car 'fuel' but it is not the normal word in all countries; in Chile they say *bencina* and in the R/P *nafta*, sometimes *el líquido*. In Venezuela, where they are specialists in the matter, *nafta* means 'high octane'; *gasolina* is the cheaper, more everyday stuff.

gastar, gasto (m). *Gasto*, 'cost', 'expense', is probably most used in the plural: *los gastos de reparación*, 'the cost of repairs'. *Gastos generales* or *comunales* are the contribution you make to the general overheads in apartment blocks/houses, i.e. lifts/elevators, lighting in hallways, etc. In advertisements for apartments you will often see the cryptogram *incl. gas. com.* which means that your rent will include these expenses.

Gastar is basically 'to spend', but extends rather further and in many contexts would equate with 'to use', or 'to take'. If you are buying, say, a collar, or anything that goes in sizes, you are likely to be asked *¿Qué número gasta?*, 'What size do you take?'; *Gasto siempre zapatos negros*, 'I always wear black shoes'. These are rather idiomatic uses so mental notes are required. If you are under a sort of impression that *gastar* means 'to waste', *v.* also **desperdiciar** (*v.* also **usar**).

gaveta. *v.* **estante.**

genial, genio (m). *Genial* is False; it does not mean 'genial'; it is the adjective for 'genius' and so means 'having genius', 'of genius': *Es un compositor genial,* 'He's a genius (of a composer)'. It is sometimes used sarcastically to describe someone who has extraordinary ideas.

For 'genial' you have to choose between *cordial, sociable, cariñoso,* perhaps *afable,* according to context.

Genio is merely Unreliable; it may mean 'genius': *Es un genio,* 'He's a genius', but without the article it means 'temperament', almost 'temper': *Es un muchacho de mucho genio* might mean 'He's a fellow with much spirit', but is more likely to mean 'He's a very quick-tempered fellow', and is often a polite way of saying 'bad-tempered'. *¡Qué mal genio!* 'What a nasty temper!'

gente (f). 'People', in a general sense, and it is important to remember that it takes a singular verb since we say people *are*: *En invierno la gente va a la sierra,* 'In winter people go to the mountains' (for skiing); *Había mucha gente,* 'There were a lot of people there'. If you wanted to say 'What a crowd!', however, it is better to say *¡Cuánta gente!* or *¡Qué gentío!* since *¡Qué gente!* tends to suggest: 'What awful people!' *Gente menuda* is 'small fry'.

In S/A *gente* was often used in the past to indicate 'whites' as opposed to Amerindians. This may be the explanation for a phrase like *Es muy gente* (R/P) meaning 'He's a good guy', 'a decent chap', or *Es buena gente* (Bolivia), meaning much the same thing. Both are interesting examples of how *gente* can be conceived of as singular when for us it feels plural. For 'a people', in the national sense, *pueblo* is indicated.

gentil. Unreliable in its quiet way; it may mean 'Gentile', possibly 'genteel', but it does not mean 'gentle'. In the past it meant 'gallant', 'courteous', and this survives in *gentileza,* 'courtesy': *Por gentileza de . . .,* 'By courtesy of . . .'. The normal word for 'courteous', 'polite', is *cortés.*

'Gentle' is uncommonly hard to translate with precision; *dulce* is too sweet, *blando* and *suave* too soft and smooth. If it is a matter of behaviour towards children then *cariñoso* is likely; if of, say, handling it (or him/her) gently, then *con cuidado*; if the 'it' is a very prized possession then perhaps *con cariño*; if docility is implied then *dócil*.

gestionar, gestiones (f. pl.). Hard to translate into English. *Gestionar* means 'to take the necessary steps', 'to negotiate', 'to get (something) organized', and tends to be associated with official procedure: *Están gestionando la devolución de los prisioneros*, 'They're negotiating the return of the prisoners'. If you made an official application to, say, erect a building, then *Están gestionando el permiso de construcción*, 'They're going through the necessary procedure to get a building permit'.

Gestión is accordingly 'the necessary procedure', 'the required step', and, as with 'step', most often used in the plural. If you consulted a solicitor/lawyer about some matter he might say: *Tendré que hacer unas gestiones*, 'I'll have to make a few preliminary enquiries'. It is essentially an action to be taken, not a mere gesture as it might seem to suggest, though it may often be a routine action. *Gestiones necesarias* might be used for 'necessary formalities', but the *necesarias* is really redundant as it is already implied in the *gestiones*. 'Una gestoria' is an agency which deals with government departments (*v.* also **trámite**).

globo (m.). 'Globe', yes, and well within the dictionary but you may not be conscious that its commonest domestic use is 'toy balloon'. These are particularly popular in Mexico and the balloon-seller uses a particular kind of whistle to announce his presence.

gol (m.). 'Goal', yes, but only in football and then only in reference to the thing scored; the place that the ball is shot into is *la meta* and it is this which is used when 'goal', in the figurative sense of 'objective', is required (*v.* also **motivo, tanto**).

golosinas (f. pl.). Usually a slightly childish word to denote scrumptious 'sweets' and 'candies', but I have seen it used as the heading on a bill of fare for the 'Sweet' course, normally known as *postres*. In Spain *goloso* means 'having a sweet tooth'; in Mexico it is the usual word for 'greedy'. *La Gula*, universally, is the Deadly Sin of Gluttony!

golpe (m.). 'Hit', or 'blow', as you no doubt know, but it is such a common word, and used metaphorically as well as literally, that I venture to draw it to your attention. The verb 'to hit' is much more likely to be *dar un golpe* than *golpear* (though this exists) and 'to get hit', *llevarse un golpe*. A metaphorical use is *golpe de estado*, 'coup d'état'. Since these 'blows of state' are not uncommon in the Hispanic world a whole jargon has grown up which is perhaps worth a little attention, partly for the entertainment but chiefly to help readers of L/A newspapers.

Golpista is a case in point; it means one who carries out, or is closely associated with carrying out, a military coup and *golpismo* is the general term for this type of political procedure. They are usually derogatory while *contragolpista* is Good. Much the same applies to *revolución/-ario* which are also Good while *contra-*

rrevolución/-ario are correspondingly Bad.

Líder and *liderismo* are a little uncertain. The normal word for leader is *caudillo* but this has become associated with 'fascism'; *líder* has been coined for the Left and connected with Fidel Castro; it is, of course, Good, but *liderismo* may savour of the 'cult of personality' which is Not so Good. Usually highly pejorative is *gorila*—a police-'thug'—and *gorilismo* is often applied to the 'fascist' type of government which relies on police-state methods. *Matón*, 'bully', is another word applied to such 'thugs'. *Cacique*, once simply an 'Indian chief', has become the word for a political 'boss'. Good, but harder to guess, is *foquista*—one who supports the Cuban theory of *un foco* ('focus/spotlight') of revolutionary activity. Nouns and adjectives are coined from proper names associated with particular activities (and likely to be Good or Bad accordingly), e.g. *macartismo* (very Bad indeed!) for those of Senator Joe McCarthy some twenty years ago, and since these seldom start with a capital letter they can sometimes be a little disconcerting when first encountered. I recall being foxed, a decade or two ago, by *naseritas* to denote the followers of Colonel Nasser (Good, because Anti-Imperialist).

Clearly those whose sympathies are on the other side of the barricades will reverse the Good and Bad images but the habit of coining words in this way is very characteristic of Spanish 'jargon', independently of political situations, and so may be of permanent value to the reader. As a guessing game he may care to exercise his brains on *policlasista, arielista, derecho de tacha, cuartelazo, entreguista*. *Policlasista*—'multi-class'; 'multi-racial' may be implied. *Arielista*—'Ivory-towerist'; derived from a book named *Ariel* by the 19th-century Uruguayan writer Rodó. *Derecho de tacha—tachar* means 'to cross out', and *derecho de tacha* is the students' 'right' to throw out (strike off the list) university teachers who fail in their duties. *Cuartelazo*—literally: 'barrack blow', i.e. a 'military coup'. *Entreguista*—nothing to do with intrigue; *entrega* usually means 'delivery' but in a military context 'surrender', and *un entreguista* is one who is willing to surrender economic and political control to the U.S. It is an adjective as well as a noun.

góndola (f). Not only the Venetian phenomenon but a fairly old word for a 'collective vehicle' which still survives in Chile where it means a 'municipal bus'.

grabadora (f). Literally 'engraving machine', but in these days the usual word in L/A for 'tape-recorder', though you may sometimes hear *máquina (de cinta)*. In Spain they call it *un magnetófono*. *Grabar* is, however, the universal verb for 'to record', whether on tape or disc. In many L/A countries this is one of those oh-so-desirable 'gringo' machines and since they can be sold there for two or three times what they originally cost they will certainly cause you trouble at the Customs. Wiser not to take one, therefore, unless you really need it and, if you do, arm yourself with the most official-looking letters from the most august institutions possible, explaining (in Spanish) why the necessity arises. Try, in any case, not to bring a brand-new one, which will be deeply suspect; a bit of shop-soiling certainly helps. For even more sophisticated equipment—video-tapes, ciné-cameras, TV sets—all this applies *a fortiori*.

gracia (f), **gracioso, -a.** An interesting evolution from the Latin *gratia*. In Spanish the essential concept is 'wit', 'amusement': *¡Qué gracia!*, 'How witty!; *Muy gracioso*, 'Very amusing'. *Tiene mucha gracia* is often said of an amusing play or movie. *Gracioso* is therefore clearly False but it is difficult to find a satisfactory equivalent of 'gracious'; *cortés*, 'courteous', is about as near as you are likely to get, perhaps *benigno*, or *elegante*.

An even more curious evolution is *gracia* meaning a person's name, usually confined to moments when somebody is obliged to ask your name and feels that *¿Cómo se llama Vd.?* is too abrupt. I think the root concept is: 'What saint has you under his protection?' In the R/P I was once asked, on the telephone *¿Cuál es su gracia?* and was somewhat disconcerted for a moment. In Spain it is regarded as rather *cursi* and in any case would apply to one's Christian name. If you have to ask somebody's name *¿Podría decirme su nombre?* is perfectly adequate.

grado (m). It is worth being aware that *grado* has two distinct meanings derived from different Latin roots. One (from Lat. *gratum*) means 'willingness' and is chiefly used in the expressions *de buen/mal grado*, 'un/willingly' and *de grado o por fuerza*, 'willy-nilly'.

The other (from Lat. *gradus*, a step) sometimes equates with 'grade': *los grados superiores de aceite*, 'the higher grades of oil', and is used for school 'grades', but perhaps more often with 'degree': *dos grados bajo cero*, 'two degrees below zero'; *un ángulo de 45 grados*, 'an angle of 45 degrees'; *No sé qué grado de amistad hay entre ellos*, 'I don't know what degree of friendship there is between them/how friendly they really are'.

'Degree', on the other hand, is not automatically *grado;'* to get a (university) degree' is *sacar un título* or *licenciarse*; 'a doctor's degree', *un doctorado*. 'By degrees' may be *gradualmente* but *poco a poco* is commoner; 'to/in some degree', *hasta cierto punto*; 'to such a degree that . . .', *a tal extremo que . . .*

grama. *v.* **césped.**

granel, a. 'Loose', in the sense of 'by the pint', etc. and mostly used in connection with liquids, such as olive-oil or eau-de-Cologne, which you can buy by the pint if you bring your own bottle. For commodities which can be broken up into separate units, as against ready-made-up packages, the expression needed is *sueltos* (*v.* **soltar**).

In the R/P *a granel* means 'in bulk': *vendidos a granel*, 'sold off in bulk', e.g. of books. In Spain this would be *al por mayor,* and *al por menor* is the contrasting 'in detail', 'individually', 'separately'. L/A has an interesting array of variants: *por mayor y menor (Arg, Pe, C/A); a mayores y menores* or *a mayoría o menoría (Bolivia); por mayor y al detal (Co); mayoreo menudeo (Me)*. It will be noted that most of them omit the *al. A granel* can be used metaphorically to mean a slightly reckless 'by the ton' and is quite a good equivalent for 'galore': *Tuve problemas a granel*, 'I had difficulties galore/wholesale'.

grifo (m). The proper word for 'tap/faucet'. *Llave* is often roughly used for a 'faucet' but really applies more strictly to the 'cock' somewhere along the pipe-line. In the Z/A 'tap' is often *caño*.

  Grifo is also used as a colloquial adjective for things which, in some sense, 'stick up'; it is often applied to hair which sticks up and will often mean 'frizzy' but it can extend to 'high' in the sense of drunk or doped.

gringo. A word you should certainly make yourself aware of, if you do not already know it, since the chances are that it means you, at all events in L/A (it is not used in Spain). It is in the same category as Limey, Dago, Wop, Kraut, Dirk, etc. and in these days usually—*but not always*—implies a North American. In the R/P it can apply to any sort of immigrant and in the past these have mostly been Italians (also called *tanos*, short for *napolitanos*). In Chile and the Z/A it applies to any light-skinned Northerner—British, Swiss, German, Swedish, etc.—and in those parts, if they expressly mean a North American, they say *un yanqui*. In Mexico, on the other hand, it definitely means a U.S. citizen. It is not always necessarily pejorative; I have been introduced at a Chilean party with *Le presento un gringo que he conocido en Londres* and good-natured laughter followed, though admittedly this was at a sophisticated level. I have heard wild speculation, and much amateur etymology, concerning the origin of the word (e.g. from the song 'Green grow the rushes-oh') but see no reason to doubt its stemming from *hablar en gringo*, a popular corruption of *griego*, e.g. to speak 'Greek' or 'Double Dutch' (cf. 'It's all Greek to me'). *Gringos* are those who speak such 'Greek'.

  Anglo-Saxons are not, of course, singled out for special treatment. Any kind of foreigner, in any country, is apt to get some such derogatory appellation, especially when thick on the ground, and I have already mentioned *tanos*. Many Spaniards still emigrate to L/A and are usually called *gallegos*, whether they come from Galicia or not, and the name has acquired deprecatory overtones. In Mexico a Spaniard is often referred to as *un gachupín* or *un gachuzo* and again it is not complimentary.

gripe (f). The universal word for 'flu', i.e. influenza, except in so far as Colombians call it *gripa*. 'To have flu' is usually *tener gripe* or *estar con gripe* but in parts of L/A you will often hear *estar agripado*.

grosero. A universal adjective for 'gross', 'coarse', and much used where we should say 'rude'. Another common word for this is *ordinario* (*q.v.*). In Venezuela *brusco* seemed to be popular; in the C/S *guarango*.

gua . . . By itself, or at least accompanied by exclamation marks, this is an exclamation of surprise in several L/A countries (or it could be of impatience, disgust, etc.). Readers may care to be aware that it often—though not always—denotes a word of Amerindian origin and is the transliteration of a sound more like our w. A mere look at the dictionary will reveal how many of these words there are. Sir Walter Raleigh, the 16th-century explorer, became a legendary figure known as *Guaterral* in the Orinoco region. In Mexico the sound is often represented by OA, e.g. *Oaxaca*, or HUA —*Chihuahua*.

guachafo (also spelt **huachafo**). An adjective used in the Z/A meaning somewhat the same as *cursi* (*q.v.*). It is interesting to note that in Peru it is considered *guachafo* to refer to one's mother and father as *mi mamá, mi papá*; one should say *madre* and *padre*—as also in Spain—very different from Mexico! (*v.* **madre**). In Venezuela *guachafo* means 'funny man', 'a comedian', though rather in a domestic than in a professional context.

guachimán (m). This seemingly Amerindian word is none other than our old friend 'watchman' in disguise. Its use is mainly confined to the Z/A round to Venezuela. More usual words for 'watchman' are *velador*, *celador* or *vigilante*.

guagua (f). 'Baby' in the Z/A. Originally a Quechua word and very onomatopoeic but note that it is feminine, even if the baby is male. In Cuba and the Canaries it means a 'municipal bus'.

guapo, -a. 'Good-looking', 'pretty', 'lovely', 'beautiful' in *Spain*. Which word you choose will depend not only on the sex of the person described but on that of the person describing. A pretty girl may safely be called *guapa* and girls may refer to a given man as *guapo* but a man who wanted to describe another man as good-looking would probably call him *bien parecido*. In the R/P *guapo* is used chiefly of men but does *not* mean good-looking; it means: 'tough', 'brave', perhaps 'gallant' and *un guapo* can be 'a tough guy', 'a bully', 'a braggart'; it is the origin, via Neapolitan Spanish, of our 'wop'.

In most of L/A the usual word for 'pretty', or 'beautiful', is *lindo* (*q.v.*). Words for a good-looking man vary but *buen mozo* is common. *Hermoso, -a* is also widely used, much more than in Spain. *Bonito, -a*—'pretty'—on the other hand, is usual in Spain for a woman but not thought suitable to describe a male, whereas in the R/P *bonito* is probably the commonest word for 'handsome'.

guarango. *v.* **grosero.**

guarda, guardia (m or f). Both words mean 'guard', and both can vary in gender. *Guarda* normally means 'watchman', but in the R/P can be a bus 'conductor' who, if female, is *una guarda*. *La guardia* implies a body of guards, e.g. of the sort changed at Buckingham Palace, but *un guardia* usually means 'policeman', or a member of the Civil Guard. A 'female policeman'—they are not numerous— would be *una guardia*, unless some special name were evolved for her.

guaya (f). It sounds very Amerindian but in Venezuela is in fact a takeover of the English 'wire'. It is usually 'small-gauge cable' of the size used for towing cars. 'Full-sized cable', e.g. ships, is *cable* universally.

Eternal vigilance is needed over words beginning with *gu* . . . In Chile 'a hot-water bottle' is *un guatero* and it would seem a fair guess that it should come from 'water' but it appears to stem from an Araucanian word *guata* meaning 'paunch' (*guatitas* is the spoken word for 'tripe' in Chile.). Perhaps in some cases there is a little of both; the Araucanian, knowing *guata* and hearing 'water', puts the two together . . .?

güero. *v.* **rubio.**

guiar. 'To guide', but used in the Z/A for 'to drive (a car)'.

guisar. *v.* **cocer.**

H

habitación (f). False, in its way, since it means 'room', not 'house', and most often implies a 'bedroom'. 'Habitation', as a general term for dwelling or abode, is likely to be *morada*, or *vivienda*.

hablar. Both 'to speak' and 'to talk', as you know. Normally it requires the preposition *con*: 'to talk to somebody', *hablar con alguien*; *¿Con quién hablo?*, 'Who's that speaking?' If the speaking is one-sided, however, it may be *hablar a*: 'He spoke to his daughter severely', *Habló a su hija en tono severo*.

In Spain a common expression is *¡Ni hablar!* 'Heavens, no!' 'I won't hear of it!', 'No fear!'

hacerse. One of the verbs for 'to become': *Se ha hecho bastante popular*, 'It's become pretty popular'; *Se está haciendo insoportable*, 'He's becoming impossible'. Also 'to get', in the sense of 'become': *Me estoy haciendo viejo*, 'I'm getting old'; *No te hagas el tonto*, 'Don't get silly', 'Don't fool around' (*v.* also **ponerse**).

hacha (f). Literally 'hatchet', 'axe', but used colloquially in Spain to mean a most effective, clever person: *¡Eres un hacha!*, 'You're terrific!'

hacienda. *v.* **estancia.**

halar. *v.* **jalar.**

¡haló! *v.* TELEPHONES.

harto. Strictly 'satiated', but very common is *estar harto de*, 'to be fed up with', 'to be sick of'. Colloquial but not in the least vulgar.

hasta. As you know, it means 'until', in relation to time and 'as far as', in relation to place; possibly 'up to', in relation to either. A more metaphorical use equates it with 'even': *Hasta los políticos deben comer*, 'Even politicians have to eat' (*v.* also **incluso**).

Probably its commonest everyday use is in the matter of leave-takings. In ordinary, formal relations with strangers 'Good-bye' is likely to be *¡Adiós, buenos días!* or *Adiós, buenas tardes!* etc., but if there is any likelihood of a further meeting then *hasta*-something will probably be added:

Hasta ahora is used when the next meeting will be almost at once and is a common ending to a telephone conversation.

Hasta luego is virtually 'See you later'. In Spain it suggests that the next meeting will be on the same day. In L/A it is by far the commonest form of 'Good-bye' and is said regardless of when the next meeting may be so that, if it is to be within a few hours, you will often hear *Hasta loguito*.

Hasta mañana obviously indicates a meeting on the following day and presupposes a definite knowledge to that effect; it is not said regardless. If it is a Friday and you will not see your colleagues until Monday then you do not say it; you say *hasta el lunes*.

Hasta la vista is more indeterminate and has something of the pious wish about it, i.e. 'Till we meet again'; if you know then you specify.

This does not exhaust the list since particular circumstance or individual fantasy may almost coin them at will: *hasta pronto* implies the hope that the next meeting will be soon; *hasta siempre* is appropriate for taking long leave, and so on, but you will see that Spanish demands more thought at such moments than our simple 'Good-bye' (*v.* also **chao**).

hay. This useful, impersonal monosyllable has no exact equivalent in English so, at the risk of teaching my grandmother to suck eggs, I give it a little attention. As you no doubt know, it is much used in crying wares: *¡Hay tomates! ¡Hay gaseosa!*; also in announcing them in writing, e.g. *Hay ancas de rana* on the wall of a restaurant to let the clients know that the special luxury of frogs' legs is available today. Most readers are unlikely to cry wares but they may well have to enquire, in a shop, whether they have any, say, oysters today and the formula is *¿Hay ostras?*.

Hay que is also useful for indicating general, impersonal necessity: *Hay que vivir*, 'One's got to live'; *Hay que respetar las opiniones de los demás*, 'Other people's opinions have to be respected'. If the necessity arises for a particular person then *tener que* is needed: *Tendrás que cuidarte*, 'You'll have to be careful'.

No hay de que, 'You're welcome', 'Don't mention it', is a common courtesy phrase (*v.* COURTESY).

hijo. 'Son', of course, but much used as an exclamation equating with 'My dear chap!', 'Good heavens, man!'. Said by an older person to a boy it can equate with 'Son', or 'Sonny', and be quite kindly but between equals its sense is more often one of protestation or impatience: *¡Pero, hijo!*, 'For heaven's sake!' The feminine *¡Hija!* is, *mutatis mutandis*, similarly used.

hipótesis (f). 'Hypothesis', certainly, but whereas, for us, this is a somewhat educated word, mostly confined to scientific or intellectual contexts, *hipótesis* is widely used in the Hispanic world and you will hear it on the lips of all and sundry: *Tiene la hipótesis de que la sequía es debida a la bomba atómica*, 'He's got a theory that the drought is due to the atomic bomb'; *Esto no es más que una hipótesis*, 'It may never happen'. The basic concept is quite Reliable; it is more a matter of realizing that you can use it freely at whatever level of education.

hogar (m). Literally 'hearth', but *el hogar* may be regarded as the Spanish for 'the home': *Artículos para el hogar*, 'Articles for the home'. Do not forget, however, the stock phrases *ir a casa,* 'to go home'; *estar en casa,* 'to be at home'; and *salir de casa,* 'to leave home'.

¡hola! It equates fairly well with 'Hello!' or sometimes 'Hi!' but it implies previous acquaintance and a certain equality of status. You would not normally use it to a stranger or to a person much older than yourself unless it were a relative or someone equally intimate. On the other hand it is used with *Vd.* at least as often as with *tú*. With *Vd.* you are likely to add *Buenos, -as días/tardes*, etc.; at the *tú* level it will probably be followed by *¿Qué tal?* It is a greeting but assumes an immediate exchange of civilities; if there is no question of this then *¡Adios!* (*q.v.*) is indicated.

In the R/P it is used when answering the telephone (*v.* TELEPHONES).

holgar. Despite its Active appearance this curious verb means 'to be inactive/idle/at leisure' (for those interested in etymology its origin is even more curious). Not quite an everyday word (though its cognate, *huelga*, a strike, of the industrial sort, is common enough); indeed *holgarse*, 'to be pleased about', may be regarded as obsolete. It survives chiefly in the expressions *huelga decir*, 'needless to say' and *huelgan los comentarios*, 'comment is unnecessary/would be superfluous'.

¡hombre! I never imagine Spaniards in conversation but I seem to hear this exclamation on their lips; it expresses their characteristically animated response to anything they are told but its very typicality makes it uncommonly hard to translate into Anglo-Saxon terms. It may be said in emphatic or enthusiastic confirmation, e.g. *¡Hombre! ¡ya lo creo!*, 'I should say so!', 'I'll say!', 'Yes, indeed!', in mild or indignant protestation: *¡Pero, hombre!* or in all-but-contemptuous refutation: *¡Pero, hombre!* . . . spoken even more emphatically and probably accompanied by a gesture. Any astonishing piece of information certainly demands *¡Hombre!* as a response, possibly followed by *¡No me digas!* (*v.* **decir**). It is used by all classes and both sexes. Men, among themselves, may well use a stronger word. It is far less used in L/A. In the Caribbean region they are likely to say *¡Manito!* (short for *hermanito*, 'little brother').

hoy día, hoy en día. Both are supposed to mean 'nowadays', but in much of L/A I found *hoy día* used meaning 'this very day', which in Spain would be *el día de hoy*.

hueco (m). As an adjective, 'hollow'; as a noun, 'cavity' (*v.* **agujero**) but used metaphorically for 'gap': *Su muerte ha dejado un gran hueco*, 'His death has left a great gap' (*v.* also **salvar**).

huella (f). In the singular, 'track', but in a wide sense; in a context of roads it will mean a rough, unsurfaced 'track', though it might mean a footprint on such a track. In the plural it is often short for *huellas dactilares* or *digitales*, 'finger prints' (needed in some countries, e.g. for an exit permit).

huerto. *v.* **jardín.**

hueso (m). Not only 'bone', but the 'stone' of a fruit (not a pip, however, which is *pipa* or *pepita*). Mark it in your mind; it is fatally easy to say *piedra* (*v.* also **espina** for the bone of a fish).

huésped (m). The dictionary will tell you 'guest', but it suggests a 'paying guest' and often equates with 'lodger'. *Una casa de huéspedes*, 'a guest house'. 'Guests' who are invited are more likely to be called *invitados*.

huevo (m). 'Egg', of course, but readers may care for some guidance as to the different ways of cooking them and the corresponding nomenclature:

'Fried', *fritos*. 'Shirred/baked', *al plato* or *flamenco* (Spain).

'Boiled', *cocidos* or *pasados por agua* (these usually imply 'soft-boiled'; if you want 'hard-boiled' add *duros*).

In Mexico 'soft-boiled' are often *tibios*.

'Poached', *escalfados*, in L/A sometimes *pochés*.

'Scrambled', *revueltos*.

There are various other terms: *Huevos rusos*, literally 'Russian eggs', and approximately what we mean by 'egg mayonnaise'; *huevos flamencos*, literally 'Flemish eggs' (no doubt dating from the days of Charles V who brought a Flemish household to Spain) —these are usually shirred in a small earthenware dish along with diced meat, etc. Sometimes you will get *Huevos a la* . . . (usually followed by the name of the restaurant); this is a bit of a shot in the dark but it is most often some form of *flamenco*.

It is only right to warn readers that in nearly all countries *huevos* is a vulgar term for 'testicles', though it can be extended to mean 'courage', 'guts'. When shopping, therefore, it is wiser to say *¿Hay huevos?* for 'Have you any eggs?' than *¿Tiene huevos?* In the R/P, however, *huevos* is used as a slang word for *pelotas* or *bolas*. In Venezuela, surprisingly, *huevo* can mean the male organ and *bolas* 'testicles'. In Paraguay it is the other way round. In Chile *un huevón* means 'twirp', 'stupid fellow'.

I

idear. A useful verb for 'to think up', 'to dream up', 'devise', 'invent': *¿Quién ha ideado esto?* 'Whose idea was this?'; *Nunca se sabe lo que va a idear*, 'You never know what he'll think of next'. Mentioned chiefly to make you aware of it.

idioma (m). 'Language', as you know, and the universal word for this. *Lenguaje* exists but is mostly applied either to the faculty of speech — language as a human phenomenon — or to particular uses of a given language: *en lenguaje científico*, 'in scientific language', perhaps 'jargon' (though this, in a derogatory sense, is usually *jerga*); *en lenguaje moderno*, 'in modern parlance'. *Lengua* equates with 'tongue' both literally and metaphorically.
'An idiom', in the sense of an idiomatic turn of phrase, is *un modismo* or *una locución*.

ignorar. Unreliable; its basic meaning is simply 'not to know', 'to be unaware' and this is usually the meaning when applied to things: *Ignoro sus señas*, 'I don't know his address'; *Ignoraba que ella le quería*, 'He didn't realize that she was fond of him'. In the negative it is quite a good equivalent of 'to be not unaware', having just the same force of understatement. Applied directly to persons, however, it usually means the same as in English: *La ignoraba completamente*, 'He took absolutely no notice of her'. Context will usually make the meaning clear but more unmistakable for 'to take no notice of' is *hacer caso omiso* (v. **caso**). Genuinely 'not to know' a person calls for *no conocer*.

igual, -mente. *Igual* means 'equal', but is much used where we should say 'same': *Son iguales*, 'They're the same'; *Es/Da igual*, 'It's all the same', 'It doesn't matter', 'I don't mind'. In a bar: *Igual que antes*, 'Same again'. *Igualmente*, 'equally', 'similarly', 'likewise', but it is the routine thing to say in reply to such wishes as *Feliz Año Nuevo*, *Felices Pascuas*, etc., i.e. 'the same to you', and can be extended to less cordial returns of compliments.

ilusión, ilusionarse, iluso (m). *Ilusión* is Unreliable and, for normal purposes, False; in psychiatry, when distinction must be made between illusions, delusions and hallucinations, *ilusión* is a false sensory impression but in everyday circumstances it means a 'hope'. 'Hope' is usually *esperanza* (*q.v.*) and *ilusión* certainly suggests a hope difficult of attainment, a 'daydream', but nevertheless one that can be realized whereas an illusion, by definition, cannot: *Sus ilusiones se realizaron*, 'His hopes were fulfilled', 'His dream came true'; *Tiene la ilusión de que . . .*, 'He cherishes the hope that . . .'; *Hacerse ilusión*, 'To be thrilled about'; *El viaje nos hace mucha ilusión*, 'We're getting very excited about the trip'; it is often one way of handling 'to look forward to'.

Ilusionarse is 'to indulge in wishful thinking'; *No te ilusiones*, 'Don't get any wrong ideas'.

The adjective *ilusionado* means 'hopeful', 'excited' and should be distinguished from *iluso* which means 'easily deceived' and borders on 'deluded'.

'An illusion' is probably best translated as *una quimera*, 'a chimera', or *un engaño*, though one may also exploit the verb *engañarse*: 'He was under no illusions', *No se engañaba. Un iluso* may be used of a man who entertains illusions, the classic case being Don Quixote; *¡Iluso!* is an exclamation directed at people who expect too much, i.e. 'You're an optimist!' Other words for a piece of wishful thinking are *espejismo* and *fantasía*.

ilustrado. Unreliable; it means 'illustrated' when applied to magazines and the like but applied to persons it means 'cultivated', 'educated': *un hombre muy ilustrado*, 'a very cultivated man'. 'Illustrious' is *ilustre* (*v.* also **culto**).

imbécil. Yes, 'imbecile', but much used colloquially to denote a 'stupid person', a 'fool', a 'twirp'. Note that it is accented on the second syllable.

importar. Transitively, 'to import'; intransitively, 'to matter'. Stock phrases you should know are: *¿Qué importa?*, 'What does it matter?' *No importa*, 'It doesn't matter'. It is often used for the polite 'mind', *¿No te importa traerme una cajetilla de cigarros?*, 'Would you mind bringing me a pack(et) of cigarettes?' (*v.* also **dar, venir**).

imprescindible. Make a mental note of this adjective; it is a wonderfully weighty word for 'essential', 'indispensable', 'vital', and not uncommon in everyday speech.

impresión (f). 'Impression', 'impress', certainly, but I have noticed it used where I think we should say 'shock': *Su muerte me hizo una gran impresión*, 'His death was a great shock to me'. It is, of course, a different kind of shock from *susto* which means a 'fright'; *impresión* means something profoundly felt.

inapreciable. *v.* **apreciar.**

incluso, inclusive. *Incluso*, literally 'included', also means 'including', but is much used where we should say 'even'. Voltaire, in the early 18th century, visited England and reported to his countrymen: 'Even the peasants eat white bread'. In current Spanish this would be *Incluso los campesinos comen pan blanco. Incluso ahora,* 'even now' (*v.* also **hasta**). As a rough guide you may say that *incluso* will mean 'even' at the beginning of a sentence and 'including' in the course of it, though inversion may sometimes hide the fact: *Todo el mundo se inquieta por el aumento de población, incluso el Vaticano,* 'Everyone is worried about the population explosion, even the Vatican'.

Inclusive is sometimes used in the same way but its proper meaning is Reliable enough: *Desde el lunes hasta el viernes inclusive,* 'From Monday to Friday inclusive', 'From Monday through Friday'.

Incluyendo/incluído may be used for 'enclosing/enclosed' in business correspondence but *adjunto* is more usual.

inconveniente. *v.* **convenir.**

incorporarse. 'To incorporate', 'amalgamate'. and extends to many acts of joining, rejoining. embodying, enlisting, etc., and in all these cases is likely to be followed by the preposition *a*. Without a preposition it will probably mean 'to stand up', or, more surprisingly, 'to sit up in bed' (not necessarily after an illness).

The equivalent of 'Inc.' is S.A., i.e. *Sociedad Anónima.*

indicado. 'Indicated', yes, but used a great deal adjectivally and then equates with 'likely', 'appropriate'; *lo más indicado,* is quite a good equivalent for our 'obvious': *La persona más indicada,* 'The obvious person'. It probably occurs most when several possibilities are being considered and 'better' or 'best' are then our most likely equations: *Un lápiz sería más indicado que una pluma,* 'A pencil would be better than a pen'; *Eso sería lo más indicado,* 'That would be the best thing'.

informal. *v.* **formal.**

ingenioso. 'Ingenious', perhaps, but it is distinctly Unreliable; *ingenio* is 'ingenuity' in the sense of 'invention', e.g. on the part of a playwright or composer, and the most usual meaning of *ingenioso* is therefore 'witty', 'amusing', though *una idea ingeniosa* could be 'an ingenious idea' in the sense of 'a happy thought' (*v.* also **ocurrencia**).

In most of the sugar-producing countries *un ingenio* means 'a sugar refinery'.

injuria (f). False; the English 'injury' usually has a physical connotation and suggests wounds and broken limbs; the Spanish is metaphorical, hence 'insult', 'cursing', 'bad-mouthing', and usually used in the plural. It is probably commoner in L/A than Spain where *insultos* is more likely.

The Spanish word for 'injury' will depend on whether it is internal or external; *una herida* (a wound) applies to external and *una lesión* to internal. Metaphorical injury is *daño*. (*v.* also **perjuicio**).

inmediato. Not confined to time, as it usually is in English, and so can be used in a physical sense: *una habitación inmediata*, 'an adjoining room'. In a literary context you may find, e.g., *la fecha inmediata*, 'the following day'.

inobjetable. This is chiefly a journalist's word but I include it as the average dictionary does not. In its small way it is False since it does not mean 'unobjectionable', which is somewhat faint praise, but 'impeccable', 'unassailable', 'unimpeachable', and so high praise.

inquietarse, inquieto. *Inquietarse* is quite a good equivalent for 'to become uneasy', 'to worry', and it might seem to follow that *inquieto* therefore means 'worried' but in fact it is something more like 'restless', 'fidgety', 'jumpy', and suggests a certain amount of physical movement. A better word for strictly 'worried' is *preocupado* (*q.v.*; also **quieto**).

inquilino (m). 'Tenant', i.e. occupant of a house or apartment and so likely to be yourself. In the Z/A it is applied to a mere 'lodger', who elsewhere would be *un huésped* (*q.v.*).

insano. Unreliable; it is more likely to mean 'unhealthy', 'insalubrious' than 'insane' which is usually *loco* or, more formally, *demente*. *Malsano* is another, rather commoner, word for 'unhealthy' (*v.* **sano**).

integrar, integridad (f). 'To integrate', yes, and Reliable in certain respects but in Spanish it is both commoner and more extended to physical contexts: *Esta exposición está integrada por obras de diversos pintores*, 'This exhibition is made up of/composed of works by various painters'; It would not occur to us to say: 'This exhibition is integrated from . . .' though I suppose it would be quite logical if we did. *Integridad* is Reliable for 'integrity', but it can also mean 'totality', 'entirety', 'the whole thing': *En su integridad*, 'In its entirety'.

intentar. One of the words for 'to try', meaning, in this case, 'to attempt': *Voy a intentar entrar*, 'I'm going to try to get in'; *Voy a intentarlo*, 'I'm going to have a go at it'. *Tratar* (*q.v.*) is almost interchangeable with it. For 'to try out', *v.* **probar**.

intermedio (m). An adjective as well as a noun and so meaning 'intermediate' as well as 'intermediary'. It is very common in the phrase *por intermedio de*, 'through', 'thanks to', 'with the help of'; not only in business letters: *Tendremos que hacerlo por intermedio de . . .*, 'We shall have to do it through . . .' (name of agency), but also in conversation: *por intermedio de Antonio*, 'with Antonio's help', or 'thanks to Antonio'. It suggests that Antonio went to some trouble on his own account in order to fix it; 'help' given on the spot would be *ayuda*.

Intermedio is also the 'interval/intermission' at the movies, the 'break' for 'ads' on TV, 'half-time' at football, etc.

interprovincial (m). A 'long-distance bus' in Peru (v. **bus**).

interruptor (m). The proper word for 'electric light switch'. In the C/S they frequently say *apagador* (literally 'switcher-offer', perhaps on the same principle as *destornillador*). In the northern parts of S/A it is usually *suiche* (m) which is admittedly less trouble to say and may win in the end. In Mexico they use *switch* but usually for the 'main' switch, i.e. the two-pronged affair in the basement. In Venezuela *suiche* often means 'ignition key'. In Spain a light switch is usually *la llave*.

intervenir. Distinctly Unreliable; its primary meaning is 'to take part in': *Intervenir en una conversación*,'To join in a conversation'. Context may suggest intervention: *La policia tuvo que intervenir*, 'The police had to intervene', but it should not necessarily be assumed that their intervention decided the matter.
    Intervención is perhaps a little more Reliable: *Hubieron llegado a los puños a no ser por la intervención de sus amigos*, 'They would have come to blows but for the intervention of their friends', but it can only be used of human intervention. In English we can say 'At this point the tea-break intervened', but for this the Spanish would have to be *A este punto llegó la hora del té* or something similar.

intoxicado. False, at all events in its associations; the English suggests drink and the Spanish food: *Está intoxicado* means, not that 'He is drunk' but 'He's poisoned'. *Tóxico*, as an adjective, means 'toxic', 'poisonous', though as a noun it is more likely to mean 'drug'. The proper Spanish word for 'intoxicated' in a court of law is *ebrio* (v. also **borracho**).

inversión (f). Unreliable; it *may* mean 'inversion' but in the contemporary world the chances are that it will mean 'investment' (of money). *Invertir*, 'to invest'.

investir. Unreliable; it means 'to invest' only in the sense of 'to confer upon': *Fue investido con los atributos de su cargo*, 'He was invested with his badge of office'. 'To invest' (money) is *invertir*.

invitado. As a noun means 'guest', and is the commonest word for this: *Vendrán unos invitados esta noche*, 'We have some guests coming tonight' (v. also **huésped** and **brindar**).

ipso facto. Oddly enough it borders on the False; it should mean the same as in English but is often, incorrectly, used to mean 'forthwith', 'immediately', or 'at the same moment'.

ir(se). *Ir* does not present any particular problems but it is worth noting that, although Spanish shares with English the use of the Present Continuous tense, e.g. *estoy leyendo*, 'I'm reading', this does not apply to *ir* and you do not say *estoy yendo*. Consequently *voy*, for example, can mean both 'I go', and 'I'm going', and if you are going, say, on foot the formula is *voy andando/caminando* (*voy a pie* is also possible); *voy terminando*, 'I've nearly finished'; *va* *anocheciendo*, 'It's getting dark'. This use of *ir* with a verb which describes some process of transformation or progression is highly idiomatic and needs a little acquiring. The English equivalent is usually 'to be getting' . . . (with an adjective): *La cuestión va complicándose*, 'The problem's getting more complicated'. It is a possible translation of 'to become'.

¡Voy! I can hardly say it should be learnt as a stock phrase but it should certainly be learnt, and it will most often mean 'I'm *coming*!' It may not have occurred to you that when you say 'I'm coming!' you are regarding the action from the other person's point of view; as far as you yourself are concerned you are going and Spanish regards it this way. We ring up and say 'I shan't be coming home to lunch, but a Hispanic will say *No voy a casa a comer.* Equally if you were calling, say, Pedro's house on his behalf to report the fact that he could not be home to lunch, you would say *Pedro no puede ir a comer.* Even within the house, if somebody calls saying lunch is ready your response should be *¡Voy!*, 'I'm coming!' In a restaurant, therefore, if you call a waiter he is quite likely to repond with *¡Voy!*, 'Coming!' He may also say *¡Va!* and here it is the waiter's turn to see things from the other person's point of view; he is saying literally 'He is going!', though still meaning 'I'm coming!' (I imagine it is this sort of inversion which leads Americans, on the telephone, to say, 'Who is this (speaking)?' where Britishers say, 'Who is that?')

A few common expressions which should be at your tongue's tip are: *Vamos*, 'Let's go', 'Let's be off' (the origin of the old Californian 'Vamoose'). Perhaps even commoner is *¡Vámonos!*, 'Here we go!' 'Off we go!' or simply 'Let's go!' In Spain *¡Vamos!* is much used (usually preceded by *pero*) to deprecate, as it were, something just said: *Es muy molesto pero ¡vamos!*, 'It's a great nuisance but there it is!' *Es muy bonito pero ¡vamos! no para valer 10,000 pesetas*, 'It's very pretty but, hell!, not worth 10,000 pesetas'.

Other exclamations characteristic of Spaniards are *¡Vaya!* which is a response to a surprising discovery or piece of information. Our equivalents are something like 'Really!', 'Fancy that!', 'Good heavens!', etc. *¡Vaya . . .!* (followed by a noun) is a stronger way of saying *¡Qué. . . (noun)!* e.g. *¡Vaya mujer!*, 'What a woman!; *¡Vaya noticia!*, 'There's a piece of news!' Note that the noun has no article.

¡Que va! is a sort of gesture of dismissal ranging (by tone of voice and context) from a polite 'I won't hear of it' (e.g. of your paying) to an impatient or contemptuous 'Nonsense!'

Irse is universally common for 'to take oneself off', 'to go', 'to depart': *Pues, me voy*, 'Well, I'm off'; *Tengo que irme*, 'I must go'; *Luego todos se fueron*, 'After that they all left'. It is more or less interchangeable with *marcharse (q.v.)*.

itinerario (m). 'Itinerary', yes, but is sometimes used for 'timetable'.

J

j. In Spain the *jota* has a fierce sound, but in L/A it is more like our 'h'.

jalar. Some dictionaries do not give this word, or else spell it *halar*. It is cognate with the English 'haul', and probably of nautical origin (the *Conquistadores* were predominantly sailors) but is the usual verb for 'to pull', in several L/A countries, notably Mexico and the Z/A. There is no question about the aspirate; it is not only distinctly audible but the word is written *JALAR*, e.g. on the double-doors of offices and the like. In these countries *tirar*, the usual verb for 'to pull', has suffered some debasement (*v.* **tirar**). In Mexico *jalar* is used a good deal colloquially meaning 'to work hard', sometimes 'to exaggerate', and *jalarse* is a familiar expression for 'to masturbate'. *Jalador* is sometimes used for a 'door handle'.

jaleo (m). 'Row', 'brawl', 'uproar', 'fuss'. The basic concept is of a lot of (probably angry) voices. *Armar un jaleo*, 'to kick up a row'. A word used in Venezuela to cover the same thing is *un bojote* (*v.* also **lío, escándalo, follón**). A more moderate word for 'upset', 'upheaval' is *trastorno*.

jaqueca (f). 'Headache', 'migraine', yes, but in the C/S it is the word for the commonest form of headache, viz. 'hangover' (*v.* **resaca**).

jardín (m). 'Garden', yes, but only that part of it concerned with flowers and recreation; if it is a matter of fruit or vegetables you have to use *huerto*.

jefe (m). 'Chief', but the universal word for 'boss'.

jerez (m). 'Sherry'. Our ancestors made a more valiant attempt to pro-nounce the word fully; in the 17th and 18th centuries it was usually called Sherries; later generations no doubt imagined this to be an unnecessary plural. *Jerez* covers all the types of wine produced in the vicinity of *Jerez de la Frontera*, from the lightest and driest *Tío Pepe* to such heavy-sweet liquids as *Pedro Jiménez*. Spaniards mostly prefer the lighter sorts and most often ask for *manzanilla* (*q.v.*).

¡Jesús! The equivalent of 'Bless you!' when anyone sneezes in Spain. In L/A they say *¡Salud!* The response to either, usually gasped into a handkerchief, is *Gracias*.

jitomate (m). As far as I know this word only occurs in Mexico and parts of C/A. It means what we normally understand by 'tomato', i.e. the red sort. *Tomates*, there, means smaller, green ones. The Mexicans ought to know since tomatoes originally came from there but I doubt whether this information will make us change our ways, either in the Hispanic or the Anglo-Saxon worlds.

joder. Omitted by nearly all dictionaries as being too coarse though it is indisputably everyday. It is one of the grossest words in the language and is the equivalent of our word 'fuck'. It is likewise used in a multitude of contexts which have nothing to do with its real meaning, mostly revolving round the notion of pestering, mucking (something or somebody) about, spoiling, ruining, 'screwing' something up, etc. In Chile it has become so identified with this meaning as to have lost most of its original force but is still slangy. In Spain, where they are great swearers, it is the extreme expletive and then in the Infinitive (but with exclamation marks) used in exactly the same way as *¡Hombre!* It is less used in Mexico as they have their own native word available (*v.* **chingar**).

joven (m or f). 'Young man/woman'; in the plural 'young people' of both sexes. It is much used in the R/P, e.g. for addressing a waiter, indeed I was once called it myself by a rather impatient young official who must have been about half my age.

jubilarse, jubilación (f). Two remarkably False Friends; *jubilación* means 'retirement', or 'retirement pension'—not always an occasion for jubilation—and the Spanish word has no emotional overtones. *Jubilarse*, 'to retire', rather suggests reaching retirement age and becoming entitled to your pension; *retirarse* could be used but it is a general word for any sort of retirement; it could be from some rough game: 'retired hurt'.

The Spanish for 'jubilee' is *jubileo* but is applied only to commemorative religious festivals and has no overtones of celebration. There is a word *júbilo* meaning 'joy' but it is little used; they are more likely to say *regocijo* or *alegría*.

juerga (f). An enthusiastic boozing bout, a 'binge'. *Correrse la gran juerga*, 'to go on a spree', 'to hang one on'; *Nos hemos corrido la gran juerga anoche*, 'We had a hell of a party last night'.

jugar, juego (m). *Jugar* means 'to play' in almost every sense except playing a musical instrument which is *tocar*. It may also mean 'to gamble', and *jugar a la lotería*, 'to buy lottery tickets'. In the window of a lottery office in Montevideo I saw *HOY SE JUEGA* meaning that the draw would be that day; in Spain this would have been *SE SORTEA HOY* or *SALE HOY*.

Juego, 'game', has several more specialized meanings very much of an everday nature: *Un juego de cama* is 'a set of bed linen', i.e. two sheets and a pillow case; *un juego de té/café*, 'a tea/coffee service'. *Hacer juego* is the verbal expression for 'to match', i.e. of colours, etc. If you are playing bridge in Spanish then *juego* means 'rubber', not 'game' which is *manga*.

junto, -a. Certainly the adjective for 'joined' but probably most used as the equivalent of our 'together': *Llegaron juntos/-as*, 'They arrived together' (for 'together with' *v.* **como**). *Junta*, as a noun, is a word we have borrowed, usually meaning a small group of men (Fascists or perhaps Army officers) who seize power (probably in some Latin-American country) and run it dictatorially. Its Spanish meaning is far less confined; it simply means a small meeting of the sort which takes place daily in offices and elsewhere and has no necessary political associations. Another common word for this is *reunión* (*q.v.*). *Junta* may also be a 'joint' in carpentry or engineering.

K

key (m). If you hit this in Ecuador it will probably mean 'cake', though *quey* is preferred (v. **queque**).

L

laburar, laburo (m). An example of Italian influence on R/P Spanish; this is a slang word for 'work' (Italian, *lavoro*) and implies very hard work: *¡Pucha, qué laburo!*, 'Christ, what a job!'

lamentar. Not really 'to lament', in quotidian circumstances; a much more precise equation is 'to be sorry', 'to regret': *Lamento mucho que no pudiera venir*, 'I'm very sorry you couldn't come'. In much of L/A it seemed to me that *lamentablemente* was the usual word for 'unfortunately', as against the Peninsular *desgraciadamente*.

lapsus (m). A 'slip' in the sense of a little mistake. We talk of a lapsus linguae and associate the word with a slip of the tongue but in Spanish it can be used of any little slip.

largo. Such a classic *Falso Amigo* that perhaps I insult you by mentioning it; it means 'long', *not* 'large', *nor* 'wide' (as in French and Italian). It is fatal to remember *Largo al factotum*, even if the Barber did come from Seville, and Handel's celebrated aria which opens his comic opera *Xerxes* was one of a multitude described by their pace ('broad'). If Spanish and not Italian had provided the terminology for music it would probably have been known as Handel's celebrated *Amplio* or *Ancho*. *Largo* may be used metaphorically for 'generous' or 'abundant' but this is far from everyday and savours of the literary, cf. a 'long' purse.

lata (f). 'Tin/can' of preserved food. For some reason it has taken on the metaphorical meaning of 'nuisance': *¡Qué lata!*, 'What a curse!' *Dar la lata* is a common expression in Spain for 'to make oneself a nuisance' (*v.* also **bote**).

leche (f). 'Milk', of course, but dictionaries tend to give *mala leche* as 'bad blood' without explaining that it is much stronger and more vulgar; *Es un tío de mala leche* is tantamount to saying 'He's a shit'. A euphemism is *de mala uva*, 'a nasty piece of work' (wine is evidently not as potent as milk): *Tiene un vino muy malo*, 'He gets very nasty when drunk'. *Leche* is also the taboo word for 'semen', hence 'spunk'.

lectura (f). False; it means 'reading', not 'lecture': *la lectura de la carta*, 'the reading of the letter'; *sala de lectura*, 'reading-room'. 'Lecture' is *conferencia* (*q.v.*; *v.* also LECTURES, CONFERENCES AND CONGRESSES).

lejía (f). 'Bleaching' fluid, a solution of lime chloride widely used for cleaning purposes. A favourite trick of lazy laundresses is to put lots of it into the water in which your clothes, handkerchiefs, etc., are soaked with the result that they come out beautifully white but disintegrate within a few weeks. It needs to be used sparingly.

leña (f). One of the words for 'wood', but it implies rough bits of wood and in practice usually means 'firewood'. 'Wood' sawn and shaped is *madera*.

lenguaje. *v.* **idioma.**

letra (f). 'Letter', yes, but of the alphabet, not the missive which, as you know, is *carta*. Do not forget, when speaking of a given letter, to refer to it as feminine: *Tendrás que buscarlo en la eme*, 'You'll have to look for it under M'; *Sólo hemos llegado a la ele*, 'We've only got as far as L'. *Letra* is also used of the 'words' of a song: 'I know the tune but not the words', *Sé la música, pero la letra, no*.

liarse, lío (m). *Liarse* is literally 'to bind oneself (to something)' but much used for 'to get down to', 'to get stuck into', taking the preposition *a*: *Se lió a hablar y no paró en una hora*, 'He got down to talking and didn't stop for an hour'.
  The noun *lío* is basically a 'tie-up' and again much used colloquially for 'mix-up', 'muck-up': *Había un lío tremendo en el Centro esta mañana* would suggest 'There was an awful traffic-jam downtown this morning', but *lío* can also be a tie-up of the affections and *Tiene un lío en su oficina* would suggest that he'd got 'tied up' with a girl there. Context usually makes things clear.

libra (f). A good old Roman word which long supplied the L in L.S.D. and still means a 'pound' sterling. British readers will be interested to know that Peru, too, has *una libra*, i.e. 10 *Soles*; you are quite likely to be told that a given article costs, say, *veinte libras*, i.e. 200 *Soles*.
  Libra has been used in the past to mean a 'pound' avoirdupois,

really meaning half a kilogram, but the practice has almost disappeared by now.

librería (f). False; it means 'book-shop', or 'book-case', *not* a library which is *biblioteca*: *Librería universitaria* is not a 'university library' but 'campus bookstore'.

licencia (f). 'Licence', in a general sense, but may have particular meanings. In the R/P it is the usual word for 'leave of absence', 'vacation': *Estuve de licencia*, 'I was on vacation' (*v.* also **permiso**). In Mexico it means 'driving licence'.

limpiabotas (m). It looks plural but is usually singular and means a 'shoeshine boy' (it will often be a man). They are a universal Hispanic phenomenon and the standard of cleaning is wonderfully high. Their call is *¡Limpia!* In the C/S they are called *lustrabotas* and the call is *¡Se lus(tra)!* In Mexico *boleros*, and the cry *¡Grasa!*

lindo, -a. The all-but-universal word for 'pretty', 'beautiful', etc. in L/A. In Spain a pretty girl is *bonita* (*v.* **bonito, guapo**). *Una lindura* is a thing of beauty, 'a beauty', which in Spain would be *una preciosidad*.

lío. *v.* **liarse.**

liquidación (f). Yes, 'liquidation', but if you took it at its face value you might think a lot of shops were going bankrupt simultaneously; in practice it usually means 'Sale' (*v.* **brutal**). *Realización* is another word used in L/A for a 'Sale'. In commercial circles it is a common word for 'settlement', 'payment'.

listo. Both 'clever', and 'ready'; which meaning is intended will depend on whether the verb is *ser* or *estar*: *Está listo*, 'He/she/it's ready'; *Es listo*, 'He/she's clever'. *Hábil* and *mañoso* appear under 'clever' in dictionaries but *hábil* suggests 'clever with the hands' and *mañoso* . . . well, 'handy' as applied to a human, perhaps 'skilful'. *Listo* involves the mind: *Es un chico listo*, 'He's a smart guy'.

In the R/P, no doubt owing to Italian influence, they use *pronto* for 'ready', and *listo* means approximately 'intelligent'; if they mean 'smart', 'astute', they mostly say *vivo* (*q.v.*).

living (m). A word which Spanish has borrowed from English; it is short for 'living-room' but does not suggest a humble dwelling where most of the living is done in one room; it means the main 'reception room', 'drawing-room', 'parlour', 'lounge', etc. I have seen some very handsome rooms which were described as *el living* in houses where there was also *un comedor*, *una biblioteca* and even *un salón de billar* (*v.* also **estancia**)

llamar, llamada (f). *Llamar*, 'to call', in a wide sense, including calling/ringing up on the telephone and 'knocking at the door' —*llamar a la puerta*, even when this means, in practice, ringing the bell. It will not, however, do for 'calling' in the British sense of coming personally to the house which would be *visitar* or *venir/ir a* ver or, if it were simply the milkman, then *venir*: *El lechero vino*, 'The milkman called'.

Una llamada is the word for 'a telephone call', though in Spain a long-distance one is *una conferencia*.

Trains and boats require other words: '(Train) calling at . . .', *con parada en . . .;* boats which 'call' at various ports *hacen escala (en)*. (*v.* also **rumbo**).

llegar. 'To arrive', of course, but one needs to develop a fairly acute sense of the act of arrival; if you wanted to say 'I hope I'm not late', would it occur to you to say *Espero no llegar tarde*? The equation will sometimes be 'to get as far as': *He llegado al punto en que . . .*, 'I've just got to the point where . . .'. Preposition may be important; *llegar a*, 'to arrive in' (a place); *llegar en*, 'to arrive in' when it is a matter of the means of transportation: *Llegará en coche/tren/avión*, 'He'll be arriving by car/train/air', or else the period: *Llegará en julio*, 'He'll get here in July'.

Very common is *llegar a ser*; it is one of the ways of handling 'to become': *Ha llegado a ser evidente que . . .*, 'It's become obvious that . . .', also 'to turn out': *Ha llegado a ser muy valioso,* 'It's turned out (to be) very valuable'. Note that an adjective is required after the *ser*; you cannot say *Ha llegado a ser que . . .* to mean 'It's turned out that . . .'; this would have to be *Ha resultado que . . .* (*v.* **resultar**).

llevar. 'To take', as you know, but 'take' is rather an all-purpose verb in English and the Spanish equivalents need a little thought. The simple act of taking something in the hand would probably be *tomar* (*q.v.*). The essence of *llevar* is 'to take along with one': *¿Puede llevar a este señor en su coche?*, 'Can you take this gentleman in your car?', but it is used for metaphorical 'taking', particularly in connection with time, which one trails behind one like a cloud of glory: *Llevábamos tres días en Guadalajara* does not mean 'We spent three days in Guadalajara', but 'We had been three days . . .', i.e. not 'to spend', but 'to have spent'; *Llevaba una vida muy triste*, 'She led a very unhappy life'; *Llevará mucho tiempo*, 'It will take a long time.'

Sometimes the translation will be 'bring' since in English we always use this when speaking to the recipient, e.g. Pablo rings Juan saying *¿Puedes traerme ese libro?*, 'Can you bring (me) that book?' An Anglo-Saxon John will reply saying 'O.K., I'll bring it tomorrow' but a Hispanic one is quite likely to say *Vale. Te lo llevo mañana* (though *Te lo traigo . . .* is also possible). (The same can apply with 'come/go'; *v.* **ir**.)

Llevarse, literally 'to take to oneself', is one of the equations for 'to get', in the sense of 'receive': *Se llevó una paliza tremenda*, 'He got/took a fearful beating'; *¡Qué susto se llevó mi madre!*, 'What a shock my mother got!' This use is somewhat colloquial but highly idiomatic.

lo. It might have been more illuminating to have put this under *le(s)* if only to draw attention to the fact that in L/A *le* and *les* are much less heard. Latin Americans are sometimes criticized for their habitual use of *lo* and *los* but in fact the arguments are in their favour.

Lo de . . . is a useful, if colloquial, way of handling '. . . and all that': *lo de 1066*, '1066 and all that'; *lo de ayer*, 'all that business yesterday'. In parts of L/A they use it like the French *chez* meaning at the house of: *lo de González*, 'the González (place)'.

One has to remember to pop in *lo* at moments when we should resort to accenting a word: 'Are you a friend of Pedro?', 'Yes, I am'—*¿Es Vd. amigo de Pedro?, Sí, lo soy*. To say merely *soy* in such a case would be too light-weight and inadequate. By implication the *lo* refers to something known, and probably just mentioned: 'But you *are*, aren't you?', *Pero lo eres, ¿No?*

local (m). As an adjective 'local'; as a noun, a useful word for 'premises'. It may also be, more specifically, a 'shop site', e.g. on the ground floor of a new apartment house. It may also occur in an address, e.g. *Avenida Bolívar 353, Local 26*. This often means that No. *353* is the building at the entrance to an arcade of shops and *Local 26* means the number of the shop within the arcade.

A reminder may be useful that *localidad*, in addition to meaning 'locality', may also be a 'seat' in a bull-ring or theatre. (The general word for a 'seat' is *asiento*.)

loco. The universal adjective for 'crazy', 'mad', 'insane', and, as in English, may be used precisely or exaggeratedly (*v.* **insano**).

In Chile it is also a kind of shellfish.

lógico. 'Logical', yes, but a very common word equating with our 'sensible', 'reasonable', 'to be expected': *Lo más lógico sería que* . . ., 'The most sensible thing would be for . . .'; *Es lógico*, 'It's only natural'. *Como es lógico* is the stock phrase for 'As might be expected'. *¡Lógico!* often equates with our 'Obviously!' 'Naturally!' The word is used far more than 'logical' in English.

lograr. *v.* **conseguir.**

lucir. A good Castilian word for 'to shine', but much used in L/A for 'to look', in the sense of appear: *Luce muy linda*, 'She looks very pretty'. In Spain they would use *parecer* in such cases. Note that the First Person Singular is *luzco*.

luego. One of the words for 'then', and needing a little distinction from *entonces*, the other main word for 'then'. *Entonces* may certainly mean 'at that time', 'at that point', but is less strictly confined to time than *luego* and so can also mean 'in that case', 'in such circumstances'. *Pues entonces*, at the start of a sentence, means no more than our 'Well, then', and the 'then' has really more reference to what has already been said. *Pues luego*, similarly at the start, means 'Well, after that . . .', and points directly to what is about to be said. If you pause when telling children a story they may say *¿ Y luego?*, 'And (what happened) then?' *Primero hizo las compras y luego fue a la peluquería*, 'First she did the shopping and then she went to the hairdresser'. People who are asked to do something will often reply simply *Luego*, meaning 'In a minute', 'Later', 'I'll do it afterwards'. *Hasta luego* is a fairly close equivalent of 'See you later' (*v.* **hasta**). In L/A (as in old Spanish) *luego* often means 'immediately', and is a common response of waiters when you try to summon them.

Luego also—and, one feels, rather improperly—means 'therefore', 'it follows that', and is the correct word for this in mathematical and logical contexts. The answer to a problem in algebra, e.g. 'Therefore x equals 7' would be: *Luego equis vale siete*, and the received translation of Descartes' *Cogito ergo sum*, 'I think, therefore I am', is *Pienso luego existo*. (This seems to savour very strongly of *post hoc, propter hoc!*)

Desde luego is the usual expression in Spain for 'of course', 'certainly', 'naturally'. In L/A they prefer *por supuesto*.

lugar, lugareño. *Lugar*, as you know, means 'place', but it is usually preferred when 'place' is metaphorical, e.g. *En su lugar habría . . .*, 'In his place I'd have . . .'. It is cognate with the French *lieu* and *en lugar de*, 'in lieu of', 'in place of'; *en su lugar*, 'in his stead'. *Sitio* is likelier for physical 'place' but the reader should not regard this as a hard and fast rule; either may be used for either.

Lugareño is a word derived from it and used, particularly in Mexico, to mean 'belonging to a place'. Most dictionaries give 'villager' but this is too limited; it is a useful word when you want to say 'native' without any pejorative intent; *indígena*, in many parts of L/A, implies 'Amerindian' and in some people's minds may sound contemptuous, just as 'native' may do in English. *Lugareño* is free from this contamination, indeed Mexicans will often say it proudly, in the same way as *típico* (*q.v.*). You may see it used to describe, say, a restaurant which aims at providing the real Mexican McCoy (*v.* also **castizo, criollo**).

lujuria (f). A very False Friend, even if not an everyday one; it is not 'luxury' but the Deadly Sin of 'Lust'. 'Luxury' is *lujo* and 'a luxury hotel' *un hotel de lujo*, so let no reader be trapped into saying *de lujuria*!

lunch (m). False, in its way, since it does not means the midday meal but some sort of cold collation taken outside normal regular meals. In Spain it is mostly associated with weddings; in Peru with something like the English 'tea-time'; elsewhere often just a 'snack' though in the R/P it suggests a '*vin d'honneur*', probably with snacks included. Various spellings occur, e.g. *lonche*, or the plural *lunchs* (*v.* also **merienda**).

lustrabotas. *v.* **limpiabotas.**

luz (f). 'Light', certainly, but often colloquially used for the domestic 'electric current': *Han cortado la luz*, 'The current's been cut off' (*v.* also **fuego**).

M

machete. A 'hacking-knife', but used metaphorically for 'mingy', 'stingy' etc. A Uruguayan once told me *Los uruguayos son muy machetes*. It was not my own experience but I was not concerned, as he was, with getting money out of people.

macho, machismo. Dictionaries give you *macho*—'male', 'he-man' —but not *machismo* though it is a common word, especially in L/A, and much has been written about it since it is deeply embedded in the Hispanic standard of values. Basically it is 'masculinity', 'virility', or at all events the need to demonstrate these qualities. I have heard the theory advanced that the high rate of road accidents in L/A, particularly perhaps Mexico, is due to notions of *machismo;* Mexicans are, admittedly, somewhat direct and impatient in their ways but the tussle to make the crossroads first—according to this theory—was activated just as much by the feeling that it would be 'sissy' to get beaten to it.

madera. *v.* **leña.**

madre (f). Should need no entry but Mexican usage makes one essential; insults connected with mothers are so common (*v.* **puta**) and so offensive that in Mexico they have steered off the word altogether when it is a matter of referring to immediate relatives and you therefore do not say *su/tu madre* for 'your/his/her mother', you say *su/tu mamá* (but *v.* also **guachafo**). By extension, also, *su/tu papá*. Certain contexts can disinfect the word; it is safe enough to say *Madre Superiora* for 'Mother Superior' and indeed it would be ridiculous to say *Mamá Superiora* but in general conversation about the family it is better to gear your mind to *mamá* and *papá* (*v.* also **abuelo**).

madrugar, madrugada (f). Familiar to students of Spanish, of course, but so common and useful that I venture to draw the reader's attention to it. *Madrugar* means 'to rise early in the morning', and 'an early-riser' is *un madrugador. La madrugada* is that period of the twenty-four hours which may be described as 'very late at night' or 'very early in the morning' according to your angle; call it 'the small hours' or 'cockcrow'. In Mexico, where lunch is very late by our standards, I was usually the first in my habitual restaurant and a waiter once said *Vd. madruga*, 'You're an early bird'.

maestro. Borders on the False as it is by no means confined to music; it can be applied, as a courtesy title, to any sort of artist or poet, and is particularly used to his face, or in his presence. In L/A it may be extended to craftsmen, indeed to any responsible worker, especially when hailing him or calling his attention. In a school context it is likely to mean specifically the 'master' of a primary school (*v*. also **profesor**).

malestar (m). A word much used by doctors and equating with our 'discomfort', in that context. It may also be used for 'hangover'.

mañanita (f). Obviously a diminutive of 'morning' but much used in Mexico and thereabouts. *En mañanita* means 'in his/her dressing gown', and *mañanitas* is the name given to the 'serenades' given by *mariachis* on *marimbas* which are so typical of those parts.

mandar. 'To order', yes, but usually in the sense of ordering people, or sending somebody to do something. Waiters in L/A will often say *Mande* or *Mándeme* when they come to take your order, i.e. literally, 'Bid me'. To send things usually requires *enviar*. *Mande* is widely used in L/A as a reply when one's name is called and then equates with 'Yes?' Equally when a person has not heard what you said and asks for it to be repeated he will say *¿Mande?*, 'Pardon me?', 'I'm sorry?', 'What did you say?' In Spain *¿Perdón?* is more likely for this.

manejar. In some respects a Good Friend of 'manage' but basically it means 'to handle', 'to operate': *¿Sabes manejarlo?*, 'Do you know how to work/use it?'; *Manejar con cuidado*, 'Handle with care'. In L/A it is often used for 'to drive' a car. It can be used metaphorically: *Ella maneja su marido*, 'She bosses her husband', but it does not extend to 'contrive to', 'succeed in': 'I managed to get in before they closed', *Logré entrar antes de que cerraran*; 'Did you manage to get the tickets?', *¿Has conseguido entradas?* (*v*. **conseguir**); 'We'll manage somehow', *Nos arreglaremos de algún modo*.

manera. *v*. **forma**.

mango (m). Unreliable; in the more tropical countries it will probably mean the fruit, viz. the large, sweet and juicy *Mangifera Indica* (not 'peppers' which are sometimes called 'mangoes' in the U.S.), and if you go to Mexico ask for *Mangos de Manila*, which have much smoother flesh.

In Spain, where the fruit is known only by hearsay, *mango* usually means 'handle'. It is impossible, unfortunately, to give the reader one word for 'handle' but *mango* is fairly all-purpose in Spain. *Manilla*, for a 'door-handle', is likely to be understood in most countries, though in Mexico they tend to prefer *manija*, in Z/A *jalador* or *chapa (q.v.)*; in Venezuela *perilla*.

A 'handle' of the lever type is often called a 'lever', i.e. *palanca*, and this is certainly the word for a 'gear(shift)-lever'.

'Handles' of the 'ear' type, e.g. of cups, or the two sides of an *olla* are usually *asas* but in parts of L/A they may be referred to as 'ears', i.e. *orejas*.

A 'handle' of the broomstick type may safely be called *el palo* in any country.

In the R/P *mango* is a slang word for 'money'.

maní. *v.* **nuez.**

manifestación (f). 'Manifestation', yes, but also the eqivalent of 'demonstration' in the matter of politics, etc. *Demostración* is more like 'show', 'display' and has no political overtones.

mano (f). 'Hand', of course, but I mention a few everyday cases where it does not mean hand: *Una mano* is used in parts of L/A to mean 'one-way street', and the notice is usually accompanied by an arrow showing which way; in card games *¿Quién tiene la mano?* means 'Whose lead is it?' *¿Quién sale?* may also be used; *mano de almirez* is the 'pestle' of a mortar and more everyday than you might imagine.

The 'hand' of a clock is usually *manecilla* and this may refer to either hand, not necessarily the small one. (*Aguja* is also used for this).

manojo (m). A 'bunch' of vegetables (beet, carrots, etc.) in Mexico and Spain; 'a bunch (of flowers)' is *un ramo* (*de flores*). Elsewhere 'a bunch' of vegetables is usually *un atado*, though in Chile *paquete* (in Chile anything tied up, even flowers, is *un paquete*).

manta (f). In Spain 'rug', or 'blanket', and the normal word for 'blanket' there. In the C/S it means the type of rug which has a slit in the middle through which you put your head, thus converting it into a sort of cape, elsewhere called *un poncho (v.* also **cobija**).

manteca (f), **mantequilla** (f), **mantecado** (m). *Manteca* is the all-but-universal word for 'pork fat', 'lard', the main exception being the R/P where it means 'butter'. *Mantequilla* is the all-but-universal word for 'butter', the exception again being the R/P. In Venezuela it is also a slang word for 'graft'.

Mantecado means 'vanilla ice-cream'; other sorts are simply *helado de fresa*, etc. *Mantecadas* are usually small cakes of the sort sold in frilled papers.

manzana. *v.* **cuadra.**

manzanilla (f). Although a diminutive of *manzana* it has no connection with apples; in Spain it is most likely to refer to a very light, dry sherry (almost salt in flavour) but even there it may be confused with 'camomile tea'. If you particularly want—or do not want —this, refer to it as *una infusión de manzanilla*; in Chile this is *una agüita*.

máquina (f). 'Machine', of course, but in appropriate contexts will mean either a 'typewriter' or a 'camera' (*v.* **cámara**). *Maquinaria* obviously means 'machinery' but is often used for a colloquial reference to 'the works', especially by people who are not very mechanically minded, meaning the machine part of some bit of apparatus.

marcar, marca (f), **marco** (m). Specialized everyday uses of *marcar* are 'to bid' (in card games) and 'to dial' (a number) (*discar* is also used in L/A). In L/A it can extend to pressing the button in an elevator and I have also heard a telephone operator say *Está marcando ahora* for 'It's ringing now'; this would normally be *llamando*.

Marca is most often used meaning 'make', or 'brand': *¿Qué marca es?*, 'What make is it?' It is *not* the word for the 'marks' you get at school which are usually *notas* or *calificaciones* (*q.v.*).

Marco—apart from being the German Mark—is most likely to mean 'picture-frame' in everyday circumstances (the 'mount' is usually *el margen* or *el passe-partout*—pronounced *paspartú*), but is also often metaphorically used for 'setting'.

marchar(se). The commonest daily use of *marchar* is the metaphorical 'to go', in the sense of doing well: *Los asuntos no marchan bien*, 'Business isn't going (too) well'. When it is a matter of machinery 'going', *funcionar* is more likely. *Marcharse* is tremendously common being the usual verb for 'to depart', 'to leave': *Se marchó a las diez*, 'He left at ten'. It is virtually interchangeable with *irse* (*q.v.*): *Si no te marchas tú me iré yo*, 'If *you* don't go *I* shall', but perhaps a little weightier.

mareado. Strictly 'seasick', but extended to being the normal word for 'dizzy', 'faint', 'sick' (and often used as a euphemism for 'drunk'). In L/A they often use *vahido* for a 'fit' of giddiness.

margen, al. *Margen* does mean 'margin', i.e. the border of a page, and *al margen* therefore may mean (and is sometimes given as) 'on the margin' or 'on the borderline' but usually means 'on the sidelines', 'in the wings' and therefore 'detached' (though interested): *Estoy al margen*, 'I'm not involved (though I may know all about it)'.

maricón (m). Several dictionaries face up to telling you that this means a 'queer' but do not add that it is also a very gross word, not suitable for mixed company. It is therefore a most pejorative insult; I cannot think of one single English word which contains so much contempt, though it can, of course, be used facetiously, as can some of our equivalents, in bantering conversations between males. *Marica*, equally common, is less blatant but nevertheless to be avoided in polite company. The female counterpart (equally vulgar) is *una tortillera*, a lesbian.

marmita. *v.* **caldera.**

martes (m). 'Tuesday', of course, but you may not know that in the Hispanic world *Martes trece*, i.e. 'Tuesday, 13th', is the equivalent of our Friday, 13th, i.e. a supposedly unlucky day.

más. 'More', as you know, but often the equivalent of 'else': *¿Que más?*, 'What else?'; *¿Algo más?*, 'Anything else?'; *¿Quien más?*, 'Who else?' (Not, however, 'or else' which has to be *si no* or, in the sense of 'alternatively', *o sea* (*v.* **ser**)). Another common equivalent is 'rather': *Es cuestión de tiempo más que dinero*, 'It's a matter of time rather than money'. *Más bien* should be at your tongue's tip for 'rather' in the sense of 'more precisely stated': *Cerró la puerta—o más bien lo intentó*, 'He shut the door—or rather, he tried to'. (For 'rather' in the sense of 'somewhat' *v.* **poco**). *No más que* is a common way of handling our 'only': *No quedan más que cuatro*, 'There are only four left'. (*Sólo quedan . . .* is another possibility.)

A highly idiomatic use of *más* is in exclamations such as 'What a . . . (adjective) . . . thing!' or 'How . . . (adjective)!': *¡Qué cosa más rara!*, 'What an extraordinary thing!', 'How extraordinary!' It is not confined to use with *cosa*: *¡Qué película más aburrida!*, 'What a boring film!' After a long acrimonious argument with her son, at a meal table, a Spanish woman I knew exclaimed to the company at large *¡Qué hijo más antipático!* It is not easy to translate such a characteristic remark; 'What an infuriating boy!' or 'There's a nice son for you!' are possibilities.

In L/A *. . . no más*, added on to (usually) an imperative, acquires the force of 'just', or 'only': *Diez escudos, no más*, 'Only ten escudos'; *Así, no más*, 'Just (leave it) like that'. I once asked a countrywoman in Peru whether I might use a particular path which led over some private property. She interrogated me briefly as to my reasons and ended with a slightly grudging *Pase, no más*. One is tempted to translate this 'Go ahead, then', but in fact she was being more polite than she sounded; *. . . no más* is much used in L/A polite phrases (*v.* COURTESY), and a better equivalent would be 'Please go ahead', or 'Go right ahead'. In a Montevideo shop I once enquired about a particular cheese and the shopman at once sliced off a small sliver of it and handed it to me saying *Pruebe, no más*, 'Please try it', or 'Just try it'.

matar. 'To kill', yes, but it implies conscious and deliberate killing, hence 'to slaughter' with reference to animals and 'to murder' with reference to humans. It is not, however, used in the Passive, i.e. you would never say *Ha sido matado*; 'He's been killed' (by whatever agency) has to be *Ha sido muerto* (*v.* **muerto**, also **ultimar**).

materia (f). 'Matter' in general but in L/A, in a university context, it means 'subject of study': *¿Qué es su materia?*, 'What's your subject?' In Spain they are more likely to say *¿Qué estudia?* Everywhere, however, *una asignatura* is used for a subdivision within the subject, e.g. of one exam paper: *Ha aprobado todas las asignaturas del curso*, 'He's passed in all subjects'. As a more general word for 'subject' *materia* does not require the article: *Esta propuesta será materia de discusiones sin fin*, 'This proposal will be the subject of endless argument'.

Conversely 'matter', a word which we use a good deal, will rarely equate with *materia*, more often with *asunto, cuestión* or *cosa*: 'It's a matter of life and death', *Es cosa de vida o de muerte* (N.B. again no article); 'The matter in hand'. *El asunto/tema de que se trata*; 'It's no laughing matter', *No es cosa de risa*. 'What's the matter (with you)?', *¿Qué hay? ¿Qué (te) pasa?* 'To matter' is *importar*: 'It doesn't matter', *No importa, Es igual* (*v.* **importar**).

Materialista normally means 'materialist' but is also applied to a person who deals in construction materials and, in Mexico, to a 'truck-driver'.

matricular(se). Fairly Reliable on the whole but, apart from college contexts (*matricularse*, 'to enrol'), it is chiefly associated with getting one's car registered. *La matrícula* is the usual word in Spain and some other countries for the 'licence/number plate' of a car (*v.* also **licencia, placa**).

matrimonio (m). 'Matrimony', yes, but in practice its most likely meaning is 'married couple'. It is often used for 'double bed' (short for *cama de matrimonio*).

máximo. 'Maximum', certainly, but used rather more in Spanish than in English and one needs to make oneself aware of its possibilities. How would you say 'as hard as he could'? Answer: *con la máxima fuerza*. Similarly with *mínimo*: 'He did as little as possible' —*Hizo lo mínimo*. Easy enough when one is wise after the event. I am merely trying to urge wisdom before it.

In Mexico *¡lo máximo!* is a common colloquial term for 'terrific!', 'way-out!', 'fabulous!' etc. (perhaps 'tops!').

mayor. Although technically Comparative and meaning 'larger', 'older', 'elder', 'senior', 'major', etc. *mayor* is often used for the Superlative: *Su hermano mayor* may mean 'his elder' or 'his eldest brother'. *Plaza Mayor* means 'Chief Place', i.e. the 'town square', and does not invite comparison with some other, smaller square. It is perhaps for this reason that many Hispanics, when wishing to stress the Comparative aspect, will say *más mayor*; strictly incorrect but it reveals how far *mayor* has lost its Comparative force. Other built-in Comparatives which get similar ill-treatment are *inferior, superior* and—though not strictly a Comparative—*antes*. A shopman may say *Esto es más barato pero es más inferior*, 'This is cheaper but it's not so good', and in L/A you may hear, e.g., *Lo había hecho más antes*, 'He'd done it earlier on'.

Used with *que*, however, *mayor* retains its comparative force: *Fernando es mayor que Ramón*, 'Fernando is older than Ramón' (and beware of saying *más viejo que* which is tantamount to saying 'more aged than').

mear. 'To urinate', but it is extremely vulgar, although universal. No need to tell you that it equates with 'piss' and it should be avoided in just the same way. *Orinar*, although very frank, is less offensive.

mecate (m). One of several words for 'rope', in the Caribbean area. It implies very thick rope, hawser, of the type used for berthing ships, though a metal 'hawser' would probably be *cable* (*v.* also **guaya**). In Mexico the expression *¡Es todo mecate!* means 'It's terrific!' (*v.* **reata**).

medias (f. pl.). Usually means 'stockings' but in much of L/A may also be applied to 'socks' for men. In Buenos Aires it is the O.K. word for 'socks', and *calcetines*, the more universal word, is considered by snobs to be rather vulgar. In Chile you may see *zoquetes*.

The expression *a medias* is useful for our 'half-', or 'not quite': *Le oigo a medias*, 'I can half-hear him'; *Lo entendía a medias*, 'I didn't quite understand'.

medidas (f. pl.). Both 'measures' and 'measurements'; *tomar medidas*, without the Article, means 'to take measures', 'to take steps', e.g. against some contingency; *tomar las medidas* is 'to take measurements', e.g. for a suit.

medusa. *v.* **aguamala.**

mejor. Obviously it means 'better', but is used a great deal where we use more words, e.g. 'It'd be better', 'I think that would be better', 'That's more like it', etc. For all of these it is sufficient simply to say *Mejor*.

A lo mejor is the commonest form of 'probably', much commoner than *probablemente* and more idiomatic: *A lo mejor llegaré a la una*, 'I'll probably get there/With any luck I'll be there by one (o'clock)'. Quite often our equation would be 'might': *A lo mejor me toca la lotería*, 'I might win the lottery'; *A lo mejor se muere*, 'He might die'.

There is a ghost to be laid here; several lexicographers, taking the dictionary of the *Real Academia* as their bible, have accepted without question a definition of *a lo mejor* which has been there longer than most of us can remember and which reads: '*loc. adv. fam. con que se anuncia un hecho o dicho inesperado, y por lo común infausto o desagradable*', as a result of which the translation of *a lo mejor* appears in several dictionaries as 'when least expected'. Readers may be assured that, for normal everyday purposes, it means nothing of the sort, nor does it necessarily herald anything unlucky or disagreeable; it can just as well be used of a desired event (*v.* **pensar**).

menos. 'Less', 'fewer' (after the definite article 'least', 'fewest'), 'minus', etc. as you know; also 'not so much/many', or 'not so . . . (adjective)'. It will often stand by itself meaning 'less so': Q. 'Is it complicated?' A. 'Yes, but not as complicated as the others'. Q. *¿Es complicado?* A. *Sí, pero menos* (simply); *¡Ni mucho menos!*, 'Far from it!' 'On the contrary.'

A very common, and rather surprising, expression is *¡Menos mal!*, equating with our 'Thank goodness!', 'Thank heaven!' or, in a less exclamatory tone of voice, 'I'm glad to hear it', 'That's good'.

mentira. *v.* **parecer.**

menu. *v.* **cubierto.**

menudo. Literally 'tiny', 'minute' but used a good deal colloquially as a deliberate understatement and implying its opposite: *Menuda tormenta tuvimos anoche*, 'That was some storm we had last night'. Much may depend on tone of voice; if a schoolboy asked a silly question the master might freeze him with a sarcastic *¡Menuda pregunta!*, 'There's a fine question!', but in another tone of voice it could equate with 'That's a good/nice question!', 'No small question!'

merecer. "To merit', 'to be worthwhile', 'to warrant'. In many contexts it is interchangeable with *valer*, particularly, perhaps, negative ones. Used positively, however, *valer* has a stronger sense of worth in terms of money: *Lo vale* is likely to mean 'It's worth' a particular sum, while *lo merece* 'It's worth while', or 'He deserves it'. The basic difference is between 'merit' and 'value'.

merienda (f). A rather movable feast. It is essentially an informal meal taken outside the normal hours or circumstances and so will often mean 'picnic'. In Spain and the R/P it is a likely word for 'tea', i.e. a snack with a cup of tea or coffee taken in mid-afternoon. In countries where the main meal of the day is eaten about 3 p.m., it may apply to the much smaller evening meal so that 'supper' is nearer the mark, though it is often little more than a snack. Anywhere it would apply to, say, sandwiches taken to eat on a train or bus.

Different countries tend to acquire words of their own for these snack-like, extra-curricular meals; Chile has *las onces*; in the R/P you may hear *el faivocló* (five o'clock) (*v*. also **lunch**).

mero. Rather Unreliable, largely because in English we have narrowed down the word 'mere' so that it borders on the deprecatory. It helps one to understand Spanish usage if one appreciates that, in origin, *mero*/'mere' meant 'pure', and a better equivalent is 'sheer': *Le ví por mera casualidad*, 'I saw him by sheer chance'. In L/A they are even more conscious of this, 'He's only a child', said compassionately, would in Spain probably be *Es sólo un niño*, but in L/A *Es un mero niño*. In Mexico they exploit the word even further: *el mero centro*, 'the very centre'; *en la mera esquina*, 'right on the corner'; *tu mero papá*, 'your own father'. All this is a very logical extension of the Latin *merus*, 'pure', 'undiluted', but it makes '*mero*' positively False.

Mero is also a fish, something like a halibut.

mesero/mesonero. *v*. **camarero.**

meter(se). There are, as you know, several verbs for 'to put' (*v*. **poner**, **colocar**); *meter* is essentially, 'to put *in*', the obverse of *sacar*, 'to take out'. A doctor telling you to put out your tongue will say *Saque la lengua* and then, having scrutinized it, *Métala*, 'Put it in again'. In a packing context *¿Has metido mis pañuelos?*, 'Did you pack (put in) my handkerchiefs?' Common verbal phrases with *meter* are *meter miedo*, 'to frighten', 'to put the fear of God into'; *meter prisa*, 'to hurry (something) up', 'to expedite'; *meter ruido*, 'to make a noise': *Haga el favor de no meter tanto ruido*, 'Please don't make such a noise'.

Meterse may mean literally, 'to put oneself into': *¡Métete en la cama!*, 'Get into bed!'; *No te metas las manos en los bolsillos*, 'Don't put your hands in your pockets', but it has many metaphorical uses, e.g. 'to poke one's nose into', 'to meddle': *Ella se* *mete en todo*, 'She pokes her nose into everything'; *Métete en lo que te importa*, 'Mind your own business'. *Meterse con* may mean 'to pick a quarrel with', but it is much used in the light-hearted sense of 'to tease': *A ella le gusta meterse con migo*, 'She likes teasing me'. In Mexico a slightly stronger form of teasing, i.e. 'to needle', 'to provoke', is *meter una pulla*.

micro. *v.* **bus.**

miedo (m). 'Fear', as you know: *¿Tiene miedo?*, 'Are you scared?' *De miedo* is a very common adjectival phrase meaning 'awful', 'fearful', 'formidable', and much used colloquially: *Era una cosa de miedo*, 'It was simply awful'. As with *bárbaro*, it can be used in a favourable sense, given an appropriate tone of voice, and will then mean 'terrific!' 'To be afraid' in the polite sense requires *temer*: 'I'm afraid I didn't quite catch your name', *(Me) temo que no oí muy bien su nombre*.

mierda (f). A rude word; too rude for some dictionaries; others will put: '(coll.) excrement' i.e. frankly, 'shit'. It is perhaps *slightly* less so than its English equivalent, but no reader should imagine that it is O.K. for him (still less her) to bandy it about his/her conversation. I feel bound to put on record, however, that in a well-to-do Spanish household I heard the hostess, a well brought up, convent-trained girl, refer to somebody she did not like as *una mierda seca*. She was being humorous and the company (all Spanish except myself) was certainly provoked into laughter but I found myself doubting whether her Anglo-Saxon counterpart, likewise *de casa bien*, would have risked its English equivalent. Readers should certainly not do so in Spanish, nor would the lady in question have done so on a less relaxed occasion.

mimar. Its commonest everyday meaning is 'to spoil (a child)'; *mimado*, 'spoilt', but it is often used about grown-ups meaning 'to make a fuss of': *No hay que mimarle tanto*, 'There's no need to make such a fuss of him' (*v.* also **echar** (*a perder*)).

mina (f). 'Mine', both as the explosive and as the burrowing in the ground but its likeliest everyday meaning is the 'lead', of a pencil, whether a wooden or a propelling/mechanical one.

mingitorio. *v.* **baño.**

ministro. (m). A 'minister' only in the governmental sense and so not the word for a Protestant parson who would be *un pastor*. In Mexico *papel ministro* means 'foolscap/legal paper', elsewhere usually *papel de oficio*.

minuta (f). 'Menu', 'bill of fare' ('minute', i.e. 60 seconds = *minuto*). *Menu* is also used. In the R/P *minuta* can apply to a dish which only takes a metaphorical minute to cook, e.g. steak, *milanesa*, chop, etc.

mirador (m). 'Look-out point', and in the past has been mostly associated with balconies on the front of houses, a 'gazebo', but nowadays is more likely to be associated with *autopistas*. The view may be breathtaking but you are not allowed to stop on the fairway; notices therefore guide you to the *mirador* where you may lawfully do so.

misión (f). Unreliable; the English 'mission' implies serious matters whereas *misión* applies to any 'job' you have been given to do. 'Job', in fact, is often the best equation: *Regular el tráfico es misión de la policía*, 'Traffic control is the job of the police'. 'Duty' is another possibility: *Sólo cumplo con mi misión*, 'I'm only doing my duty'. 'Business' is yet another, provided it is business you have been sent to do and not your own private business. *Tiene sentido de misión* is often said of people who have a sort of bee in their bonnet about some course of action, i.e. who like to feel they are obeying external dictates though in fact very self-impelled.

mismo. Needs little comment from me, except perhaps to remind you that it means both 'same' and 'self': *La casa misma* or *la misma casa* can both mean either 'the same house', or 'the house itself'. Common uses are: *Lo mismo*, 'same again' (e.g. in a bar) and *dar lo mismo*, 'to come to the same thing': *Me da lo mismo*, 'It's all the same to me'. 'I don't mind'. *Por lo mismo que*, 'By the very fact that'.

mistificar. Not a common verb but, in so far as it is used, it is False since it implies deliberate intention 'to deceive'. The difference shows up most clearly in the Past Participle, *mistificado*, which means, not 'mystified', but 'taken in', 'hoodwinked', 'led up the garden'. Used of things it usually means 'adulterated'. A variant spelling is *mixtificar*.

mitad (f). The noun for 'half' as opposed to the adjective (*v.* **medio**) but much used for 'middle'; *en mitad de* is often more or less interchangeable with *en medio de*. *A* (*la*) *mitad de* (Article not essential) is 'half-way through', and implies motion.

mitin (m). A borrowing from the English 'meeting' but its use is confined to large-scale, usually open-air, political meetings and it tends to be associated with popular indignation and demagoguery (*v.* also **manifestación, junta, reunión**).

modo (m). Included to remind you to have at your tongue's tip such expressions as: *de este modo*, 'this way'; *de todos modos*, anyway'; *de cierto modo*, 'in a way', 'to a certain extent'.

A fairly common and widespread expression is *a grosso modo*, 'by and large', 'roughly speaking', 'approximately'. It is really a piece of Latin, hence the double *s* (French and Italian have borrowed it, too) (*v.* also **manera**). In Mexico they are fond of the phrase *¡Ni modo!*, meaning 'Just too bad!', 'Nothing to be done about it' (*v.* also **paciencia**).

'Mode', meaning fashion, is *moda*. *Pasado de moda*, 'old-fashioned'.

molde (m). 'Mould', in the sense of 'shape' (the fungus is *moho*). You are likely to meet it in connection with bread; 'a loaf of bread' is normally *un pan* which may be of varying size of shape; *pan de molde* means a loaf which has been baked in a rectangular pan. In Mexico they call this *pan de caja*.

Another common use is in connection with lettering. On forms that require filling you will often see *Se ruega escribir en letras de molde*. Strictly speaking *letras de molde* are printed script, as opposed to linear, but 'Please write in block letters' is intended.

In the Z/A *molde* is applied to the 'pattern' which ladies use to pin to material when making a dress. Elsewhere this is *el patrón*.

molestar, molestia (f), **molesto**. *Molestar*, 'to molest', but this word savours of the law courts in English whereas *molestar* is an everyday verb equating with 'to bother', 'trouble', 'pester', 'disturb', etc. It is much used in polite phrases (*v.* COURTESY).

Molestia is a noun for 'nuisance!'; *molesto* an adjective but often used as a noun: 'What a nuisance!' could be either! *Qué molestia!* or ¡*Qué molesto!*; *Es una situación muy molesta*, 'It's a very irritating situation', but 'It's very annoying' could be either *Es muy molesto* or *Es mucha molestia*.

montón (m). Means 'heap', but is much used colloquially for 'heaps', 'piles', etc.: *Tengo un montón de cosas que hacer*, 'I've got a thousand things to do'.

moqueta. *v.* **carpeta**.

morenales (m. pl.). 'Shanty towns' in Honduras (*v.* **suburbio**).

moreno. *v.* **rubio**.

mostrar. *v.* **enseñar**.

motivo (m). Unreliable. Perhaps through much reading of crime stories Anglo-Saxons have a fairly precise idea of the meaning of 'motive' and for us it has been a comparatively educated word. For Hispanics it has not and as a result its meaning is very often 'purpose' or 'reason': *Con motivo de*, 'for the purpose of', 'by reason of', 'owing to', even 'in order to'. *El motivo de no escribirte* seems to suggest that I deliberately refrained from writing but in fact means 'The reason why I didn't write to you' and I then go on to explain what prevented me (*v.* also **propósito**).

moto (f). 'Motorcycle'. No need to be surprised at its being feminine; it is short for *motocicleta*; in L/A sometimes for *motoneta* (motor scooter).

mudar(se). *Mudar* is 'to mutate', and not a common verb though *mudar de propósito*, 'to change one's mind', is a rather more literary version of *cambiar de idea*. *Mudarse*, however, is very common and in most countries is likely to mean 'to move (house)' (*v.* also **trasladar**). Fairly universal is *mudarse de ropa*, 'to change one's clothes', though it suggests underclothes and *una muda* means 'a change of (under)clothes'. 'To change one's suit' or 'dress' is *cambiarse de traje* or *de vestido*.

muelle (m). 'Spring', but this is an all-purpose word in English; Spanish is more precise about different types of spring. *Muelle* is the sort which a layman might describe as 'spiral', e.g. 'chain springs', 'bed-springs', the 'springs' used on those old-fashioned scales on which goods are hung while an indicator points the weight. A laminated 'spring', e.g. of a car, is *una ballesta*. A coiled 'spring', of the type used in clockwork, is *un resorte*. (For really ancient clockwork it was *cuerda*, i.e. in a grandfather clock when the weights hung on cords, and this survives in the expression *dar cuerda* for 'to wind up' a clock or watch.)

In harbour circumstances *muelle* means 'mole', or 'quay'.

muerto. Perhaps this should have been put under *morir* but it is only the past participle, which deserves attention. *Muerto* means, basically, 'died', and therefore automatically 'dead'. In, say, a hospital context, *El enfermo ha muerto* equates with 'The patient has died', i.e. when the death is—dare I say?—hot news. The complications start when referring to that so-permanent condition since here Spanish uses that very auxiliary verb which—we are told in Part I, Lesson I—is applied to temporary conditions!: 'He is dead', *¡Está muerto!* *Ser muerto* means 'to be killed': *Un hombre fue muerto a tiros*, 'A man was shot dead' (*v.* also **matar**).

In card games *muerto* means 'dummy'.

mugre (m). 'Dirt', but it has different images in different places; in the R/P I found it used as the ordinary word for 'dirt' and it could apply to such mild things as 'grubbiness', whereas in Spain it is a strong word and equates with 'filth'. With *suciedad* the roles are almost reversed in the two places.

murmurar. Yes, 'to murmur', 'to whisper', and we can extend these in English to muttered protests. In Spanish *murmurar* extends even further: it means 'to gossip', usually maliciously: *No murmures*, 'Don't tell tales', 'Don't spread nasty stories around'. *Murmuración* is definitely malicious gossip.

N

nacional. Not only 'national', but applied to products of local manufacture or production, hence 'local', 'native', 'indigenous', 'home': 'Home products', *productos nacionales*. If you order a brandy in the C/S you are likely to be asked by the waiter *¿Quiere nacional?*, i.e. 'Do you want the local product?' or a (much more expensive) brandy imported from Europe?

nada. *v.* **courtesy.**

nafta. *v.* **gasolina.**

ñapa (f). Other forms are *yapa* and *llapa*; it is a Quechua word indicating something thrown in for good measure or, more strictly, for luck. It can also mean the 'one for the road', i.e. 'the last drink', 'one more for luck'; in other circumstances 'tip' (I struck this in Venezuela), since it is obvious that what is *una propina* for the waiter may be regarded as *una ñapa* by the client. Readers who know Louisiana may be aware of the word lanyap, or lagniappe, meaning something thrown in as a bonus. It seems fairly certain that this was taken over from the French who in turn got it from the Spanish/Quechua.

natural, -mente, naturaleza (f). *Natural*, though certainly meaning natural, is used where we should say 'real', or 'plain': *agua natural*, 'plain water' (as opposed to carbonated); *flores naturales*, 'real flowers' (as opposed to artificial).

    Naturalmente seems as if it ought to be the word for 'naturally', but in fact is a shade literary and is seldom used in conversation; in Spain they say *desde luego* and in L/A *por supuesto*; *claro* or *claro está* are also common—and universal.

    Naturaleza is Nature, with a capital N, but it may also mean 'place of birth', and you likely to hit it when filling up forms. If you are questioned verbally in such matters then *¿De dónde es Vd. natural?* is quite a likely one and means 'Where were you born?' Your answer requires the name of a place, not of a country, though *naturalización* does mean naturalization.

negar(se). *Negar* means not only 'to deny' a fact, or an assertion: *Negó que había estado*, 'He denied having been there'; but also 'to refuse' to perform an act, permission, etc.: *Me negó el saludo*, 'He ignored my salutation', 'He cut me'; *Le negaron el paso*, 'They refused to let him in'. You might therefore be tempted to imagine that *negarse* means 'to deny oneself' but in fact it usually means 'to refuse': *Pues, si viene me voy a negar a verle*, 'Well, if he comes I shall refuse to see him'. We are rather fond of such phrases as 'I shall deny myself the pleasure', but for this the Spanish is *privarme*. 'Self-denial' would be *autoprivación*.

    Desnegar is another word for 'to deny' an assertion; it is particularly likely to be used in a political or legal context; *desmentir* is very similar. *Rechazar* is 'to rebut, to refute'.

nene. *v.* **chaval.**

nervioso. It means 'nervous' when applied to a temporary state: *Me está poniendo nervioso*, 'You're making me nervous', but applied to temperament or disposition it means 'highly-strung, 'nervy', 'excitable'. Even applied to a temporary state it may mean 'worked up': *No te pongas nervioso*, 'Take it easy', 'Don't get excited'. *Una crisis nerviosa*, 'a nervous breakdown' (*v.* **excitar(se)**).

ni. 'Neither', 'nor', but often used to mean 'not even': *No tenía ni un céntimo*, 'I hadn't (even) a cent on me'. *Ni idea* is the stock phrase for 'No idea!' It is the Spanish way of handling cases where we are likely to use a heavy stress (in the above cases on 'cent' and 'idea'). Hispanics may give a stress too but the *ni* is slipped in almost unconsciously to reinforce it. *¡Ni modo!* is the usual expression in Mexico for 'Just too bad!', literally 'not even a way' (of doing something about it) (*v.* MISCELLANEOUS NOTES, p. 21).

Even more colloquial is *ni ná, ni ná*, short for *ni nada, ni nada*; it is added at the end of a series of 'nors', meaning 'nor anything else': *No fuma ni bebe ni ná ni ná*, 'He doesn't smoke nor drink nor anything else/nor any damn thing'.

noche. *v.* **tarde.**

nombrar. 'To name', 'to nominate', 'to appoint', but also useful for our 'to mention': *Ha nombrado Vd. al Sr. Fulano*, 'You mentioned Mr. So-&-So'; *Este muchacho que nombraste*, 'This guy you were talking about'. We are unlikely to say 'this guy you named'.

nombre. *v.* **apellido.**

norma. (f). 'Norm', but much used, even in conversation, where we might say 'standard': *Según sus normas*, 'by their standards'. *Normal* is also the adjective 'standard' and useful for our 'average'. *Fue un día normal*, 'It was an average sort of day' (*v.* also **término**).

norteamericano. Normally means a 'U.S. citizen'. Opinions vary as to whether it includes Canadians and the latter are advised to describe themselves as *canadienses*. It is a good idea to make oneself conscious of the word. We all get into the habit of identifying the word 'American' with the United States, 'all', that is, that is, except Hispanics, but it should come as no surprise that they have their own word for those who live north of the Mexican border, just as we use Latin American for those south of it. U.S. readers, in particular, are advised to be on their guard against letting the adjective *americano* slip out as applying to themselves or 'what we do at home' and to implant *norteamericano* in its place. It is good diplomacy—as well as common politeness—to show some recognition that the other Americas are just as American as you are, indeed, where Amerindians are concerned, even more so. If you go to Mexico it is also useful to know that its official title is *Estados Unidos de México* so that even *Estados Unidos* may be tricky there (it is O.K. elsewhere). *México,* within Mexico, usually means 'Mexico City'.

noticia (f). Best regarded as False; its commonest form is in the plural and *noticias* means 'news': *Boletín de noticias*, 'News bulletin'. *Una noticia* is not a notice but 'an item of news'; 'a notice' is usually *un aviso* or *anuncio*. A play or performance which 'gets good notices', *tiene buenas reseñas* or *críticas*. 'At short notice', *a corto plazo*; 'worthy of notice', *digno de atención*; 'until further notice', *hasta nuevo aviso*; 'without notice', *sin aviso* or *sin avisar*.

Dar noticia de might conceivably equate with 'to give notice of', in a context where this was synonymous with 'give news of', but *notificar* is better for 'to give notice of', 'to notify', 'to announce'. Neither will do for 'to give notice' in the sense of 'to fire/sack' which would be *despedir* or, less formally, *echar*. *Tener noticias de*, 'to have news of,' 'to hear from'. For 'to take notice', *v.* **caso.**

notorio, notoriedad (f). *Notorio*, though more used in L/A than Spain, may be regarded as False since it means 'famous', 'well-known', even 'obvious', and implies nothing disgraceful or undesirable. *Notoriedad* is universal but again means 'fame', not 'notoriety'. A good equation for *notorio* is often 'manifest'. If a context already implies 'ill-fame' then *notorio* will serve for 'notorious'; if not then *de mala reputación* is indicated.

novio, -a. 'Boy-friend/girl-friend' will often serve though in most countries 'fiancé(e)' would be more accurate since they take these things seriously. It has, however, become sufficiently vague in some L/A countries for *afianzado, -a* to be used by those who are anxious to show that it really is serious. *Noviazgo* is an 'engagement' (usually very long by our standards) (*v.* also **pololo**).

Nueva York. Obviously 'New York', but it is as well to know that they have their own version of it; also that the final *k* is rarely pronounced so that you hear a sound like *nuevayor* and might be mystified if you were not warned. The adjective is *neoyorquino* but you will often hear *nuevayorquino*.

nuevo. 'New', of course, but we use the word in two senses; 'a new car' may mean one that is brand-new or one recently acquired, different from its predecessor, etc. In Spanish the distinction is made by word order: *un nuevo coche* is a 'different' car and *un coche nuevo* is a brand-new one.

nuez (f). Ought to mean 'nut', but, surprisingly, Spanish has no generic word for nut and *nuez*, in most countries means 'walnut'. Other nuts have different names: *avellana*, 'hazel-nut'; *almendra*, 'almond'; *castaña*, 'chestnut'; *nuez de Brasil*, 'Brazil nut', etc. 'Pea-nut' varies: it is *cacahuate* in Mexico, *cacahuete* in Spain and usually *maní* elsewhere.

In Mexico they have their own version of the walnut, viz. the pecan nut, so *nueces*, in Mexico, means 'pecan nuts'; for 'walnuts' they say *nueces de Castilla*. For 'cashew nuts' they often say *nueces de India* though these are usually *nueces de acachú*.

A 'nut', meaning the counterpart to a bolt, is *una tuerca*.

O

ocurrencia (f), **ocurrente.** *Una ocurrencia* may mean 'an occurrence' but is much more likely to mean 'something that has just occurred to one', hence 'bright idea', 'brainwave' and often a witty remark, though it can of course be used sarcastically to mean a ridiculous idea: *¡Qué ocurrencia!*, 'What an idea!' (tone of voice can indicate whether it was a good idea or a bad one).

    Similarly, *ocurrente* means 'bright', 'entertaining', 'amusing': *Una persona muy ocurrente*, 'A person of lively, witty conversation', or one to whom bright ideas occur.

odómetro (m). 'Odometer', or—as most dictionaries give it—'hodometer'. British readers may not be aware that this is what we call a 'milometer'. I found it only in Mexico. In most countries they say *cuentakilómetros*; more of a mouthful but it has the advantage of being self-explanatory.

oficina (f). 'Office', of course, but in Spain a distinction is made between the office in general and an individual's private 'office' which is *despacho*. Most L/A countries do not bother about this difference but in the R/P they are fond of *escritorio* for a private 'office' and lawyers, architects and accountants—as well as artists—often refer to their offices as *estudios*. *Oficio*, 'office' in a metaphorical sense, e.g. 'the cares of office', in these days usually means 'trade', or 'skill', in connection with workers.

¡oh! Mentioned chiefly to warn you that Hispanics do not use this exclamation, although dictionaries give it. The equivalent of a mild 'Oh', e.g. when you have just been reminded of something, is *¡Ah!*: *¡Ah, sí!*, 'Oh yes!'; *¡Ah, eso!*, 'Oh, that!', but for phrases like our 'Oh, how exciting!', they do not say anything, i.e. they would simply say *¡Qué suerte! ¡Qué alegría!* etc. For a stronger emotion *¡Ay!* is indicated; by and large you may say it is a reaction to bad news—or to pain—but 'bad' is obviously a relative term; a mother might well exclaim *¡Ay! ¡ay! ¡ay!* to see her child dribbling jam down its bib.

oír. 'To hear', as you know, but you should be aware of *¡Oiga!/¡Oye!* which are the normal way of calling anyone's attention and thus equate with 'I say!', 'Excuse me!', 'Look!', etc. 'Listen!' is more precisely *¡Escuche!* If you went into a shop and there was no one behind the counter, what would you say to call attention? The answer is certainly *¡Oiga!* When a telephone conversation is renewed after a break *¡Oiga!/¡Oye!* serves to take it up again.

¡ojalá . . . ! Readers may be interested to know that this curious word is a piece of Arabic and means literally, 'Would to Allah that . . .!' It is one of the few words (apart from a scattering of nouns and place-names) that Spanish has taken over, a fact all the more ironic when one considers their past attitude to the 'infidel'. As usual with such borrowings, it supplies a need; it expresses wishing with a strong desire and modern equivalents are 'I do wish/hope . . .!', 'If only . . .!', etc. It takes the subjunctive without any intervening *que*: *¡Ojalá se dé prisa!*, 'I do wish he'd hurry up!'; *¡Ojalá fuese verdad!*, 'Let's hope it's true!' By itself: 'Let's hope so!', 'I do hope you're right!', etc.

¡olé! Anglo-Saxons have half-annexed this word and so we confidently imagine that we know what it means, viz. an ejaculation of cheerfulness something like 'Whoopee!' or else a sort of gay encouragement to some performance. In fact it is rather more deeply felt. If you have heard records of *flamenco* singers you may have noticed that there is usually an audience included, since *flamenco* singers find it as difficult to perform *in vacuo* as radio comedians, and a response is needed to stimulate them to their best efforts. When, at the end of some protracted arabesque of almost cadenza-like proportions, the singer and his guitarist bring the music to its inevitable Phrygian cadence there is immediately a *tutti* of *¡Olé!*s from those present to round the movement off but it is not necessary for them to wait until the end before uttering the cry; if the music stirs them deeply enough they may do so at any time, much as a believer is provoked into the occasional Alleluia! in the middle of a prayer at a revivalist meeting.

Olé, Hola and *Ojalá* all come from the Arabic and all invoke Allah. *Hola* may be equated with *a Dios* (*v.* **adios**); *olé* with *por Dios* and *Ojalá* with *y quiera Dios*. In other words those who exclaim *¡Olé!* at a *flamenco* session are in fact ejaculating 'By God!'

olla (f). A very Hispanic 'saucepan', deeper than it is broad and with two little handles, one on each side. In the past it was made of earthenware, and may still be, but in these days aluminium is more likely. The two little handles are called *asas* and as they are often made of aluminium too they become infernally hot so that you will need a pair of cloths to grab the thing when it is boiling over (and if you use the two ends of one cloth be sure that the middle doesn't catch fire!).

Una ollita, 'a small pot', is, in Mexico, specifically devoted to the making of *mezcal*. A normal saucepan is usually *una cacerola*.

once. *v.* **merienda.**

Oporto (m). The town in Portugal but also 'port wine'.

oportunidad (f). Squares fairly well with 'opportunity', but often used where we should say 'occasion': *En esa oportunidad*, 'On that occasion'. Conversely, when we talk about 'an opportunity', Hispanics will often say *la posibilidad:* 'I saw an opportunity of talking to him', *Vi la posibilidad de hablar con él* (*v.* also **chance**).

oración (f). Wiser to regard it as False since it nearly always means 'prayer', and is rarely used for an 'oration' which would be *discurso* or sometimes *arenga* (harangue). We have a cognate, if somewhat archaic, version, via the French *oraison*, in 'orison': 'Nymph, in thy orisons Be all my sins remembered' (*Hamlet* III, i, 89). Music lovers will know the *Oración del torero*, 'The bull-fighter's prayer', by Turina.

In a grammatical context it means 'sentence', and here we might well say 'speech': *Partes de la oración*, 'parts of speech'.

orden (m & f), **ordenar.** It is important to distinguish between the genders since they indicate which type of order is intended. *El orden* means 'order' in the sense of 'sequence', hierarchy or regularity: *En el orden correcto*, 'in the correct order'. *La orden* in the sense of 'command': *a la orden*, 'at your orders'—chiefly a military expression in Spain but very common in L/A, e.g. in a shop or restaurant, equating with 'What can I get you?' and in some parts it is also used *post hoc*, and even as a private civility, for 'You're welcome', 'Don't mention it', etc.

Ordenar means 'to put (something) in order', but I have heard it used in Mexico for 'to give an order', i.e. in a restaurant. This is not common, perhaps not even 'correct'; 'to order' something is *pedir* and 'to order' a person, *mandar*.

ordinario. Undoubtedly False when applied to persons as it means 'rude': *Es un muchacho muy ordinario*, 'He's a very rude boy'. It has implications of 'commonness' as well. Used of things it is rather more Reliable but better equations for 'ordinary' are *normal, corriente, regular*.

oriental. Both 'oriental' and 'eastern' and most often likely to mean the latter. In Uruguay it has quite a special meaning; Uruguay did not become a separate state until 1828 and until then was the eastern province—*la Banda Oriental*—of Argentina. Its official title is still *República Oriental de Uruguay* and *un oriental*, there, usually means a 'compatriot', i.e. simply an 'Uruguayan'. It is very frequently used, e.g. on the radio or in newspapers.

otro. Not only 'other' but 'another' and one often has to keep awake about this, especially for 'and another' which is simply *otro*: 'Give me a nail . . . now another . . . and another' (e.g. when hanging pictures), *Dame un clavo . . . otro . . . otro*.

Otro can also mean 'next', and in both a forward and a backward direction so that it will sometimes equate with 'last', or 'previous'. If you are driving along a street and are wondering whether the next intersection is the one you want you might say *¿Es ésta?* If the reply is *No, la otra* it means 'No, the next one', but if it is *No, era la otra* it means 'No, it was the last one'; in other words you have to watch the tense used. To say *la última* would suggest 'the final one', no more to come. *El otro día* is, however, a stock phrase for 'the other day', and always refers to the past. 'The next day' is *el día siguiente*.

Unos con otros is a useful phrase for 'taking one (thing) with another', 'on an average', and provides a device for handling our 'to work out at': *Unos libros con otros resultaron a 1000 pesetas*, 'The books worked out at 1000 pesetas (apiece)'. Note that it is possible to insert a noun; in this case *libros* (*v.* also **término**).

P

PA, PB and PC, i.e. in lifts/elevators. PA stands for *puerta abierta* and PC for *puerta cerrada* so you press the former if you want to hold the doors open and the latter if you want to hasten their closing. PB stands for *piso bajo* or *planta baja* and means 'ground floor' where this is not called the '1st Floor' (*v.* **piso**).

paciencia (f). 'Patience', of course, but used as an exclamation in the R/P equating with 'Just too bad!', i.e. when some disappointment must be philosophically accepted. There is no ready-made equivalent of 'Just too bad' in Spanish, but *v.* **ni** for Mexico.

padres (m. pl.). Might mean 'fathers' but is much more likely to mean 'parents' (*v.* **pariente**).

paella (f). One of the most typical and popular of Hispanic dishes, though you often have to order it half-an-hour beforehand. Its main constituent is rice; the other ingredients are lumps of fish, chicken, shellfish, or what not. Quite often the shellfish will be in their shells so do not count on keeping your fingers clean.

paja (f). 'Straw', as you probably know, and quite often a 'drinking straw' though *pajita* is commoner for this in L/A (*v.* also **bombilla**). *Meter paja* is a common phrase which most dictionaries do not mention; literally 'to stuff with straw', it is used figuratively for 'to pad', i.e. with superfluous verbiage, or whatever. *Hacerse una paja/las pajas* is a vulgar but surprisingly universal expression for 'to masturbate'. In Spain the usual expression for this is *meneársela*.

palmatoria (f). 'Candlestick', but essentially a humble one. More glorious affairs of silver are likely to be *candelabros* (note the gender). Candelabras which hang from the ceiling are often called *arañas* (spiders).

paño (m). A universal word for 'cloth', and it may be applied to any old bit of kitchen cloth. *Pañuelo*, its diminutive, is, as you know, a 'handkerchief'. *Trapo* is another widespread word for a 'cloth'.

papa (f). The L/A word for 'potato'; in Spain this is *patata* which in L/A means 'sweet potato'. Be sure of your genders: *el Papa* means 'the Pope'.

In most of the Hispanic world *papas/patatas fritas* means what Americans call 'chips' and the British 'crisps'. If you want what the British call 'chips' and the Americans 'French-fried' ask for *francesas*.

As a Central American footnote let me add that in Salvador chips/crisps are *papas colochas* and in Guatemala *papalinas*. In Mexico *una papalina* means 'a booze-up/drinking session'.

papel (m). Obviously 'paper', but rarely used for the 'daily paper' which is *periódico* or *diario*. It is, however, much used, even in conversation, in the figurative sense of 'rôle': *Jugó un papel importante en el asunto*, 'He played an important part in the affair'. Within the theatre *interpretar un papel* is the proper expression for 'to play a part' but outside it *hacer el papel de . . .* or *emprender el papel de . . .* is often used for 'to undertake the job of . . .', 'to act as . . .' usually implying an amateur capacity: *Consuelo hace el papel de mi secretaria*, 'Consuelo acts as my secretary' or 'does the job of secretary' so that one equation can be 'job'.

Papelera is a universally understood word for 'waste-paper basket', but *v.* also **canasta**.

paquete. *v.* **cajetilla, manojo.**

para. As you well know, it means 'for' in the sense of 'with a view to'; I mention it because in most of L/A (all, I think, except the R/P) it is used in telling the time: *Veinte para las nueve*, 'Twenty of/to nine', as opposed to the *Las nueve menos veinte* which is usual in Spain and the R/P. It is not merely colloquial; radio announcers use it.

Tener para is a common telescoped expression for 'to have (the money) for' and so 'to afford': *No tengo para el viaje*, 'I can't afford the fare'.

parada (f), **paradero** (m). *Parada* means a 'stop', e.g. on a bus. Strictly speaking it means the act of stopping: *Tres paradas más allá*, 'three stops further on', but is also widely used to mean 'bus stop', i.e. the place where you stand and wait for it. *Paradero* is also sometimes used in L/A for a 'bus-stop', but its normal use is for 'whereabouts', of things that move, usually humans: *¿Sabe Vd. el paradero del Sr. Fulano?*, 'Do you know where Mr. So-&-So is (at the moment)?' For the whereabouts of places, *v.* **ubicación**.

parar. Basically 'to stand still', and so a universal verb for 'to stop', i.e. to come to a standstill. In L/A they have segregated the standing part of it so that it has also become the usual verb there for 'to stand', with *parado* for 'standing': *Estaban parados en el comedor*, 'They were standing in the dining-room'; a lady is likely to say *No se pare* for 'Please don't get up'. They do, however, understand, and sometimes use, the more precise *levantarse* for 'to get up', as well as *estaban de pie* for 'they were standing'.

It is perhaps hardly necessary to add that it is also used in L/A for 'to stand' in the sexual sense, usually in the form *tenerlo-la parado/-a*.

parecer. 'To appear', yes, but in a general sense, hence 'to seem', 'to be (in various ways) like (something else)', and therefore valid for 'to look like', 'taste like', 'sound like', 'feel like', 'smell like', 'seem like'. *Parece una bomba* could mean 'It sounds like a bomb going off', or 'It looks like a gasoline pump', according to context. It should be distinguished from *aparacer* which is much more strictly confined to visual appearances while not inviting comparison with anything else: *De repente apareció,* 'He suddenly appeared'.

Stock phrases you should have handy are: *Me parece que sí/no,* 'I (don't) think so', and *¿Qué le/te parece?,* 'What do you think?', 'How does it seem to you?' A curious, and rather idiomatic, one is *Parece mentira* equating with 'Would you believe it?', 'You'd hardly credit it!', 'Believe it or not'.

In much of L/A they use the verb *lucir* (*q.v.*) for 'to look like'.

paréntesis (m). 'Parenthesis/bracket', of this type: ( ); 'square' brackets [ ] are *corchetes* and *una corchetera* is 'a stapling machine' in Chile since the individual staples, before the blow, look like square brackets. *Entre paréntesis,* 'in brackets', is much used in ordinary conversation where we might say 'by the way', or 'incidentally', i.e. when going off at a brief tangent.

pariente (m or f). False; it does not mean 'parent' but 'relative', 'relation', in the family sense (and note that *relación* (*q.v.*) is also False). 'Related to', in the family sense, is *emparentado con.* 'Parents' are *padres*.

parte. (f). Means 'part', right enough, but be aware of *en alguna parte,* 'somewhere'; *en ninguna parte,* 'nowhere'; also of *¿De parte de quién?* (*v.* TELEPHONES).

participar. Unreliable; used with *en* it means 'to participate in' but without the preposition: 'to inform', 'to impart', 'to let know': *Tenemos el gusto de participarles,* 'We have pleasure in informing you'. It is particularly used in giving notice of such things as weddings and funerals on specially printed cards and I take the opportunity of warning readers that if they receive *una participación de bodas* it does not necessarily mean that they are expected either to send a present or to be present. Some English acquaintances of mine once did both and only discovered years later that they had been the only non-relatives there. *La participación* merely informed them of the event.

particular. False; it means 'private', 'personal': *Una casa particular,* 'a private house'. The difference is not always apparent and so must be watched. It is tempting to translate 'I have particular reasons', as *Tengo razones particulares* but this means 'private reasons', which is not the same thing; you should say *razones especiales.* 'I particularly wanted to see him', *Quise verle especialmente*; if you said *particularmente* it would mean 'personally'. 'In a particular case', *en un caso determinado. Especial* is usually the best equivalent of 'particular'; it can even apply to persons: *Es muy especial en* *estas cosas,* 'He's very particular about such things'—and so a non-slangy word for 'fussy'.

partido, partidario. *Partido* is a 'party' in the political sense; also 'game/match', in sporting context. It is not, however, the word for a convivial 'party' which, in these days, is usually *fiesta*.

Partidario means 'partisan' but is much used in colloquial contexts where we should say 'in favour of': *Soy partidario de dárselo,* 'I'm in favour of giving it to him'; *Soy muy partidario de las naranjas,* 'I'm very fond of/partial to oranges'. For a 'partisan' in the sense of a 'supporter', *v.* **adicto.**

pasar. 'To pass', certainly, but in colloquial contexts one of the commonest equivalents of 'to happen': *¿Qué pasa?,* 'What's happening?', 'What's going on?'; *A veces pasa que . . .,* 'It sometimes happens that . . .'; *Pasar con,* 'to happen *to*': *¿Qué ha pasado con él?,* 'What's happened to him?', 'What's become of him?'

Pasar a máquina is the verb for 'to type' (on a typewriter).

¡Pase! is 'Come in!' in response to a knock at the door, though *¡Adelante!* is perhaps better for this. Equally, when ushering someone in or out of a door *¡Pase Vd!* is the phrase you need. If you want 'After you!' then *Vd. primero.*

A useful idiom is *Siempre pasa igual/lo mismo,* 'It's always the same', and the 'with' which so frequently follows is handled by the insertion of the appropriate pronoun: *Siempre le pasa igual,* 'It's always the same with him/her/you'; *Siempre me pasa lo mismo,* 'I'm always having the same trouble'.

Paso—'I pass'—is the equation for 'No bid/pass,' at cards.

paseo (m). A 'walk' for recreational purposes. It may be a 'ride' or an 'outing' in, or on, a vehicle: *dar un paseo,* 'to go for a walk/ride/drive/spin'. Hispanics are not great ones for country walks, however, and in most places *el paseo* is the evening stroll in the streets for the purpose of seeing, and being seen by, one's fellow-citizens. *La hora del paseo* is towards sunset and the streets are usually full to overflowing then.

pastel (m). It may mean 'pastel', but in everyday circumstances is more likely to mean 'cake'; also 'pastry', though Hispanics do not go in for pastry to the same extent and, when they do, it is nearly always of the 'puff', *mille feuilles,* variety.

pasto *v.* **césped.**

pata (f). Not only the 'paw' of an animal but also the 'leg' of a chair or table. It is very easy to say *pierna* by mistake so a mental note is indicated. *Meter la pata* might be described as an Unreliable Idiom since it may mean 'to put one's foot in it', 'to blot one's copybook' but also 'to poke one's nose into', 'to interfere', 'to butt in'.

patio (m). No doubt every reader will imagine he knows what this means and will visualize the delightful courtyard, probably with plants and a little fountain, which is characteristic of so many Hispanic houses and has a history going back beyond the Roman

Empire. With regret at having to spoil the image I have to record that it can also mean the, often very dingy, area or 'well' within an office or other big city building.

Since we are concerned with values as well as meanings, I feel it may be worth mentioning another aspect of the matter: the beauty of Hispanic houses usually lies within, and they often turn very bleak and blank cold shoulders to the road, in sharp contrast to most Anglo-Saxon houses. There may be some correlation between this tendency and the reluctance of most Hispanics to invite outsiders into their private house, which for the most part remains a family sanctum.

patrimonio (m). 'Patrimony', yes, but sometimes short for *Impuesto al patrimonio*, i.e. 'death duties/inheritance tax'. In Spain these are *derechos reales*.

pay (m). If you take care to pronounce this Spanish-fashion you should have little difficulty in realizing that it means 'pie'. In the more touristy places it may be written *pie* but since this means 'foot' one can hardly blame them for preferring their own spelling. (*Pai* is another possibility.) It occurs chiefly in Mexico; further south, where such 'pies' exist, they are likely to be called *tortas* (*q.v.*).

pedante. Strictly a noun meaning 'pedant', but much used as an adjective and carrying a different image from 'pedantic'; the latter suggests nothing worse than a fuss-pot about unimportant details of scholarship, whereas *pedante* means 'pompous', 'conceited', 'self-important': *El jefe era muy pedante*, 'The boss was a pompous ass'.

pedazo (m). An everyday word for 'piece', and most readers will be well aware of it but may not be conscious of the distinction between it and *trozo*, the other, equally common, word for 'piece'. In many contexts there is no need to distinguish; either will do, but *pedazo* suggests a separate piece that can be handled apart whereas *trozo* may mean a part of something larger which has not in any way come adrift but is merely being considered separately, e.g. *En este trozo del parque hay mucho ruido*, 'There's a lot of noise in this bit of the park'. You could not use *pedazo* here. *Trozo* is more likely to be used for anything three-dimensional, so 'lump', 'chunk', are possible equivalents. Where a hunk of, say, bread is concerned either word will do, but you would say *un pedazo de papel* (only technically three-dimensional) and to use *trozo* here would be a little like referring to a 'lump' of paper.

pegar. 'To stick' (i.e. with glue, gum, etc.) but also a common word for 'to hit (someone)': *¡Pégale!*, 'Hit him!', 'Sock him one!' It borders on slang but is widely used. It implies the hitting of one human by another. The accidental hitting of things calls for *tropezar, topar* or *dar (con, en)*.

pelo (m). 'Hair', in a wide sense including the fur of an animal. Dictionaries give you *cabello* but this is almost obsolete in Spain and considered rather *cursi* in Buenos Aires. Stick to *pelo* therefore.

A common expression is *tomar el pelo*, the equivalent of our 'to pull (someone's) leg': *Me está tomando el pelo*, 'You're pulling my leg' (*v.* also **vacilar**). A word for 'a head of hair' is *una melena*; in the past normally a woman's, but *melenudos* is applied— pejoratively, of course!—to young men with long hair (*v.* **macho**). On an equally ephemeral note 'skinheads' may be *pelados*, a pun on 'peeled'.

pelota (f). *v.* **bola.**

peluquería (f). 'Barber shop'; literally 'wiggery', just as barber shop, *barbería*, means 'beardery'; neither seems to take much account of hair-cutting though this is obviously their main activity. A ladies' wiggery is more likely to be called *Salón de belleza*, 'beauty parlour', but you may find *peluquería de señoras.*

pena (f). 'Trouble', 'misfortune', 'sorrow', but used a great deal colloquially and our equation will often be 'pity': *¡Qué pena!*, 'What a pity!', 'What a shame!' Very common is *No vale la pena*, 'It's not worth the trouble'. It nevertheless remains a serious word when required: *Le causó mucha pena*, 'It was a great sorrow to her', indeed it is a better word for 'sorrow' than *dolor*, which suggests physical pain.

penal, penalty (m). *Penalty* is easy enough when you see it written but you may have more difficulty in remembering to say it with the accent on the second syllable. Since *-al* is a common Spanish word-ending, *penal* comes easier, being also short for *un tiro penal*, and is on its way to becoming a noun. The English vocabulary for sports is becoming as universal as the Italian vocabulary for music did in the past but where the spoken word is concerned you have to be on the look-out for strange noises, especially as it is not always the most educated part of the population that is interested in, say, football. I recall being mystified by a word which sounded like *orsay*, only to discover that it was my old enemy 'off-side', though the official term is *fuera de juego*. If you hear two Latin-Americans discussing boxing look out for how they handle words like 'heavy-weight'; you might hear *peso completo* or *peso pesado* but are quite likely to hear a sound like *yavi*. How about *jonrón*? Would you have recognized it as 'home run'?

pendejo (m). Strictly 'pubic hair', but widely used in the Caribbean region, from Mexico to Colombia, to mean 'twirp', 'fool', etc.— and when I say 'widely' I mean that quite nice women often use it. *Una pendejada* is a 'curse', a 'bloody nuisance'.

pensar. 'To think', but in the sense of 'consider', 'reflect'; in English we use 'think' a great deal in the sense of 'believe' or 'assume'; Spanish differentiates: 'Her mother heard the noise/And thought it was the boys' would be *creyó*; one does not imagine she spent much time meditating the point. *Creo que no vendrán* means 'I don't think they'll come'; *Estoy pensando que (a lo mejor) no* *vendrán*, 'I'm beginning to think they won't come', 'I'm wondering whether they'll come'. Note the Continuous Present with *pensar*. It is hard to imagine any context where you would want to say *estoy creyendo*; belief excludes meditation. Further expressions with *pensar* are: *Lo pensaré*, 'I'll think about it'; *pensándolo bien*, 'on reflection, thinking it over'; *tener pensado*, 'to intend, to have in mind to': *Tenemos pensado venir en agosto*, 'Our idea is to come in August'; *en el momento menos pensado*, 'when least expected' (*v*. **mejor**).

pensionista (m or f). Usually 'boarder', but in L/A it can extend to 'subscriber', a person who makes regular payments. In a Mexican parking lot I saw a notice addressed to *los Sres. Pensionistas*, i.e. those clients who paid to park their cars there daily, as opposed to occasional *ad hoc* parkers. If they had said *clientes* it could have referred to anyone who used the parking lot. A more normal word would have been *Sres. Abonados*. *Pensionista* does, after all, mean 'pensioner', a person to whom regular payments are made.

perder. 'To lose', of course, but used in connection with *tiempo* where we should say 'waste': *No debes perder tiempo*, 'You mustn't waste (any) time' (*v*. also **gastar**); also 'to miss', in connection with trains, buses, etc. A common expression is *Nada se pierde*, 'There's no harm (done)': *Nada se pierde por intentar*, 'There's no harm in trying'.

perdón. *v*. COURTESY.

perjuicio (m). Should be distinguished from *prejuicio* since it is the latter which means 'prejudice'. *Perjuicio* means 'damage' of the figurative sort; 'damages' in a court of law is *daños y perjuicios*; *en mi perjuicio*, 'to my detriment'. *Perjudicar* is 'to harm', or 'damage', in this sense, and is frequently used in conversation about the acts of, say, neighbours, which cause more than usual indignation. In L/A it may extend to maligning, slandering (*v*. also **murmurar**).

permiso (m). 'Permission', but often used for 'leave', i.e. time off, especially for youths doing military service, but not confined to them (*v*. also **licencia**). A phrase you should certainly have at your tongue's tip is *con permiso* (*v*. COURTESY).

perseguir, persecución (f). A little Unreliable; *perseguir* has a stronger sense of chasing than our 'persecute' and 'to pursue' would sometimes be a better equivalent: *Me persiguieron*, 'They were after me'. It should also be distinguished from *proseguir* (*v*. **seguir**).

persona (f), **personal**. *Persona* equates well enough with 'person', though remember that it remains feminine even when applied to a man. A phrase much used is *Es muy buena persona*; we might well say: 'He/She's a very nice person', but goodness, reliability, honesty and high character are all suggested in addition to niceness.

Personal, in addition to being the adjective for 'personal', is also the noun (m) for 'personnel'.

perspectiva (f). 'Perspective', yes, but the English word is rather associated with drawing and architecture. *Perspectiva* is the everyday word for 'prospect', 'outlook', both literally and metaphorically: *¡Qué perspectiva!*, 'What a prospect!' It is not used metaphorically in the sense of 'proportion'; 'to get/see things in (their proper) perspective' is *poner/apreciar las cosas en su sitio, . . . en su justo valor*, or *debidamente*.

pesado. Literally 'weighed', but the universal adjective for 'heavy', both literally and figuratively, and a common word for 'boring'. *Fue muy pesado*, 'It was an awful bore'.

pescado (m). For domestic purposes 'fish', but you should be aware of the word *pez* which applies to the living creature. *Pescado*, literally 'fished', suggests the fish market, the kitchen or the meal table. If you go in for tropical fish, in an aquarium, do not go to the shop and ask for *unos pescados*, ask for *unos peces*.

pesero (m). Something for which one pays a *peso* and the usual word in Mexico City for a *colectivo* taxi, hence *pesear*, 'to ply for hire'.

pibe. *v.* **chaval.**

picante. 'Hot', in the sense of 'highly-peppered', and an everyday word, particularly in L/A; beware of saying *caliente* which applies only to the food's temperature. In Peru you may even see *Picantería* meaning a restaurant which specializes in 'hot' food. *Picante* should be distinguished from *picado* which, in connection with meat, means 'minced', or 'chopped up fine' (*v.* also **piqueo**).

pichón (m). 'Pigeon', when it is a matter of the bird on the table or as a target for the gun; *tiro de pichón*, 'pigeon-shooting'. The live, unmenaced bird is *la paloma*. 'Pigeon-fancying', *colombofilia*.

pico (m). Basically 'point', and you no doubt know of Falla's opera *The Three-cornered Hat*, '*El sombrero de tres picos*'. It has a wide extension of other meanings, serious and colloquial, of which 'beak' is one of the commonest. Domestically it can mean a 'spout' of the longer type, e.g. of a tea or coffee-pot, and in Mexico can apply to the spout of a mere jug. In Colombia it may mean a 'kiss'. In Chile it *may* mean a rather nightmarish, surrealistic-looking shellfish which, like oysters, has to be eaten not only raw but alive, but it is also the vulgar word for the male organ in that country.

A very common expression (except of course in Chile) is *y pico*, meaning 'and a bit', '-odd': *Mi padre tiene 50 años y pico*, 'My father is fifty-odd'; *Diez dólares y pico*, 'Ten dollars and a bit'. If, however, you are referring to, say, the 1930's you do not say *los treinta y pico* but *los treinta y tantos* or *los años treinta*. In Chile, to avoid the embarrassments of *pico* they say *y tanto* or *y fracción*.

piedra (f). 'Stone', yes, but also the 'flint' of a cigarette-lighter (and *not,* incidentally, the 'stone' of a fruit, *v.* **hueso**).

pieza (f). I am half-tempted to damn this as False since although, by and large, it means 'piece', it is seldom used where we say 'piece', and vice versa. For *las piezas* (*de la máquina*) we say 'the parts (of the machine)'; *una pieza de ajedrez*, 'a chessman'; *una pieza de teatro* or *de música* border on the obsolete; much more usual is *una obra*.

In midstream there is the phrase *de una sola pieza*, 'all of a piece', and no doubt a scattering of others, but on the further side 'a piece' of sugar is *un terrón*, 'a piece of clothing', *una prenda de vestir* and the general words for 'piece', or 'bit', are *trozo* or *pedazo* (*q.v.*).

In L/A *una pieza* often means 'a room': *un apartamento de tres piezas*, 'a three-room apartment/flat'.

pila (f), **pileta** (f). *Pila*, in everyday circumstances, is likely to mean 'dry battery', needed for your *linterna* or your *transistor*, and you may care to know that 'leak-proof' is *hermética* (a 'wet battery' is *batería*) but it might also mean the 'kitchen sink'. It is basically a 'stone basin' and, in a church, means 'font' (*nombre de pila* is the official term for a 'Christian' name.). *Pileta* is technically a diminutive but in the Argentine is often used for 'swimming pool' (as against the usual *piscina*) or even a 'wash-basin' (as against the usual *lavabo* or *lavamanos*). In a garage it might mean 'sump', though I have heard it used of the 'trench' over which cars are placed so as to get at them underneath. *Pila/pileta*, in short, border on the 'all-purpose' and you may expect to find them used for other things.

píldora (f). A universal word for 'pill', and already identified with 'the Pill'; the Mexican version of 'Make love, not war!' was *¡Guerra no! ¡Píldora sí!* At a rather more humdrum level I put on record that in the R/P *pildoritas* are the 'baby' Frankfurter sausages used at cocktail parties.

pimiento, -a, pimentón (m). Slightly Unreliable terrain since usage may vary regionally, but *pimienta* is pretty universal for 'pepper', i.e. the powder shaken out of pepper pots. *Pimientos* are usually the green or red 'peppers', i.e. capsicums (sometimes called 'mangoes' in the States), eaten as vegetables; they are not necessarily *picante* (*q.v.*). *Chile* is also used for this vegetable and is more often, though not invariably, 'hot'; in Mexico the 'sweet' ones are called *poblanos* and the 'hot' *chicheros*. *Pimentón* is 'red pepper', 'paprika', again powdered, and you can often choose between *dulce*, which is not especially 'hot', and *picante* which *is* (Cayenne pepper, I fancy).

pinche. Strictly 'scullion', 'kitchen boy', but much used as a slang adjective in Mexico corresponding to our 'blasted', 'accursed', 'damn', 'goddam', 'bloody': *un pinche molesto*, 'a goddam nuisance'; *esa pinche mujer*, 'that bloody woman'. Note that it is invariable in gender.

pinta (f). In a Spanish translation of, say, Dickens, it might mean 'pint', but in ordinary circumstances is more likely to mean 'appearance', though it is distinctly colloquial: *Un señor de buena pinta*, 'a nice looking man' (not only good-looking but well dressed too). *Tener . . . (adj.) . . . pinta* is often used where we should use 'look': *¡Qué mala pinta tiene esta comida!*, 'This food doesn't look too good!' Less colloquially one would use *parecer* or, in L/A, *lucir*.

In card games *¿A qué pinta?* means 'What's trumps?', though the 'trumps' themselves are *triunfos*.

piqueo (m). The 'first course' of a slap-up, *típico*, Peruvian meal; it is the local equivalent of *entremeses* but the dishes composing it are not cold; on the contrary they are likely to be hot in both senses. They are also both tasty and voluminous and unless you have a large appetite it is wiser not to go too hard at them since, after this *hors d'oeuvre*, you get down to some serious eating. In an ordinary restaurant you are less likely to find *piqueo*; 'the first course' will probably be called *la entrada* and will be cold. The restaurants where they are available are called *picanterías* (v. **picante**).

piropo (m). There is no one English word to equate with this; it applies to a very Hispanic phenomenon, viz. the 'compliments' called out to women. It is not unknown in the North for an attractive young woman to be whistled at by admiring males but Hispanics are more articulate in such matters and have a long tradition to back them up. The compliment may be no more than an appreciative *¡Chata!* or *¡Guapa!* but it may well be much longer, sometimes unblushingly outspoken and obviously, whether well or badly turned, will hinge on the bedworthiness of the lady concerned.

Since you, reader, may well be a young lady, it is more than likely you will have *piropos* shouted at you and therefore right that you should know how to react in such circumstances. In a certain sense, of course, you must not react at all; you must continue straight ahead, looking neither to the right nor the left, and making a very obvious show of paying no attention. Be sure, however, that it is obvious; really to appear not to have heard seems almost rude, expecially if the *piropo* is a good one; after all no woman really minds being thought desirable. If the *piropo* is quite a polite one you may allow your features to draw into a half-smile but you must on no account look at the man who made it—and it will not always be a workman; it may very well be a respectably-dressed, middle-aged man, sitting in a café, who looks as though he ought to know better. If you are walking with another young lady then you may even, if the *piropo* is respectable enough, allow yourselves to start giggling together, once past the scene of the crime. This will be much appreciated and no danger attaches, but if the *piropo* is rather 'high'—or *verde*, as they say—then danger does begin to attach if you react too favourably.

Clearly you would like to be given a few examples of *piropos verdes* so as to be warned but it would be impossible to begin, so wide is the range. The chances are that you will not understand them, anyway, and perhaps it is as well you should not since, if you did, you might burst out laughing there and then, with worse than fatal results. It is, however, above all in southern Spain and in the Argentine that you are most likely to get them.

pisco (m). A rather agreeable spirit produced in Peru and Chile and named after a town in the former. It is similar to gin and its quality is likely to vary with its price so the higher-priced brands are recommended. A *pisco sour*, made of *pisco*, icing/powdered sugar and lemon juice is an excellent cocktail.

piso (m). 'Floor', or 'story', of a building: *Un edificio de diez pisos*, 'a ten-story building'. It should be distinguished from *suelo* which really means 'ground', but is the word for 'floor' as seen from the inside of a room: *Cayó al suelo*, 'It fell on the floor'.

In Spain it is commonly used for 'apartment/flat', so that you can say *Le invité a mi piso* for 'I invited him to my apartment', but *apartamento* is gaining ground, even there.

Countries vary as to how they number their floors. In Mexico and the R/P, in accordance with the usual European practice, the 'ground floor' is called the *planta baja* or *piso bajo* (and marked PB on the lift button); the '1st Floor', *primer piso*, will be one up and the others above it counted from then on. In the Z/A the North American practice is followed and the ground floor is also the 'first' floor.

In the Z/A it also means 'mat': *piso de baño*, 'bathmat'.

pista (f). 'Track', including a running or racing track, but in these days most often the 'runway' of an airfield. *Autopista* is the commonest word for a 'motorway/turnpike', though *autovía* also exists. There are several different words for the 'lane' of a highway—*banda* (Spain), *vía* (Colombia), *canal* (Venezuela), *carril* (Mexico), *trocha* (Argentina)—but *pista* will generally be understood in such a context.

pisto (m). A very Spanish dish, being a sort of mash of marrow/squash, peppers, beans, tomatoes and other odd vegetables fried in olive-oil. Well made, it is delicious. The French equivalent, perhaps better known, is *ratatouille*. In C/A and thereabouts *pisto* is a slang word for 'money'.

pitar, pito(s), pitillo (m). Dictionaries mostly confine themselves to giving 'whistle' for this but in modern times *pitar* is the normal word for 'to honk (one's car horn)'. In Colombia *los pitos* means 'car horn', and 'to honk' is *dar los pitos*. In Mexico and some other countries 'a car horn' is *un claxón*. *Pito* is often a colloquial word for the male organ.

Pitillo, the diminutive, is the colloquial word for 'cigarette', in Spain, but in Venezuela means 'drinking straw'.

placa (f). Literally, 'plaque', and quite valid for this but in Mexico and Colombia it is likely to be more specifically the 'licence plate' of a car (short for *placa de matrícula*). The diminutive *plaquita* is likely to be used for 'brass plate', e.g. outside the front door.

placard (m). False; it does not mean 'placard' but 'built-in cupboard'. Its use seems to be confined to the R/P (*v.* **armario** and **closet**). There is an old word *placarte* but it is never used for 'placard' which is universally *cartel*.

plan (m). 'Plan', but used a good deal colloquially in Spain: *en plan de*, 'as if': *Salieron en plan de novios*, 'They went about together (for all the world) as if they were engaged'; *en este/ese plan*, 'this/that sort of way'.

planchar, plancha (f). *Planchar* is the universal word for 'to iron', and *una plancha* is 'an iron'—of the domestic sort—but the word extends to other sorts of 'ironing', usually grilling: *champiñones a la plancha*, 'grilled mushrooms'. *Jamón planchado* might seem to mean 'grilled ham' but here yet another sort of 'ironing' is intended; it usually means 'pressed ham', i.e. pressed into a squarish shape, after having been boned. *Hacer una plancha* is an expression used in the C/S for 'to put one's foot in it'.

planta. *v.* **piso.**

plata (f). 'Silver', but the usual word in many parts of S/A for 'money': *No tengo plata*, 'Can't afford it'. A common expression in the C/S is *¿Con qué plata?*, 'Where are you going to get the money from?', 'What are you going to use for money?' In Mexico this is *¿Con qué dinero?* In Spain usually *¿Con qué cuentas?*

plausible. False; it means 'praiseworthy', 'laudable', i.e. 'worthy of applause', so do not let dictionaries lead you astray. There is no very satisfactory equivalent of 'plausible'—*verosímil, especioso* ('specious'), *creíble* ('believable') might serve but they would need a context to make the meaning apparent.

plomero. *v.* **gasfitero.**

plumero. *v.* **zorros.**

poblano. *v.* **pimiento.**

pocillo (m). Some dictionaries tell you 'chocolate cup' but it is just as likely to be 'coffee cup', i.e. the small size. In Colombia it is the normal word simply for 'cup'. In Buenos Aires top circles, however, the O.K. word for 'coffee-cup' is *tacita* and *pocillo* is not considered 'high class'.

poco. One grasps without difficulty, in early stages, that *poco* means 'little', and quickly learns such phrases as *un poco de pan*, etc. but its full range is a good deal more idiomatic. It seems a light-weight word and we do not always appreciate how much positive weight it can take. Used as an adjective it not only inflects but can come at the end of a sentence, e.g. *Todas las precauciones son pocas.* Our equivalent is certainly not 'All precautions are little'; we should probably say 'inadequate', one aspect of little, but a much weightier word; more idiomatically, perhaps, 'You can't be too careful'.

Other idiomatic aspects of 'little' are 'not many', 'not much', 'very few': *Hizo muy poco,* 'He didn't do very much'; *Tengo poco dinero,* 'I don't have much money'; *Hay pocas,* 'There aren't many/are very few (there)'; *Poco da,* 'It doesn't make much difference'; *Hace poco,* 'Not long ago'; *Es poco ¿No?,* 'That's not much, is it?'

'Not very', is a likely equivalent for the adverbial use. If you wanted to say: 'I won't be very long', would it occur to you to say *Tardaré poco,* or for 'This meat isn't properly done/is underdone', *Esta carne está poco hecha?* The adverbial phrase *por poco* is also worth digesting, equating with 'nearly', or 'almost'. A man arriving home on the late side for lunch might well say *Por poco no vengo a comer,* 'I very nearly didn't come home for lunch'; *Por poco le nombraron Ministro,* 'They nearly appointed him Minister'.

Applied to an adjective *poco* is often a good equivalent of 'hardly': *poco probable,* 'hardly likely', especially in cases of understatement. Another possibility is the prefix 'un-': 'undignified', *poco formal, poco serio;* 'rather un-British', *poco británico;* yet another is 'seldom': *poco visto,* 'seldom seen'. Its positive counterpart is *algo,* 'somewhat/rather': *algo difícil,* 'rather difficult'; *algo distinto,* 'somewhat different'.

poder. Pretty basic, but *Se puede . . .?* followed by an infinitive is a phrase you should have in stock: *¿Se puede ver?,* 'May I see?' *¿Eso se puede hacer?,* 'Is that possible?', 'Can you manage that?' *¿Se puede?* by itself usually means 'May I come in?' (*v.* COURTESY).

polla (f). Strictly 'female chicken', 'hen', but in Chile it means 'lottery', and is interchangeable with *lotería.* It can also be used of a 'pool' of the football type. In Spain the word should be avoided as it is the commonest vulgar word for the male organ.
Pollera, in rural circumstances, is 'hen-coop', but in the R/P a 'woman's skirt'.

pololo, -a. 'Boy-friend/girl-friend', in Chile, and it suggests a 'steady', not a mere casual one. *Pololear,* 'to go steady (with someone)'. I am told that the word derives from a local species of bird in which the male and female are always about together.

polvo (m). 'Dust', also 'powder'; but a common expression, particularly in Spain, is *hacer polvo,* used colloquially for 'to shatter': *Estoy hecho polvo.* 'I feel pulverized/exhausted'; *Esta carretera hace polvo las cubiertas,* 'This road simply ruins the tyres'. *Echar un polvo* is a slangy expression for 'to screw' (taboo).

poner. One of the verbs for 'to put' (*v.* also **meter**), and essentially 'to put on', or 'to put ready': *Se puso el sombrero,* 'He put his hat on'; *La mesa está puesta,* 'The table's been laid'. *Poner con* is 'to put (someone) through', on the telephone: *¿Puede ponerme con la Señorita . . .?,* 'Can you connect me with Miss . . .?'

Ponerse is one of the verbs for 'to become' (*v.* also **hacerse, llegar**) and 'get' will therefore often be the equation: *Cuanto más tiempo pasa más fuerte se pone,* 'It gets stronger as time goes on' (e.g. of tea); *No te pongas tonto,* 'Don't get silly'. In most contexts *ponerse* and *hacerse* are interchangeable but there are a few cases where *ponerse* always seems to be used: *ponerse colorado* is the stock phrase for 'to blush', and similar temporary states seem to invite *ponerse,* e.g. *Me estás poniendo nervioso,* 'You're making me nervous'. Not always temporary: *Se ha puesto muy fea,* 'She's become very unattractive'.

portavoz (m). One might imagine that it means a radio 'loudspeaker', and it can in fact mean a megaphone but by far its commonest use is in the newspaper for 'spokesman'—White House, Whitehall, White-have-you: *Un portavoz del Kremlin dijo . . .,* 'A Kremlin spokesman said . . .' *Vocero* is another word for 'spokesman'.

porteño, -a. Basically 'port-dweller', and likely to be particularized in different countries; in the R/P it means a 'citizen of Buenos Aires'; in Chile, of Valparaiso, and so on, in relation to the big port if there is one. In the same category are *costeño,* 'coast-dweller', and *serrano,* 'a man from the *sierra*', both of which can have a specific reference in particular countries.

portero (m). Usually the man who guards the entrance to an apartment house/block of flats, though in a football context 'goalkeeper', i.e. the man who guards the entrance to the goal. Their rôles are not entirely dissimilar. The *portero* at the entrance to your apartment is likely to know far more about you than you might imagine. You may be a stray foreigner, living in someone else's flat, and he may be rather hazy about the spelling of your name, but the chances are that he will have received on the grapevine a fairly precise notion of who and what you are, and he is in a position to defend your interests when necessary. Treat him as a human being (the regular weekly or monthly *propina* does no harm) and you will often find him a valuable ally. He is, however, tending to be replaced by *porteros eléctricos* which provide each apartment with a separate bell-push.

posponer. In parts of S/A, thanks to Anglo-Saxon influence, it may mean 'postpone' but its proper meaning is 'to put after' (in order of merit, etc.), 'to subordinate'. It is not a common verb; one might hear: *Pospuso su interés al bien público* for 'He subordinated his private interests to the common good' but it would be decidedly high-flown and rhetorical and *Subordinó su interés . . .* would be more normal. The normal word for 'to postpone' is *aplazar.*

practicante (m). It seems to mean 'practitioner' but in fact implies something less than full medical honours. In some countries it can mean a 'quack', i.e. someone who practises without proper qualifications, but is usually more particularized.

In Spain it normally means a 'male nurse', who in L/A be *un enfermero*. In Mexico it means a 'final-year medical student' who has reached the stage of 'walking' the wards under supervision. In Chile it means 'injectionist', and he usually has separate premises so that you have to pay him a special visit armed with the necessary *ampolla* which you will have bought at the *farmacia* under the doctor's prescription. Other countries may have other meanings and readers are recommended to make enquiries locally, before jumping to conclusions.

prado. *v.* **césped.**

precario. Borders on the Unreliable as it means simply 'doubtful', 'uncertain', 'unpredictable', and does not have such strong overtones of impending disaster as 'precarious' does: *En vista del precario futuro económico*, 'In view of the uncertain economic outlook'. Like 'precarious', however, its use is confined to things and it could not apply to a person who was uncertain or unpredictable.

precioso. A popular adjective which has been annexed, particularly by ladies, for 'beautiful', 'charming', 'exquisite', etc., and is much used in social chit-chat. *Encantador (-a)*, 'charming', is another common word in such conversations. Anything that really is 'precious' is likely to be described as *valioso* or *de gran valor*.

preciso, precisar. *Preciso* means 'precise' only when used to describe a noun: *Llegó en el momento preciso*, 'He arrived at that very moment'. Used with a verb it takes on the surprisingly different meaning of 'necessary': *¿Es preciso que vaya yo?*, 'Is it necessary for me to come?' *No es preciso decir que . . .*, 'It goes without saying that . . .'. If you want 'precise' in connection with a verb then *exacto* or *correcto* are indicated (and beware of **cierto,** *q.v.*).
  The adverb *precisamente* can be even more disconcerting. It is perfectly valid for 'precisely', 'quite so', but if, for example, you call a friend asking whether he knows where a third party is you may get the answer *¡Está precisamente aquí!*, 'It just so happens that he's here!', i.e. *precisamente* means 'it just so happens that'.
  Precisar is a verb meaning 'to fix the details': *Hay que precisar un poco*, 'It's time to get down to brass tacks' (*v.* also **concretar**).

preferir(se). Strictly speaking 'to prefer', but Hispanics are not always strict and often use the verb when it is a matter of choosing out of a whole selection and not merely between two. It is much associated with the offering of drinks and *¿Qué prefiere?* means 'What'll you have?'
  Preferirse is also used for 'to push oneself forward': *Se estaba prefiriendo para el puesto*, 'He was gunning very hard for the job'.

preguntar. 'To ask', in the sense of 'enquire', and you will no doubt have distinguished it, in your mind, from *pedir* which means 'to ask for'. *Preguntarse* can be used for 'to wonder' in the sense of 'to ask oneself' but we use 'to wonder' in various other ways and are often at a loss to know how to handle it in Spanish so an exhaustive inquest is offered:

As usual with words for which there is no one equivalent, one has to examine the real meaning—as well as watch for spontaneous exclamations on the lips of natives—and an examination of 'to wonder' reveals five possible senses:

1. Genuine surprise—*sorprender(se)*, *extrañar(se)*: 'I wonder she didn't bring the cat as well, while she was about it', *Me extraña que no se haya traído también el gato de paso*; 'I shouldn't wonder if . . .', *No me sorprendería que . . .* (N.B. not *si*); 'I don't wonder', *No me sorprende.*

2. Turning over in one's mind—*dar (a uno) vueltas a . . .*, 'I wondered about that for a long time', *(Le) di muchas vueltas a eso.*

3. Uncertainty—*no saber (si)*: 'He wondered whether to go on', *No sabía si seguir adelante*; 'I wonder whether I ought to', *No sé si debería*; 'If you're wondering how to do it', *Si no sabes cómo se hace.*

4. Curiosity. If it is curiosity you are about to satisfy then *A ver si*: 'I wonder whether the milkman's been yet', *A ver si el lechero ha venido*, but if it is more 'academic' or remote in time then *no saber si* followed by the Future: *No sé si el lechero habrá venido*, or the Conditional or Subjunctive: 'I wondered whether it might have been the children', *No sabía si habrían sido los niños.*

5. Politeness. Usually *gustarse* with the Conditional or Subjunctive: 'I wonder whether I might come and see you', *Me gustaría ir a verle*; 'We were wondering whether you'd care to come to dinner', *Nos gustaría que vinieran a cenar.*

A small pointer to difference in approach is that we often want to put a question mark after a sentence beginning with 'I wonder' though it is technically a statement. The Spanish is more definitely a statement, hence the positiveness of *no sé si* or *me gustaría*. It is largely the tenses—Future, Conditional, Subjunctive—which provide the element of uncertainty but that this does not prevent an interrogative note from sounding through these phrases.

preocuparse. 'To be preoccupied', perhaps, but it is the normal and universal verb for 'to worry': *No se preocupe (por eso)*, 'Don't worry (about that)'. We might say 'bother' and it is wise to distinguish *preocuparse* from *molestarse* which means 'to bother' in a physical sense: *No se moleste*, 'Don't trouble (yourself)', 'Don't put yourself out'. *Preocuparse* refers to mental bother. *Está muy preocupado por los exámenes* may seem to mean 'He's very busy with his exams', but in fact means 'He's very worried about his exams'. *Preocupado* is the normal adjective for 'worried' and so a far commoner word than our 'preoccupied'. It is true that the use of the prepositions *con* or *de*, rather than *por*, gives a stronger sense of our meaning but if you want to stress this sense then *absorto* (absorbed) is more unmistakable. The noun for a 'worry' is *preocupación*; a preoccupation of the sort someone is 'always on about' is usually *un tema*. *Despreocupado* can mean 'unworried', 'casual', 'free-and-easy' but also, in other contexts, 'impartial', 'disinterested'. (N.B. not 'uninterested' which would be *poco interesado*; 'to be uninterested', *no tener interés*).

preparación (f), **preparado.** Quite Reliable, on the whole, but they have become a little particularized; *preparado* is often used as an adjective meaning 'able', 'competent', 'well-informed', and is applied to somebody who knows his business inside-out: *Es un muchacho muy bien preparado*, 'He's a very competent young man'. *Preparación*, therefore, may often mean 'ability', 'competence'.

presentar(se). Unreliable; *presentar* means 'to present', only in the sense of 'introduce' (*v.* COURTESY). 'To present *with*', i.e. give a present, is *regalar* or *obsequiar*.
  Presentarse is most used in connection with examinations when it means 'to sit': *Se presentó a examen de doctorado*, 'He sat for his doctorate'. In L/A they mostly do not make it reflexive and are more likely to say *Presentó su doctorado* (for 'pass/fail.' *v.* **aprobar, suspender**).

presente. Unreliable; if 'present' means 'at the present time' then the word needed is *actual*, and it is certainly not the word for 'a gift' which is *regalo* or *obsequio*. It is probably commonest in business letters when it means 'the present letter'; and when we should probably say 'hereby' or 'herewith': *Le comunicamos por la presente*, 'We hereby inform you'. Rather oddly, it is used in L/A typed on an envelope to mean: 'By hand'. *Tener presente* is 'to bear in mind'.

pretender. False; it does not mean 'to pretend' but 'to aim to', 'hope to', and its commonest everyday equation is probably 'to try to': *Pretende hacernos creer que es casada*, 'She's trying to have us believe she's married'; *Pretende entrar en el Cuerpo Diplomático*, 'He's hoping to get into the Diplomatic Corps'. In much of L/A *pretender a* can mean 'to aspire to the hand of': *Ramón pretende a Isabel*, 'Ramon's hoping to get engaged to Isabel'.
  There are various possibilities for 'to pretend': *fingir* ('feign'), *aparentar*, *hacer como si*, sometimes *hacerse el . . .*: 'He pretended to be asleep', *Se hizo el dormido*.

prevenir. Unreliable to the point of Falsity; by far its commonest meaning is 'to warn', and if a Hispanic meant 'prevent' he would use *impedir*. The Spanish equivalent of the proverb 'Forewarned is forearmed' is *Hombre prevenido vale por dos*.

primordial. Not merely 'primordial', but simply 'first in order', and so a much commoner word: *Eso es primordial*, 'That's top priority'. Our equation would sometimes be 'primary/over-riding': *Un asunto de importancia primordial*, 'A subject of primary importance'.

prisa (f). 'Speed', 'hurry'. It is greatly used in Spain where *darse prisa* is the usual expression for 'to hurry up'; in L/A *apurarse* or *correr* are more usual: *¡Date prisa!*, 'Hurry up!' *Tendrá que hacerlo de prisa*, 'He/she /you'll have to do it quickly'. *Meter prisa*, 'to hurry something up', 'to expedite'. *Tener prisa* and *estar de prisa* are, however, fairly universal for 'to be in a hurry'.

probar. It may mean 'to prove', but its commonest everyday meaning is 'to try', in the sense of 'put to the test'. If there were some strange-looking dish on the menu one might say *Voy a probarlo*, 'I'm going to try it'. It should be distinguished from *tratar* and *intentar* (*q. v.*) (*v.* also **procurar, pretender, buscar**).

problema (m). There is nothing False about this Friend (except that he is masculine) but the word is widely used where we should say 'trouble', 'difficulty', 'snag': *No habrá problema*, 'There won't be any difficulty'; *Siempre hay problemas*, 'There are always some snags'. The only problem is to remember to use it.

procesar. In connection with things it may mean 'to process', an increasingly common verb, but applied to persons in legal cases it means 'to try (in court)', 'to take to court', 'to prosecute'.

procurar(se). Best regarded as False since its most usual meaning is 'to try', 'to take steps to', 'to contrive': *Procura que no te vea nadie*, 'Take care nobody sees you', 'Mind no one sees you'; *Procura llegar temprano*, 'Try to be here early', 'Be sure to be here early'; *Procuró que los estudiantes lo hiciesen por sí mismos*, 'He tried to get the students to do it for themselves'.

The Reflexive *procurarse* is a good deal more Reliable since it implies some success in the attempt and 'procure' would therefore often fit though perhaps 'acquire' is nearer the mark. It is not a common verb but might be used when one is in a slightly evasive mood and where we, instead of baldly saying 'I bought a tie', say 'I got myself a tie', or even 'I procured a tie' (*v.* also **proporcionar**).

profesor (m). Something of a classic in the way of False Friends; you must be aware that it does not mean 'professor', but simply 'teacher'. A professor, in the sense of holder of a university chair, is usually *catedrático*. Attached to somebody's name it may do service in either language but you should be aware that it carries far less prestige in Spanish. If Hispanics want to award you some 'honorary' title to which you are not academically entitled they mostly prefer *Doctor*.

pronto. 'Soon', as you know, but in the R/P the older meaning of 'ready' still survives, helped, perhaps, by the large numbers of Italians who have emigrated there. Elsewhere 'ready' is *listo*. Expressions worth being aware of are: *de pronto*, 'all of a sudden, without warning'; *al pronto*, 'at first, to begin with'; *por lo pronto* or *por de pronto*, 'for the moment, for the present, provisionally', sometimes 'at all events'. *Pronto* used to describe a person means 'quick, sharp, keen'.

proporcionar. 'To supply', 'provide', 'get hold of' (something for somebody). It implies some difficulty, and perhaps ingenuity, in the process: *Mi tío me proporcionó esta colocación*, 'My uncle found me this job'; *Voy a proporcionarme una bebida*, 'I'm going to (see if I can) get hold of a drink'. It is one of those pleasantly imprecise words which suggest that the exact means of provision need not be too closely looked into: *Conseguí proporcionarme un encendedor*, 'I managed to "acquire" a lighter'. It is not reflexive but always requires a pronoun since the essence of it is getting hold of something for somebody, even if the somebody is yourself.

propósito (m). Seems to mean 'proposal' but a better equivalent is 'purpose' though it can often mean an 'intention' or a 'resolution' of the New Year type (*v.* also **resolución** and **motivo**).

A propósito is the usual phrase for 'on purpose' but may also mean 'apropos', 'incidentally'. Which it means will usually depend on whether it comes at the beginning or the end of a sentence: *Lo hizo a propósito*, 'He did it on purpose'; *¿A propósito, has comprado mis cigarros?*' 'By the way/Incidentally/That reminds me, did you get my cigarettes?' *De propósito* may also be used for 'on purpose' but in my experience is less common. Other words for 'on purpose' are *adrede* and *aposta*, or *apostadamente*.

In English a common alternative to 'on purpose' is 'deliberately' and it may be worth remarking here that *deliberadamente*, though it exists, is not common in conversation and in any case has a much stronger sense of 'with deliberation'; it equates better with 'quite (or very) deliberately'.

proseguir. *v.* **seguir.**

prospecto (m). False; it is not a 'prospect' but a 'prospectus'. 'Prospect' needs diverse handling; if it means a 'view', i.e. of scenery, then *vista* or *panorama* are indicated; if it is the figurative, 'What a prospect!', then *¡Qué futuro!* or, in the R/P *¡Qué esperanza! Perspectiva* is a word which certainly means 'the view ahead' but it is less used than 'prospect' in English and a phrase like 'I'm delighted at the prospect of meeting you', would probably be simply *Me encantará verle* or *conocerle*.

provecho (m). 'Profit', but usually in the figurative sense, so that 'benefit' is better. Financial 'profit' is likely to be *beneficio* (*v.* also COURTESY).

provocar. A little Unreliable; 'provoke' suggests anger whereas *provocar* has a much stronger sense of exciting, inciting, or tempting. In the northern countries of S/A a head waiter may often ask you *¿Qué le provoca?*, 'What do you fancy?', 'What tempts you?' More universal for this is *¿Qué le apetece?*

prudencial. 'Prudential', yes, but this is mostly associated with a well-known insurance company and in neither language is the word at all common but in Spanish it is associated with the cliché *un tiempo prudencial* which is quite a good equivalent of 'a decent interval', e.g. *Dejó pasar un tiempo prudencial*, 'He allowed a decent interval to elapse'. Certainly the normal word for 'prudent' is *prudente*, and for 'decent', *decente*.

público (m). 'Public', perhaps, but it is the usual word for 'audience': *¿Hubo mucho público?*, 'Was there a large audience?' *¡Respetable público!* is about as common as *¡Señoras y Caballeros!* for 'Ladies and Gentlemen!' If you mean 'the general public' it is better to say *el gran público*. *Una audiencia* is the sort of thing the Pope gives.

puente (m). 'Bridge', but universally used in a figurative sense for what might be termed a 'long week-end', i.e. when a public holiday falls on a Thursday, Friday or Monday. *Hacer puente* means 'to take time off' for the whole period, including any days in between which are not officially *fiestas*.

puerta (f). 'Door', of course, but also 'gate'. An iron gate may be called *una verja* and the street door of an apartment block is *el portal* but most often it is only the context which indicates whether 'door' or 'gate' is to be understood.

pulla (f). A (nasty) 'crack', i.e. of the verbal type. *Meter una pulla* is an expression used in Mexico for 'to needle', 'to provoke', 'to tease'.

pulpería (f). You might imagine that this was a 'squid shop' but in L/A it means 'grocery store'. The shop itself is unlikely to have this name outside, however; it will probably announce itself as *Abarrotes* or *Comestibles*. In remote districts it is likely to mean 'general store' and in the past could almost be an 'inn'.

punto (m). 'Point', yes; also 'spot', 'dot', hence 'full stop/period'; *punto y coma*, 'semi-colon'; *dos puntos*, 'colon'; *punto y aparte*, 'paragraph' (when you are dictating; a completed paragraph is *un párrafo*). *Punto muerto* is 'dead centre' in a mechanical context and 'neutral' in a car. *En punto* is a very common phrase for 'punctually', 'on the dot': *A las tres en punto*, 'At three o'clock sharp'. Within the home *el punto* is likely to mean 'knitting'; *hacer punto*, 'to knit'.
   Punto is not used in the sense of 'the essential fact/aim', etc. which is usually *caso* (*q.v.*): 'the whole point is that . . .', *Lo único que importa es que . . .*; 'I don't see the point of . . .', *Yo no veo la necesidad de . . .*; the 'point' of a joke or story is *la gracia*. 'A nice point!', *¡Menuda cuestión!*

pupilo (m). False; it usually means 'ward', i.e. a young person, usually an orphan, who is looked after administratively by an older person though not normally educated by them. In other contexts it may mean a 'boarder' or 'inmate' of some institution. A 'pupil' is *un alumno* though schoolchildren are mostly referred to as *escolares*. The 'pupil' of the eye is *la pupila*, though this could obviously also mean a female ward.

puro (m). As a noun this means 'cigar', and do not let dictionaries mislead you into thinking that this is *cigarro* which practically always means 'cigarette', though *cigarrillo* is no doubt commoner. As an adjective *puro* means 'pure', but is useful also for 'sheer':

Fue puro prejuicio, 'It was sheer prejudice'; *seda pura*, 'sheer silk' (*v.* also **mero**).

puta (f). It would be unkind, and certainly exaggerated, to say that *puta* is one of the commonest words in the Spanish language but it is certainly universal throughout the Hispanic world, as well as one most likely to figure in 'graffiti', and touches a nerve within their values which reveals a deep preoccupation. *Puta* means 'whore', and *hijo de puta* is one of the strongest of Spanish insults, far stronger than 'son-of-a-bitch'. When Hemingway, in *For Whom the Bell Tolls*, puts into the mouth of one of his characters 'I obscenity in the milk of thy whore of a mother' he is translating —though softening down—*¡Me cago en la leche de tu puta madre!*, thus attempting to convey the passionate contempt, the most insulting *injurias* that a Hispanic can think up when he is furious. The Shakespearian 'whoreson' reveals that chastity among women was once a preoccupation in the Anglo-Saxon world but the slowly achieved equality of the sexes has deprived the word of much of its force, and indeed its use.

'Whore' is not really an adequate translation. We associate the word with a professional who takes money for her services; for a Hispanic it can signify any woman who has had carnal knowledge outside marriage. Since many Hispanics, especially Spaniards, rather fancy themselves as Don Juans nothing delights them more than a conquest and they are greatly attracted to northern girls who, with any luck, can be conquered with ease by their standards. It should not be imagined that they will be especially grateful, and the easier the conquest the less so. Appearances are very important in the Hispanic world and Anglo-Saxon girls are advised, in their own interest, to keep them up with the utmost rectitude, otherwise the word *puta* will be bandied contemptuously about. Do I seem to be teaching my grandmother to suck eggs? Most of our grandmothers would have needed no such instruction and they had probably heard an old music-hall song about 'The Spaniard who blighted my life'. It is their grand-daughters, and a generation that knew not 'Alfonso', that I am thinking about.

Q

q.e.s.m. These letters stand for *Que estrecha su mano*, 'Who shakes your hand', and were the normal ending to business letters in the past but are now tending to become obsolete. In latter-day correspondence more usual is *Le saludo atentamente*, sometimes simply *Atentamente*, equating with 'Yours faithfully', 'Yours truly' (*v.* **atento**).

For slightly more personal letters, in cases where we might use 'Sincerely yours', *Cordialmente* is appropriate. As with 'sincerely' it implies personal knowledge of one's correspondent but, given this, it can be used in business letters. If in doubt then *Atentamente* is safe enough. Either may be strengthened with a *muy*.

For really personal letters *Afectuosamente* is useful and is not quite as strong as 'Yours affectionately'; it can be used between males. Very common is *Abrazos* and this again is not as strong as it may look; *abrazos* means 'embraces', not 'kisses', and implies no more than the formalized embraces which are customary, even between males, in the Hispanic world. If you do not wish to be quite so heartfelt, then use *Su/tu buen amigo, -a.* Even more affectionate endings can no doubt be left to the ingenuity of the reader. For beginnings, v. **querer.**

que. Everyone knows this word but there are idiomatic uses of it which would-be speakers of Spanish ought to be alert about. *Que* is used a great deal implying—but without stating—some antecedent use of the verb *decir* and it is quite common for a sentence to begin with *Que.* The English equivalent mostly involve using the word 'tell': *Que venga* (implying *Dígale que venga*) equates with 'Tell him to come', 'Let him come'; *Que lleve Manolo su máquina,* 'Tell Manuel to take his camera'.

Que is therefore much used as an intensifier. Childish disputes of the "Tis!"—"Tisn't!" variety are *¡Que sí!—¡Que no!* in Spanish and this use is by no means confined to children. If, in reply to the question, say, 'Are you going swimming?', you wanted to answer with something stronger than a mere 'Yes', viz. 'Yes, I *am*', the Spanish would be *Sí, que voy,* and if you were being more emphatic still then *¡Que sí! ¡Voy!,* even *¡Que sí! ¡Que voy!,* 'I tell you I *am*!' If we do not actually use the word 'tell' then our equivalent is a heavy stress. The context need not necessarily be hotly contentious. Both *qué sí* and *que no* can be said in a quietly positive tone when you want to indicate that you really mean what you are saying.

¿Qué? at the end of a sentence is the equivalent of our 'What about . . .?' at the beginning: *¿Y de mí? ¿Qué?*, 'What about me?'; *¿Y de los obreros? ¿Qué?*, 'What about the working classes?' The *Y* at the start is part of the formula; it is essential to put it in, indeed it is often sufficient if previous talk explains it and an interrogative tone of voice is used: *¿Y los demás?* '(And) what (will you do) about the others?'

quedar(se). 'To remain', 'to be left', but one needs to make oneself conscious of its force as it is often used as a stronger form of 'to be'. *Queda entendido que* . . . is a common wording in contracts and agreements and equates with 'It is understood that . . .' or 'It is agreed that . . .', i.e. not merely 'to be', but 'to remain in being'. At a more domestic level, if you wanted to say 'Is there any wine left?' would you remember to say *¿Queda vino?*; or *No queda* for 'There isn't any more'?

Other idiomatic uses may come easier if you are aware of the word's Latin origin, viz. *quietare*, 'to quieten', 'pacify', and therefore 'settle'. *Quedar en*, 'to come to an agreement about something': *¿En qué quedamos?*, 'What have we decided?' and so 'What's it to be?' or 'When's it to be?' It is particularly used when fixing times or dates. *Quedar con* is 'to agree to meet', and so 'to have a date with': *He quedado con Paquita para las seis*, 'I've got a date with Francisca at six'. It need not be necessarily a 'date'; it may apply to quite a serious appointment.

Quedarse is not always strictly reflexive; it is often simply a more emphatic form, just as *irse* is a more decisive form of *ir*, e.g. *Me quedé tres días en Burgos*, 'I stayed three days in Burgos'. *Quedarse con* is a common colloquial phrase for 'to retain', 'to keep', 'to hang on to': *Se quedó con uno y tiró los demás*, 'He kept one and threw the rest away'. If you said *guardó uno* it would suggest that he put it away for safe-keeping; *se quedó con* merely means that he retained it and no more. In a shop, when choosing an article out of several, you are likely to say *Me quedo con éste* for 'I'll take this one', 'I'll settle for this one'.

queque (m). You might imagine this to be some Indian word but in fact it is merely our old friend 'cake' in disguise. It is widely used in L/A though the type of cake it represents will vary. *Panqueque* also occurs and is rather more recognizable (*v.* also **key**).

querer, querido. Readers will no doubt have recovered from their surprise at learning that this verb means both 'want' and 'love'. It may help if they appreciate that it is cognate with our 'quest' and normally means 'want' when applied to things, and 'love' when applied to persons. The verbal phrase *querer bien* is also worth appreciating; you may say it means 'to like', and it can be used to someone of the same sex, but it is associated with occasions involving the saying of something unpleasant. A typical use is *Te digo esto porque te quiero bien*, literally 'I say this because I like you', but what it really conveys is 'for your own good', 'in your own interest'. More usual ways of rendering 'to like (a person)' are *apreciar* (*q.v.*) or *tener afecto* (*v.* also **cariño**).

Sin querer—'involuntarily'—is well within the dictionaries but they do not usually have space to add that it is useful for our 'didn't mean to', 'couldn't help it', etc. *Lo hizo sin querer*, 'He didn't mean to do it', 'He couldn't help doing it'. In a poker context *quiero* is the word for 'I'll see you' (*v.* also **remedio**).

Querido, by and large, means 'dear', but as an opening to a letter it does not equate with our conventional 'Dear . . .' as it means what it says and so is too affectionate for many purposes. This is therefore a good moment to consider the whole problem of *Modes of address in letters*:

The ordinary, minimum form of address is usually *Muy Señor mío*, equating with 'Dear Sir'. It is a purely routine expression and does not presuppose any previous acquaintance with the person addressed (*v.* also **consideración**).

If you are writing to an individual and wish to seem polite, either because of his exalted office or reputation, or from a desire to suggest such, then *Distinguido Señor* is appropriate but Hispanics are very title-conscious and you should first be sure that the man is not a Doctor or whatever, since then you would say *Distinguido Doctor*. In L/A lawyers, engineers and others come into this category so that *Distinguido Licenciado* or *Ingeniero* are quite common. They do not imply that you have met him personally but they do suggest that you know about him and consider him to be above routine.

If you have come to know your correspondent either personally or from previous correspondence then possibilities are *Apreciado* or *Estimado Señor/Doctor*, etc. They equate with 'Dear Mr. So-&-So', but note that in Spanish there is seldom any need to mention the man's name. To do so increases both the cordiality and the personal nature of the communication and *Apreciado,* being a shade formal, is then less likely. Cordiality may also be increased by strengthening these adjectives with *Muy*.

Querido does not enter the picture until you have established a personal friendship and even then the most likely form will be *Querido amigo*, again without mentioning the man's name; and again, mentioning it makes it more personal and indeed affectionate. *Querido amigo Juan* is about as far as one man is likely to go in addressing another. Women are allowed by convention to be more outspokenly affectionate and may therefore extend to *Querida Juana* or even *Querida Juanita*. If a man addresses a woman in this way, or vice versa, it clearly indicates an acknowledged love affair between them. Anyone addressing the opposite sex and not wishing to be thought too affectionate could say *Estimado amigo, -a*, or even *Querido amigo, -a*, which correspond, more or less, with 'Dear . . . ' and 'My dear . . .' respectively.

For letter endings, *v.* **q.e.s.m.**

quien. Not only 'who', but 'he who', and sometimes 'one' or 'a man': *Como quien dice* is a common idiom for 'As they say', 'As one might say', 'As it were'. 'Whoever' is another possibility; *A quien corresponda* is the stock phrase for 'To whom it may concern'; *para quien lo encuentre*, 'for whoever finds it'. I quote from the Uruguayan author Juan Burghi a highly idiomatic example of it which offers a nice little exercise in translation: '*Dos detalles atraían la atención de quienes lo veíamos*', 'Two details attracted the attention of (those of) us who saw him' (the 'of us' is contained in the *-amos*).

Cada quien is a common method of saying 'each one', 'everyone': *cada quien tiene el derecho a su opinión*, 'Everyone/A man has a right to his own opinion'.

quieto. Borders on the False as it does not mean 'quiet' but 'still': *¡Estese quieto!*, 'Keep still!', or 'Keep calm!'. It is true that *¡Quieto!* addressed to children or a dog might be used where we should say 'Quiet!' but a Hispanic would probably have been more worried by the restlessness than the noise. Anyone commanding silence is more likely to say ¡*Silencio!* and the received translation of Greene's book, *The Quiet American*, is '*El Americano Impasible*' (*v.* also **inquieto**).

quinta (f). Originally a 'country house' or 'country seat' but nowadays more likely to be applied to a suburban residence in much the same way as our 'villa'. Its image will vary from one country to another and in Spain it may be regarded as obsolete.

quitar(se). *Quitar* may be classed as False as it does not mean 'quit'; it is transitive and is a very common, all-purpose verb for 'to take away', much as *sacar* is all-purpose for 'to take out'. It is often used meaning 'to steal': *Le quitaron el reloj*, 'He had his watch pinched', but *Primero hay que quitar la rueda*, 'You have to take the wheel off first'. Note that the preposition *a* is used when taking something away from a person and *de* when from a thing: *Quitó la tapa de la caja*, 'He took the lid off the box', but *Quitar un caramelo a un niño*, 'Taking candy from a kid'.

   Quitarse is used—perhaps a little colloquially—for 'to take oneself off', hence 'to push off', or 'to get out of the way': ¡*Quítate!*, 'Get out of the way!'; *Vamos a quitarnos de aquí*, 'Let's get (the hell) out of here'. In this last case it might just equate with 'Let's quit'.

R

radio (f or m). The word is usually feminine, and in Spain always so, but in parts of L/A they make a distinction between 'radio' in general, i.e. the waves on the ether, which is *la*, and a 'radio-set', which is *el*: *Voy a comprar un radio*. *Radio* also means both 'radium' and 'radius' and will be masculine in these cases too.

raja. *v.* **rebanada.**

rancho (m). So much associated with the Rancho Grande that one confidently assumes it to mean 'ranch' but this is not always so. One of its earlier meanings was a modest 'hut' or 'encampment' and in Venezuela it is applied to a 'shanty' of the shanty-towns of which Caracas has such a copious supply. In Spain it is only known as the 'communal meal', e.g. for soldiers or prisoners, and is mainly associated with the army.

   In Mexico *salsa ranchera* is one of the peppery sauces of which they are so fond. It is a green colour and often waiting on the restaurant table, it being assumed that you will want some.

raro. You may call it False since, in everyday circumstances, it practically never means 'rare'; it means 'odd', 'peculiar', 'funny' and is
a very common word. *¡Que raro!*, 'How extraordinary!'; *Pues es
una manera muy rara de hacerlo*, 'Well it's a very funny way of
doing it'.

Raro is correct for, say, a 'rare' stamp but *poco frecuente* is
more likely in practice.

rato (m). Nothing to do with 'rat', which is *rata*; it means a 'while'; *un
ratito*, 'a little while': *Salió hace un ratito*, 'He went out a short
while ago'. 'A long while', in English, is often boiled down to
'long': e.g. 'Have you been waiting long?' and *un largo rato*,
similarly boiled down in the same sort of context, is *mucho rato*:
¿Ha esperado mucho rato?, but it should be noted that the length
of *rato* cannot exceed a day, nor last overnight, and is usually not
more than an hour or two. 'A long while ago' is therefore a very
relative term and may need quick thought; if it extends beyond the
confines of a day then it would be *hace mucho* or *hace muchos
días/semanas/meses/años*, etc.

raya (f). 'Line', of the sort drawn on paper, but it has some more specialized meanings, e.g. 'parting', of one's hair; also the 'crease' in
one's pants/trousers. It is not, however, used for 'line' in the sense
of 'queue', which is *cola*. *Rayar* is 'to draw a line', and is often
used in L/A for 'to cross out', 'delete' (*v.* **borrar**); *papel rayado*,
'lined paper'. It should be distinguished from *rallar*, 'to grate' or
'shred', which sounds much the same in many mouths.

razon (f). Not only 'reason' and 'right': *tener razón*, 'to be right'; but
also 'ratio': *en razón de 2 a 1*, 'in a ratio of 2 to 1'. 'Rate' is another
possibility: *La población aumenta a razón de 1,000,000 cada año*,
'The population increases at the rate of a million a year'.
'Rationale' is yet another possibility. *Dar razón de* means 'to give
an account of, to report on'.

realizar. Unreliable and, for everyday purposes, may be regarded as
False; it means, literally, 'to bring into reality', hence 'to carry
out', 'to perform': *Esperamos realizar este proyecto*, 'We hope to
carry out this plan' (*v.* also **verificar**). *Lo realizó con sumo éxito*,
'He brought it off triumphantly'. It is much used of the performance of plays and music: *El estreno de la obra se realizó en
Madrid*, 'The work was first performed in Madrid'. In this Passive
sense it can come close to our 'to be realized', e.g. *Sus ilusiones se
realizaron*, 'His hopes were realized', but it will not do for our
everyday use of 'realize' which is usually *darse cuenta* (*v.* **cuenta**,
also **caer, caso, enterar, ignorar**).

reata (f). The usual word for 'rope', in Mexico. They also have a figurative use for it: *Es muy reata*, 'He's a great friend of mine' (*v.*
mecate).

rebanada (f). 'Slice', usually of bread or cake. Spanish has different
words for slice, mostly according to the thing sliced, much as we

talk about a 'rasher' of bacon. 'A slice' of meat is likely to be *una lonja* (in L/A often *loncha*) or *un filete*, but any 'slice' which is more or less circular is likely to be *rueda, rodaja*, sometimes *medallón*, and this can apply not only to, say, sausages but even fish or an onion. A 'slice' of fruit, e.g. melon, is usually *raja*. A more general and rather colloquial word for slice is *tajada*; strictly speaking it means a 'cut' but is used with an easy imprecision, and can often equate with 'helping'.

rebasar. Strictly speaking 'to go beyond', and could sometimes mean 'to trespass', but in Mexico and some countries south it is the usual word for 'to overtake/pass', in a car. Our equation would sometimes be 'to top': *Las ventas rebasaron el millón*, 'The sales topped the million mark'.

receta (f), **recetar.** Unreliable; it does not mean 'receipt', which is usually *recibo*, it means 'recipe', in the kitchen, and 'prescription', at the drug store. *Recetar* means 'to prescribe', but is often used when one speaks as an amateur physician: *Te receto una vacación*, 'What you need is a holiday'.

recién. Most dictionaries make clear that this is short for *recientemente* and only to be used before a past participle, e.g. *recién nombrado*, 'recently appointed'. In L/A, however, you will often hear it used by itself, no doubt because it is less trouble to say, and it usually equates with 'just now', 'a moment ago'. I recall a man on the telephone who had been cut off and asked, rather impatiently, to be put back to *la señorita con que hablaba recién*.

reclamación (f). Unreliable to the point of Falsity; its commonest meaning is 'claim', or 'complaint'. There are many Spanish words beginning with *re-* where this suffix is merely a strengthener and does not imply 'back' or doing a thing for the second time (e.g. *recortar, recolección, resolución*). Equally False is *reclamar* which does not mean 'to reclaim' but 'to put in a claim', 'to stake a claim'.

For the 'reclamation' of (waste) lands *recuperación* is indicated.

recoger. Another case where the *re-* is chiefly a strengthener, though it does imply some previous activity; it means 'to collect', 'to pick up': *¿Tenemos que ir a recogerlos?*, 'Do we have have to go and collect them?'; *Van a recogerlo*, 'They're going to call for it'. 'To collect', in the sense of 'make a collection', is *coleccionar*.

recolección (f). Unreliable, since the Spanish is physical and the English metaphorical. In an agricultural context it is likely to mean 'harvest', i.e. 'the gathering-in'. In city circumstances, notably in L/A, it means the 'collection' of garbage, dustbins, trashcans, etc.; in Spain this is *la recogida*. The English 'recollection', i.e. remembrance of things past, would be *recuerdo, recordación* or *rememoración*.

recomendado. Clearly the past participle of *recomendar* but the usual word in L/A for 'Registered', in connection with mail. In Spain the word is *Certificado*. I take this opportunity of mentioning that 'Poste Restante/General Delivery' is *Lista de Correos*.

recordar. False; it does not mean 'to record' but 'to recall', or 'remind': *Recuérdame que escriba a Alvaro*, 'Remind me to write to Alvaro'; *¿Recuerda?*, 'Do you remember?' *Recordar* and *acordarse* are more or less interchangeable for 'to remember', but only *recordar* will do for 'remind'.

'To record' is *grabar* when it is a matter of putting something on tape or disc, but *registrar*, *inscribir*, *hacer constar* or *dejar constancia de* if it is a matter of putting something on record in writing.

recorrer. *v*. **correr.**

recortar, recorte (m). *Recortar* seems as though it ought to mean 'to cut again' but in fact means 'to cut away', 'to trim'. In the R/P *un recorte* is 'a trim' at the barber's. In Spain this is *un arreglo*, in Colombia *una revista*. *Un recorte* is also fairly universal for a 'newspaper cutting/clipping'.

recuperar(se). 'To recuperate', yes, but only when reflexive, otherwise it is the normal equivalent for 'to recover', 'to get back', 'to make up for': *Recuperar el tiempo perdido*, 'to make up for lost time'. *Recuperación de tierra/terreno*, 'reclamation of land'.

refrán (m). Strictly False; our image is musical, 'the chorus' of a song; the Spanish is verbal, 'a tag', 'a proverb': *Un refrán conocido*, 'a well-known saying'. 'The old refrain', *el viejo refrán*, said rather cynically, may do service in either language but the difference is still between words and music. A musical 'chorus' is *un estribillo*.

regalar. False; it means 'to present', in the sense of making a gift, and 'a present' is *un regalo* (or *obsequio*). 'To regale oneself with' would be *darse el lujo de* or something of the sort.

regio. Basically 'kingly', but often exploited for less august purposes, particularly, perhaps, in advertisements for apartments, etc. and will then equate with 'sumptuous', 'superb'.

registrar, registro (m). A rather Unreliable pair, especially *registrar*, one of whose commonest meanings is 'to search', in the police sense: *Durante su ausencia la policía registró su apartamento*, 'During his absence the police searched his apartment'; *Le han registrado en la aduana*, 'They searched him at the Customs'. Basically the verb means 'to record for official purposes', which might be regarded by some as characteristic of the disinfected police attitude in the matter of searching.

Un registro can therefore mean 'a police search', though it can also mean simply 'an official record'. *Registro Civil* means the City Records or Archives (births, marriages, deaths, etc.); St. Catherine's House in London and/or a Department of Vital Statistics in the U.S. are both *Registros*. It can also mean 'recording': *Registro sonoro amablemente cedido por . . .*, 'Sound recording kindly supplied by . . .', and is then more or less interchangeable with *grabación*.

In the reverse direction 'to register', e.g. for some course of study, is *matricularse*. 'A registered letter' is *una carta recomendada* in L/A, *certificada* in Spain. In a musical context, *registro bajo*, 'lower register'.

regla (f). Both 'rule' and 'ruler' (of the sort one draws lines with). It is also commonly used of a woman's 'period'. *Tener la regla* is the usual expression for this.

regodeón. An adjective for 'fussy', 'self-indulgent', in the Z/A. It may also be used as a noun for a 'pet'.

regresar, regreso (m). The usual words for 'return', in L/A. A 'round-trip/return ticket' is *ida y regreso*. In Spain it is *volver* and *ida y vuelta*.

regular. Both a verb and an adjective. The verb is straightforward for 'to regulate', 'to control', but the adjective is Unreliable and its commonest everyday meaning is 'so-so', 'not bad', 'ordinary': *¿Qué tal era? Regular,* 'What was it like?' 'Not bad', 'Much as usual', 'Fair to middling'. It is not suitable for persons, e.g. a 'regular' customer, nor for 'regular' in the sense of real, genuine, e.g. Gilbert's 'regular royal queen', which would have to be *auténtica* or *verdadera*. 'Regular' requires such words as *metódico, ordenado, regulado, uniforme, exacto* (and some careful thought).

relación (f). Unreliable; it may mean 'relation' in the general sense, e.g. *tenían relaciones oficiales*, 'Official relations existed between them', but if a man *tiene relaciones con* a woman, or vice versa, it means specifically 'is engaged to', and does *not* mean 'has a liaison with'. *Relación* has another common meaning which is quite distinct, viz. 'list': *¿Puede darme la relación de socios?*, 'Can you give me the list of members?' (*Lista* is also used).

'Relations' in the family sense are *familiares* or *parientes*, and 'related to', or 'a relative of', is usually *emparentado con: Ha roto las relaciones con todos sus parientes (*or *familiares),* 'He's broken off relations with all his relations'.

remedar. A word little used in Spain though surviving in L/A. It does not mean 'to remedy', as you might imagine, but 'to mimic' (its origin is 're-imitate') and it should be distinguished from *remediar* which does. *Remedaba al jefe,* 'He was mimicking the boss'; *remediaba la situación,* 'he was remedying the situation', 'he was solving the problem'.

remedio (m). 'Remedy', yes, but *No tener más remedio,* 'Not to be able to help it', is such a common and idiomatic verbal phrase that it should certainly be in your repertory: *No tengo más remedio,* 'I can't help it', 'I don't have any option'.

remover. May be regarded as False; it has quite a different image from 'remove', viz: 'to turn (things) over, to move (objects/ material) around', hence, in the kitchen, 'to stir, to turn things over' (e.g. in a frying pan); in the garden 'to dig', 'to turn the soil'. 'To remove' is usually best handled by *quitar (q.v.)*.

rendir. A verb for which the dictionary will give you a remarkable array of equivalents. Basically it means 'to render', 'yield', 'produce', and in everyday circumstances its commonest use is probably in the phrase *Rinde mucho,* said of somebody who produces a lot. The best equations are probably 'He gets through a remarkable amount of work', or 'He produces an astonishing amount of stuff'. In a school report *No rinde* would equate with 'Doesn't try hard enough', 'Could do better'. The much greater length of the English equivalents indicates what a useful little verb it is.

renta (f). Tends to have a different image in Spanish as it is more associated with money coming in i.e. dividends, pension, unearned income, and in the plural this is what it is most likely to mean. In recent decades *la renta* has come increasingly to be used for 'the rent' but the official word for rent is *el alquiler* and this word is by no means obsolete; *alquilar* is the universal verb for 'to rent' though *rentar* is used in places.

reparar. 'To repair', both literally and metaphorically, hence also 'to restore, make amends' etc. *Reparaciones* is valid for both 'repairs' and 'reparations'. Dictionaries give *reparar en* 'to take heed of' without making clear that it is somewhat antiquated, though the expression *sin reparar en las consecuencias*, 'regardless of the consequences', survives as a stock phrase. A common expression, however, is *poner reparos* 'to be difficult, to raise objections, find fault', even 'to be squeamish'.

repartir. A useful, all purpose verb for 'to dish out, deal out, share out, distribute, hand round' etc; it can mean 'to deliver' when it is a matter of general delivery to many as opposed to a single individual: *Se reparte a domicilio,* 'Home delivery service'.

repente. Nothing to do with 'repentance'; it means a 'start', a 'sudden movement', and *de repente* is the normal adverbial phrase for 'suddenly'. *Repentinamente* and *súbitamente* exist but are unlikely in conversation.

reprobar. *v.* **suspender.**

resaca (f). A 'hangover' in Spain. Not surprisingly there is a multitude of different words for this: *jaqueca* (R/P), *cruda* (Mexico), *guayabo, chucháqui* (Colombia, Ecuador), *ratón* (Venezuela), *papalina (q.v.)* (Spain). If you want to refer to the state more euphemistically then *malestar* is indicated.

reserva (f). 'Reserve', and *de reserva* is a useful adjectival phrase for 'spare', or perhaps 'extra': *Tengo uno de reserva,* 'I've a spare one'. In a car context a 'spare' wheel is usually *de repuesto,* i.e. 'a replacement'. *De sobra* is another possibility for 'extra' (*v.* **sobrar**) but this implies rather one 'left over' and suggests chance whereas *de reserva* suggests planning.

resolución (f). 'Resolution', perhaps, but it is a reinforced form of 'solution', and can apply to the act of solving, e.g. a problem or even a cross-word puzzle. In the R/P I found it extended to 'finishing off', 'completion': *A la resolución de sus actividades*, 'Having completed their task'. A 'resolution' of the New Year type is handled by *propósito* (*q.v.*).

resorte (m). 'Spring', but can also mean 'springiness', 'elasticity' (*v.* **muelle**).

responsable. 'Responsible', yes, but most often used as a noun: *Ser el responsable de . . .*, 'to be responsible for . . .'; *No es el responsable*, 'He's not responsible'. In conversation 'responsibility' is often *cuenta*; *Eso es cuenta tuya*, 'That's your responsibility'.

restar. False; it has nothing to do with 'rest', it is a transitive verb and means 'to subtract', 'deduct', being the normal word for this at school: *Resta el número que habías pensado*, 'Take away the number you first thought of'. *Sustraer* exists but is mainly used in a physical sense (*v.* **sustraer**). *Restar* may be used figuratively: *Le resto importancia* (literally, 'I subtract importance from it'), 'I don't give it much importance'. *Restar* (*la pelota*) is 'to return (the service)' in tennis. 'To rest' is *descansar*.

resultar. 'To result', yes, but in English we mostly use it with the preposition 'in'; in Spanish it is much used without any preposition and equates with 'to turn out': *Las fotografías han resultado bien*, 'The photographs have turned/come out well'. A very common conversational expression is *resulta que*, 'so that', 'with the result that': *. . . resulta que sus esfuerzos fueron completamente inútiles*, '. . . so that her efforts were completely wasted'.

resumir. Unreliable; it only means 'to resume' in the sense of 'to give a résumé', 'to summarize'. 'To resume' in the sense of 'take up again' is either *reasumir*, usually of duties or responsibilities, or *reanudar*, of journeys; sometimes simply *empezar otra vez*, or *volver a*.

retorno (m). Basically a 'return', usually some form of repayment; the 'return' of a person is *regreso/vuelta*. You will, however, see *Retorno* on Mexican motorways to indicate a place where you are entitled to turn round.

retrasar, retraso (m) 'Delay', 'hold-up', and if you do much travelling you will certainly become aware of *un retraso de* (*dos*) *horas*, 'a (two)-hour delay', *retrasado* (sometimes *atrasado*) has virtually become an adjective—and unfortunately a common one—for 'backward', in connection with countries. If you prefer 'developing' say *en desarrollo*.

retrete. *v.* **baño**.

reunir(se), reunión (f). *Reunir* is the transitive verb for 'to join', 'to reunite' things which have come apart. *Reunirse* applies to people and means 'to meet', though it implies a meeting of more than two people and suggests a coming together from different quarters. *Reunión* is a 'meeting' in this sense but suggests a small meeting and has not the limitation of a reunion of friends; it is applied to meetings in office circumstances (*v.* also **junta**). A large 'meeting' would be *una asamblea* (*v.* also **mitin**).

revés (m). Basically a noun meaning 'the other side': *El revés de la medalla*, 'the other side of the coin/medal', but the adverbial expression *al revés* should certainly be in your repertoire as it offers, in three unvarying syllables, the equation for 'up-side-down', 'inside-out', 'wrong way up', 'wrong way round', 'back to front', 'conversely', 'vice versa' . . . there may well be others. Hispanics do, however, also say *vice versa*, and *al revés* in the sense of 'conversely' is usually said at the end of a sentence when the converse needs no explanation, in other words meaning much the same as vice versa. 'Conversely', in mid-sentence, is more likely to be *en cambio* (*v.* **cambiar**).

The verb 'to reverse' is not quite so simple. 'To put a car into reverse' is *poner en marcha atrás*, and 'to drive a car in reverse' is *dar marcha atrás*: 'He reversed the car into the gatepost', *Al dar marcha atrás chocó con el poste de la puerta.* 'To reverse the charges' on the telephone is *cobrar al número llamado* (*v.* **cobrar**).

revisar. Unreliable because we use the verb 'to revise', in two senses; viz. 'to correct', 'alter', 'modify' (e.g. Revised Version) and, on the other hand 'to check', 'to go over the work again', as in preparation for exams. In Spanish *revisar* has only the latter meaning. 'To revise', in the sense of 'correct', would be *corregir*, *repasar*, *modificar*, etc.

revolver. I refer to the verb, not the noun, which has an accent on the *o*. *Revolver* is the ordinary domestic word for 'to stir', though it can extend to a more figurative 'stir up', but in Mexico I found it being used in a transitive sense for 'to revolve': *Estaba revolviendo la rueda*, 'He was turning the wheel round'. Quite a logical use but more idiomatic is *dar vueltas(a)* which is the usual verbal expression for 'to revolve', whether transitive or intransitive (*v.* **preguntarse**).

rico. 'Rich', when applied to persons, but one of its commonest applications is to food and it then equates with 'nice', or 'delicious'. Children are daily encouraged to eat up their food *porque es muy rico* (*v.* **delicioso**).

rodaja. *v.* **rebanada.**

rubio. 'Blond', 'fair-complexioned'; a word which I feel inclined to call extremely common, though I suspect this may be because it applies to so many of us Gringos. In Mexico they usually say *güero, -a* for 'blond', and in Venezuela *catire* (feminine *catira*). *Rubio* is also applied to tobacco in contradistinction to *tabaco negro* which Hispanics mostly prefer, though 'dark-complexioned, brunette' is *moreno*.

rudo. 'Rude' in the sense of 'rough, crude, unpolished' but not of 'impolite' which would be *descortés* or *ordinario* (*q. v.*).

rumbo (m). A nautical word for 'course, direction': *cambiar de rumbo*, 'to change course'; *con rumbo a*, 'bound for, heading for'. It is used of other forms of transport which require some sort of 'navigation' and *con rumbo a . . .* is likely to occur in announcements as the equivalent of 'calling at . . .' followed by a series of place-names.

rural. (m). As an adjective 'rural', but used as a noun in the C/S for 'station waggon', and in Colombia for 'long-distance bus'. A station waggon is more commonly *una camioneta*. In countries where they have a *Guardia Rural*, *un rural* can mean a member of the Rural Police.

S

saber. Usually well attended to in grammar books and dictionaries so that I need do no more than remind you that the equation is sometimes 'to speak': *¿Sabes ruso?*, 'Can you speak Russian?'; or 'to hear about': *Así supe del accidente*, 'That was how I heard about the accident'. A few stock phrases are perhaps worth a mention:

¿Qué sé yo?, 'How should *I* know?', 'Don't ask me!'; or, in a different tone of voice: 'One never knows'; *Me dijo que vendría pero ¿qué sé yo?*, 'He said he'd come but how can one be sure?' It is a sort of verbal substitute for a shrug of the shoulders.

Y no sé qué y no sé cuánto, 'and so on and so forth', '. . . and I don't know what all'.

¡Tú qué sabes!, a crushing remark usually made in rather a sarcastic tone of voice and equating with 'How do *you* know?', 'What do *you* know about it?', 'Wise guy!' As in the English equivalents, it is something of a legacy from childhood, hence the Second Person Singular. It is unlikely to be said in the 'Polite' form.

sabroso. *v.* **delicioso.**

sacar. A tremendously common, and very all-purpose, verb meaning, as you know, 'to take out', 'pull out', 'get out', 'fish out', or, less colloquially, 'to extract', 'remove', etc: *Voy a sacar el coche*, 'I'm going to get the car out'; *¿Puede sacar este corcho?* 'Can you get this cork out?' It is much used colloquially in preference to a more precise verb, e.g. *Voy a sacar cuentas con él* for 'I'm going to have it out with him', when the usual expression for this is *arreglar cuentas*. In a Colombian (or was it Peruvian?) bank I was told *Han sacado el descuento*, 'They've deducted the discount', when the 'correct' verb is *restado*. One has to be on the look-out for such uses and, of course, with growing confidence, one may try the odd sally oneself. There are, however, certain contexts where you may regard it as obligatory and where no native is likely to avoid it, viz.:

Sacar un pasaporte, 'to obtain a passport' (it can apply to other types of official document, e.g. a driving licence).

Sacar una fotografía, 'to take a photograph'.

Sacar una copia (*más*), 'to take a(n extra) copy'.

Sacar buenas notas (*en un examen*), 'to get good marks (in an exam)'.

Sacar la cuenta, 'to work out a given numerical problem'.

Sacar is also the almost invariable verb for 'to serve', in tennis, and 'to kick off', in football: *¿Quién saca?*, 'Whose service is it?' I fancy it may likewise apply to other types of 'starting' in other sports and readers should be on the alert for it. I particularly recommend a mental note about *sacar una fotografía*; it is fatally easy to say *tomar* before you manage to think about it.

Echar (*q.v.*) is another all-purpose verb for to 'out' in a wide variety of senses and readers anxious to distinguish between them may regard the basic concept of *sacar* as 'extract' and *echar* as 'eject'. It is largely a difference in unconscious standpoint; *echar* sees the action from within and *sacar* from without. There may, therefore, be overlaps, especially in 'rough' usage, e.g. *sacar cuentas* and *echar cuentas*, both of which mean 'to have it out (with somebody)'.

saco (m). 'Sack', e.g. of the sort used for potatoes. Rather suprisingly it is also the usual word in L/A for 'jacket', 'short coat', whether for men or women. In Spain this is *chaqueta*. If there is any likelihood of confusion in L/A they will say *bolsa* or *bolso* for 'sack', though they will understand *chaqueta* well enough.

sala (f), **salón** (m). *Sala* is the normal word for 'drawing-room', 'parlour', 'sitting-room', in a private house; *salón* suggests a 'reception-room' in a large house. Surprisingly, perhaps, *sala* is also the word for a 'concert or lecture-hall', 'auditorium'. The 'hall' in a private house is likely to be *el pasillo* or *la entrada* (*v.* **correr**).

saldar, saldo (m). *Saldo* means 'residue', 'remainder', usually in connection with accounts, and in some contexts will mean 'outstanding'. When trying to decipher your electricity bill you may find the letters *SA* against one of the figures; this stands for *Saldo Anterior* and means 'Outstanding' from last month. *Saldo* is sometimes used for a 'Remainder' Sale, though perhaps *liquidación* (*q.v.*) is commoner. The verb *saldar* means 'to pay the balance'.

salir. As you know 'to come out', 'go out', 'emerge', but it extends to figurative uses and then equates with 'turn out', 'work out': *Ha salido bien*, 'It's come out nicely'; *A lo mejor no me sale*, 'It probably won't work (when I try it)'; *Sale igual/lo mismo*, 'It works out the same', 'It comes to the same thing' (*v.* also **resultar**).

Salir is used in card games: *¿Quién sale?*, 'Whose lead is it?', 'Who goes first?' In the kitchen it may be used reflexively, for 'to leak': *Esta cacerola se sale*, 'This pan leaks'.

salpicón (m). A sort of salad, usually of shredded raw vegetables (notably onion) and no doubt some *ají*. It implies a cold dish and is particularly popular in Peru. At the start of Don Quixote we read that he had '*Salpicón las más noches*' which Jervas, in the early 18th century, translated: '. . . the fragments served up cold on most nights'.

salto (m). 'Jump', or 'leap'; also 'waterfall', but a common domestic expression is *salto de cama*, 'negligée', 'déshabillée': *en salto de cama*, looking as though she had jumped out of bed, i.e. 'in her dressing-gown' (*v.* also **mañanita**). *Salto* may also be used figuratively; *Un gran salto adelante*, 'a great step forward'.

salvaje. *v.* **brutal.**

salvar. 'To save', 'salvage', 'rescue'; also 'to overcome', and used in the R/P for 'to pass' an examination (not necessarily by the skin of one's teeth). It is used for 'to cross/negotiate/get round' some obstacle (with the implication of not being held up by it): *Salvó el foso de un salto*, 'He crossed the trench in one bound'; *El avión salva la distancia en 3 horas*, 'The plane covers the distance in 3 hours' (i.e. when the overland journey would take as many days or weeks); *salvar el hueco*, 'to bridge the gap'. The normal word for 'cross' is of course *cruzar*; *salvar* is more like 'to cross/jump/get clean over' or '. . . right over'.

sancionar. Better to class it as False as it leads in quite the opposite direction to our 'sanction' which usually means 'to permit'. The Spanish sense is rather of imposing sanctions and if you read that certain types of activity will be *sancionado* do not imagine they will be permitted; it means that they will be 'prosecuted'.

sandwich (m). Tends to have a different image, except in the more touristy places, being usually a bread roll cut in two with meat, or whatever, inserted, and it may well have been this that Lord Sandwhich took with him to the gaming table at the word's birth. *Bocadillo* (*q.v.*) is also used for this but if you want to be sure of getting sliced bread ask for *un sandwich de miga* (i.e. crumb as opposed to crust).

sano. Largely False; it means 'healthy, sound, whole(some)'; *sano y salvo* is the stock phrase for 'safe and sound'. 'Sane' is *cuerdo* (*v.* also **insano**).

santo (m). 'Saint', obviously, but also 'Saint's Day': *El jueves es mi* santo, 'It's my Saint's day on Thursday'. Most Christian names in the Hispanic world are names of saints and every saint has his day. On the whole they are regarded as more important than birthdays and require the giving of presents rather more than a *cumpleaños*. The system has its advantages. If you know a person's name then you know—or can readily find out—when his or her *santo* is and send a present accordingly. You may also care to know that boys named *Jesús* usually celebrate their *santo* at Christmas. *Es lógico, ¿no?* Of recent decades there has been a tendency, particularly in L/A, to give names which are classical rather than strictly 'Christian', e.g. *Artemio, Aquiles*. In such cases it is perforce the *cumpleaños* which is celebrated.

schop. *v.* chop.

secretaria (f). With the accent on the first *a*, it means a 'secretary' (female) but *secretaría* with an accent on the *i* means 'secretariat', and is the usual word for a government department.

seguir. 'To follow', yes, when used with a noun or pronoun, and may be used figuratively: *¿Me sigues?*, 'Do you follow me?'. More important and idiomatic are the cases when it is followed by the Gerund since then its meaning is 'to continue', 'to go on (doing)', 'to still (do)': *El barbero siguió afeitando*, 'The barber went on shaving'; *Sigo cometiendo los mismos errores*, 'I go on making the same (old) mistakes'; *Sigo pensando lo mismo*, 'I still think the same'. For negative sentences, e.g. 'I still don't . . .', the formula is *seguir sin*: *Sigo sin comprender*, 'I still don't understand'; *Sigue sin decidirse*, 'He still can't make up his mind'.

Without either a noun or a gerund *seguir* usually equates with 'to get on', in the sense of making progress: *¿Cómo sigue?*, 'How's he/it getting on?', is likely to be asked of, say, someone who is ill, or a boy at school or of some work in progress (*v.* also **cundir**), and in reply to some such enquiry you are quite likely to say *Sigue igual* for 'No change', 'Much as usual'. *Sigue* is the equivalent of 'Go on', in almost any kind of context (*v.* also **adelante**).

Lo siguiente, 'the following', is also widely used in conversation, even by people of little education, far more, in fact, than 'the following' in English. How many readers would, in the course of ordinary chit-chat, say: 'He said the following . . .' and then proceed to quote? Very few, I suspect, but in Spanish it is quite usual.

Proseguir borders on the False; it looks like 'prosecute' but in fact is a stronger and more formal version of *seguir*. If you were giving an account of some occurrence and were interrupted, your hearer would normally say *Sigue* for 'Carry on', 'Go on', etc. but if you were making a statement to a policeman he would probably say *Prosiga*, 'Proceed'. 'To prosecute', in the legal sense, is *procesar*; in the sense of 'carry out', *llevar a cabo* or possibly *realizar* (*q.v.*).

En seguida is the normal expression in Spain for 'at once', 'right away', 'right now'.

según. 'According to', 'as'; the four Gospels are entitled *El Evangelio según . . .(S. Mateo, S. Marcos, S. Lucas y S. Juan)*, and in a serious, scholarly work you may see *Según vamos a ver en el próximo capítulo*, 'As we shall see in the next chapter', but it is also much used in conversation and our equations are usually less august: *Según Pablo hay nueve*, 'Pablo says there are nine'; *Pues, es según*, 'Well, it (all) depends'; *Según dicen*, 'so they say'. Our equivalents often involve the verb 'to say'.

seguro, -amente. *Seguro* undoubtedly means 'safe', 'certain', 'sure', and a common expression is *Es seguro*, or simply *Seguro*, meaning 'Certainly', 'That's for sure'. You might be tempted to think this is an alternative way of saying *Seguramente* but in fact there is an important, though subtle, difference; *Seguramente* equates with 'no doubt', and just as 'no doubt' immediately allows for uncertainty, so does *seguramente*: *Seguramente van a estar contentos*, 'They'll no doubt be pleased'; *Es seguro que van a estar contentos*, 'They'll certainly be pleased' (and beware of **cierto**, *q.v.*).

sello (m). Traditionally 'seal', and still the proper word for this on documents which require one, as well as for the special stamps which sometimes have to be put on such documents. In office circumstances, however, it is likely to mean 'rubber stamp' (short for *sello de goma*). In Spain it is the ordinary word for a 'postage stamp'; in L/A this is usually *estampilla* though *timbre* (m) is also used.

seña (f). Mostly used in the plural, meaning 'particulars' of some sort. *Señas particulares* on, say, a passport means 'distinguishing marks', 'special peculiarities' (e.g. scar above left eyebrow). In everyday circumstances its commonest meaning is 'address': *¿Puede darme sus señas?*, 'Can you give me his address?', but if you asked *¿Puede darme las señas del Director del Colegio?* it might suggest that you wanted his name as well. It is perhaps commoner in Spain than L/A.

sencillo. 'Simple'; sometimes 'single': *Una habitación sencilla* is the normal expression in Spain for a 'single' room (for 'double', *v.* **matrimonio**). In the Z/A it is the usual word for 'small change': *¿No tiene sencillo?* 'Don't you have anything smaller?' (In Spain this is *calderilla*) (*v.* also **simple, soltar, feria**).

sensato. 'Sensible', especially as applied to persons: *Es un muchacho muy sensato*, 'He's a very sensible fellow'—and you should warn yourself off *sensible* (*q.v.*). *Sensato* may be applied to things, e.g. a 'sensible' line of conduct, but in practice a native is much more likely to use *lógico*.

sensible. False; it does not mean 'sensible' but 'sensitive', at all events when applied to persons. Applied to things it might mean 'considerable', 'appreciable': *Una pérdida sensible*, 'an appreciable loss'. 'Sensible' would normally be *sensato* (*q.v.*) though sometimes *práctico*. 'I am very sensible of the honour you do me' would be *Estoy muy consciente de . . .* or *Aprecio mucho . . .* Musicians may be interested to know that *la sensible* is the 'leading note', i.e. the seventh note of the scale.

sentencia (f). Unreliable; in legal contexts it may mean 'sentence', but in some countries, owing to their legal systems, would equate better with 'verdict'. In most countries 'a sentence' (in the law courts) is *una condena*. In grammar a 'sentence' is usually *oración, frase* or *claúsula*.

sentido (m). A noun which started life as past participle of *sentir* but now has several particularized meanings. One is 'direction', 'way', whether metaphorical or literal: *No vamos en este sentido*, 'We're not heading that way' (*v.* **dirección**). Another, and perhaps the commonest, is 'sense': *Eso tiene sentido*, 'That makes sense'; *sentido común*, 'common sense'. 'Meaning' is another: *un doble sentido*, 'a double meaning'; in music: *tocar con sentido*, 'to play with feeling'.

ser. I shall not embark on an examination of this verb but will remind readers in passing that one may say either *es casado* or *está casado* for 'he is married'; also that, for that even more permanent state, death, one has to say *está muerto* for 'he's dead', since *ser muerto* means 'to be killed' (*v.* **muerto**). A few idioms are worth a little attention:

O sea is a tremendously common phrase and is really a strengthened form of *o*, 'or', which is a very light-weight monosyllable: *Así que es rico . . . o sea, que no es pobre*, 'So he's rich . . . or, at all events, not poor'. It's force is something like: 'or in other words'.

Soy yo, literally 'I am I'. It appears to be stating the obvious but is really quite logical, though the English practice is to view oneself with more detachment; we say 'it is' instead of 'I am', and in the past were more grammatical about it: 'It is I, be not afraid', '*Soy yo, no temáis*'. Nowadays, I fear, most of us would say 'It's me', or 'That's me'. Louis XIV's, '*L'état, c'est moi*', is *El estado, soy yo*, but if he had been speaking in modern English he would have to have said '*I* am the state', with a heavy accent on the *I*. The same principle applies when, instead of saying *yo*, you give your name, e.g. on the telephone: *Soy Antonio*, where we should say 'It's Antonio speaking'. It is not confined to the First Person Singular: *Son catorce*, 'There are fourteen of them'; *Éramos ocho en el coche*, 'There were eight of us in the car'; *Eres tu el culpable*, 'You're the one to blame', 'It's you who's to blame'.

Mention of *soy yo* prompts the recommendation that all visitors to Hispanic countries should ascertain what their own names are likely to sound like on the lips of a native, e.g. 'Smith', which sounds like *Esmí*, 'Jones', *Honess*, etc. (also to watch out for their middle name being taken as a surname, *v.* **apellido**). It is quite common at banks, tourist offices, customs and the like, for names to be called out and failure to recognize it may lead to loss of your place in the queue; and when you do hear it your response should be *Soy yo.*

sereno. May mean 'serene', 'calm', but also 'sober', i.e. not drunk, and is the formal word used in a court of law. As a noun it means the man who guards the block at night and lets you in or out after 11 p.m. (10.30 in winter). Perhaps he is another of the old Spanish customs which is tending to disappear but he still survives in the larger Spanish cities, notably Madrid. (The word derives from the mediaeval night-watchman who went round calling; 'Three o'clock and all's well!, *¡Las tres de la noche y sereno!* (referring to fine weather). It was no doubt his ample vocalization of the last word which gave him his name.) If you live in an apartment house you should try to persuade the *dueño* to let you have a key of the *portal* but as he so often has no duplicates left you may well need the services of the *sereno* to get in, and friends of yours who leave late may need him to get out.

To attract his attention you either call out *¡SERENO!* in a stentorian voice or clap your hands. When he hears he usually responds by tapping the pavement with his stick to show that he is coming or he may call out *¡Voy!* If he does not know you, he may enquire who you are going to see since it is his business to know the name of every flat-owner in the block. Getting out may be rather more of a problem as it is less easy to shout from within the *portal* and in any case many of these have metal grilles with a glass pane behind. The technique is then to tap on the glass with a coin, which can make a most formidable racket (and is perhaps why these panes are so often cracked) but one may sometimes pass an entrance late at night which seems to have caged beasts behind the bars. These are likely to be somebody's departing guests who have so far failed to attract the *sereno's* attention. He should, of course, be rewarded for his pains.

I am not aware that he exists anywhere in L/A. The *portero eléctrico* is in any case gaining ground in all countries (*v.* **portero**).

serrano. *v.* **porteño.**

servicios. *v.* **baño.**

servir. 'To serve', of course, but *servir para* is very common where we should say 'to be (used) for'. If you wanted to say 'This cloth is for (cleaning) the windows' I dare wager you would say *Este trapo es para (limpiar) las ventanas* but a native would almost instinctively say *Este trapo sirve para* . . . A stock phrase is . . . *no sirve para nada*, '. . . is useless'. *No me sirve*, 'I can't use it', 'It doesn't serve my purpose', 'It's no good to me'.

sí. Means 'yes', of course, but is often used as an intensifier where we should get by with a strong emphasis: *Yo no quiero pero ellos, sí*, 'I don't want to, buy *they* do'. *Eso, sí* is worth adding to your stock; it often equates with an accented 'do' or 'have' and is much shorter than the English 'Yes, I do like/have seen, etc. that (one)'; *Los argentinos no lo dicen pero los españoles, sí*, 'Argentinians don't say it but Spaniards do', and conversely in the negative, mutatis mutandis (*v.* also **píldora**).

¡Sí señor! is universal for 'Yes indeed!' 'Yes, sirree!' and is used to women in the same form and not modified to *Sí señora*— except sometimes facetiously.

Sí pues is an expression much used in the Z/A. Its general sense is to confirm something just said so that it means, approximately, 'Of course', but it is usually said rather idly. A more positive 'of course' would be *por supuesto*.

siempre. 'Always', but a common way of handling our 'usual': *como siempre*, 'as usual'; *lo de siempre*, 'the usual thing'; *del modo de siempre*, 'in the same old way'.

sifón (m). The proper word for 'syphon/siphon', but in Spain it has become so identified with soda that it usually means that: *Coñac con sifón*, 'brandy and soda'. In Colombia, in bars and restaurants where they serve draught beer, *un sifón* is likely to mean 'a beer' (draught beer is normally *de barril*). In these days soda is usually *soda*, especially as it mostly comes in bottles. In Spain you may occasionally come across *seltz* (pronounced *sél*), standing for Seltzer water, though in fact meaning soda water, but this too is tending to disappear.

significado. Distinctly Unreliable; as an adjective it means 'well-known', 'reputable', 'important': *Un significado político de derechas*, 'A well-known right-wing politician'; and, as a noun, 'meaning'; *¿Cuál es el significado de este recado?*, 'What is the meaning of this message?', a different matter from 'significance' which would be *significación* or *importancia*.

simpático. Rather a classic *Falso Amigo*; it does not mean 'sympathetic' but 'nice', as applied to a person, i.e. of attractive personality, 'easy to get on with', etc.: *Es un muchacho muy simpático*, 'He's a very nice fellow'. English seems to be the only European language where it has the connotation of 'compassionate', 'condoling', 'understanding', for which the Spanish is *compasivo* or *comprensivo* (*v.* also **persona**). Equally common is *antipático* for the opposite, viz. 'not nice', 'nasty', 'objectionable', 'disagreeable'; you may say it means 'antipathetic' but is vastly more everyday.

The verb *simpatizar* is a little more Reliable since it is possible to say, e.g., *simpatiza con los rebeldes*, 'his sympathies are with the rebels', but in narrower, domestic circles it is more likely to mean 'to get on (well) with': *Simpatiza bien con sus colegas*, 'He gets on well with his colleagues', and 'to sympathize' is usually best handled by *compadecer*.

simple. Unreliable; applied to things it means 'simple', as in English: *La solución es muy simple*, 'The answer's quite simple', but applied to persons it means 'simple-minded' and is sometimes a euphemism for 'stupid', 'A simple person', i.e. straightforward, unaffected, would be *una persona sencilla*.

sino. As a noun it means 'Fate', but as a conjunction it is highly idiomatic and needs a bit of acquiring; it means 'but' in the pattern 'not . . . but . . .': *No fue la comida sino el vino*, 'It wasn't the food but the wine'; *No anglos sino ángeles*, 'Not Angles but angels'. One has to programme one's mental computer with this pattern inserting *sino* in place of *pero*.

siquiera, ni. *Ni siquiera* is given in most dictionaries—quite correctly—as 'not even', but it is often used where we should say 'practically (not)', 'virtually (not)' or 'hardly': *Pasó con tanta prisa que ni siquiera lo vi*, 'It went so fast I hardly saw it', '. . . practically didn't see it'.

sobrar. A curious verb meaning 'to be left over', 'to remain', 'to be surplus'. It is one of the verbs that it is difficult to remember to use in time, though the most illiterate Hispanic will use it a dozen times a day. You should be conscious of the difference between it and *quedar* which also means 'to remain'; if you said *¿Queda vino?* it would mean 'Is there any wine left?' but suggest that you were still sitting at the meal-table and could do with some more; *¿Sobra vino?* means 'Is there any wine left over?' and suggests a hostess surveying the table after the guests have gone: *Después de repartir las cartas sobraba una*, 'After dealing the cards there was one left over'; *No me sobra tiempo*, 'I haven't any spare time'.

The phrase *de sobra* is useful for 'plenty', 'extra': *Tengo uno de sobra*, 'I have one extra'; *Tenemos tiempo de sobra*, 'We've tons of time'. 'To be superfluous' is another possibility: *Tú sobras aquí* is the sort of thing one says to anyone who is 'getting in the way'. The normal verb for 'to be in the way' is *estorbar* (*v.* COURTESY).

In L/A *sobretiempo* is sometimes used—rather roughly—for 'overtime' though the official term is *horas extraordinarias* or *tiempo suplementario*. In the R/P they use an adjective *sobrador* to mean 'stuck-up', i.e. anxious to think himself above his fellows.

socorro (m). 'Help', and cognate with our 'succour'. The normal word for 'help', as you know, is *ayuda* but if you are ever unlucky enough to have to shout for help then shout *¡SOCORRO!* It is much more shoutable than *ayuda* as well as being the right word in such circumstances.

soler. I hesitate to say that it means 'to be wont to', 'to be in the habit of', since it is so defective that even the infinitive chiefly exists in dictionaries. Such fragments as do survive, however, are useful for 'I/he/she/they always . . .': *Suelen salir a las seis*, 'They usually come out at six o'clock'; also for our Simple Present tense when it denotes habitual actions: *Suelo fumar unos veinte cigarros al día*, 'I smoke about twenty cigarettes a day'. It is less used in L/A where *usar* is more likely.

solicitar, solicitud (f). 'To request', perhaps 'earnestly request', and nothing like so specialized as 'solicit'. It is quite usual in business correspondence: *Hemos solicitado una copia/un ejemplar*, 'We have requested a copy'. Equally *solicitud* mean 'request', 'application', 'petition': *presentar una solicitud*, 'to make an application'. 'Solicitude' is probably best handled by the adjective *solícito*: *Se mostró muy solícito por . . .*, 'He showed great solicitude for . . .'; though *solícito* is also useful for 'concerned', 'thoughtful', sometimes 'anxious'.

solo. Barely my business but do not forget that, when used as an adjective, it inflects: *Lo hizo solo*, 'He did it alone'; *lo hizo solita*, 'She did it all by herself'. As an adverb it remains unchanged (except for an accent) and means 'only': *Sólo me quedan dos cigarros*, 'I've only two cigarettes left'. (N.B. not 'the only' which is *único*.) In music it can be a noun, as in English; within the orchestra *solistas* means 'single desks'.

soltar. Another of the verbs which it is difficult to remember to use, though it is very common. It means 'let go (of)', 'release', sometimes 'to leave alone', and it may help some readers to appreciate that in origin it meant 'isolate'. If someone is holding something and you want them to let go of it then *¡Suéltelo!* is the word that should spring to your lips. A mother chiding her child might also say *¡Suéltalo!*, 'Put it down!', 'Leave it alone!' In Victorian melodramas the heroine was accustomed to say *¡Suélteme, canalla!* for 'Unhand me, villain!'

    Suelto, the past participle, has come to have a life of its own. As an adjective it means 'single', 'separate', 'isolated' from others of its kind. If you wanted to buy a single volume of a work in several volumes you would ask *¿Se venden sueltos?*, 'Do you sell them separately?' and *cigarros sueltos* means 'loose' cigarettes, i.e not sold in packets (though these are rarer in these days of affluence). In L/A they even extend it to liquids, e.g. olive oil, molasses, etc. (bring your own bottle), though the proper phrase for this is *a granel* (*q.v.*). 'Separate sheets' of paper, 'loose leaves', are *hojas sueltas*.

    Suelto is also much used as a noun meaning 'small change'. If you offer a 500 note on a bus the *cobrador* is quite likely to say *¿No tiene suelto?*, 'Don't you have anything smaller?'

    I once saw a child drop some of those minute 'sweets' known as 'hundreds and thousands' and her elder brother consolingly said to her *Tendrás que recogerlas sueltecitas*, 'You'll have to pick them up one by one'.

solvencia (f). Universally valid for financial 'solvency' but, in the R/P, journalists are fond of a very metaphorical use of it meaning 'ability', 'competence': *Un solista de gran solvencia*, 'A soloist of great brilliance', and *solvente* can there mean 'talented', 'gifted'. In Venezuela, on the other hand, *una solvencia* means 'an Income Tax clearance certificate'.

sonar(se). *Sonar*, as you know, is 'to sound', 'to ring', but is much used, as in English, for 'to ring a bell' in the figurative sense: *Eso* *me suena*, 'That rings a bell', i.e. 'that reminds me of something'; also to 'look like', 'sound like': *Eso me suena a trampa*, 'It sounds like a racket to me'. *Sonarse* seems a little disconcerting for 'to blow one's nose', but is really short for *sonarse las narices*, 'to sound the nostrils'.

soportar. Unreliable; the Spanish meaning is nearly always figurative, viz. 'to put up with', 'to endure', 'to bear': *No puedo soportar el sonido de su voz*, 'I can't stand the sound of his voice'. We are unlikely to say 'I can't support . . .'; this sounds like a foreigner speaking.

'To support' has a variety of translations: 'to support' a family, *mantener* or *sustentar*; 'to support' a roof, or 'to back (somebody) up', *apoyar (v.* also **aguantar**).

s.r.c. If you come across these initials on an invitation, etc. you should know that they stand for *Se Ruega Contestación*, 'Please reply'. You may say that they equate with 'R.S.V.P.' but they are a good deal less usual.

suave. 'Smooth, even', but it also has to do service for 'gentle': *una brisa suave*, 'a gentle breeze'; *colores suaves*, 'soft/delicate colours'. The equation will often be 'soft' but soft to touch is best handled by *blando*. There is no exact word for 'gentle' (though in the past *manso* might have served); 'He touched it gently' might be *Lo tocó tierna/ligera/delicadamente* according to context. 'He spoke to her gently' would probably be *Le habló suavemente* whereas 'He spoke to her softly' would be . . . *en voz baja*. 'Suave' is probably best handled by *zalamero* though this borders on 'flattering, cajoling'. *Afable, cortés* and *fino* are other possibilities but they would need a context to make the nuance apparent.

subir. False for those who know some French; it means 'to go/come up', not 'to undergo': *Está subiendo la escalera*, 'He's coming up the stairs'.

substraer. *v.* **sustraer.**

suburbio (m). False in its associations rather than its strict meaning; it does mean the regions on the outskirts of a city but in the Hispanic world such quarters tend to be very poor, often shanty towns, and if you say *Vivo en los suburbios de Londres* the average Hispanic might think you live in a slum. 'High-class suburbs' (a contradiction in terms for a Hispanic) have other names, one of the commonest being *colonia*, which applies in Madrid and Mexico City. Caracas uses *urbanización*. If you want a neutral word to refer to the 'outskirts' of a city use *afueras (v.* also **urbanización**).

It is perhaps suprising that, although shanty towns are a universal phenomenon in L/A, there is a different word for them in nearly every country, though *arrabales* is generally understood. I have therefore made a collection of them and some readers may care to benefit from it: *callampas* (Chile), *barriadas* (Peru), *villas miserias* (Argentina), *cantegriles* (Uruguay), *barracas, orillas* (Mexico), *morenales* (Honduras), *clandestinos, tugurios*

(Colombia), *ranchos* (Venezuela). Although outside the province of this book I feel inclined to add *favelas* for Brazil. I feel sure this does not exhaust the list.

sucedáneo. Two well-known dictionaries give 'succedaneous' for this. Does that leave the reader any further on? My first reaction was that the lexicographers did not know themselves (I have now some experience of the game) but perhaps this was unfair; not only has the word 'succedaneum' been known in English for some three centuries but we now mostly use a word which, according to the *Oxford Dictionary*, first appeared in 1919 and did not come into general use until the 1930's, viz. 'ersatz', 'substitute material', 'surrogate'. It can be used as a noun or an adjective: *un sucedáneo del café*, 'coffee substitute'.

suceder, suceso (m). Classic False Friends; *suceder* can mean 'to succeed' only in the sense that a king succeeds to a throne and its normal meaning is 'to happen': *¿Qué sucedió entonces?*, 'What happened then?' It does, however, contain the notion of a succession of events and the most usual way of saying 'What's happening?' is *¿Qué pasa?*

Un suceso is emphatically not 'a success'; nor 'a succession' to the throne, which is *sucesión*, it is simply 'event', 'incident', 'happening', and an alternative for the rather longer *acontecimiento*. *Fue un suceso extraordinario* means, not that it was a 'huge success', but an 'extraordinary occurrence'. 'Success' is *éxito* (*q.v.*), another False Friend.

sueldo (m). A fairly universal word for 'wages', 'salary', 'pay packet'.

suelo (m). 'Ground', but the reader should note that, inside the house, the 'floor' is regarded as the 'ground' so that its usual domestic meaning is 'floor': *Cayó al suelo*, 'It fell on the floor'. (It might, of course, be one of the fragments of *soler*, *q.v.*)

suelto. *v.* **soltar.**

suiche. *v.* **interruptor.**

sujetar, sujeto. Unreliable; we use 'subject' mostly in metaphorical senses; in Spanish *sujetar* is basically physical: 'to hold tight/firm/down, to fasten': *Sujetó la puerta*, 'He held the door (open)'; *Sujetó los papeles con un clip*, 'He fastened the papers with a clip'; *Sujétalo bien*, 'Hold it tight'. It is true that *sujetarse a* can be used for 'to subject oneself to' but 'to be bound by, to abide by, to submit to' are better equivalents and 'to subject' is better handled by *someter*.

The adjective *sujeto* is therefore 'tight, firm, fastened': *El nodo estaba bien sujeto*, 'The knot was firmly tied'. *Sujeto a*, however, equates fairly well with 'subject to, liable to'.

Sujeto as a noun borders on the False; only in grammar does it mean 'subject' (sometimes in medicine for an anonymous 'patient') and applied to a person it means 'individual, character', usually in a pejorative sense: *Es un sujeto algo raro*, 'He's rather an odd individual'. 'Subject' in the sense of 'topic' is *asunto*, and of 'citizen', *súbdito*: 'A British subject', *un súbdito británico*.

suma (f), **sumar**. *Suma* means 'sum' in the sense of 'total': *Una suma global*, 'a lump sum'; *suma y sigue* is the equation for 'carried forward' in accounts. Metaphorically it can be used for 'summary' but *resumen* or *sumario* are more normal for this. 'Sums' of the sort one had to do at school are *cálculos*. *Sumar*, therefore, is 'to add up': *¿Cuánto suma?*, 'How much does it come to?' (*v.* also **añadir**).

'Sumo' is an adjective meaning 'the greatest/highest/utmost'. The article is not required unless it refers to the highest in rank: *la suma autoridad*, 'the highest authority'; using it as a superlative one simply says: *con suma dificultad*, 'with the utmost difficulty'; *en sumo grado*, 'in the highest degree'; *con suma destreza*, 'with consummate skill' (*v.* also **realizar**).

suponer. Quite a Good Friend of 'to suppose' for everyday purposes: *Supongo que sí*, 'I suppose so', but it has a greater range and extends to 'presuppose, assume, take for granted, guess, imagine': *Ya puedes suponer lo que sucedió*, 'You can guess/imagine what happened then'; *Eso supone que él no estaba*, 'That implies that he wasn't there'; *Supondrá grandes gastos*, 'It will involve a lot of expense'.

supuesto. Past participle of *suponer* but the phrase *por supuesto* is extremely common, especially in L/A. You might imagine it to mean 'supposedly' or 'presumably' but in fact it means 'of course', 'naturally', and *¡Pero, por supuesto!* is a polite phrase for 'You're welcome!', 'Please do!' In Spain 'of course' is nearly always *desde luego* (*v.* COURTESY).

suspender. 'To suspend', certainly, but it has a particularized use in Spain which may be of importance to some readers; it means 'to fail (someone) in an examination': *Le han suspendido*, 'He's (been) failed'. In L/A they mostly use *reprobar*, literally 'to reprove', but similarly particularized (*v.* also **aprobar**).

susto (m). Not beyond the dictionary but a common word for 'fright', 'scare', a '(nasty) turn': *¡Qué susto me has dado!*, 'What a fright you gave me!', 'How you scared me!' *Dar un susto* is 'to give a shock'; when it is a matter of receiving one you use *llevarse un susto*. *Asustar*, 'to shock', also exists but is far less common colloquially.

sustraer. May be regarded as False; the Spanish is usually physical, i.e. 'to extract', and much associated with illicit extractions so that it usually means 'to pinch', 'to steal', 'to pick a pocket'. Perhaps you know a line of Shakespeare: 'The king was slily finger'd from the deck' (3 *Henry VI*, V, I, 44); *sustraído* would describe exactly what happened to that card. *Me han sustraído la cartera*, 'They've pinched my wallet'. For 'to subtract', *v.* **restar**.

T

tabla (f). Unreliable; it does not mean 'table' but 'board', 'plank', 'slab'. A rough trestle-table might be described as *una tabla* but 'board' should be understood. 'A tablet' of stone might be called *una tabla* if it were horizontal but if it were fixed vertically in a wall it would more likely be *una placa*. 'Table', as you know, is *mesa*.

tacana (f). A slang word for 'police', in the R/P.

taco (m). 'Heel', in Peru; elsewhere this is *tacón*. In Mexico it is a very common dish consisting of meat and/or vegetables rolled up in a *tortilla*, i.e. a maize pancake. It is a favourite snack and you can buy a single one and eat it with your fingers. In Spain *taco* means 'swearword': *¡No digas tacos!,* 'Don't swear !' There are various other uses, mostly revolving round the concept 'wad', in a rather rough sense.

tal. 'So', or 'such', as you know, but a very common word and used in many contexts where we should not use 'such': *El señor Tal* is one way of saying 'Mr. So-&-So', and an alternative to *Fulano (q.v.)*. *Tal, tal, tal* (often accompanied by a gesture) is a way of saying 'etcetera, etcetera', when hopping briefly over understood or unimportant details.

   ¿Qué tal? is a very common form of greeting between people who have met before and are on comparatively equal terms and is not necessarily as familiar as it might seem; it is used as much with *Vd.* as with *tu* and one may greet a fairly slight acquaintance with *¿Qué tal está Vd.?* A familiar friend would be greeted *¡Hola! ¿Qué tal?,* or, if it really is an enquiry, then *¿Qué tal estás? ¿Qué tal?* by itself barely requires an answer, it equates with 'Hello!' or 'Hi!' and is likely to get another *¡Qué tal!* in exchange.

   It is important to distinguish between *ser* and *estar* when using *¿Qué tal? ¿Qué tal está?* means 'How is he/she?', whereas *¿Qué tal es?* means 'What's he/she/it like?'

   ¿Qué tal si . . .? is a useful phrase for 'How about . . .?', 'Suppose we . . .?'

   Con tal que . . . is useful for 'so long as': *Con tal que nadie me vea,* 'So long as nobody sees me'.

tamal (m). A dish consisting of a hash of meat and maize/corn-flour wrapped in a leaf. In Colombia it is usually a banana leaf and comes as quite a parcel which you unwrap on your plate. In Mexico, where *tamales* are tremendously popular, it is the leaf of a corncob and many small shops exist solely to supply them hot for taking away. In Guatemala they are called *chuchos* or *chuchitos*, in the Z/A *humitas*, in Honduras *nacatamales,* in Venezuela *hallacas*.

tamaño (m). Normally a noun meaning 'size', as you no doubt know:

¿De qué tamaño?, 'How big?' Its origin is *'tan magno'*, 'so big', and in L/A it is often used adjectivally: *Hay tamaña casa en nuestro pueblo,* 'There's a building that big in our village'. In some countries it has come to mean 'huge', 'tremendous': *Nunca he visto toro tamaño,* 'I've never seen such an enormous bull'; *Un tamaño retrato del Presidente,* 'A colossal picture of the President; *No cometerá tamaña locura,* 'He won't do anything so stupid'.

tampoco. 'Neither', 'nor', 'not either', as you know, but you have to remember to say it for 'No' whenever there is a series of negatives: *¿Has visto a Lolita? No. ¿A Paquita? Tampoco.* 'Did you see Lolita? No. Paquita? No, I didn't see her either', and you continue to say *tampoco* for every succeeding 'No'. A person interrogated in a game of 'Twenty Questions' would find himself continually saying *tampoco.* Basically it means 'equally little' and you have to remember to use it the moment there is anything to be equally little to; *Yo tampoco,* 'Neither am/have/do, etc. I', 'Nor me'. Correspondingly *también* is used for affirmative replies and our equivalent in such cases is not 'Also' but 'That too' or, more often, simply 'Yes'.

tan. 'So', as you know, but in Mexico (possibly elsewhere) they use *¿Qué tan . . .* (adjective)*?* for questions which in English start with 'How . . .?': *¿Qué tan pronto?,* How soon?'; *¿Qué tan lejos?,* 'How far?'. It will not do for all of them; 'How long?' might be *¿Qué tan largo?* for physical length but if it meant 'How much time?' then the usual *¿Cuánto tiempo?* would be used.

tano. *v.* **gringo.**

tanto. Little to add to the dictionaries which usually cover this word fairly well but you should be aware of *tantos* for '-odd': *Ha durado unos cincuenta y tantos años,* 'It's been going on for fifty-odd years'. How would you translate 'the 1920's' into Spanish? Answer: *los veintitantos* or *los años veinte* (*v.* also **pico**). *Estar al tanto de lo que pasa* is a useful phrase for 'to know what's going on'. In the R/P they have a way of saying rather rhetorically *¡Tanto! ¡Tanto!* meaning 'There was a fearful lot of it!' but I suspect this is taken fairly directly from the Italian.

Tanto can also be a noun, usually meaning 'chip', or 'counter', in such games as poker. These are sometimes counted in fives and *cinco tantos* equals *un marreco. Tanto* can also mean a 'score' and in a foot-ball context is likely to mean 'goal', though *gól* is also used.

tapa (f), **tapón** (m), **taparse.** Words with a rather disconcerting variety of meanings but *tapa* revolves around the notion of 'lid' or 'cover' and *tapón* of 'plug' or 'stopper'. *Tapón* is fairly universal for the 'plug' of a wash-basin though in Mexico it is also a 'fuse', i.e. the porcelain plug within the fuse-box. *Tapa* will usually apply to a 'lid' of the 'cap' type and in Mexico is applied to the 'hub-cap' of a car (*v.* CARS).

In Spain *tapas* is a colloquial word for the little snacks served with drinks. A more official name is *aperitivos* (*q.v.*).

In Venezuela (and possibly elsewhere) *taparse* is used meaning 'to get blocked up'—more usually *atrancarse*—and it may be used for a car over-heating (through getting blocked up). Elsewhere *taparse* may mean 'to put on one's hat', i.e. 'to cover oneself'.

taquilla. *v.* **boleto.**

tarde (f). 'Afternoon' or 'evening', and one needs to appreciate how Hispanics subconsciously divide their day in their minds. *Mañana,* by and large, is the period between getting up and lunchtime but where they have their *comida* (*q.v.*) very late, *Buenos Días* will only apply up to noon; and they can often be astonishingly noon-conscious and greet you with *Buenas tardes* at 12.5 p.m. *Tarde* is roughly the period between noon/lunchtime and nightfall. *La noche* begins with the dark and is quite distinct from our 'evening' which is normally the time between finishing work and going to bed. For us 'Goodnight' is used only for departure; for a Hispanic it is a greeting as well, provided night has fallen by the time it is uttered. When you meet somebody after nightfall, therefore, you say *Buenas noches,* as well as again on leaving. *Buenas tardes* will only do for 'Good evening' if it is still daylight.

Apart from greetings and partings *de tarde* and *de noche* may serve to distinguish, say, the two 'houses' at the movies, even when it is dark for both your houses. A mental note is desirable where the adjective is concerned; the Spanish for 'to be late' is not *estar tarde* but *llegar tarde* (*v.* **llegar**).

tarea (f). 'Task', 'chore', 'drudgery'. Readers will not be surprised to learn that is also the universal word for a child's—or student's —'homework': *¿Has terminado tu tarea?*, 'Have you finished your homework?'

tarro (m). Basically a 'pot' or 'large jar' made of earthenware but it is one of the words that may be used rather indiscriminately for all kinds of containers, e.g. a 'waste-paper basket', a 'garbage can' or even, in Chile, for the 'can' of, say, preserved fruit.

tata (m). An Amerindian—I fancy Quechua—word for 'father', 'papa'. *El tata* may be used to refer to a 'priest'. When Amerindians hear the word *tatarabuelo* they probably understand it as meaning 'the father of a grandfather'.

templo (m). 'Temple', yes, but commonly used in L/A to refer to a Protestant 'church'.

tener. Very common and idiomatic in Spanish is the use of *tener* with a noun where we should use 'to be' with an adjective or adjectival phrase, e.g. *Tener un disgusto*, 'To be fed up'; '*tener un despiste*', 'to be all at sea'; *tener una borrachera*, 'to be drunk'. Such expressions can almost be coined at will and readers should be on the alert for them.

Tener que is the commonest way of expressing 'must'. *Tengo que irme*, 'I must go', in ordinary domestic circumstances. *Deber* is more likely to be used when it is a matter of one's duty: *Debo ir* rather suggests that you have a moral obligation to go, though it would be unwise to draw a hard and fast line between them. *Debo de ir* is rather stronger and equates with 'I (simply) must go'. *Hay que* implies general necessity, not attached to a particular person.

tentativo,-a. As an adjective, 'tentative' but *una tentativa* is the normal noun for 'an attempt': *hacer una tentativa*, 'to make an attempt, to have a try'.

término (m). Dictionaries usually give one a rather dismaying list of words for 'average', so it may be worth mentioning that *término medio* is the most likely in everyday conversation, with *por término medio* for 'on an/the average'. For the adjective, *mediano* is appropriate if you are being precise but we often use the word somewhat figuratively, e.g. It was an 'average' sort of day, and for this a native would probably say *normal, regular or corriente*. For an imprecise 'by and large' *a grosso modo* is indicated (*v*. **modo**). For 'to work out at', *v*. **otro**.

    Término is also used to indicate relative distances in connection with pictures, or the theatre: *primer término*, 'foreground'; *segundo término*, 'middle distance', and *tercer* or *último término*, 'background'. In the theatre *último término* is in effect 'upstage' but *en el fondo (de la escena)* is often used for this; *ir hacia el fondo*, 'to move upstage'.

tertulia (f). Dictionaries do not normally have space to explain the meaning this word. It is a 'social gathering', 'meeting of friends', yes, but usually in a café and centred round an outstanding figure, a writer, say, or artist who, as it were, holds court there while literature, philosophy, politics, etc. are discussed. It is not a purely Hispanic phenomenon but it is highly characteristic and perhaps arises from the fact that entertainment in the home is less customary. It is mostly in cafés that the 'debate', on which human society depends for sorting out its thoughts, chiefly continues.

tiempo (m). Not only 'time', but weather': *¿Qué tiempo hace?,* 'What's the weather like?' *Tiempo* is also used when discussing the ages of children who are too young for it to be assessed in years: *¿Qué tiempo tiene? Tiene tres meses*, 'How old is he? Three months'. When he is old enough to be measured in years then *¿Cuántos años tiene?*

    In music it may mean 'tempo', but also 'movement': *El segundo tiempo*, 'the second movement' (e.g. of a symphony), though in a context of games *el segundo tiempo* means 'the second half'.

tinto. Mentioned to remind you that it is the word for 'red' in connection with wine; it is all-too-easy to say *rojo* by mistake. In the Z/A it is also used for a 'black' coffee.

tío (m). Strictly 'uncle', but also a light-hearted word for 'chap', 'guy', 'fellow': *¿Qué tal es, el tío ese?,* 'What's he like, that guy?' It is a little patronizing, even for a man, and for a woman *una tía* can suggest the oldest profession. *¡Qué tío!* 'You're a fine one!'

típico. Not only 'typical', but in many contexts 'national' or 'regional': *Bailes típicos* means dances characteristic of the country or region where you happen to see them (*v.* also **lugareño).**

tipo(m). 'Type', yes, but also 'chap, guy, fellow': *Es un tipo bastante simpático*, 'He's quite a nice fellow'. For other words see **sujeto, tío.**

tirar(se), tiro (m). Very all-purpose, mainly revolving round the concept 'discharge'. The commonest everyday use of *tirar* is probably 'to throw away', but there is an important exception to this; in the Z/A the word has gone downhill (in the same direction as *coger* in the R/P) and should be avoided there; for 'to throw away' they mostly say *botar* (*v.* also **arrojar).** If shooting is regarded as an everyday matter then the reader should know that *tirar* also means 'to shoot' (to discharge a firearm) and *un tiro*, 'a shot'. *A tiro,* 'within range', or 'within reach', can be extended to 'at your disposal'; I saw it in the R/P written above a pile of brochures to which one was invited to help oneself, so the equation would be 'Please take one'. In Chile a very everyday expression is *al tiro*, 'like a shot', and equating with 'at once', 'right now'.

Tirarse is often used for 'to spend', in connection with time: *Me tiré tres horas haciéndolo*, 'I spent three hours doing it', 'It took me three hours to do' (*v.* also **llevar).**

The above is very far from exhausting the possibilities but may serve as a pointer to the kind of thing to expect. The concept often has to be extended into 'pull' and 'draw 'in which case it is followed by *de*: *Tiró de la cartera*, 'He pulled out his wallet'. 'Pull' on a door will often be *Tirad* (*v.* also **jalar).**

título (m). 'Title', yes, but commonly used of almost any document which in some way proves your title to something, cf. title-deeds, and the word tends to suggest a document to native ears. In Venezuela it is the usual word for a driving licence, but it can equally be applied to, say, a diploma or certificate.

tlapalería (f). The usual word in Mexico for 'hardware store/iron-monger', though they do also use the more universal *ferretería*.

tocar. Not only 'to touch' but also 'to play' a musical instrument: *¿Toca Vd. la guitarra?*, 'Do you play the guitar?' For these purposes a gramophone/phonograph counts as a musical instrument: *Están tocando unos discos*, 'They're playing some records'. *Un tocadiscos,* 'a record-player'. An electric bell also counts as a musical instrument: *tocar el timbre*, 'to ring the bell'.

Tocar a with a personal pronoun, though within most dictionaries, should certainly be added to your stock; it is the usual way of indicating turns, e.g. in a game: *¿A quién toca?*, 'Whose turn is it?', *Me toca a mí*, 'It's my turn' (*v.* also **turno).**

tomar. One of the verbs for our all-purpose 'take'; its main force is 'to take to oneself', so that it often applies to eating and drinking, particularly the latter. Given an appropriate context *¿Qué va a tomar?* is pretty universal for 'What'll you have?' (v. also **preferir**). In Chile and Mexico it is unlikely to mean anything else. Teetotallers, there, are described by saying *No toman*; what it is they don't take needs no definition. For other words for 'take', v. **llevar, sacar, coger, cobrar.**

tontería (f). A very common word. *Tonto*, as you know, means 'stupid', 'silly'; *una tontería*, literally 'a stupidity', equates with 'a silly thing to do/say': *¡Qué tontería!*, 'What a silly thing to say!', 'Isn't that stupid!; *Sería una tontería . . .* (Infinitive), 'It would be silly to'. The plural *tonterías* is the usual equivalent of 'nonsense', 'rubbish': *No digas tonterías*, 'Don't talk nonsense'.

tope (m). 'Protuberance', 'impediment', but if you do go to Mexico by car you should be warned of *los topes*—a row of very large 'studs' set across the road in order to make you slacken speed. It is a most drastic way of doing so since, if you do not know they are there —and they turn up in the most unexpected places unannounced— you may well be in for a broken spring.

tópico. It may be used in L/A to mean a 'topic' of conversation (thanks to Anglo-Saxon influence) but by and large it is better regarded as False since, as a noun, its primary meaning is 'catchphrase, cliché, platitude'. Its force is somewhat pejorative therefore. It has a secondary meaning of a subject of conversation which people can't let alone, are always 'on about', hence, no doubt, the L/A usage, but the proper word for 'topic' is *asunto* or *tema* (m).

   As an adjective it is chiefly used in medical contexts to mean 'local' in the sense of 'belonging to a particular part of the body': *para uso tópico*, 'for local (external) use', 'to be applied locally'. 'Topical' is *actual, de interés actual* or *sobre cuestiones del día* (v. **actual**).

tormenta (f). False; it does not mean 'torment' but 'storm', including a 'thunderstorm'. 'Torment' is *tormento* (m) or *suplicio*.

torta (f), **tortilla** (f). *Torta* has a variety of meanings, even within the field of food; in most of S/A it usually means some sort of sweet cake; in Mexico a 'sandwich' of the *bocadillo* (q.v.) type; in Spain a 'pancake'. *Tortilla* is equally diverse; in Spain it means an 'omelette'; in the R/P more precisely a 'Spanish omelette'—a fairly solid affair containing, inter alia, potatoes, and often eaten cold—and there an omelette is *un omelet*. In Mexico (and Guatemala) *una tortilla* means a 'maize pancake'—rather like a *chapati*—and an essential part of Mexican cuisine. If you want an 'omelette' in Mexico ask for *una torta de huevos*.

   Una tortillera is a vulgar, but widespread, expression for a 'lesbian'.

toxicómano. v. **adicto.**

trabajo (m). 'Work', as you know, but it can be used with the indefinite article and *un trabajo* means 'a job of work': *Tengo un trabajo que hacer*, 'I have a job to do'. 'A work', meaning a work of art, etc. would be *una obra* (*v.* also **papel**).

trago (m). By and large 'drink' but it really implies the amount drunk at one swallow, hence 'draught, pull, swig'; *echarse un trago*, 'to have a swig'; *¿Quieres un trago?*, 'Do you want a drop?' (usually of wine). In L/A it is used without the article as a generalized word for 'liquor, booze': *Bebimos mucho trago*, 'We drank a lot of liquor'; *aficionado al trago*, 'fond of the bottle'. The universal, all-purpose word for a 'drink' of any sort is *bebida*.

trámite (m). Mostly used in the plural and very common for 'business, procedure, formalities', in a not-too-precise sense: *Tengo que hacer todos los trámites para el viaje*, 'I have to make all the arrangements for the trip'. It could sometimes equate with 'red tape'.

trampa (f). A somewhat slangy word for, 'racket', 'wangle', 'fiddle', any piece of trickery. There is a saying *Hecha la ley, hecha la trampa* which might be translated 'There's your law and there's your racket', i.e. no sooner is any given law passed but someone will have discovered a means of making money by circumventing it. *Hacer trampa* is 'to cheat', e.g. at cards.

tránsito (m). 'Transit', yes, but in many parts of L/A it also means 'traffic', and in places is almost becoming identified with 'one-way' (*v.* **dirección**).

trasbocar. A word used—quite formally—for 'to vomit', in the Z/A. More universal is *vomitar* which will always be understood.

trascendencia, -ental. 'Transcendence, —ental' in the Kantian sense but the verb *trascender* can be used of physical things, e.g. smells, in the sense of 'permeate, penetrate' and is used figuratively for 'to leak out, become known, spread to, have a wide effect': *Procuraron que no trascendiera la noticia*, 'They contrived to prevent the news from leaking out'. *Trascendencia*, therefore, is 'wide effect', hence 'importance, consequence, far-reaching implications': *El discurso no tendrá mucha trascendencia*, 'The speech won't have much effect'. *Trascendental*, 'far-reaching, momentous, vital'.
It can be spelt *transcen-* but this has become unusual.

trasladar. Not to translate but 'to transfer': *Me han trasladado al departamento extranjero*, 'I've been transferred to the foreign department'. In much of S/A *trasladarse* is used for 'to move house', which in Spain is *mudarse* and in Mexico *traspasar*.

traspasar. Do not equate it with 'trespass'; it can be used metaphorically as 'to go beyond, to overstep the mark' but its main force is physical: 'to go (right) through': *La bala le traspasó el brazo*, 'The bullet went right through his arm' (and therefore came out the other side). It is used of liquids for 'soak through': *La* *humedad traspasa el techo*, 'The damp comes through the roof', as well as for 'to sell/transfer/convey' a going concern; if you saw a notice outside a shop reading *'Se traspasa por jubilación'* would you appreciate that the business was being sold owing to the proprietor's retirement? 'Trespass' in the legal sense is *intrusión, entrada ilegal* or *penetración en finca ajena;* 'Trespassers will be prosecuted', *Prohibida la entrada.* 'Forgive us our trespasses', *'Perdónanos nuestras deudas'*.

tratar. 'To treat', but *tratar de* has become the normal, and commonest, verb for 'to try (to)': *Trataba de entrar en la casa*, 'He was trying to get into the house'. It is more or less interchangeable with *intentar. Tratar con* is 'to deal in/with, to have dealings with': *No tratan con particulares*, 'They don't deal with private individuals'.

An indispensable phrase is *Se trata de*, 'It's a matter of', 'It's a question of', or simply 'It's about . . .'. When you arrive in somebody's office and have to explain your business you are likely to start *Se trata de . . .*, 'It's about . . .'.

tren (m). 'Train', but also 'tram/streetcar' in Mexico.

trillizo (m). *v.* **cuate.**

trocha. *v.* **pista.**

trozo. *v.* **pedazo.**

tú, tutear. No doubt many readers, noticing the numerous examples in this book couched in the Second Person Singular, will wonder whether they should learn to *tutear* and some indications of its use are therefore desirable.

Probably the only people visiting the Hispanic world who can manage without it will be tourists who, in these days, hardly need know any Spanish at all. If they are more conscientious and prefer to make some contact with the people they will almost certainly want to speak to children and to address small children as *Usted* sounds ridiculous.

Young readers who go to Hispanic countries, either as students or to work, should certainly master it. There is a kind of free-masonry of students the world over and it is quite usual for them to *tutear* from the very first word, certainly within a few days of first acquaintance. Much the same applies in offices, even for the not so young; there is the same sense of confraternity. Any situation, as it were between colleagues, is likely to call for the use of *tú*, though countries vary slightly in their practice when *tú* crosses the sex barrier. In Spain it is quite normal but when I first used it to a female colleague in Uruguay a few eyelids were fluttered. On the other hand a business man who has got to know his secretary well is quite likely to call her *tú* though he might hesitate to do so from the start in case he should seem to be treating her like a servant.

The use of *tú* is not necessarily two-way; youth and age can affect the situation. I frequently got to know students and the like well enough to call them *tú* but they always—and I think unconsciously—called me *Vd.* without in the least feeling that I was talking down to them. Certainly between young people of the same sex to *tutear* is virtually a 'must' and to reply with *Vd.* can sound cold and unfriendly even when they make allowance for your ignorance.

Visitors to Spain will have the additional complication of *vosotros* (*q.v.*) and, to the R/P, of *vos* (*q.v.*).

tugurios. *v.* **suburbios.**

turno (m). Almost a Good Friend since in many contexts it equates well enough with 'turn', but it implies a roster or schedule so that *Estoy de turno* means 'I'm on duty'. In such circumstances we might say 'It's my turn', but the roster pattern in the background is essential; other possibilities are 'watch', 'shift', 'stint of duty': *El turno de noche,* 'the night shift'. For 'turn' in a context of games, *v.* **tocar.**

You are likely to come across it in connection with drug-stores since those in each quarter of a city whose duty it is to remain open all night will usually have an illuminated sign saying *TURNO*, sometimes *GUARDIA*; others, though closed, will indicate whose 'turn' it is and give the address. They may sometimes look rather shut but may be roused by pressing a bell—provided the sign is lit up. After some delay a little speak-easy window opens up and a face asks you what you want and it is a great advantage, at this point, to know exactly what you do want by its local trade-name. People roused from their slumbers in the small hours are not always at their most helpful.

U

ubicar(se). The commonest form of this verb is probably *ubicado* meaning 'situated', and *ubicación,* 'situation', is a useful word for 'whereabouts', in connection with things immobile (for the 'whereabouts' of persons, *v.* **parada**). In L/A they often extend its meaning so that *ubicar* may mean 'to find out the whereabouts': *He conseguido ubicar la calle Valdivia,* 'I've succeeded in tracking down Valdivia Street'. *Ubicarse* may be similarly used for 'to find one's way about', though in the R/P it will more probably mean 'to take up one's abode', 'to settle in'.

ultimado. Means 'finished', 'wound up', but L/A journalists are rather fond of it as a high-falutin word for 'killed': *Seis personas ultimadas,* 'Six people killed'.

ultramarinos. *v.* **abarrotes.**

único, -a. 'Unique', certainly, but in English we rarely use this word with the definite article whereas in Spanish *el único* is the normal way of saying 'the only': *Será la única oportunidad*, 'It'll be the only chance'. 'Sole' is another possibility: *el único superviviente*, 'the sole survivor'. 'One-way' is *(de) dirección única* or *(de) sentido único*.

urbanización (f). The general word for 'urbanization', but it will often mean a modern 'housing estate', and tends to be associated with the better sort of housing so that it is often the word for a respectable 'quarter' of a city. In Spain a quarter, in this sense, is *un barrio*, but in L/A *barrio* suggests a poor quarter (*v.* **suburbios**). 'Town-' or 'city-planning' is *urbanismo* (*v.* also **colonia**).

usar. 'To use', yes, and it will often be figurative exactly as in English: *Nunca usaba* (or *acostumbraba*) *hacerlo como joven*, 'I never used to do it when I was young'; Spanish, however, employs it quite consistently, in the Present tense as well: *No uso tomar té o café*, 'I don't (usually) drink tea or coffee' (*v.* also **soler**). 'To wear' is another meaning but it rather implies 'to be in the habit of wearing': *Siempre usaba una falda negra*, 'She always wore a black skirt'; if she was wearing one on a particular occasion then *llevaba una falda negra* is more likely. *Usado*, again quite consistently, is the adjective for 'worn' in the sense of 'worn out': *muy usado*, 'very worn', but be alert about such phrases as 'Skirts are worn'; if your meaning implies 'very long this year' or something of the sort, then *Las faldas se usan . . .*, not *están usadas*.

V

v. Called *uve* in Spain; *bé corta* in the R/P and *bé chica* elsewhere.

vacilar. 'To waver', 'hesitate', 'stagger', certainly, but I heard it used intransitively in Mexico for 'to tease', 'to pull someone's leg'. If the context were light-hearted enough it could be used for 'to equivocate'.

vago. Unreliable; it means 'vague', when applied to things: *fue una respuesta muy vaga*, 'it was a very vague reply', but applied to persons it means 'lazy', 'good-for-nothing'. *Un vago*, 'a layabout', 'a loafer', even 'a tramp', 'a bum'. Care should therefore be taken about such sentences as 'He was very vague in his reply'.

vale (m). 'Promissory note' is certainly a correct definition but *vale* is universally an everyday word and applies to any little slip of paper marked, or scrawled, with some amount owed, hence 'I.O.U.', 'chit', 'bill/check', etc. In many parts of L/A you do not pay a waiter or shop assistant direct but receive from them *un vale* which you then pay at the cash desk. In the Caribbean region it may be used figuratively for 'chum', 'pal', 'buddy' (*v.* also **valer**).

valer. 'To be worth', 'to be as good as', and often 'to be O.K.'. It is such a common verb and its uses often so idiomatic that I reiterate some of the expressions given in the better dictionaries as they are worth learning by heart: *¿Cuánto vale?*, 'How much?; *No vale la pena*, 'It's not worth it/the trouble'; *lo mismo vale para . . .*, 'the same goes for . . .'; *¿Vale ésto?*, 'Will this (one) do?'; *Si, vale*, 'Yes, that'll be O.K. *¡Vale!* by itself, is the word for 'O.K.', 'That's right', 'That's correct', even for 'Good enough!' A man, having counted his change and found it correct, will say *Vale*; or choosing, say, a screw out of a mass of them and finding one that will fit, he will say *Ésto me vale*, 'This'll do me', 'This'll fit'; or when a crane is lowering some object which the crane-driver cannot see and a second man is calling out instructions, then the latter will call out *Más . . . más aún . . .* and finally *¡Vale!* whereupon the crane-driver stops. Its use is not confined to the 3rd Person: *¿No valgo yo un poco de consideración?*, 'Don't *I* deserve a little consideration?'

No vale is used in games as an equivalent of 'No ball' or, in tennis, 'Out'. In games which do not allow for this type of 'no ball', however, e.g. in most games of cards, *No vale* or *Esto no vale* might almost amount to accusing somebody of cheating though in other circumstances it could simply mean 'it doesn't count'. *No valen*, 'They don't have to be taken into consideration'.

Más vale often equates with '(is) better': *Más vale tarde que nunca*, 'Better late than never'. Even when the equation is 'worth', e.g. *Más vale pájaro en mano que ciento volando*, 'A bird in the hand is worth two in the bush', note that the phrase *starts* with *Más vale* when it is matter of stating a general principle.

vario(s). Nearly always used in the plural. It seems to mean 'various', but borders on the False as it really means 'several', and the differences are not always apparent though sometimes real: *Hay varias maneras de hacerlo* equates well enough with 'There are several/various ways of doing it', but if you wanted to say 'The ways of doing it are very various', you would say *muy diversas, distintas* or *diferentes*. One cannot add *muy* to *varios*, any more than one can add 'very' to 'several'.

vaso (m). There are points of Falsity here, for the unwary. In the first place it does not mean 'vase', which is *florero* or *jarrón* (the latter if it is not for flowers). One learns early on that it means 'glass', 'tumbler', and has no difficulty in asking for *un vaso de agua* but if you were asking for 'a glass of wine' would you remember to say *una copa de vino*? (*v.* **copa**). In Peru it can also mean 'hub cap'.

Vaso de noche—'chamber-pot' though *orinal* is more usual.

velatorio (m). One must needs call this pre-funeral ceremony a 'wake'. Though less wild and incantatory than the occasions one associates with Ireland (perhaps thanks to Synge), they are nevertheless grim enough, unless you like that sort of thing. For twenty-four hours after death the corpse is displayed in its coffin and it is a strong social obligation, at all class levels, to visit the bereaved, probably survey the deceased, and utter words of praise for the latter and condolence to the former. Not only relatives, but friends and even acquaintances, if they happen to be in the vicinity, *tienen que cumplir* (*v.* **cumplir**, also **ardiente**).

If you find yourself thus obligated you may be glad to have at your tongue's tip the phrase *Le acompaño en el sentimiento* as the appropriate thing to say to the bereaved. In the matter of written condolence you should be conscious of the noun *pésame* (literally 'it weighs on me') meaning 'expression of sympathy'; the formula *mi más sentido pésame* may prove useful.

vencer. 'To defeat', yes, but also 'to expire' of time; you may hit it on a parking meter: *Tiempo vencido*, 'Time expired'. I put on record a notice put up by the Town Clerk in San Miguel de Allende (Mexico) concerning some houses about to be demolished and requiring those claiming compensation to apply by a certain date '. . . *ya que, vencido este plazo, no habrá lugar a reclamación alguna*'. In L/A *vencer* is used for 'to win', in a sports context. Its basic meaning is 'to conquer'. More usual for this is *ganar*.

venir. 'To come', of course, and fairly Reliable by and large. It is worth being aware, however, of *venir bien*, 'to be convenient, suitable': *Eso me viene bien*, 'That suits me nicely'; also its counterpart *venir mal*: *Me viene mal ir a tu casa esta tarde*, 'It's not convenient to come and see you this evening'. Both are used of clothes etc. that '(don't) suit' (*v.* also **convenir**).

'Comes to', in the sense of 'amounts to, works out at' is usually *viene a ser*: *Viene a ser lo mismo*, 'It comes to the same thing' (*sale lo mismo* is also possible, *v.* **salir**); *Viene a ser más difícil que habíamos pensado*, 'It's turning out more difficult than we thought'.

ver. 'To see', of course; I draw attention to a few phrases which should certainly be in your stock:

No *tener nada que ver con*, 'to have nothing to do with'; *Pues ¿qué tiene que ver con migo?*, 'Well, what's it (got) to do with me?' It is all too easy to say *hacer con*, or rather to have said it before you remember.

A ver, 'Let's see', 'Let's have a look', 'Show me'. More politely *¿Se puede ver? A ver* is not impolite but it is familiar and direct. *A ver si* . . . , 'Let's see if . . .', is a useful way of conveying 'I wouldn't be surprised if . . .', or even 'I'll bet (he, etc) . . .', 'Just like him/life to . . .'.

Vamos a ver, though not necessarily colloquial, is tremendously common, equating with 'We shall see', 'Let's see', 'Let's go and have a look', 'Time will show', 'We shall find out in due course', etc.

The past participle, *visto*, has a certain life of its own, e.g. *bien visto*, 'the O.K. thing', 'the done thing', sometimes 'popular'; *mal visto*, 'not done', 'unpopular': *Eso sería bastante mal visto*, 'That wouldn't go down at all well'. *Por lo visto*, 'by the look of things' is a common and idiomatic equivalent for 'apparently', 'I suppose so', and is a way of handling our 'to look as if': *Por lo visto no va a venir*, 'It looks as though he isn't coming'. (*Al parecer* is another possibility.)

verdad (f). 'Truth', and often used as a positive affirmation, much as in English: *Es (la) verdad*, 'That's true'. Used interrogatively it is an all-purpose, 'Isn't that so?', i.e. a tail question that can be tacked on to the end of any statement like the French *n'est-ce pas?* and where we use such a horrifying variety of permutations and combinations: 'don't we?', 'haven't they?', 'can she?', 'isn't it?', etc. *¿Verdad?* covers the lot (*v.* also **así**).

verga (f). I include it with diffidence but if you go to Mexico you are almost sure to hear it, especially the phrase *Me vale verga*, 'I don't give a damn', and should perhaps be warned that it is the vulgar word for the male organ. For once it is not a euphemism; it has borne this meaning for several millennia (the Latin was *virga*) but I do not recall hearing it used anywhere except Mexico and C/A.

vergüenza (f). 'Shame', but beware of thinking that *¡Qué vergüenza!* means 'What a shame!' since this, in English, has come to mean 'What a pity' (*¡Qué lástima!*); *¡Qué vergüenza!* means 'What a scandal!', 'Isn't it outrageous!', 'How disgraceful!', etc. *Un sinvergüenza* means 'a shameless person', 'scoundrel', and is a fairly strong word, not to be lightly used to anyone's face, or rather only lightly—i.e. playfully, not seriously.

verificar. Unreliable; it might sometimes equate with 'verify' but this is usually better handled by *cerciorarse* or *confirmar* or, if it is a matter of putting something to the test, then *comprobar*. *Verificar* means literally 'to make true', hence 'to carry out', 'to perform'; *Harán falta tres semanas para verificar este trabajo*, 'It will take three weeks to do this job'. In a laboratory context: *Verifíquese la siguiente prueba*, 'Carry out the following test/experiment' (*v.* also **realizar**). *Verificar* suggests physical action and a tangible end-product.

vermouth (m) (pronounced *vermú*). Usually it means simply the drink but in much of L/A it has become identified with the cocktail hour. In cinemas, for example, you will see *Matinée 4h.*; *Vermouth 7h.*; *Noche 10h.* to indicate the times of the three programmes. In this context it is usually feminine.

vez (f). As you know, it means a 'time', a 'go': *la primera vez*, 'the first time'; *a la tercera vez*, 'at the third go'. It is much used for handling 'often', which is *muchas veces*, with its counterparts *pocas veces*,

'seldom', and *algunas veces* or *a veces*, 'sometimes' (*v.* also
frecuencia). *De vez en cuando*, 'from time to time'. *En vez
de*—'instead of'. *Alguna vez* is often the equivalent of our 'ever':
¿Has visto alguna vez . . .? 'Have you ever seen . . .?'

It is also worth being conscious of *cada vez más*, 'more and
more': *cada vez más lento*, 'slower and slower', as it offers a way
of handling 'increasingly': *Se puso cada vez más evidente que
. . .,'* It became increasingly clear that . . .' It has a counterpart in
cada vez menos, 'less and less', 'decreasingly'. There are also *cada
vez mejor/peor*, 'better and better/worse and worse'. *Cada vez
que* is one way of handling 'whenever' (*v.* **cualquier**). You will
already be aware of *tal vez*, probably the commonest form of
'perhaps'. Much less common is *toda vez que*, 'since', 'as', an
alternative to *ya que*.

villa miseria. *v.* **suburbio.**

violento. Unreliable; applied to persons it is likely to mean 'violent',
but it can be applied also to situations and then means 'awkward':
Fue un momento un poco violento, 'It was rather an awkward
moment'. Similarly, used with *ser* it will mean violent: *Fue un
hombre muy violento*, 'He was a very violent man', but used with
sentirse will mean 'embarrassed'; *sentirse violento* is almost interchangeable with *sentirse confuso* for 'to feel embarrassed' (*v.* also
embarazada).

vistar. A verb coined out of *vista* and used in L/A for 'to have a (good)
look at', 'to look over', 'look around'. The equivalent in Spain is
echar un vistazo which is also a little slangy.

vivo. 'Alive', 'lively', 'smart', 'quick', but much will depend on the
whether *ser* or *estar* is used: *Está vivo* means 'He/it is alive', while
es vivo (or sometimes *es un vivo*) means 'He's a pretty smart guy',
'a pretty wily bird'.

volante (m). As an adjective 'flying', but as a noun may mean either a
'steering wheel' or a 'fly-wheel'. In an office context it will mean
some document, usually on a single sheet of paper.

voluble. False; applied to things, e.g. prices, it means 'easily moved
about' and to people 'changeable'; *un tipo muy voluble* means a
chap who's always changing his mind and is not very sure of
himself, 'vacillating'. Spanish possibilities for 'voluble' are
locuaz, *hablador* or *facundo*.

volver. A verb with a vast array of uses, most of which the reader is
bound to have studied. I therefore confine myself to a few
comments.

For the sense of 'to go back', 'to return', *volver* is usual in Spain
but in L/A it is usually *regresar*. Its basic meaning, however, is
'turn' and, used transitively, it will mean this: *Vuélvalo*, 'Turn it
over'. If it is something which can revolve, and where we should
say 'Turn it round', then *dar vueltas*, or *dar una vuelta* are needed
(*v.* also **preguntarse**). In a car context the phrase for 'to turn

round' is *dar la vuelta*: *Tenemos que dar la vuelta y volver/ regresar*, 'We'll have to turn round and go back again'.

Volverse is a somewhat colloquial expression for to 'turn' in the intransitive sense. *Me estoy volviendo loco*, 'I'm going (turning) crazy'.

Vuelto, -a has an even more active life as a noun than most Past Participles; in addition to the basic 'turn' mentioned above it is the usual word for the 'other side' of some two-sided object: *Pon la vuelta*, 'Put the other side on' (e.g. of a record); *A ver la vuelta*, 'Let's see the other side' (of a piece of paper, cloth, etc.). In Spain it is also the 'return' half of a journey and *Ida y vuelta* (in L/A *Ida y regreso*) is the phrase for 'round trip/return ticket'. *Lo haré a la vuelta*, 'I'll do it when I get back'. *De vuelta* is accordingly the adjectival phrase for 'back': *¡Está ya de vuelta/regreso!*, 'Are you back already!'

By no means least, *vuelta* (L/A *vuelto*—perhaps because their units of currency are usually masculine, e.g. *peso*) means 'change', i.e. money back: *Estoy esperando la vuelta/el vuelto*, 'I'm waiting for my change'.

vos. In Argentina, Uruguay and vestigially in Costa Rica there is this curious survival of more honorific times, a mode of address which was, so to speak, 'holier than thou' (still is if you are addressing, say, the Pope), and the Second Person counterpart of the royal 'we' but which, like *tú*, becomes even more intimate when turned to more personal purposes. It is less a survival than an adaptation; it is cognate with the French *vous* and Italian *voi*—indeed with old English 'ye'—but in modern times is entirely Singular. It does not (now) have an Objective/Accusative case; *te* is used instead and *tuyo* instead of *vuestro*.

The form of the verb is usually the Second Person Singular accented on the second syllable, e.g. *tú sabes* becomes *vos sabés*, *tú quieres*—*vos querés* (when there is no accent the *i* is of course dropped; likewise *tú puedes* becomes *vos podés*), *tienes*—*tenés*, *varías*—*variás*. It is simplest to regard it as being formed from the Infinitive, changing the final *r* to *s*: *venir*—*venís*, *estar*—*estás*, *leer*—*leés*, etc. By this mode of reckoning the only Irregular ones are:

  ser—*sos*
  ir—*vas*
  creer—*cres*

For other tenses than the Present the ordinary *tú* forms are used.

Almost part and parcel of the use of *vos* is the exclamation *¡Che!*, untranslatable, but something like: 'Hey!' or 'Say!' *¡Che vos! ¿Qué decís?* has perforce to be rendered 'Hey you! What news?', but is not really as cheeky though the whole form is extremely personal. It is also extremely *criollo*, especially in Buenos Aires; even across the river in Montevideo *tú* tends to be commoner though *vos* is common enough. Some of the local purists disapprove of it and have even tried to get it officially abolished but when were such efforts ever successful? ('Che'

Guevara earned this nickname because he was an Argentinian and no doubt unconsciously used *¡Che!* in his conversation.)

vosotros. You will only need this in Spain since throughout L/A a plural 'you' (you-all) is always *Ustedes*, even between children or intimate scoundrels. In Spain, on the other hand, other people become *vosotros* the moment they are in company with somebody they know on *tú* terms, even if they are complete strangers, and since Spaniards get on *tú* terms fairly quickly you should certainly learn it up if you expect to spend any time there. Students will undoubtedly need it: *¿Sois todos de la misma Facultad?*, 'Are you all from the same Faculty?', *¿Qué vais a tomar?*, 'What are you-all drinking?'; *Tan pronto como estéis listos*, 'As soon as you're all ready'.

It is not difficult to acquire. For nearly all Present tenses you change the final *r* of the Infinitive to *is*: *poder—podéis*; *estar —estáis*, etc.; verbs in *ir* become *is*: *venir—venís*, etc. Exceptions are: *ser—sois* and *ir—vais*. For most of the other tenses it is a matter of inserting *i* into the Second Person Singular: *llamabas —llamabais*; *querías—queríais*; *compres—compréis*, etc. Exceptions to this are the Future, where *-ás* changes to *-éis* and the Past Perfect/Aorist/Preterite, in which *-aste* or *-iste* change to *-asteis* or *-isteis*.

vuelto, -a. *v.* **volver.**

vulgar. Borders on the False since it means 'popular', in the sense of belonging to the people, rather than vulgar, e.g. *Canciones Vulgares*, 'Popular Songs', a title that might be most misleading if you were not warned. Tone of voice may suggests 'commonness' but not indecency. *Vulgarización* is definitely False since it means 'popularization', and suggests such things as Adult Education rather than dragging down the level of the refined. 'Vulgar' is probably best handled by *ordinario* or *soez* or, if it means 'indecent', then *indecente*.

W

w. Called *uve doble* in Spain, *vé doble* in S/A and *doble u* in Mexico.

Y

y. For sentences beginning with *Y* and ending with *¿Que?*, *v.* **que.**

ya. One of the commonest words in the language and extending some distance beyond the 'already' and 'now' given by the dictionary. Quite often our equation would be simply 'Yes', e.g. when somebody is explaining something and his hearer gives an occasional *Ya . . . ya . . .* to show he follows or agrees. Equally if he suddenly tumbles to it he will come out with *¡Ah, Ya!*, 'I see!', 'Yes, of course!', 'I get it!' A person answering an impatient ringing at the bell will mutter *¡Ya! ¡Ya!* as he walks towards the door.

Ya is also much used in conjunction with various verbal phrases to indicate something approaching obviousness or well-knownness: *Ya lo sabes* or *Como ya sabes*, 'As you know', 'You know very well', etc. A stock exclamation is *¡Ya lo creo!*, 'I'll say!', 'I can well believe it!', 'You bet!', 'I certainly do/have/must', etc. *Ya veo que vamos a tener problemas*, 'I can see we're going to have trouble'. You might be tempted to say *Puedo ver* but a Hispanic would almost instinctively say *Ya veo*. How would you translate 'Well, that's something!'? Answer: *Pues, ¡ya es algo!* It is one of the particles put in where we get by with a heavy stress (*v.* Miscellaneous Notes, p. 20).

A common equation is 'now', especially when there is a sense of overdueness: *Ya me voy*, 'I'm off now'; *Ya es hora*, 'It's high time'; *Ya viene*, 'Here he comes!', 'He's coming now'. There is a Christmas carol which runs *Pastores venid, Pastores llegad, A adorar al niño que ha nacido ya* and a fitting translation (which also fits the tune) would be '. . . who is born today', another aspect of 'now'. In a negative sentence *ya no* has the force of 'no longer': *Ya no viene*, 'He doesn't come now/any more'. *Ya que* is the commonest way of expressing 'as', 'since', 'now that': *Ya que está terminado*, 'Now that it's over', 'Since it's finished' (*v.* also **vez**).

No dictionary could teach you all these uses, nor is it really necessary. Once you acquire the sense of immediacy or obviousness you should have no great difficulty in slipping it in.

yapa. *v.* **ñapa.**

yesquero (m). Formerly 'tinder-box', but commonly used in S/A for 'cigarette-lighter', usually called *un encendedor*, or in Spain, *mechero*.

yuca (f). 'Manioc' or 'cassava' and a popular vegetable in the tropical countries. It has no connection with 'yucca', the State flower of New Mexico.

Z

zócalo (m). Dictionaries give you 'socle'. Does any reader know what that is? Yes, a 'pedestal' or 'plinth', e.g. of a statue, but in everyday circumstances in Spain it means 'skirting board', 'base board' . . . in Mexico the 'central square', of a town or village, presumably because such squares so often have a statue in the middle. In the Z/A they call this the *Plaza de Armas*, in most other countries *Plaza Central* or *Plaza Mayor*, in Venezuela usually *Plaza Bolívar* and in Guatemala *el Parque*.

zorros (m. pl.). A bunch of rags tied to a stick (hence the plural form) and used for dusting. The technique is to flap around with it so as to remove the more obvious evidences of dust. In S/A *los zorros* are sometimes dignified with the name of *plumero* which is really a 'feather-duster', and maids will sometimes beat around the walls with it at an early hour of the morning in a manner calculated to banish sleep for all occupants of the house.

Special Vocabularies

Note: Words marked with an asterisk appear in the main Spanish-English text and should be consulted there for a fuller explanation.

Cars

English–Spanish

accelerator, acelerador (m)
accident, choque (m)*
axle, eje (m), flecha (f) (*Me*)
axle-shaft, palier (m), semi-eje (m) (*Pe*), punta de eje (f) (*Ve*), ejemando (m) (*Co*)

baggage-grid, baca (f), porta-equipajes (m), parrilla (f)
ball-bearings, rodamiento (m), rodillo (m), balero (m) (*Me*), balinera (f) (*Co*)
battery, batería (f)
bill/invoice, factura (f)
blinkers, intermitente (m), luz vuelta (f) (*Me*)
bolt, perno (m) (nut, tuerca (f))
bonnet, capó(t) (m), cofre (m) (*Me*)
boot, maleta (f), cajuela (f) (*Me*), baúl (m), maletera (f) (*Pe*)
brake, freno (m) (to brake, frenar) (see entry on echar)
breakdown, avería (f) (*Sp*), descompostura (f) (*Me*), pana/e (f or m) (*S/A*), accidente (m) (*Ve*)
brush (dynamo), cepillo (m)
bulb, bombilla/-o (f or m), foco (m) (*Me*)

bumper, parachoques (m), paragolpes (m), defensa (f) (*Me*)

camshaft, árbol de levas (m)
car, coche (m), auto (m), carro (m) (*L/A*)
carburettor, carburador (m)
chain, cadena (f)
choke, aire (m) (*Sp*), ahogador (m) (*Me*), chok(é) (m) (*Z/A*), cebador (m) (*R/P*)
clutch, embrague (m), cloche (m) (*L/A*)
coil, bobina (f)
condenser, condensador (m)
connecting rod, biela (f)
contact points, platinos (m. pl.)
crankcase, cárter (m)
crankshaft, cigüeñal (m)
crash, to, tener un choque*, estrellarse*
cylinder block, bloque (m), monobloc (m) (*Me*)

dashboard/panel, panel (m), tablero (m)
dashbox/pocket, guantera (f), cajuelita (f) (*Me*)

231

diesel truck, camión de diesel (m), camión de petróleo (m) (*Z/A*), camión de gasoil (m) (*Ve*)
differential, diferencial (m)
dip (lights), to, bajar
dipstick, varilla (f), cala (f)
direction indicator, intermitente (m), luz vuelta (f) (*Me*)
distributor, delco (m), distribuidor (m)
drive, to, conducir, manejar (*L/A*)
driving licence, licencia (f), título (m) (*Ve*), brevete (m) (*Z/A*), carnet (m), libreta (f) (*R/P*), permiso (m) (*Sp*)

engine, motor (m)
exhaust, escape (m), exosto (m) (*L/A*)

fan, ventilador (m)
fanbelt, correa (f), polea (f), faja (f) (*Pe*), banda (f) (*Me*)
fender, aleta (f), salpicadera (f) (*Me*), guardafango (m)
filter, filtro (m)
flat, pinchazo (m) (*Sp*), llanta baja (f),ponchadura (f) (*L/A*)
flywheel, volante (m)*
footbrake, freno de pie (m)

garage, garaje (m)
garage (private), cochera (f) (*Me*)
'gas', gasolina (f), nafta (f) (*R/P*), bencina (f) (*Ch*)
gas-tank, depósito (f), tanque (m) (*L/A*)
gasket, empaque (m)
gear box, caja de velocidades/cambios (f)
gear (shift) lever, palanca (f)
gearing, engranaje (m)
gears, cambios (m. pl.), velocidades (f. pl.)
glove compartment, guantera (f), cajuelita (f) (*Me*)
grease, grasa (f) (**to grease,** grasar)
greasing, engrase (m), lubricación (f)

hammer, martillo (m)
handbrake, freno de mano (m)
headlight, luz (f), faro (m) (*Sp*), linterna (f) (*Co*)
hood, capó(t) (m), cofre (m) (*Me*)
horn, bocina (f), claxón (m) (*Me*), pito (m) (*Co*), corneta (f) (*Ve*)
horse-power, (potencia (f) en) caballos (m. pl.)
hub-cap, tapón (de rueda) (m), taza (f) (*R/P*), vaso (m) (*Pe*), copa (f) (*Co*)

ignition (key), llave (f), suiche (m) (*L/A*)
inner-tube, cámara (f), tripa (f) (*Ve*), manguera (f) (*Co*)
instrument panel, panel (m), tablero (m), salpicadero (m) (*Sp*)

jack, gato (m), gata (f) (*Pe*)

key, llave (f), suiche (m) (*Ve*)

lever, palanca (f)
licence-plate, matrícula (f), placa (f), chapa (f) (*R/P*)*
lubrication, engrase (m)
luggage-grid, baca (f), parrilla (f), portaequipajes (m)

milometer, cuentakilómetros (m), odómetro (m) (*Me*)
motorcycle, motocicleta (f)

neutral, punto muerto, neutro (*Ve*), neutral (m) (*Me*)
number-plate, matrícula (f), placa (f)
nut, tuerca (f) (**bolt** = perno (m))

odometer, cuentakilómetros (m), odómetro (m) (*Me*)
oil, aceite (m)
oil-seal, retén (m), estopero (m) (*Me*)
overhaul(ing), ajuste (m) (*Me*), recorrido (m), revision (f) (*Sp*)
over-rider, uña (f), tacho (m) (*Pe*)

overtake, to, adelantar, rebasar (*Me*), sobrepasar

park, to, estacionar, aparcar, atracar (*P/R*), cuadrar (*Z/A*)
parking-light, piloto (m), mica (f) (*Ve*), cocuyo (m) (*Co*)
petrol, gasolina (f), nafta (f) (*R/P*), bencina (f) (*Ch*)
petrol tank, depósito (m), tanque (m) (*L/A*)
piston ring, segmento (m) (*Sp*), aro (m) (*R/P*), anillo (m) (*Z/A*, *Me*)
pulley-wheel, polea (f)
pump, bomba (f)
pump, to, hinchar, inflar, bombear, dar aire (*Sp*)
puncture, pinchazo (m) (*Sp*), llanta baja (f), ponchadura (f) (*Me*)

radiator, radiador (m)
rear light, piloto (m), calavera (f) (*Me*), cocuyo (m) (*Ve*)
repairs, reparaciones (f. pl.), composturas (f. pl.) (*Me*)
re-treading, recauchado (m), reencauche (m) (*Z/A*), recauchutaje (m) (*R/P*), vulcanización (f)
reverse, marcha atrás (f) (*Sp*), reversa (f) (*Me*), retroceso (m) (*Ve*), reverso (m) (*Co*)
roofrack, baca (f), parrilla (f), portamaleta (m), portaequipajes (m)
run over (someone), to, arrollar, atropellar
running in, en rodaje

screw, tornillo (m)
screwdriver, destornillador (m) (*Sp*), desarmador (m) (*L/A*)
seat, asiento (m)
self-starter, (puesta en) marcha (f), arranque (m)
'service', engrase general (m), servicio (m)
shock-absorber, amortiguador (m)

sidelight, luz de estacionamiento (f), mica (f) (*Ve*), cocuyo (m) (*Co*)
silencer, silenciador (m), mofle (m) (*Me*)
skid, patinazo (m), patina (f)
skid, to, patinar(se)
spanner, llave (f), española (f) (*Me*)
spare, de repuesto, de auxilio
spare parts, repuestos (m. pl.), refacciones (f. pl.) (*Me*)
spark(ing) plug, bujía (f)
speedometer, velocímetro (m)
spring (laminated), ballesta (f)
spring (spiral), muelle (m)
stall, to, calarse
start up, to, arrancar
starter, arranque (m), (puesta en) marcha (f)
steer, to, dirigir, manejar (*L/A*), guiar (*Z/A*)
steering wheel, volante (m)*, timón (m) (*Z/A*)
stop, to, parar
studs (road), topes (m. pl.) (*Me*)
switch off, to, apagar
'super' (gas), super (m), nafta (f) (*Ve*)

tail lamp, piloto (m), calavera (f) (*Me*), cocuyo (m) (*Ve*)
tire/tyre, cubierta (f), neumático (m) (*Sp*), llanta (f) (*L/A*), goma (f) (*R/P*), caucho (m) (*Ve*)
toll (gate), peaje (m), cuota (f)*
top gear, directa (f)
tuning, afinación (f) (**to tune,** afinar)
traffic, circulación (f), tránsito (m), tráfico (m)
traffic lights, semáforos (m. pl.)
transformer, bobina (f)
trunk, maleta (f), cajuela (f) (*Me*), baúl (m), maletera (f) (*Z/A*)
turnpike, autopista (f), carretera de peaje (f)

turn round, to, dar la vuelta
turn signal, intermitente (ṁ)
tyre, *v.* **tire**

universal joint, cruceta (f), junta universal (f)

ventilator, polea (f)
ventilator fan, ventilador (m)

washer, arandela (f), suela (f)

(*L/A*), empaque (m) (*Me*), huacha (f) (*Z/A*)
wheel, rueda (f)
windscreen/shield, parabrisas (m)
windscreen-wiper, limpiaparabrisas (m)
wing, aleta (f)
wire, alambre (m)
wrench, llave (f), española (f) (*Me*)

Spanish–English

accidente (m), breakdown
aceite (m), oil
acelerador (m), accelerator
adelantar, to pass, overtake
afinación (f), tuning
afinar, to tune up
ahogador (m), choke (*Me*)
aire (m), choke (*Sp*)
ajuste (m), overhaul (*Me*), adjustment
alambre (m), wire
aleta (f), fender, wing
amortiguador (m), shock-absorber
anillo (m), piston-ring (*Me, Z/A*)
apagar, to switch off
aparcar, to park
arandela (f), washer
árbol de levas (m), camshaft
aro (m), piston ring (*R/P*)
arrancar*, to start up
arranque (m), starter
arrollar, to run over (someone)
asiento (m), seat
atracar, to park (*R/P*)
atropellar, to run over (someone)
avería (f), breakdown (*Sp*)

baca (f), roofrack, luggage-grid
balero (m), ball-bearings (*Me*)
balinera (f), ball-bearings (*Co*)
ballesta (f), spring (laminated)
banda (f), fanbelt (*Me*)
batería (f), battery
baúl (m), boot, trunk

bencina (f), gasoline (*Ch*)
biela (f), connecting rod
bloque (m), cylinder block
bobina (f), coil, transformer
bocina (f), horn
bomba (f), pump
bombilla (f), bulb
brevete (m), driving licence (*Z/A*)
bujía (f), spark(ing) plug

caballos (m. pl.), horse-power
cadena (f), chain
caja (de cambios) (f), (gear)box
cajuela (f), trunk/boot (*Me*)
cajuelita (f), glove/dash pocket (*Me*)
cala (f), dipstick
calarse, to stall (engine)
calavera (f), tail-light (*Me*)
calentar(se), to heat up, overheat
cámara (f), inner-tube
cambios (m. pl.), gears
camión (m), truck/lorry
capó(t) (m), hood/bonnet
carburador (m), carburettor
carné(t) (m), driving licence (*Ch*)
cárter (m), crankcase
caucho (m), tire/tyre (*Ve*)
cebador (m), choke (*R/P*)
cepillo (m), dynamo brush
chocar*, to collide
choque (m)*, crash, accident
cigüeñal (m), crankshaft
cloche (m), clutch

cocuyo (m), side/tail-light, parking light
cofre (m), hood/bonnet (*Me*)
composturas (f. pl.), repairs (*Me*)
copa (f), hub-cap (*Co*)
corneta (f), horn (*Ve*)
correa (f), fanbelt
cruceta (f), universal joint
cuadrar, to park (*Z/A*)
cubierta (f), tire/tyre (*Sp*)
cuentakilómetros (m), odometer, milometer
cuota (f)*, toll (turnpike) (*Me*)

depósito (m), tank
defensa (f), bumper (*Me*)
delco (m), distributor
descompostura (f), breakdown (*Me*)
desarmador (m), screwdriver (*L/A*)
destornillador (m), screwdriver (*Sp*)
directa (f), top/high gear
dirigir, to drive, steer
distribuidor (m), distributor, exit from motorway (*Ve*)

eje (m), axle
ejemando (m), axleshaft (*Co*)
embrague (m), clutch
empaque (m), gasket
engranado, in gear
engranajes (m. pl.), gearing
engrase (m), lubrication
engrase general (m), 'service'
escape (m), exhaust
española (f), wrench, spanner (*Me*)
estacionar, to park
estopero (m), oil seal
estrellarse*, to crash (seriously)

factura (f), bill, invoice
faja (f), fanbelt (*Z/A*)
faro (m), headlight (*Me*)
flecha (f), axle (*Me*)
foco (m), bulb (*Me*)
frenazo (m), sudden jamming on of brakes

gato (m), **-a** (f), jack
goma (f), tyre/tire (*R/P*)
guantera (f), glove compartment
guiar, to drive (*Z/A*)

hinchar, to inflate, pump
huacha (f), washer (*Z/A*)

inflar, to inflate
intermitente (m), turn signal

libreta (f), driving licence (*R/P*)
licencia (f), driving licence (*Me*)
limpiaparabrisas (m), windscreen-wiper
linterna (f), torch, headlight (*Co*)
llanta (f), tire/tyre (*L/A*)
llave (f), key, tap, spanner/wrench
luz (f), light
luz vuelta (f), turn signal (*Me*)

maleta (f), trunk/boot
maletera (f), trunk/boot (*Pe*)
manejar, to drive, steer
manguera (f), hosepipe, inner-tube (*Co*)
marcha atrás (f), reverse
martillo (m), hammer
matricula (f), licence plate
mica (f), side/parking light (*Ve*)
mofle (m), silencer (*Me*)
monobloc (m), cylinder block (*Me*)
muelle (m), spring (spiral)

nafta (f), gasoline (*R/P*)
neumático (m), tire/tyre (*Sp*)

palanca (f), lever
pana (f), **-e** (m), breakdown (*Z/A*)
panel (m), panel, dashboard
parabrisas (m), windshield/screen
parachoques (m), bumper
paragolpes (m), bumper
parar, to stop
parrilla (f), roof rack, luggage grid
parquear, to park (*L/A*)

patina (f), **-zo** (m), skid
patinar, to skid
peaje (m), toll
peatón (m), pedestrian
perno (m), bolt
petróleo (m), diesel (*R/P*)
piloto (m), tail or parking light
pinchazo (m), puncture/flat (*Sp*)
pito (m), horn (*Co*)
placa (f), licence/number plate
platinos (m. pl.), contact points
polea (f), pulley, fanbelt
portaequipajes (m), luggage carrier
portamaleta (m), roof rack, luggage grid
punta de eje (f), axleshaft (*Ve*)
punto muerto (m), neutral
puesta en marcha (f), starter

rebasar, to pass/overtake (*Me*)
recauchado (m), **-chutaje** (m), retreading
recorrido (m), overhaul, driving-time (*Me*)
refacciones (f. pl.), spare parts (*Me*)
repuesto, de, spare, replacement
retén (m), oil-seal
retroceso (m), reverse (*Ve*)
revisión (f), overhaul

rodaje, en, running in
rodamiento (m), ball-bearings
rodillo (m), ball-bearings
rueda (f), wheel

salpicadero (m), dashboard/instrument panel (*Sp*)
segmento (m), piston ring
semáforos (m. pl.), traffic lights
semi-eje (m), axleshaft (*Pe*)
servicio (m), service
suela (f), washer (*L/A*)
'super' (m), gasoline (*Ve*)

tablero (m), dashboard, instrument panel
tapón (m), lid, hub cap
taza (f), hub cap (*R/P*)
timón (m), steering wheel (*Z/A*)
título (m), driving licence (*Ve*)
topes (m. pl.)*, road studs (*Me*)
tornillo (m), screw
tuerca (f), nut

uña (f), over-rider (of bumper)

varilla (f), dipstick
vaso (m), hub cap (*Pe*)
velocidades (f. pl.), speeds, gears
velocímetro (m), speedometer
ventilador (m), fan
volante (m), flywheel, steering wheel
vuelta, dar la, to turn round

Courtesy

Politeness is the lubricating oil of society; it is also very much a matter of doing as Rome does and is not a department in which originality is likely to be successful. Its conventionality, its clichés, are largely an indication of a desire for things to proceed smoothly and most of us will say Thanks! or Excuse me! or Sorry! a dozen times a day when in technical fact we have nothing to thank or to apologize for—sometimes rather the contrary—but it is important to know what is said locally for one's passage to be successfully lubricated. When Ali Baba said: 'Open barley!' instead of 'Open sesame!' the cave failed to oblige. Fortunately the Hispanic world does not offer great problems but certain expressions used in Spain tend to be regarded as excessive, or affected, in Latin America and conversely some Latin Americanisms as crude or *cursi* in Spain, and no reader will want to risk that tiny degree of alienation which comes of saying the wrong thing. Let me start, however, with words and phrases which are universally valid:

'May I introduce Mr. So-&-So?', *¿Puedo presentar . . .?* or *¿Se puede presentar (al) Señor Fulano de Tal?* (The *al*—or *a la* for a *Señora*—is not essential but it suggests 'the well known'.)

'How d'you do/Pleased to meet you', *Mucho gusto* or *Tanto gusto* (routine) or *Encantado* (a little more cordial). Ladies, of course, say *Encantada*.

'How are you?' (implying previous acquaintance)—*¿Cómo está Vd.?* or more familiarly *¿Qué tal está Vd.?* (*v.* note under **hola**).

'May I . . .?', *¿Se puede. . .?* is the conventional introduction to any polite request. Used by itself it is likely to mean: 'May I come in?' though circumstances will obviously affect this, but it can be followed by whatever Infinitive is appropriate: *¿Se puede ver?*, 'May I see?; *¿Se puede saber su nombre?*, 'May I know your name?' (For 'May I know who's speaking?' *v.* TELEPHONES.) For more routine, rhetorical requests, when you are already taking action, *¿Vd. permite?* or *Con permiso* are indicated; for more genuine—but familiar—ones *¿No le/te importa . . .?*, 'Would you mind . . .?' is appropriate.

'Excuse me!' If this is a genuine apology, equating with the British 'Sorry!' or 'I'm so sorry!' then *¡Disculpe!* or, more fulsomely, *¡Discúlpeme, por favor¡* though *¡Perdón!* will do when there is nothing much to apologize for. *¿Perdón?* also serves universally as a request for something to be repeated, e.g. the American 'Pardon me?' and British 'Sorry?'—but in parts of L/A, notably Mexico, they say *¿Mande?*

In addition to apologies there are what might be termed the disclaimers, e.g. 'Don't mention it!' 'Not at all!' 'You're welcome!' For these, fairly universal is *No hay de que* (literally 'There's nothing to thank me for'), though in the R/P they usually say *¡No hay por que!* and in the Z/A, when it is routine enough, simply *De que*. In Spain, when they have their full party manners on, they may say *No faltaba* *más* (see below). A more routine (and universal) disclaimer is *De nada*, or even *Nada*, which equates with the German *Bitte* and the Italian *Prego*. This is something which we do not quite have an equation for. We tend to say, 'Thanks!' or 'Thank you!' a good deal oftener than Hispanics say *¡Gracias!* but when you do get a *¡Gracias!* then *De nada* should follow like a conditioned reflex, unless circumstances warrant the more fulsome *No hay de que*.

'Please do!', 'Go right ahead!' Here there are transatlantic variations; in Spain they say *No faltaba más* or *No faltaría más* (literally 'No more was to be expected') which equate with the French *Mais, je vous en prie!* When the urging is really strong this is preceded by *¡Por Dios!* and it should not be supposed that this equates with 'For God's sake, do!' which implies exasperation; *¡Por Dios!*, in such a context, is extremely polite and suggests rather self-reproach for having failed to anticipate the request it is a reply to. In most of L/A this is likely to be regarded as excessive and affected; 'Please do!' is there either *¿Cómo no?* or . . . *no más* tacked on to some Imperative, e.g. in reply to the question *¿Se puede fumar?* they would say *¡Siga no más!* (*v.* entry under **más**).

By and large Hispanics use the Imperative a good deal more than we do and it is not necessarily rude. A polite 'Please' is often *Haga el favor (de)* . . . (between intimates, even *Haz el favor* . . .) literally 'Do (me) the favour (of) . . .', which sounds pretty frigid to our ears but is quite a good equivalent of 'Would you be good enough to . . .?', or: 'Do you mind . . .?'; in Spain it could be muttered when getting off a crowded bus; in L/A *Con permiso* is more likely in such circumstances. *No se moleste* is universal for 'Please don't trouble', without any *favor* being mentioned. The Diminutive, too, often provides a way of softening down an Imperative and indicating that the request is polite; *Espere un momento* is a phrase much used by telephone operators and is not felt as nearly so abrupt as 'Wait a moment', but if she were particularly anxious to show cordiality she would probably say *Espere un momentito*, 'Do you mind waiting *one* moment?'

Another way of phrasing a formal request—above all when addressing a company rather than an individual—is *Se ruega . . .*: *Se ruega silencio*, 'Pray silence . . .', but it is what a Hispanic is likely to say when trying to get the party quiet so that the guest of honour can make a speech and 'May I have your attention for a moment?' is more like it. Most of our polite phrases are in the form of questions, or else prefixed by: 'Please . . .'. I would hazard a guess that Hispanics do not say *por favor* as much as we say 'please'; they rely on other devices to convey its effect. The Diminutive has been mentioned; the Passive Voice is another, e.g. *Se ruega* and *Se puede* . . . Yet another softening device is the use of the Subjunctive tense and readers are referred to the entry under **preguntar(se)** for the handling of 'I wonder . . .'

There are a few words which should certainly be in your 'polite' vocabulary:

Agradecido, -a, 'grateful'; *muy agradecido*, 'most grateful'.

Amable, 'kind'; *Vd. ha sido tan amable (que de)* . . ., 'You've been so kind (as to) . . .' (*v.* also **atento**); *Gracias, muy amable*, 'Thank you so much'.

Cortés, 'polite'. *Cortesía*, 'politeness'.

Desear, 'to wish'; *Le deseo un feliz nuevo año*, 'I wish you a happy New Year'; *Le(s) deseo un feliz viaje*, 'I hope you have a good trip'.

¡Enhorabuena!, 'Congratulations!' *Tengo que darle la enhorabuena (por su* . . .), 'I must congratulate you (on your . . .)'.

Estorbar, 'to be in the way', and likely to be needed when travelling; *Espero que no le estorbe*, 'I hope it's not in your way'.

Gusto, 'pleasure'; not only *Mucho gusto* (see above) but *Da gusto* . . ., 'It's nice to . . .'.

Levantarse, 'to get (stand) up', and of particular use to ladies; *No se levante*, 'Please don't get up'. In L/A this is usually *No se pare* (*v.* **parar**).

Molestar, 'to be a nuisance'; *No se moleste*, 'Please don't trouble'; *Espero que no le molesto*, 'I hope I'm not being a bother'.

Sentir, lamentar, 'to regret', 'to be sorry about': *Lo siento mucho*, 'I'm so sorry' (e.g. 'to hear it' though it can also mean 'I do apologize'). *Lamento mucho que* . . ., 'I very much regret that . . .'.

In the matter of travel there is a delicate convention which you should be aware of when it is a matter of eating or drinking in the presence of others who are not strictly of your company. Hispanics are acutely sensitive to such occasions and the humblest peasant, particularly in Spain, is unlikely to get out his sandwiches and start eating without making a token offering of them to you, saying *¿Vd. gusta?* The conventional response to this is *Buen provecho* or *Que le aproveche* and you are not expected to accept the offer. I still recall with embarrassment an occasion in a train when some sailors offered me their just-uncorked bottle of wine with an *¿Vd. gusta?* and I in my ignorance accepted and drank a very small amount from the neck. To my surprise they then corked it up again, rather impatiently, and put it in the luggage rack and it was only afterwards that I learnt I should have declined with a *Buen provecho*. One does not, however, need to wait to be asked before saying it. If you suddenly surprise someone in the act of eating—in any circumstances—the first thing for you to say is *Buen provecho* (in L/A they often word it *Buen apetito*). Conversely, if you get out your own sandwiches in the presence of others, do not forget to say *¿Vd. gusta?* If you really want them to accept you will need to use a different wording and insist rather harder.

A more social convention arises when somebody admires, say, the dress that a lady is wearing. Her response is *A su disposición*, literally 'It's at your disposal', but this will not be taken literally; she is in no danger of having the offer accepted but it gives her something cut-and-dried to say in place of a rather embarrassed 'Do you like it?' or 'Yes, it is rather nice, isn't it?' (*v.* also entries under **cumplir, participar, velatorio, delicioso, esposo, importar, anfitrión, solicitar.**)

Visitors to Buenos Aires may care to know of one or two usages among the 'best people' there. They are in the same category as the use of 'table napkin' as opposed to 'serviette', or 'wireless' instead of 'radio' in Britain, viz.:

tacita (f), 'coffee cup',	instead of *pocillo* (m)
cinta (f), 'film',	instead of *película* (f)
medias (f. pl.), 'socks',	instead of *calcetines* (m. pl.)
pelo (m), 'hair',	instead of *cabello* (m)
balón (m), 'brandy glass',	instead of *copa* or *copita* (f)

There may well be others. If they have learnt their Spanish on the Peninsular model then perhaps the warning about *coger (q.v.)* had better be repeated.

Food

English–Spanish

almond, almendra (f)
anchovies, anchoas (f. pl.),
  boquerones (m. pl.)
apple, manzana (f)
apricot, albaricoque (m), damasco (m) (*L/A*)
artichoke, alcaucil (m), alcachofa
  (f)
artichoke (Jerusalem), cotufa (f)
asparagus, espárragos (m. pl.)
aubergine, berenjena (f)
avocado, aguacate (m), palta (f)
  (*C/S*)

bacon, jamón ahumado (m),
  tocino (m) (*Me*)
bass (fish), robalo (m), lubina (f)
bay leaf, laurel (m)
beans, judías (f. pl.), frijoles (m.
  pl.), porotos (m. pl.) (*Ch*),
  habichuelas (f. pl.)
beans (green), judías verdes (*Sp*),
  chauchas (*R/P*), vainitas (f.
  pl.) (*Z/A*), ejotes (*Me*),
  porotos verdes (m. pl.) (*Ch*)
beef, carne (f) (*C/S*), res (f) (*Me*),
  vaca (f) (*Sp*)
beet, remolacha (f) (*Sp*), betabel
  (m) (*Me*), betarraga (f) (*Ch*)
biscuit, galleta (f), galletita (f)
  (*R/P*)
boiled, cocido (*v.* **cocer**)
brains, sesos (m. pl.)
bread-roll, bollo (m), bolillo (m),
  pan (m), birote (m) (*Me*)
broad beans, habas (f. pl.)
brown bread, pan de centeno (m)
butter, mantequilla, manteca*

cabbage, col (m), repollo (m)
cake, pastel (m), torta (f)*,
  queque (m)
caramel custard, flan (m)

carrot, zanahoria (f)
cassava, yuca (f)
cauliflower, coliflor (m)
celery, apio (m)
chapati, tortilla (f) (*Me*)
cheese, queso (m)
cherry, cereza (f), **(black),** guinda
  (f)
chicken, pollo (m)
chickpeas, garbanzos (m. pl.)
chips/crisps, papas/patatas fritas
  (f. pl.)
chop, chuleta (f)
cinnamon, canela (f)
cocktail sticks, palillos (m. pl.)
cold meats, fiambres (m. pl.)
conger eel, congrio (m)
coriander, cilantro (m), culantro
  (m)
corn/maize, mazorca (f), elote
  (m) (*Me*), choclo (m) (*Z/A*)
cornflour, maicena (f)
courgette, calabacita (f)
crab, cangrejo (m), jaiba (f)
  (*L/A*)
cracker, cookie, galleta (f)
cream, nata (f)
crisps, papas/patatas fritas (f.
  pl.)
crumb, miga (f)
custard, natillas (f. pl.)
custard (egg), flan (m)
custard apple, chirimoya (f)
cutlet, chuleta (f)
cuttlefish, calamares (m. pl.),
  chipirones (m. pl.)

doughnut, churro (m)*, berlina
  (f) (*L/A*), rosquilla (f) (*Sp*)
draught, de barril, de presión
drinking straw, paja (f), popote
  (m) (*Me*), pitillo (m) (*Ve*),
  bombilla (f) (*R/P*)
duck, pato (m)

241

eel, anguila (f)
egg, huevo (m)*
egg plant, berenjena (f), lúcuma (f) (Z/A)

fat, grasa (f)
fig, higo (m), **(black)** breva (f)
fillet, lomo (m)
fish, pescado (m)
French fried, papas/patatas francesas (f. pl.)

garlic, ajo (m)
giblets, menudillos (m. pl.)
grape, uva (f)
grapefruit, toronja (f), pomelo (m)
gravy, salsa (f), jugo (m)
grease, grasa (f)
grill, parrilla (f), plancha (f)
grouper, mero (m)
guava, guayaba (f)

halibut, halibut (m)
ham, jamón de York (m)
hazel nut, avellana (f)
herring, arenque (m)
honey, miel (f)
hors d'oeuvres, entremeses (m. pl.)
'hot' (highly spiced), picante

jam, mermelada (f)
jelly, jalea (f), gelatina (f)
jerked beef, tasajo (m) (Me)
juice, jugo (m), zumo (m), almíbar (m)

kebab, pincho moruno (m) (Sp), anticucho (m) (Pe)
kidney beans, frijoles (m. pl.)

lamb, cordero (m), lechal (m)
'lard', manteca (f)*, tocino (m)
lemon, limón (m), lima (f) (Me)
lentil, lenteja (f)
lettuce, lechuga (f)
Lima beans, habas (f. pl.)
loaf, pan (m), barra (f) (Sp)
lobster, langosta (f)

loin, lomo (m)
lump of sugar, terrón (m), pancito (m)

malt, malta (f)
manioc, yuca (f)
marrow, calabacín (m)
marrow (bone), tuétano (m)
mashed, puré
mayonnaise, mayonesa/mahonesa (f)
meat, carne (f)
meat-ball, albóndiga (f)
meat pie, empanada (f)
melon, melón (m)
meunière, molinera
minced, picado
mint, menta (f)
mussel, mejillón (m), cholga (f) (Ch)
mustard, mostaza (f)
mutton, cordero (m), capón (m) (R/P)

nut, v. entry under **nuez**

olive-oil, aceite (m)
omelette, tortilla* de huevos (f)
orange, naranja (f)
oxtail, rabo de buey (m) (Sp), cola de res (f) (Me)
oyster, ostra (f), ostión (f) (Me)

palm-shoots, palmitos (m. pl.), chonta (f) (Z/A)
pancake, torta (f) (Sp), panqueque (m) (L/A)
pancake (maize), tortilla (f) (Me)
papaw/pawpaw, papaya (f), lechosa (f) (Ve)
parsley, perejil (m)
partridge, perdiz (f)
peach, melocotón (m), durazno (m) (L/A)
peanut, cacahuete (m) (Sp), maní (m) (S/A), cacahuate (m) (Me)
pear, pera (f)
peas, guisantes (m. pl.) (Sp), chícharos (m. pl.) (Me),

alverjas/arvejas (f. pl.)
(*S/A*)
pepper, pimienta (f)*
pepper (red), pimentón (m)*
peppers, pimientos* (m. pl.),
morrones (m. pl.) (*R/P*),
poblanos (m. pl.) (*Me*)
peppermint, menta (f)
pheasant, faisán (m)
pigeon, pichón (m)
pineapple, piña (f)
plaice, platija (f)
pork, puerco (m), cerdo (m),
marrano (m), chancho (m)
(*Z/A*), coche (m) (*Gu*)
pork, belly of, tocino (m)
potato, patata (f) (*Sp*), papa (f)
(*L/A*)
poultry, ave (f)
prawns, gambas (f. pl.) (*Sp*),
camarones (m. pl.)
prickly pear, higo de chumbo (m)
(*Sp*), tuna (f) (*Me*), penca (f)
(*Z/A*)
pulse, legumbres (f. pl.)
pumpkin, calabaza (f), alcoyota
(f) (*Ch*), zapallo (m) (*R/P*)

raisins, pasas (f. pl.)
raw, crudo, natural
red-snapper, guachinango (m)
red wine, vino tinto (m)
rice, arroz (m)
rissole, albóndiga (f), croqueta (f)
Russian salad, rusa (f), ensaladilla (f)
rye (cereal), centeno (m)

salad, ensalada (f)
salami, chorizo (m)
salmon, salmón (m)
salt, sal (f)
salted beef, cecina (f), tasajo (m)
(*Me*)
sardine, sardina (f)
sauce, salsa (f)
sausage, salchicha (f), sal-
chichón (m), chorizo (m),
embutido (m)

scone, arepa (f) (*Ve*), allulla (f)
(*Ch*)
sea urchin, erizo (m)
shellfish, mariscos (m. pl.)
sherry, jerez (m)
shrimp, camarón (m), gamba (f)
(*Sp*), langostina (f)
shrimp, small, quisquilla (f)
sirloin, solomillo (m) (*Sp*)
skewer, brocheta (f)
slice, rebanada (f)*, raja (f),
tajada (f), rueda (f)
smoked, ahumado
snails, caracoles (m. pl.)
soft drinks, refrescos (m. pl.)
sole, lenguado (m)
soup, sopa (f), caldo (m)
soup (thin), consomé (m)
sour, agrio
spice, especia (f)
spinach, espinacas (f. pl.), acelga
(f) (*R/P*)
sponge-cake, bizcocho (m),
pudín (m) (*R/P*)
squash, calabacín (m), zapallo
(m) (*R/P*), alcayota (f)
(*Ch*)
squid, pulpo (m), calamar (m),
chipirón (m)
steak, asado (m), solomillo (m)
(*Sp*), bife (m) (*L/A*), churrasco
(m) (*R/P*), entrecot (m)
'stock', caldo (m)
strawberry, fresa (f), fresón (m),
frutilla (f) (*C/S*)
string beans, judías verdes (f. pl.)
(*Sp*), ejotes (m. pl.) (*Me*),
chauchas (f. pl.) (*R/P*),
vainitas (f. pl.) (*Z/A*)
sucking pig, cochinillo (m),
lechona (f)
sugar, azúcar (m)
sweetbreads, mollejas (f. pl.)
sweet course, postre (m)
syrup, almíbar (m), siro

tea, té (m)
tip, propina (f)
tomato, tomate (m), jitomate (m)
(*Me*)*

tripe, callos (m. pl.), mondongo (m), pancita (m) (*Me*)
trout, trucha (f)
tunny fish, atún (m)
turbot, rodaballo (m)
turkey, pavo (m), pavipollo (m), guajalote (m) (*Me*)
turnip, nabo (m)

vanilla, vainilla (f)
veal, ternera (f)
vegetables, verdura (f)

vermicelli, fideos (m. pl.)
vintage, cosecha (f)

waiter, camerero (m) (*Sp*), mesero (m) (*Me, Co*), mesonero (m) (*Ve*), garzón (m) (*R/P*), mozo (m) (*Z/A*)
walnut, nuez (f)*
water cress, berro (m)
water melon, sandía (f), patilla (f) (*Ve*)
whiting, pescadilla (f)

Spanish-English

aceite (m), olive oil
aceitunas (f. pl.), olives
acelga (f), form of spinach
agrio, sour
aguacate (m), avocado pear
ahumado, smoked
ají (m), chili
ajo (m), garlic
albaricoque (m), apricot
albóndiga (f), rissole, meat-ball
alcaucil (m), **alcachofa** (f), artichoke
alcayota (f), pumpkin
allulla (f), scone (*Ch*)
almejas (f. pl.), cockles, clams
almendra (f), almond
almíbar (m), syrup
alverjas (f. pl.), **arvejas** (f. pl.), peas (*R/P*)
anchoas (f. pl.), anchovies
anguila (f), eel
anticucho (m), kebab (*Pe*)
apio (m), celery
arenque (m), herring
arepa (f), griddle cake
arroz (m), rice
arvejas (f. pl.), peas (*R/P*)
asado, roast
atol (m), sort of thick sweet soup
atún (m), tunny fish
ave (f), poultry, chicken
avellana (f), hazel nut

bacalao (m), cod (usually salted)

bechamela (f), white sauce
berenjena (f), aubergine, eggplant
berro (m), water cress
betabel (m)/**betarraga** (f) (*Me*), beet
bife (m), steak (*R/P*)
bizcocho (m)*, spongecake
blanquillo (m)*, white of egg
bocadillo (m)*, sandwich
boquerones (m. pl.), fresh anchovies
botana (f), snack (*Me*)
brevas (f. pl.), black figs
brocheta (f), spit, skewer
budín (m), cake, trifle

cacahuate, -uete (m), peanut
calabacín (m), marrow/squash
calabacita (f), courgette, zucchini
calabaza (f), pumpkin
calamares (m. pl.), cuttlefish
caldo (m), broth, stock
callos (m. pl.), tripe
camarones (m. pl.), shrimps, large prawns
camote (m), sweet potato (*Me*)
cangrejo (m), crab
capón (m), mutton (*R/P*)
caracoles (m. pl.), snails
caramel (m), fresh sardine
caramelo (m), caramel, sweet/candy

carbonada (f), chop or steak
carne (f), meat (usually beef)
cazuela (f), stew
cebiche (m)*
cebolla (f), onion
cecina (f), smoked beef or pork
centeno (m), rye (**pan de centeno**, brown bread)
cerdo (m), pork
cereza (f), cherry
champiñón (m), mushroom
chancho (m), pork (*Z/A*)
chauchas (f. pl.), green beans (*R/P*)
chícharos (m. pl.), peas (*Me*)
chipirones (m. pl.), squid
chirimoya (f), custard apple
choclo (m), corn on the cob (*Z/A*)
cholgas (f. pl.), mussels (*Z/A*)
chonta (f), palm-shoot (*Z/A*)
chorizo (m), salami
chucrút (m), sauerkraut
chuleta (f), chop
churrasco (m), beefsteak (*R/P*)
churro (m)*, doughnut, fritter (*Sp*)
cigala (f), Norway lobster
cilantro (m)/**culantro** (m), coriander
ciruela (f), plum
coche (m), pork (*Gu*)
cochinillo (m), sucking pig
col (m), cabbage
cola (f), tail (usually oxtail)
coliflor (m), cauliflower
congrio (m), conger eel
consomé (m), thin soup
cordero (m), mutton
corvina (f), sea bass, croaker
cosecha (f), vintage
cotufa (f), Jerusalem artichoke
croqueta (f), rissole, croquette
crudo, raw, fresh

damasco (m), apricot (*L/A*)
dieta (f), sort of stew (*Pe*)
durazno (m), peach (*L/A*)

ejotes (m. pl.), green beans (*Me*)
elote (m), corn on the cob (*Me*)

embutidos (m. pl.), sausages
empanada (f), meat pie
enchiladas (f. pl.)*
ensalada (f), salad
ensaladilla (f), Russian salad
entrecot (m), steak
entremeses (m. pl.), hors d'oeuvres
epazote (m), Mexican herb tea
erizo (m), sea urchin
escabeche (m), sauce of vinegar, oil, garlic and bay leaves
espada (f), sword fish
española (f), 'hot' Mexican sauce
espárragos (m. pl.), asparagus
especia (f), spice
espinacas (f. pl.), spinach
estofado (m), stew

faisán (m), pheasant
fiambres (m. pl.), cold meats
fideos (m. pl.), vermicelli, spaghetti, etc.
flan (m), egg custard
frambuesa (f), raspberry
francesa (f)*, French-fried/chips
fresa (f), wild strawberry
fresón (m), strawberry
frijoles (m. pl.), kidney beans
frito, fried
fruta (f), fruit
frutilla (f), strawberry (*C/S*)

galleta (f), biscuit/cracker, cookie
gallina (f), chicken
gambas (f. pl.), shrimps/prawns
garbanzos (m. pl.), chickpeas
guisantes (m. pl.), peas

helado, ice(d)
huevo (m)*, egg

jaiba (f), small crab (*L/A*)
jalea (f), jelly
jamón (m), ham (sometimes bacon)
jerez (m), sherry
jitomate (m)*, tomato (*Me*)

judías (verdes) (f. pl.), beans (green) (*Sp*)
jugo (m), juice, gravy

langosta (f), lobster
langostino (m), small lobster, jumbo shrimp
laurel (m), bay leaf
lebranche (m), fish resembling mullet
lechal (m), young (sucking) animal
leche (f), milk
lechona (f), sucking pig
lechosa (f), pa(w)paw (*Ve*)
lechuga (f), lettuce
legumbres (f. pl.), pulse
lenguado (m), sole
lentejas (f. pl.), lentils
licor (m), liqueur (not liquor)
lima (f)/limón (m), lemon
llaucha (f), meat pie (*Bo*)
lomo (m), steak, rib, loin
lubina (f), sea-bass

macha (f), sort of shellfish (*Ch*)
mahonesa (f)/**mayonesa** (f), mayonnaise
maicena (f), maize/cornflour
malta (f), malt
maní (m), peanut
mantecado (m), vanilla ice-cream
manzana (f), apple
manzanilla (f)*
mariscos (m. pl.), shellfish, seafood
marrano (m), pork (*Co, Me*)
matambre (m), cold meat brawn (*R/P*)
mazorca (f), corn/maize
medallón (m), slice (circular in shape)
mejillones (m. pl.), mussels
melocotón (m), peach
melón (m), melon
membrillo (m), quince jelly
menta (f), peppermint
menudillos (m. pl.), giblets
merluza (f), hake
mermelada (f), jam, conserve

mero (m), grouper
miel (f), honey
miga (f), crumb, soft part of bread
milanesa (f), fried in batter
mojo (m), garlic sauce (*Me*)
mole (f), 'hot' black chilli sauce (*Me*)
molinera (f), meunière (fried in butter)
mollejas (f. pl.), sweetbreads
mondongo (m), tripe
morrón (m), sweet pepper (vegetable)
mostaza (f), mustard

nabo (m), turnip
naranja (f), orange
nata (f), cream
natillas (f. pl.), custard
natural, raw, fresh
nuez (f)*, walnut

ostras (f. pl.)/**ostiones** (f. pl.), oysters

paella (f)*
palillo (m), cocktail stick, toothpick
palmitos (m. pl.), palm-shoots
palta (f), avocado pear (*C/S*)
pan (m), bread
pancita (f), tripe (*Me*)
pancito (m), lump of sugar
papas (f. pl.)*/**patatas** (f. pl.), potatoes
papaya (f), pa(w)paw
pargo (m), fish (*Co*)
parrilla (f), grill
pasas (f. pl.), raisins
pato (m), duck
pavo (m)/**pavipollo** (m), turkey
penca (f), prickly pear
pepino (m), cucumber
pera (f), pear
perdiz (f), partridge
perejil (m), parsley
pescadilla (f), whiting, codling
pescado (m), fish
picado, minced

picante, highly peppered, 'hot'
pichón (m), pigeon
pimiento (m)*, **-ta** (f), **pimentón**
piña (f), pineapple
piqueo (m)*
pisco (m)*
pisto (m)*, ratatouille
plancha (f)*, grill
platija (f), plaice
platilla (f), water melon (Ve)
poblanos (m. pl.), peppers (Me)
pollo (m), chicken
pomelo (m), grapefruit
popote (m), drinking straw (Me)
porotos (m. pl.), beans (C/S)
postre (m), dessert, sweet course
pudín (m), usually a sort of trifle
puerco (m), pork
pulpo (m), squid
puré, mashed

queque (m), cake
queso (m), cheese
quisquilla (f), shrimp (very small)

rabo (m), oxtail
raja (f), slice (usually of fruit)
rebanada (f)*, slice
refrescos (m. pl.), soft drinks
remolacha (f), beet
repollo (m), cabbage
res (f), beef (Me)
robalo (m), bass (fish)
rodaballo (m), turbot
rosquilla (f), doughnut (Sp)
rueda (f), slice (circular in shape)
rusa (f), Russian salad

saisi (m), minced beef with vegetables and rice (Bo)
sal (m), salt
salado, salted
salchicha (f), **-ón** (m), sausage
salmón (m), salmon
salmonete (m), red mullet
salpicón (m)*, shredded vegetables

salsa (f), sauce, gravy
sangría (f), 'claret cup'
saltena (f), highly spiced meat (Bo)
sandía (f), water melon
sardina (f), sardine
sargo (m), flatfish (R/P)
seviche (m), v. cebiche*
sesos (m. pl.), brains
siro (m), syrup
solomillo (m), sirloin steak
sopa (f), soup

taco (m)*
tacu-tacu (m), mash of rice and beans (Pe)
tamal (m)*
tasajo (m), jerked beef
té (m), tea
tinto (m), red (wine), black (coffee) (Z/A)
ternera (f), veal
terrón (m), lump of sugar
tocino (m), belly of pork, bacon (Me)
toronja (f), grape-fruit
torta (f)*
tortilla (f)*, omelette
trucha (f), trout
tuétano (m), marrow (bone)
tuna (f), prickly pear

uvas (f. pl.), grapes

vainilla (f), vanilla
vainitas (f. pl.), green/string beans (Z/A)
verdura (f), greens, vegetables
vinagre (m), vinegar

yuca (f), manioc, cassava

zanahoria (f), carrot
zapallo (m), squash/marrow
zumo (m), fruit juice

Household Words

English–Spanish

A.C. (current), corriente alterna (f)
absorbent cotton, algodón (m)
apron, mandil (m), delantal (m)
armchair, butaca (f)
ash-tray, cenicero (m)

baby's dummy, chupete (m)
bag, bolsa (f)
bake, to, asar
ball-valve, flotador (m)
bandage, venda (f)
basement, sótano (m), subterráneo (m)
basket, canasta (f), cesto (m)
bathing suit, traje de baño (m)
bath-mat, alfombrilla (f), piso (m) (*L/A*), tapete (m) (*L/A*)
bathroom, cuarto de baño (m)
bath-tub, bañera (f), tina (f)
beach-wrap, bata (f), batín (f)
beater, batidor (m)
bed, cama (f), catre (m)*
bedroom, habitación (f)
bell (electric), timbre (m)
bell (clapper), campanilla (f)
bib, babero (m), bebida (f) (*R/P*)
bill/invoice, factura (f)
bleaching fluid, lejía (f)
blanket, manta (f) (*Sp*), cobija (f) (*L/A*), frazada (f) (*C/S*)
blocked up, atrancado (m), atorado (m)
blow/fuse, to, fundir
board, tabla (f)
boil, to, hervir
boil (eggs), to, cocer*
boiler, caldera (f)
bookcase, librería (f)*, estante (m)*
bottle top, tapón (m), chapa (f)
bottle-opener, abridor (m)

bowl, tazón (m), taza (f), palangana (f) (*Z/A*)
box, caja (f)
brass, bronce (m)*, latón (m)
brassière, sostén (m)
broom, escoba (f)
brush, brocha (f)*, cepillo (m)
brush, to, cepillar
bucket, cubo (m), balde (m), tobo (m) (*Ve*)
built-in, empotrado
bulb (electric), bombilla (f), lámpara (f), foco (m) (*Me*), ampolleta (f) (*Ch*), bombita (f) (*R/P*)
bunch (flowers), ramo (m)
bunch (veg), atado (m), paquete (m) (*Ch*)
burn out, to (lamps), fundir
button, botón (m)

'can'/'john', baño (m)*
can-opener, abridor (m)
can/tin, lata (f), bote (m)
candle, vela (f)
carpet, alfombra (f)
carving knife, trinchante (m)
chair, silla (f)
chamber-pot, vaso de noche (m), orinal (m)
chest of drawers, cómoda (f)
china, vajilla (f), cerámica (f)
cistern, depósito (m), tanque (m)
cloth, trapo (m), paño (m)*
clothes peg/pin, pinza (f)
coat-hanger, percha (f)
cocktail stick, palillo (m)
coffee-cup, pocillo (m)*
colander, colador (m)
comfortable, cómodo
conservatory, invernadero (m)
cook, to, cocinar *, guisar
cook (by boiling), cocer*

cork(screw), (saca)corcho(s) (m)
corn (on foot), callo (m)
cotton, cotton wool, algodón (m)
counterpane, colcha (f)
crate, bulto (m), cajón (m)
crossword puzzle, crucigrama (m)
cruet, alcuza (f)
cuff-links, gemelos (m. pl.), mellizos (m. pl.) (*L/A*)
cup, taza (f), pocillo (m) (*Co*)
current (electric), luz (f), corriente (f)
curtain, cortina (f)
curtain (thin), visillo (m)
cushion, cojín (m), quilla (f) (*R/P*)

darn, to, zurcir
D.C., corriente continua (f)
deep-freeze, congeladora (f)
dent, abollo (m); **to dent,** abollar
desk, escritorio (m)
detergent, detergente (m)
diaper, pañal (m)
dining-room, comedor (m)
dish (oval), fuente (f)
disposal unit, trituradora (f)
door-bell, timbre (m)
door-handle, mango (m)* (*Sp*), perilla (f), pestillo (m)
doormat (coconut), felpudo (m)
drainpipes, cañería (f)
drawer, cajón (m), gaveta (f)
drawing-room, sala (f), living (m)
dress, vestido (m)
dressing-gown, bata (f), batín (m), mañanita (f) (*Me*)
drill, taladro (m), (**dentist's**) turno (m)
drum (butane gas), bombona (f)
drying-cloth, secador (m), repasador (m) (*R/P*), trapo (m)
dust, polvo (m)
dustbin, balde (m), cubo (m), tobo (m) (*Ve*)
duster, gamuza (f), pulidor (m), trapo (m)

ear-rings, pendientes (m. pl.), caravanas (f. pl.) (*C/S*)
egg-whisk, batidor (m)
elastic, elástico (m), goma (f), jebe (m) (*Z/A*)
evening-dress (male), traje de etiqueta (m)

faucet, grifo (m), llave (f), caño (m) (*Pe*)
feather-duster, plumero (m), zorros (m.pl.)*
file (nail), lima (f)
floor-cloth, bayeta (f), jerga (f) (*Me*)
floor-polisher, enceradora (f)
flower vase, florero (m)
fold, to, doblar
fork, tenedor (m)
fry, to, freír (**fried** = frito)
frying-pan, sartén (f)
furniture, muebles (m. pl.)
fuse, fusible (m), tapón (m) (*Me*), plomos (m. pl.) (*v.* entry under **fundir**)

garbage, basura (f)
garbage-can, balde (m), cubo (m), tobo (m) (*Ve*)
'give', to (stretch), dar de sí
glass, vidrio (m), cristal (m)
glass (tumbler), vaso (m)
grate, to, rallar

hall, sala (f), pasillo (m)
hallway, pasillo (m)
hammer, martillo (m)
handbag, bolso (m)
handkerchief, pañuelo (m)
handle, mango (m)*
hang, to, colgar
hinge, bisagra (f), gozne (m)
hook, gancho (m)
hosepipe, manguera (f)
hot-water tank, termo (m)

ice-compartment, congelador (m)
inch-tape, metro (m)
incinerator, quemador (m)
inventory, inventario (m)
iron, plancha (f); **to iron,** planchar

jacket, chaqueta (f), saco (m) (L/A)

jar, jarra (f), tarro (m)

jig-saw puzzle, rompecabezas (m)

jumper, chomba (f)*

kettle, caldera (f)*, pava (f), marmita (f) (Me)

key, llave (f)

knife, cuchillo (m)

knitting, punto (m), labor (f)

ladder, escalera (f)

ladder (stocking), carrera (f)

lamp, lámpara (f)

lawn, césped (m), pasto (m), (R/P), prado (m) (Z/A), grama (f) (Ve)

lay, to (table), poner (la mesa)

leak, fuga (f); **to leak,** fugarse, salirse *

leg (of furniture), pata (f)

lever, palanca (f)

lid, tapón (m), tapa (f)

light, luz (f)

light, to, encender

lining (of clothes, etc.), forro (m)

lipstick, palo/lápiz (m) de labios

lock, cerradura (f); **to lock,** cerrar (v. **echar**)

market, mercado (m)

mat, alfombra (f), piso (m), tapete (m) (L/A), estera (f)

mat (coconut), felpudo (m)

match, to, hacer juego con

matches, fósforos (m. pl.), cerillas (f. pl.) (Sp), cerillos (m. pl.) (Me)

material (textile), tela (f)

mattress, colchón (m)

measure, to, medir

measurements, medidas (f. pl.)

melt, to, derretir

mend, to, reparar

meter (gas, etc.), contador (m)

milkman, lechero (m)

mirror, espejo (m)

mixture, mezcla (f), **to mix,** mezclar

mortar, almirez (m)

mower, segador(a) (m/f)

nail (hands), uña (f)

nail (metal), clavo (m)

'nappie', pañal (m)

necklace, collar (m)*

needle, aguja (f)

nightdress, vestido de noche (m)

opener, abridor (m)

oven, horno (m)

overall(s), bata (f), mandil (m), mono (m)

padlock, candado (m)

pajamas, pijama (m)

pane (glass), luna (f)

panties, bragas (f. pl.), bombachas (f. pl.) (R/P)

pants (Amer.), pantalones (m. pl.)

pants (Brit.), calzoncillos (m. pl.), truza (f) (Ve)

paper bag, bolsa (de papel) (f), talajo (m) (Co)

passage, pasillo (m)

penknife, navaja (f)

pestle, mano de almirez (f)

picture, cuadro (m)

picture-frame, marco (m)*

pill, píldora (f), comprimido (m), pastilla (f)

pillow, almohada (f), cojín (m)*

pillow-case, funda (f)

pin, alfiler (m), **to pin,** alfilar

pincers, alicate(s) (m. (pl.)), tenazas (f. pl.)

pipes (water, etc.), cañería (f)

plaster, yeso (m)

plate, plato (m)

pliers, alicate(s) (m. (pl.)), tenazas (f. pl.)

plug (electric), enchufe (m), chavija (f) (Me)

plug (washbasin, etc.), tapón (m)

plumber, fontanero (m), plomero (m) (R/P), gasfitero (m) (Z/A)*

postman, cartero (m)

pot, tarro (m)
prescription, receta (f)
put away, to, colocar
put right, to, poner en condiciones
pyjamas, pijama (m)

recipe, receta (f)
reel (cotton, etc.), carrete (m), bobina (f)
refrigerator, refrigerador (m), nevera (f), heladera (f) (*R/P*)
repair, to, reparar, componer (*v.* entry on **condición**)
ribbon, cinta (f)
ring, to (the bell), tocar (el timbre)
roll-top desk, buró (m)
rope, cuerda (f), mecate (m), soga (f)
rouge, colorete (m)
rug, manta (f), frazada (f) (*Z/A*), cobija (f) (*Me*)
run (stocking), carrera (f)

safety pin, imperdible (m)
sand, arena (f)
sandpaper, lija (f)
sanitary towel, paño (m), tampón (m)
saucepan, cazerola (f), olla (f)*
saucer, platillo (m)
scales, balanza (f)
scissors, tijeras (f. pl.)
screw, tornillo (m), **to screw,** atornillar
screwdriver, destornillador (m), desarmador (m) (*L/A*)
scrub, to, fregar*
service/set (linen, crockery, etc.), juego (m)*
serving dish, fuente (f)
sew, to, coser; **sewing,** costura (f)
shammy, gamuza (f)
shed, cobertizo (m)
sheet, sábana (f)
shelf, estante (m)*, balda (f), repisa (f)
shirt, camisa (f)
shoe, zapato (m)

shoe-lace, cordón (m), pasador (m) (*Pe*)
shoe-horn, calzador (m)
shopping, las compras (f. pl.)
shopping-basket, canasta (f)
shorts, pantalón corto (m)
shred, to, rallar
shrink, to, encoger
sieve, criba (f), tamiz (m)
sink, pila (f)*, pileta (f), lavabo (m) (*Ec*)
sink disposal unit, trituradora (f)
sitting-room, sala (f), living (m)
skewer, brocha (f), brocheta (f)
skirt, falda (f), pollera (f) (*R/P*)
slab, tabla (f), bloque (m)
slipper, zapatilla (f), pantufla (f) (*R/P*)
sock, calcetín (m)
sour, to go, cortar (*Sp*), malograr (*L/A*)
sour, agrio
spade, pala (f), laya (f)
spill, to, tirar (*Sp*), derramar (*L/A*)
spoon, cuchara (f)
spout, pico (m)*
spread, to (e.g. butter), untar
spring, muelle (m)*
squeezer, exprimidor (m)
stain, mancha (f), **to stain,** manchar (f)
stairway, escalera (f)
starch, almidón (m)
stew, (to,) estofa(r)
stir, to, revolver, remover
stitch, puntada (f)
stocking, media (f)
stool, banqueta (f)*, taburete (m)
stopper, tapón (m)
string, cuerda (f), soga (f), mecate (m) (*Me*)
sugar bowl, azucarero (m)
suit, traje (m), vestido (m)
suitcase, maleta (f), valija (f) (*R/P*)
sweater, suéter (m)
switch, apagador (m), interruptor (m)*, llave (f)
switch off, to, apagar

switch on, to, encender

table, mesa (f)
table-cloth, mantel (m)
table-cloth (ornamental), tapete (m), carpeta (f) (*Co*)*
table napkin, servilleta (f)
tablespoonful, cucharada (f)
tampon, paño (m), gasa (f)
tank, depósito (m), tanque (m)
tank (hot water), termo (m)
tap, grifo (m), llave (f), caño (m) (*Pe*)
tape, cinta (f)
teaspoon, cucharilla, -ita (f)
'temperature', fiebre (f), calentura (f)*
thermos flask, termo (m)
thimble, dedal (m)
thread, hilo (m)
thumb-tack, chincheta (f)
tie, corbata (f)
tiles (glazed), azulejos (m. pl.)
tiles (of roofs), tejas (f. pl.)
toaster, tostador (m)
toilet paper, papel higiénico (m)
tools, toolkit, herramiento (m), -a (f) (*Sp*)
torch, linterna (f)
towel, toalla (f)
trash, basura (f)
trash-can, balde (m)*, cubo (m)
tray, bandeja (f)
trim, recorte (m), **to trim,** recortar, arreglar

trousers, pantalones (m. pl.)
trunk, baúl (m)
tweezers, alicate(s) (m. (pl.)), tenazas (f. pl.)

underpants, calzoncillos (m. pl.)
undershirt, camiseta (f)

vacuum-cleaner, aspiradora (f)
vase, florero (m)
vase (ornamental), jarrón (m)
vest (Amer.), chaleco (m)
vest (Brit.), camiseta (f)
volt, voltio (m)

waistcoat, chaleco (m)
wall-to-wall carpet, moqueta (f)*
washbasin, lavabo (m), lava-manos (m) (*Z/A*)
washer (e.g. of tap), arandela (f), suela (f)
washing-machine, lavadora (f)
wash up, to, fregar (*Sp*), lavar los platos/trastos (*Me*)
waste(paper) basket, cesto (m), papelera (f)
watt, vatio (m)
wax-polisher, enceradora (f)
wine-glass, copa (f)
wire, alambre (m)
wool, lana (f)

zipper, cremallera (f), rache (m) (*Ve*)

Spanish–English

abollo (m), dent, **abollar,** to dent
abridor (m), opener
agrio, sour
aguja (f), needle
alambre (m), wire
alcoba (f)*, bedroom
alfiler (m), pin
alfombra (f), carpet, mat
algodón (m), cotton, cotton wool
alicate(s) (m. (pl.)), pliers, pincers

almidón (m), starch
almirez (m), mortar
almohada (f), pillow
ampolleta (f), ampoule, bulb (*Ch*)
apagar, to switch off, put out
arena (f), sand
arrugar*, to crease
asar, to bake, roast
aspirador(a) (m or f), vacuum cleaner

atorarse, to get blocked up
atrancarse, to get blocked up
azucarero (m), sugar bowl
azulejos (m. pl.), tiles (glazed)

babero (m), bib
balanza (f), scales
balda (f), shelf
balde (m)*, dustbin, trashcan, bucket
bandeja (f), tray
bañera (f), bath tub
baño (m)*, bath, 'toilet', 'john'
banqueta (f)*, stool
basura (f), rubbish, garbage, trash
basurero (m), trashcan, dustbin
bata (f), overall(s), beach wrap
batidor (m), beater, egg whisk
batidora (f), electric beater
batín (m), dressing gown
baúl (m), trunk
bayeta (f), floor cloth
bebida (f), drink, baby's bib (*R/P*)
bizagra (f), hinge
bobina (f), spool, reel
bodega (f), cellar, storeroom
bolsa (f)*, bag
bolso (m), handbag
bombachas (f. pl.), panties (*R/P*)
bombilla (f), bulb (electric), drinking straw (*R/P*)
bombona (f), 'drum' (of butane gas)
botón (m), button
bragas (f. pl.), panties
brocha (f)*, brush
brocheta (f), skewer, spit
bronce (m), bronze, brass
buró (m), roll-top desk
butaca (f), armchair
butano (m), butane, 'calor' gas

caja (f), box
cajón (m), drawer, crate
calcetines (m. pl.), socks
caldera (f)*, boiler, kettle
callo (m), corn (on foot)

calzador (m), shoe-horn
calzoncillos (m. pl.), underpants
cama (f), bed
camisa (f), shirt
camiseta (f), undershirt, vest (Brit.)
canasta (f), basket
candado (m), padlock
cañería (f), pipes, drainpipes
caño (m), tap, faucet (*Pe*)
caravanas (f. pl.), earrings (*C/S*)
carrera (f), ladder/run (stocking)
carrete (m), reel, spool
cartero (m), postman
cazerola (f), saucepan, oven dish
cenicero (m), ashtray
cepillo (m), brush (*v.* **brocha**)
cerámica (f), china, porcelain
césped (m), lawn
cesto (m), basket, waste(paper) basket
chaleco (m), waistcoat/vest, pullover (without sleeves)
chapa (f)*, brass plate, bottle cap
chaqueta (f), jacket
chavija (f), electric plug (*Me*)
chinche (m), **chincheta** (f), thumb tack, drawing pin
chomba (f)*, jumper
chupete (m), baby's dummy
cinta (f), tape, ribbon
clavo (m), nail (for hammering)
cobertizo (m), shed, outhouse
cobija (f), blanket, covering (*Me*)
cocer*, to cook by boiling
cocina (f)*, kitchen
cocinar, to cook
cojín (m)*, cushion
colador (m), colander
colcha (f), counterpane, coverlet
colchón (m), mattress
colgar, to hang
collar (m)*, necklace
colocar, to put away, put in place
colorete (m), rouge
comedor (m), dining-room
cómodo, comfortable
compras (f. pl.), shopping
comprimido (m), pill
congelador (m), ice-compartment

congeladora (f), deep-freeze
contador (m), meter
copa (f)*, wineglass
corbata (f), tie
corcho (m), cork
cordón (m), shoelace
cortar, to cut, shorten
cortarse, to go sour (*Sp*)
cortina (f), curtain
cremallera (f), zipper
criba (f), sieve
crucigrama (m), crossword puzzle
cuadro (m), picture
cuarto (m), room
cuarto de baño (m), bathroom
cubo (m), bucket, dustbin, trash-can
cuchara (f), spoon
cucharada (f), tablespoonful
cucharilla, -ita (f), teaspoon
cuchillo (m), knife
cuerda (f)*, cord, string, rope

dar de sí, to 'give', stretch
dedal (m), thimble
delantal (m), apron, overall(s)
depósito (m)*, tank, storeroom (*R/P*)
derramar*, to spill
derretir, to melt
desarmador (m), screwdriver (*L/A*)
destornillador (m), screwdriver (*Sp*)
detergente (m), detergent
doblar, to fold

empotrado, built in, embedded
encender, to light, switch on
enceradora (f), wax-polisher
enchufe (m)*, electric plug
encoger, to shrink
escalera (f), ladder, stairway
escoba (f), broom
escritorio (m), writing-desk
espejo (m), mirror
estante (m)*, shelf, bookstand
exprimidor (m), squeezer

factura (f), bill, invoice
falda (f), skirt
felpudo (m), coconut mat
fianza (f), surety, deposit (money)
fiebre (f)*, fever, temperature
florero (m), flower vase
flotador (m), ball valve
foco (m), electric bulb (*Me*)
fontanero (m), plumber
forro (m), lining (of clothes, etc.)
fósforos (m. pl.), matches
frazada (f), blanket (*C/S*)
fregar*, to scrub, wash up
freir, to fry (**frito** = fried)
fuente (f), serving dish
fuga (f), leak
funda (f), pillow case
fundir*, to blow/fuse
fusible (m)*, fuse

gamuza (f), yellow duster, shammy
gancho (m), hook
gasa (f), gauze, tampon
gasfitero (m)*, plumber (*Z/A*)
gaveta (f), shallow drawer
gemelos (m. pl.), twins, cuff-links, binoculars
grama (f), lawn (*Ve*)
gramo (m), gramme/gram
grifo (m), tap/faucet
guisar, to cook

habitación (f), room (usually bedroom)
herramienta, -o (f/m), tools, toolkit
hervir, to boil
hilo (m), thread
horno (m), oven
huacha (f), washer (*Z/A*)

imperdible (m), safety pin
interruptor (m)*, electric switch
inventario (m), inventory
invernadero (m), greenhouse, conservatory

jarra (f), jug, jar
jebe (m), elastic (*Z/A*)

jerga (f), floorcloth (*Me*)
juego (m), 'set' (linen, china, etc.)
    hacer juego con, to match with

labor (f), knitting, sewing
lámpara (f), lamp
lana (f), wool
lápiz de labios (m), lipstick
latón (m), brass
lavabo (m), lavamanos (m),
    wash-(hand) basin
lavadora (f), washing machine
lavatorio (m), wash-basin (*C/S*)
laya (f), spade
lechero (m), milkman
lejía (f), bleaching fluid
leña (f), firewood
librería (f)*, bookcase
lija (f), sandpaper
lima (f), file
linterna (f), torch
living (m), main sitting-room
llave (f), key, tap, faucet,
    spanner, wrench, switch
luna (f), pane of glass
luz (f)*, light (often used of
    current)

maleta (f), suitcase
malograr, to go wrong/sour
mancha (f), stain, manchar, to
    stain
mandil (m), apron
mango (m)*, handle
manguera (f), hosepipe
mano (de almirez) (f), pestle
manta (f)*, blanket, rug (*Sp*)
mantel (m), tablecloth
marco (m)*, picture frame
marmita (f), kettle (*Me*)
martillo (m), hammer
mecate (m), string, cord (*L/A*)
medias (f. pl.), stockings
medidas (f. pl.)*, measurements
medir, to measure
mercado (m), market
mesa (f), table
metro (m), inch-tape
mezcla (f), mixture, mezclar, to
    mix

minifalda (f), miniskirt
moqueta (f)*, wall-to-wall carpet
mueble (m), piece of furniture

navaja (f), penknife
nevera (f), ice-box, refrigerator

olla (f)*, saucepan

pala (f), spade
palanca (f), lever
palangana (f), bowl (*L/A*)
palillo (m), cocktail stick, tooth-
    pick
palo de labios (m), lipstick
pañal (m), diaper, 'nappie'
paño (m), cloth, tampon, sani-
    tary towel
pantalones (m. pl.), trousers/
    pants
pantufla (f), slipper (*R/P*)
pañuelo (m), handkerchief
papel higiénico (m), toilet paper
papelera (f), waste-paper basket
pasto (m), lawn (*L/A*)
pata (f),* leg (of furniture)
pava (f), kettle
pendientes (m. pl.), earrings
percha (f), coat/dress-hanger
perilla (f), door-knob (*Ve*)
pestillo (m), door-knob (*L/A*)
pico (m)*, spout
pijama (m), pyjamas/pajamas
pila (f)*, pileta (f)*, sink, dry
    battery
píldora (f), pill
pinza (f), clothes peg/pin
piso (m)*, mat (*Sp*)
plancha (f) iron, planchar, to iron
plato (m), plate, dish
platillo (m), saucer
plomero (m), plumber (*R/P*)
plumero (m), feather duster
pocillo (m)*, coffee cup (*L/A*)
pollera (f), skirt (*R/P*)
polvo (m), dust
poner en condiciones, to set right,
    to repair
poner la mesa, to lay the table
prado (m), lawn (*Z/A*)
pulidor (m), polisher, duster

pulpería (f), grocery store (*L/A*)
puntada (f), stitch
punto (m)*, knitting

quemador (m), burner, incinerator
quilla (f), cushion (*R/P*)

rache (m), zipper (*Ve*)
rallar, to grate, shred
receta (f), recipe, prescription
reparar*, to repair
revolver*, to stir

sábana (f), sheet
sacacorchos (m), corkscrew
sala (f)*, sitting-room, parlour
sartén (f), frying pan
secador (m), drying cloth
segador(a) (m/f), mower
serrucho (m), handsaw
servilleta (f), table napkin
sierra (f), saw (usually mechanical)
soga (f), string, rope
sostén (m), brassière
sótano (m), basement, cellar
suela (f), washer (*L/A*)
suéter (m), sweater

tabla (f), slab, board
taladro (m), drill
talego (m), cloth bag
tamiz (m), sieve
tapa (f)*, lid
tapete (m), mat
tapón (m), stopper, plug, bottle-cap
tarro (m), pot, mug, can
taza (f), cup, bowl
tazón (m), bowl
tejas (f. pl.), tiles (roof)
tela (f), material (textile)

tenazas (f. pl.), pincers, pliers
tenedor (m), fork
tenida (f), dress (*L/A*)
termo (m), hot water tank, thermos flask
terno (m), man's suit (*Z/A*)
tetera (f), tea-pot, kettle
tijeras (f. pl.), scissors
timbre (m), bell (electric)
tirar*, to throw away, spill, pull
toalla (f), towel
tobo (m), bucket, garbage can (*Ve*)
tocar*, to ring (the bell)
tornillo (m), screw
tostador (m), toaster
traje (m), suit, costume
trapo (m), cloth
trastos (m. pl.), dirty dishes (*Me*)
trinchante (m), carving knife
trituradora (f), sink disposal unit

vajilla (f), crockery, china
valija (f), suitcase (*R/P*)
vaso (m)*, glass (tumbler)
vatio (m), watt
vela (f), candle
venda (f), bandage
verter, to pour out (deliberately), to empty
vestido (m), dress
vestido de noche (m), nightdress
visillo (m), thin transparent curtain
voltio (m), volt

yeso (m), plaster

zapato (m), shoe (**zapatilla** (f) = slipper)
zorros (m. pl.)*
zurcir, to darn

Lectures, Conferences and Congresses

It frequently happens that 'specialists' on a variety of subjects have to visit the Hispanic world for the purpose of lecturing on their subject and with no more than a smattering of Spanish. They are usually well looked after by their sponsors but there may be moments—especially, perhaps, when giving a lecture illustrated by slides—when they would prefer not to be too hopelessly dependent on third parties. Equally common is attendance at congresses—or reading the proceedings thereof—and for this, too, a knowledge of the jargon may be useful.

The Spanish for 'lecture' is *conferencia* (*q.v.*), and for 'conference', *congreso*. A 'lecturer', in the general sense, is therefore *un confereciante*. With a capital L, in university circles, however, he will be *Profesor Adjunto* or sometimes, in L/A, *Docente*. Readers may care to know that *conferencia* is a slightly august word for a 'lecture' so that a man might sound a little pompous if he referred to his own as *mi conferencia*; more modest to refer to it as *mi charla*, 'my talk'. Delicacy of this sort will be much appreciated. 'A talk' followed by a discussion is usually referred to as *un coloquio*. 'A lecture-hall' is *una sala de conferencias* though the word *aula* is a good deal used. In the particular matter of illustrated lectures, when direct communication with the gentleman operating the slides is often urgent, the following vocabulary may help:

Dar/pronunciar/dictar (L/A) *una conferencia,* to give a lecture
Una diapositiva, 'a slide', *un cliché* may be used of a glass slide
Una película, 'a film'
El proyector, 'the projector'
La pantalla, 'the screen'
Un puntero, 'a pointer'; *palo,* 'stick', may also be used
Al revés, 'upside-down', 'wrong way round'
La luz, por favor, 'Lights, please'
Señalar or *hacer señal,* 'to make a signal'

In the matter of conferences and congresses:

Congresista, 'anyone attending the congress'.
Comunicación, usually a 'paper' offered by a *congresista* who, in the course of it, will refer to himself as *el comunicante*.
Ponencia, an 'address' given in plenary session, usually by invitation. The man who gives it is *el ponente* and refers to himself as such.
Resumen, literally résumé, usually called an abstract, whether for the programme or for a press hand-out.

It is conventional, on these occasions, to refer to oneself in the Third Person, i.e. instead of saying 'I discovered', one says *el comunicante/ponente descubrió*; 'it appeared to the writer', *parecía al comunicante/ponente*, etc. To us it sounds a little pompous but since it is the convention there is danger of sounding conceited if one uses the First Person for anything of which one is rather proud. Wiser to do so only for the occasional, parenthetical confession of failure or when emphasizing that an expression of opinion is purely personal. We are, after all, fairly used to 'the writer' or 'the present writer' in written communications and *el comunicante/ponente* is quite a logical extension of this. The lst person plural may also be used.

Office Matters

accountant, contable (m. or f.), contador (m)
accounts, contabilidad (f)*, contaduría (f)
addressing letters, *v.* **querer; apellido**
addressing-machine, máquina de direcciones (f)
adhesive tape, (e)scotch (m)
appointment, compromiso (m), cita (f)

ball-point pen, bolígrafo (m), pluma atómica (f) (*Me*)
bill, factura (f)
blotting paper, secante (m)
brackets, paréntesis (m)*
brackets (square), corchetes (m. pl.)

carbon paper, (papel) carbón (m)
card (of card index), ficha (f)*
card-index, fichero (m)
cash, efectivo (m)*, moneda (f)
cash-desk, caja (f)
cashier, cajero (m)
clip, clip (m)
colon, dos puntos (m. pl.)
copy, copia (f)*, ejemplar (m)
correcting fluid, corrector (m)
counter, mostrador (m), mesón (m) (*Ch*)
cover, under separate, por separado
cross out, to, tachar, borrar*

dash/hyphen, guión (m)
'Dear. . .', *v.* **querer**
desk, mesa (f), escritorio (m)
dictate, to, dictar
directory, guía (f)
dispatch/despatch, envío (m); **to dispatch,** expedir*

dossier, carpeta (f)*, expediente (m)*
double-spacing, a dos espacios
draft (of letter)*, borrador (m)
drawing-pin, chinche (f)*, chincheta (f)
duplicator, mimeógrafo (m), multicopista (m)

enclosed, incluído (m), adjunto (m)
enclosing, incluyendo
enclosure, carta (etc.) adjunta
envelope, sobre (m)
expedite, to, despachar, meter prisa, expeditar (*L/A*), apurar (*L/A*)

fair copy, to make, copiar en limpio
file, carpeta (f), archivo (m), expediente (m) (*R/P*)*
filing cabinet, archivador (m)
fire/dismiss, to, despedir, destituir*
fold, to, doblar
full stop, punto (m)

glue, cola (f)

heading, título (m)*, encabezamiento (m)
hyphen, guión (m)

ink, tinta (f)
inverted commas, comillas (f. pl.)

key (typewriter), tecla (f)

lead (of pencil), mina (f)
leave, vacaciones (f. pl.), permiso (m), puente (m)*

259

management, gerencia (f),
  dirección (f)
manager, director (m), gerente
  (m. or f.)
meeting, reunión (f)*, junta (f)*
memorandum, escrito (m),
  volante (m)*
message, recado (m), mensaje (m)
messenger, muchacho (m),
  botones (m)*
mind, to (telephone), atender*
modes of addressing letters, *v.*
  querer, apellido
modes of ending letters, *v.*
  q.e.s.m.

office, oficina (f)*

pad, borrador (m)*, block (m)
paper clip, clip (m)
paper weight, pisapapeles (m)
paragraph, párrafo (m)
paragraph, punto* y aparte
parenthesis, paréntesis (m)*
payment, giro (m), liquidación (f)
pen, bolígrafo (m), pluma (f)
pencil, lápiz (m), bolígrafo (m)*
pencil-sharpener, sacapuntas (m)
period (full stop), punto (m)
priority, top, primordial*
punch, taladro (m), perforadora
  (f)

quotes (in), (entre) comillas (f.
  pl.)

ribbon, cinta (f)*
roller (typewriter), rodillo (m)
roster, turno (m)*
rubber stamp, sello de goma (m)
ruler, regla (f)*

safe, caja fuerte (f)
scissors, tijeras (f. pl.)

scotch (*reg. trade mark*) **(adhesive) tape,** (e)scotch (m), cinta
  adhesiva (f)
scribbling-pad, borrador (m)*
sellotape (*reg. trade mark*), *v.*
  scotch tape
semi-colon, punto y coma (m)
settlement, liquidación (f)
send off, to, expedir*
sheet (of paper), hoja (f), volante
  (m)*
shorthand, taquigrafía (f), steno-
  grafía (f)
shorthand typist, stenógrafa, -o
sign (signature), firmar (firma (f))
single-spacing, a un espacio
space-key, espaciador (m)
stamp (post), sello (m), estampilla (f) (*L/A*)
stamp (rubber), sello (de goma)
  (m)
stapler, grapadora (f), corchetera
  (f) (*Ch*)
stencil, matriz (f), cliché (m),
  (e)stencil (m)
stick, to (gum), pegar*
stroke (/), barra (f)

thumb-tack, chinche (f), chincheta (f)
transfer (money), to, girar
tray, bandeja (f), gaveta (f)
type, **to,** pasar/escribir a
  máquina
typewriter, máquina (de escribir),
  (f)
typist, stenógrafa (f), -o (m),
  mecanógrafa (f), -o (m)

'window' (ticket, etc.), ventanilla
  (f), taquilla (f)
writing pad, block (m)
'writing, in', por escrito

'Yours . . .', *v.* **q.e.s.m.**

Spanish–English

apurar, to expedite, hurry
archivador (m), filing-cabinet or -clerk
archivo (m), file
atender*, to 'mind' (the telephone)
atentamente, faithfully

bandeja (f), tray
barra (f), stroke (/)
block (m), writing pad
bolígrafo (m), ball point pen
borrador (m)*, draft, scribbling pad
borrar*, to draft, cross out
botones (m), office boy

caja (f), cash desk
caja fuerte (f), strong-box, safe
cajero (m), cashier
calco, papel de (m), tracing-paper
carbón (m), carbon paper
carpeta (f)*, file
chinche (f), thumb tack, drawing-pin
cinta (f), tape, ribbon
cita (f), appointment
cliché (m), stencil
clip (m), paper clip
cola (f), glue
coma (f)*, comma
comillas (f. pl.), quotes, inverted commas
compromiso (m)*, appointment
contabilidad (f)*, accounts
contable (m), **contador** (m), accountant
contaduría (f), accounts
copia (f)*, copy
corchete (m), square bracket, staple (*Ch*)
corchetera (f), stapler (*Ch*)
corrector (m), correcting fluid

despacho (m), private office (*Sp*)
despedir, destituir*, to dismiss
dictar*, to dictate
doblar, to fold

efectivo (m)*, cash
ejemplar (m), copy (*v.* **copia**)
encabezamiento (m), heading
envío (m), despatch, sending off
(e)scotch (m), adhesive tape
escritorio (m), writing desk
espaciador (m), space key
espacio(s) (m), **a un/dos,** single/double-spacing
estampilla (f), postage stamp (*L/A*)
(e)stencil (m), stencil
estudio (m), private office (*R/P*)
expediente (m)*, file, dossier
expedir*, to send off

factura (f), bill
ficha (f)*, card (of card index)
fichero (m), card index
firma (f), signature, **firmar,** to sign

gaveta (f), shallow drawer, tray
gerencia (f), management
gerente (m), manager
girar, to transfer (money)
giro (m), money transfer
grapa (f), **-dora** (f), staple, -r
guía (f), guide, directory
guión (m), hyphen, dash, 'script'

hoja (f), sheet (of paper)

incluido (m), included, enclosure

junta (f), meeting

lápiz (m), pencil
limpio, hacer en, to make a fair copy
liquidación (f), payment (of bill)

máquina (de escribir) (f), typewriter
matriz (f), stencil
mensaje (m), message
mesa (f), desk, table
mimeógrafo (m), duplicator
mina (f), lead (of pencil)

moneda (f), coin, cash
mostrador (m), counter
multicopista (m), duplicator

párrafo (m), paragraph
pasar a máquina, to type
pegar*, to stick, glue
perforadora (f), punch, perforator
pisapapeles (m), paper-weight
primordial*, top priority, first in order
prisa, dar, to hurry up
puente (m)*, 'long week-end'
punto (m)*, full stop, period (**dos puntos,** colon)
punto y aparte, paragraph
punto y coma, semi-colon

q.e.s.m., see entry

recado (m), message
regla (f), rule, ruler
reunión (f)*, meeting
rodillo (m), roller

sacapuntas (m), pencil sharpener
secante (m), blotting paper
sello (m), stamp (*Sp*)
sello de goma, rubber stamp
separado, por, under separate cover
sobre (m), envelope
stenógrafa (f), **-o** (m), shorthand typist (*L/A*)

taladro (m), punch, drill
taquigrafía (f), shorthand
taquilla (f), ticket, etc. window
tecla (f), key (of typewriter)
tijeras (f. pl.), scissors
tinta (f), ink
título (m)*, heading
turno (m)*, roster

ventanilla (f), 'ticket' window (i.e. for serving public)
volante (m), fly-sheet, loose sheet of paper

Telephones

The word 'telephone', with minor variations of spelling, is international and one might have expected that 'Hello!', which is pretty international in the northern hemisphere, might have been valid for the Hispanic world likewise, but this is not the case; the word for it varies from country to country. There are other differences but since the greater part of the vocabulary is fairly universal perhaps it is better to deal with that first:

¡Al habla!, 'Speaking!' Another possibility is *¡Soy . . . (yo)!* (*v.* **ser**).

Atender, 'to mind' the telephone: *Tendrá que atender el teléfono* is a fairly common instruction to a secretary or servant. (In the R/P *atender* means 'to answer' the telephone, *v.* **coger**.)

Auricular, strictly 'earpiece', but often used where we say 'receiver'.

Central (f), 'exchange', but words vary for a private exchange (see below).

Colgar, 'to hang up', 'ring off': *No cuelgue*, 'Don't ring off', 'Hold on!'

Descolgar, literally: 'to unhang', i.e. 'to pick up' (receiver). This is the official word but in domestic circumstances a Spaniard is likely to say *coger* (*q.v.*). Since this is 'out' in the R/P they say *atender*.

Disco, 'dial'.

Ficha (*q.v.*), 'dummy coin' needed for many public telephones.

Guía, directory.

Llamar, llamada, 'to call/ring up', and a 'call' respectively.

Marcar (*un número*), 'to dial (a number)'. In L/A you will sometimes hear *discar* but *marcar* is universal currency.

Micrófono, 'mouthpiece'.

¡Oiga!, 'Hello!', but of the kind you say when you are trying to call someone's attention, often in the fear that they are about to hang up or be cut off. For the 'Hello!' uttered initially see below.

Parte, 'behalf', but it almost always occurs in the phrase *¿De parte de quién?*, 'Who is it speaking?' a stock phrase you should memorize.

Poner con, 'to put through to', 'to connect', and I commend particular attention to the *con* which also applies in *hablar con*, 'to speak to. . .'. Phrases for memorization are: *¿Se puede hablar con el Señor . . .?*, 'May I speak to Mr . . .?; *¿Puede ponerme con . . .?* 'Can you connect me with . . .?' It is not unduly abrupt to say *Póngame con. . . .*

Ranura, 'slot', for putting coins or *fichas* into.

Recado, 'message': *¿Quiere dejar un recado?*, 'Do you want to leave a message?' or *¿Puede darle un recado?*, 'Can you give him/her a message?' should be added to your stock. In L/A they sometimes say *mensaje*.

Señal, 'signal', 'dialling tone'. *Tono* is sometimes used for the latter but *señal* is self-explanatory and so universally understood.

Sonar, 'to ring': *Está sonando*, 'It's ringing now'.

Another universal usage which should be engraved on your mind is to say simply *¿Está . . . ?* for 'Is . . . there?' and refrain from adding *allí* or *allá;* also to understand *No está* as meaning 'He/she isn't here'.

Since readers cannot be in more than one country at a time I take the regional variations country-wise:

Spain: 'Hello!' on first answering is *¡Diga!* or *¡Dígame!*
    'Busy/engaged', *comunicando*
    'Private exchange', *centralita*
    'Extension', *extensión*
    'A long-distance call', *una conferencia*

Mexico: 'Hello!' on answering, *¡Bueno!*
    'Busy/engaged', *ocupado*
    'Private exchange', *conmutador*
    'Extension', *extensión*
    'Pardon me!/Sorry, I didn't quite catch', *¿Mande?*

Venezuela: Usually *¡Haló!* on answering; otherwise much as for Mexico.

R/P: 'Hello!' on answering, *¡Hola!*
    'Busy/engaged', *ocupado*
    'Extension', *interno*

Z/A: 'Hello!' *¡Haló!;* in Colombia often *¿A ver?*
    'Private exchange', *conmutador*
    'Extension', *anexo.*

In Chile ''phone', or ''phone number', is nearly always *fono.*

The above will not always be rigorously adhered to nor is the barrier between the different usages rigid. Latin Americans who have travelled are in any case rather fond of saying *¿Haló?* when first answering, sometimes just to show how cosmopolitan they are.

Latin-American Usage and Pronunciation

Spanish, like English, has become a mother-tongue in many countries beyond that of its birth and it is only to be expected that there should be some regional variation in local accent and vocabulary. There is, however, no need to make heavy weather of these differences.

When I first approached the shores of South America it was with some trepidation; I recalled Wilde's remark 'We and the Americans have much in common but there is always the language barrier' and the fact that it was not my mother-tongue. My apprehensions seemed to be justified when, on the sea-front in Guayaquil, I saw a notice: 'PROIBIDO VOTAR BASURA'. The concept of 'voting' rubbish was a new one and although I shortly discovered that it was a misspelling of *botar* this verb is so little used in Spain that I had never come across it. A couple of days later I saw a swing-door in a Peruvian bank marked JALAR; another new one. In the event I need not have worried. The Spaniards Christianised and Hispanised their dominions with remarkable thoroughness and I was far more struck by the ease of communication than by what one well-known dictionary, even as recently as the 1940's, stigmatized as 'grotesque and barbarous usage'. No doubt the fact that Spanish was not my mother-tongue made me less sensitive to words and phrases that would have jarred on the ear of a Spaniard but these never seemed more than a small element in what was manifestly 'Spanish' and — as everywhere — the higher the level of education the less they were noticeable.

My insensitivity will also have made me less alert to differences in regional pronunciation but this at least is evidence that they are not formidable. It is always those closest-up who are most conscious of such differences and so most likely to talk about them; Americans will immediately identify a Canadian accent which to the average Britisher sounds simply 'American'. In the Cono Sur I was told about the extraordinary way Mexicans talk and led to believe I should find them hard to understand but in fact found them among the easiest; Mexicans usually articulate clearly and do not speak very fast, at least as compared with Spaniards who fire away like machine-guns. Those I found hardest to understand, in the initial stages, were Chileans who, like Andalusians, tend to drop their *s*'s, sometimes substituting an 'h' sound, as well as using a great deal of slang. Venezuelans, too, are very fond of slang, indeed it is widespread throughout Latin America, but to cover it adequately would require a different book from this (and a rather larger one). A few general comments, however, may be worth making:

One thing common to all Latin America is pronouncing *z and c* (before *e* or *i*) like *s*, as opposed to the Castilian 'th'. It is the source of endless spelling mistakes as well as confusion, e.g. in a lift when somebody appears to want floor *dos* or *tres* but turns out to want *doce* or *trece*. Another fairly universal trait (also common in Spain) is in not distinguishing between *ll* and *y*; both sound like our 'y', except in so far as they sound like our 'j' in the R/P. The practice of extending a vowel, to emphasize a point, is also widespread, e.g. *l-e-e-e-jos* as opposed to the Peninsular *lejísimo*. In places, notably Mexico, it has a counterpart in very lightly stressed syllables, e.g. *Muchas gracias*, which in Spain would have four almost equally stressed syllables but which there will often come out as *much's graci's* so that it almost sounds like Portuguese. As mentioned under Miscellaneous Notes, the 'best Castilian' does not go in for heavy (or light) stresses and the higher the level of education the more this is universally true.

Another L/A trick is a prolific use of the Diminutive. In the First Edition I remarked that, in Spain, the Diminutive is used to convey cordiality, indeterminacy or understatement. This is just as true of L/A but the practice is even more widespread and has become, one suspects, simply a habit (*v.* MISCELLANEOUS NOTES, p. 22).

In the matter of vocabulary there are a few words which are common to most of the Americas:

boleto, 'ticket' (*Sp. billete*)
caminar, 'to walk' (*Sp. andar*)
chico, 'small/little' (*Sp. pequeño*)
lindo, 'pretty/beautiful' (*Sp. bonito*)
lucir, 'to look/appear' (*Sp. parecer*)
papas, 'potatoes' (*Sp. patatas*)
plata, 'money' (*Sp. dinero*)
regreso, -ar, 'return' (*Sp. vuelta, volver*)
terminar, 'to finish' (*Sp. acabar*)

Cancha is also used for any field or court where games are played whereas in Spain it is mostly confined to the game *pelota*. There are also words which, although universal, have become debased in certain countries and for which substitutes must therefore be sought, *v.* **coger, fregar, jalar, pico, polla, tirar.** Here we get on to local variations and the innumerable Amerindian contributions to the Spanish language, particularly in the Z/A and in Mexico, and here I have to give up since their number is enormous. Dictionaries of 'Americanisms' exist but they badly need reprinting and bringing up to date. At the moment they are hard to come by, even in second-hand shops, so that it is little use telling readers their titles, but they involve a tremendous amount of work by whole committees of experts and so are outside the brief of this book which is primarily concerned with the 90 per cent which needed no justification. Let me therefore confine myself to a few comments on regional pronunciation:

In the River Plate area Italian influence has been strong and seems to have affected their manner of speaking. They tend to give—by Peninsular standards—exaggerated stresses; they use *pronto* for 'ready', instead of the usual *listo* (*q.v.*); they rarely use the Past Indefinite tense (nor do Chileans); they use *vos* (*q.v.*) and they pronounce *ll* and *y* like the English 'j', e.g. *galletitas* (biscuits/cookies) which sound as though they were little gadgets.

In Colombia, Venezuela and thereabouts, not excluding Mexico, their *j*'s, *ge*'s and *gi*'s are a good deal less guttural than in Spain and often hardly more aspirated than an English 'h'. On the other hand they will sometimes give the same light aspiration to words beginning with *h*: *hijo* comes out almost as *jijo; humo* as *jumo*, etc. Also when a Diminutive involves two *t*'s the second is usually converted into *c*: *galletitas* becomes *galleticas*; *momentito, momentico*, etc. (a practice not unknown in some parts of Spain).

I heard many opinions expressed as to where the 'best' Spanish is spoken outside Spain and the answers usually revolved around Colombia and Peru. I suspect this chiefly meant that the ruling classes in those countries have clung with the greatest conservatism to the original Spanish (and good Castilian still commands some respect) but they are also countries with a very high percentage of Amerindians whose tongues (notably Quechua) have greatly added to their vocabulary. In the same way Nahuatl, the language of the old Aztec empire, has contributed to Mexican speech (and indeed the world's; what about such everyday words as 'chocolate', 'tomato', 'potato', 'tobacco'?). It is perhaps particularly in the matter of food that they are most noticeable; no doubt because in the earliest days 'Mamá' was an Amerindian.

During recent years, and particularly since the advent of television, processes have been at work in the Hispanic world similar to those in the Anglo-Saxon. A profusion of North-American films find their way to Hispanic screens but in what sort of Spanish are they to be dubbed? The problem has been squarely confronted and there now exists—I believe in Puerto Rico—a dubbing centre which keeps its eye on death-traps and is producing a kind of mid-Atlantic Spanish which will be understood everywhere and not cause too much shuddering or giggling. As a result even conservative Spain is coming to accept usages which in the past might have been denounced by the *Real Academia*.

This, one feels, must be all to the good. It would be a world of pities if Spanish fragmented into several Hispanic tongues in the way that Latin did in the Dark and Middle Ages. Despite the diverse beauties of the Romance languages, Towers of Babel are not to be desired, nor are they really necessary. A language which is hospitable can assimilate foreign words while still remaining unmistakably itself, indeed being enriched thereby. Purists look backwards, not forwards, and a Frenchman, say, who shudders at the barbarities of French-Canadian speech has probably never asked himself how Vergil or Horace would have reacted to the Frankish treatment of their classical Latin.

With modern communications there is now less danger of fragmentation but it is worth bearing in mind that a language can fragment horizontally as well as vertically; this happened to Latin which remained the *lingua franca* of educated Europe until the 18th century when nationalism finally killed it. There are some who would settle for a 'mandarin' speech for the educated, leaving the groundlings out of account but in fact no class is 'an Iland intire of it selfe'; we are all 'a peece of the Continent' — by now of several Continents — and have to appreciate that it takes all sorts to make a language. Aldous Huxley remarked that a language is a work of genius — but a collective one, formed over the millennia by all and sundry in a multitude of diverse circumstances, and slowly made apt for all occasions. The wit, widsom and wording of proverbs are analogous to the subtle curves of an axe-handle. Individual geniuses have greatly extended the range of this 'Common Man's' speech but without it they could not have started.

It is, of course, always in process of change, a continuum in which new words and usages emerge while others fade away. Pronunciation also changes; The Great Vowel Shift of the 15/16th century knocked the speech of Chaucer into quite a different shape. What seems much more resistant to change is the 'lilt', the deep underlying rhythm which is the heartbeat of every language, imposed on it perhaps by the form of its words and structures but nevertheless one of its most characteristic features. It was this that produced most of our verse forms and for those with ears to hear it sounds through Chaucer/Shakespeare/ Wordsworth/Longfellow/Yeats/Eliot as it does through *El Cid*/ Vega/Cervantes/Lorca/Neruda/Borges . . . If we could hear how the Common Roman spoke Latin at the time, say, of the Antonines — no doubt with much use of *ille, iste* and *unum* — I would guess that we should hear a tune recognisably like modern Italian. It would be fascinating to know how it compared with the provincial speech of *Hispania*. A latterday Spaniard regards Italian as excessively stressed and mocks its sentimental, 'effeminate' lilt. By comparison Spanish is spoken vigorously; an Italian mocks it for its brutal *b/v*'s — no distinction between the two — and its guttural *j*'s — making a noise like retching — and sets one wondering to what extent Spanish diction was influenced by Visigothic and Arabic.

Whatever the truth of the matter — and we shall probably never know — it seems clear that language needs processing by the 'folk' who knock it into manageable and potentially poetical shape. The French word *courage* was given the Stratford-atte-Bowe treatment several centuries ago so that it is now 'correct' to pronounce it 'kurridge', whereas *garage*, a much more recent acquisition dating from the days when it was mostly the educated who possessed cars, is still only half-way to 'garridge'. Similar processes were at work in Spain where *ferrum* was being turned into *hierro*, *miraculum* into *milagro*, 'parable' into *palabra* and various bits of Visigothic (*rico, ganso*), Basque (*izquierda*) and Arabic (*olé, ojalá*) assimilated, thus evolving the uncommonly beautiful continuum we now know as 'Spanish'. Language, like charity, undoubtedly begins at home but it does not end there; it ranges through all levels of society and psyche, our vital and subtle means of inter-communication. It is not a finished artefact belonging to a definite past, nor the possession of ideological 'schoolmen' with bees in their bonnets. Handle words with sufficient skill and it is wonderful how you can handle your fellow creatures but this ability is not simply a matter of class, sex, nation or education (some of the 'schoolmen' speak — and write — abominably). If we speak 'badly' then the fault, dear *brutos*, is ultimately in ourselves.

It goes without saying that the process continues even now in Latin America and there, away from the shadow of the *Real Academia*, Spanish has shown itself more hospitable than in Spain. English itself has been responsible for some of the assimilations; *posponer*, for example, is often used there to mean 'postpone' though it strictly means 'to put after' in the sense of 'rank lower' and 'postpone' is *aplazar*; *tópico* is used for 'topic' though its proper meaning is 'catchphrase, cliché, platitude'. Transatlantic dubbings result in Spaniards hearing, e.g., *remover* used for 'to remove', *audiencia* for 'audience', etc. and the process seems likely to continue. I should not like to suggest that it is *all* to the good. Foreign borrowings are justified when they provide something not previously available, even if only a nuance, but not when they mask ignorance. I find myself irritated to hear people say 'disinterested' when they really mean 'uninterested' or 'hopefully' when they mean 'I/we hope', since it reveals a failure to appreciate their own language. Serious writers, however, are bound to consider the proper use of their own language and the literature of Latin America is increasingly a 'must' for educated people. Linguistic innovations will find their way into it, will even come to be accepted by the *Real Academia*, but that is the way with language. (Latin America, moreover, despite an addiction to ideology in poltics, has been less plagued with linguistic ideology than the Anglo-Saxon world.) Human beings have an understandable tendency to regard history, and therefore language, as finishing 'now' simply because, for the moment, we have reached the last page, but there are clearly many more exciting chapters ahead and some of them will undoubtedly be written in Spanish.

Language, in short, like charity, yes, and money and politics, is a means to a greater end, not an end in itself, and is as good as those who use it. By exploring and exploiting its riches, past and present, they will often discover themselves to be better than they modestly imagined. A fine mother-tongue with a long tradition and a great literature is a priceless inheritance. The main thing required of legatees is to appreciate it.

English–Spanish
Cross-Reference Index

IMPORTANT NOTE: The words *cross-reference* cannot be too strongly emphasized; the following pages merely provide a means of tracking down information, not of providing it ready-made. The average dictionary is a two-way affair but since, in this handbook, it would obviously be a waste of space to give the commentary twice over, all this is concentrated in the Spanish-English section. The index which follows will, I hope, make it fairly easy to find but in many cases it will be indicated under *the very word you should not use*. Where False Friends are concerned the Spanish word is shown in brackets in the hope that readers will be discouraged from thinking it is a translation but the Unreliables cannot always be handled in this way.

Readers should also be conscious that words coming under the heading of CARS, FOOD, HOUSEHOLD WORDS, OFFICE MATTERS, COURTESY, TELEPHONES, LECTURES, CONFERENCES and CONGRESSES will not appear in this index unless there is some reason for comment in the Spanish-English section.

A

abandon, to, abandonar
abide by, to, sujetar
ability, condición, preparación, solvencia
able, to be, saber
abortion, (aborto)
about, alrededor, argumento, eso, tratar
abrupt, brusco
absent-minded, despistar
absolute(ly), absoluto, completo
absurd, disparar, tontería
abuse, to, (abusar)
A.C. (current), corriente
academic, escolar
accessory, accesorio
accident, accidente, casual
accidentally, accidentado
acclimat(iz)e oneself, to, ambiente
accommodate, to, caber
accompany, to, asistir

according to, según
accost, to, (acostarse)
account(s), contabilidad, cuenta
account(s), to settle, echar
account, to take into, cuenta
accuse, to, acusar
ache, dolor
achieve, acabar
acknowledge, acusar
acquaintance, to make, conocer
acquiesce, to, condescender
acquire, to, proporcionar, procurar(se)
act as, to, papel
actually, efectivamente, (actual)
A.D., a. de J.C. (p. 30)
add, to, añadir, sumar
addict, toxicómano, (adicto)
addition to, in, como
address, dirección, señas
address oneself to, to, fijar, (acostar)
adequate, (adecuado)

adjoining, inmediato
adulterate, to, mistificar
advance, to, adelantar
advance, in, anticipación
advantage, convenir, aprovechar
advert, to, (advertir)
advertise, to, anunciar
advise, to, advertir, (avisar)
affected, cursi, guachafo
affection, cariño, (afección)
afford, to, alcance, para
afraid, miedo
afternoon, tarde
afterwards, luego
against, to be, partidario
agency, intermedio
agility, destreza
agony, (agonía)
agreement, conforme, quedar
ahead, straight, adelante, allá
aim at, to, apuntar, buscar
aim to, to, pretender
air hostess, azafata, aeromoza
air-conditioned, condicionar
alert, to be, estar
alias, apodo
alienate, to, extrañar
alive, vivo
all at sea, (tener), despistar
all right, regular, valer
all the same, dejar
all for, to be, partidario
all that, and, lo, tal
allow, to, dejar
almost, poco
alone, solo
along?, how far, altura
aloud, alto
already, ya
alter, to, (alterar)
always, siempre, soler
amalgamate, to, incorporarse
amends, to make, reparar
American, norteamericano
amiable, (amable)
amorous, (amoroso)
amount, cantidad
amount to, to, efectivamente, alcance
ample, (amplio)

amusing, divertido, entretener, gracia, ingenioso, ocurrencia
and-er-and-um, este
angry, echar
announce, to, (anunciar), denunciar
annoyed, -ing, disgustar, fastidiar, molesto
another, otro
answer, contestar, atender
anticipate, to, adelantar, anticipación
anxious, solícitar
anybody, cualquier, quién
any more, ya
anyway, forma, modo, ser
apart, aparte
apart from, fuera
apartment, apartamento, piso, departamento
ape, to, remedar
apologize, to, (apología)
appalling, funesto
apparatus, -dora
apparently, ver, parecer, como
appear, to, parecer, lucir
appearance, pinta
appetize, to, provocar
applaud, celebrar
applause, worthy of, plausible
applicable, extender
application, solicitud
apply oneself, to, dedicarse, fijar
appoint, to, nombrar
appointment, comprometer, concertar, esperar, quedar
appreciable, sensible, (apreciable)
appreciate, caer, caso, apreciar, enterarse
appropriate, adecuado, apto, convenir, corresponder, indicado
approve of, to, aprobar
approximately, alrededor, así, modo
apropos, propósito
apt, apto
area/well, patio
argue, to, discutir

beard, barba
beautiful, guapo, lindo, precioso
beauty parlour, peluquería
become, to, hacerse, ponerse, ir, llegar, convertirse
become of, to, pasar
bed, catre
bed (double), matrimonio
bed, to go to, acostarse
bedbug, chinche
bedroom, alcoba, cuarto, habitación
beforehand, antes, anticipación
begin again, to, (resumir)
begin with, to, pronto
behave, to, culto, educación
'behind', culo
beho(o)ve, to, corresponder
believe it! Would you, fijar
bell, campana
bell captain, conserje
bell-hop, botones
belong, to, corresponder
bench, banqueta
benefit, provecho
bet, I'll, ver
betoken, denunciar
better, best, indicado, mejor, valer
better and better, vez
beverage, trago
bewilder, to, despistar
beyond, allá, rebasar, fuera
bid, to (cards), marcar
big? How, tamaño
'big-mouth', -azo
bill/check, cuenta
bill of fare, cubierto
billing (theatre), cartel
bin, balde
birthday, (santo)
birthplace, naturaleza
bit/piece, pedazo
bit, and a, pico, tanto
black-out, desmayo
blame, culpa
blanket, manta, cobija
bleaching fluid, lejía
'blessed', este
'Bless you!', Jesús
block letter, molde

block (city), bloque, cuadra
blocked, to get, tapa
blond, rubio
blood, bad, leche
'bloody', bárbaro, brutal
blot one's copybook, pata
blow, a, golpe
blow, to (fuse), fundir
blow one's nose, to, sonar
blue, pale, celeste
blush, to, acholarse
board, tabla
'boarder', pensionista, pupilo, huésped
boarding-house, huésped
boil, to, cocer, hervir
boiler, caldera
bones (fish), espina
bookcase, estante, librería
bookshop/store, librería
booze, trago
borderline, margen
bored, boring, aburrido, pesado
born, natural
boss, golpe, jefe
boss, to, manejar
bother, to, molestar, preocuparse
bottle, hot water, bolsa, guaya
'bottom', culo
bound by, to be, sujetar
bound for, to be, rumbo
bound to, to be, tener
bowling alley, bolero, boliche
boy, chico
boy-friend, novio, pololo
box, P.O., aparte
bracket, paréntesis
brainwave, ocurrencia
brake, to, echar
brand, marca
brand-new, flamante
brass, bronce
brass plate, chapa, placa
brass tacks, precisar
brawl, jaleo
brazen, caradura
break-down, accidentado, descomponer, composturas
break-down, nervous, crisis
break into, to (e.g. a run), echar

break, to (change money), feria, sencillo
break (e.g. for tea), descanso, intermedio
break (lucky), chance
breath, dying, agonía
breathe down one's neck, to, apretar
breathe in, to, aspiración
breeding, culto, educación
bridge the gap, to, salvar
bridges, to cross, adelantar, anticipar
briefcase, cartera, portafolio
'bright' (of persons), ocurrente
bring, to, llevar
bring off, to, realizar
broad, amplio
broadcast, to, anunciar, echar
broadcasting, divulgación
brochure, prospecto
bronze, bronce
bruise, cardenal
brunette, (rubio)
brush, brocha
brusque, brusco
bucket, balde
buddy, cuate
bugger, (cagar)
build (stature), complexión
built-in, armario
bulk, in, granel
bum, vago, culo
bumpy (roads), accidentado, agujero, calamina
bunch (flowers, etc.), manojo
burn out, to, fundir
burst out, to (e.g. laughing), echar
bus, bus
business, lo, misión, trámites
business, to be one's, allá, corresponder, cuenta, meter
business, to know one's, preparado
bus-stop, parada
busy (v. TELEPHONES)
busy, to get, apurar
but, sino
butane gas, bomba

butcher, to, matar
butt in, to, pata
butter, mantequilla
butter to (fig.), engreír
by and large, modo
by oneself, solo
by, to put, aparte
by the way, paréntesis, propósito

C

cabin, rancho, barraca
cable, guaya, mecate
cake, pastel, torta, queque
call, to, llamar, calificar
call for, to, recoger
calm, (calma), quieto
camera, cámara, máquina
'camomile' tea, manzanilla
camping, campo
can/tin, bote, lata, tarro (*Ch*)
'can', baño
cancel, to, (cancelar)
can't quite, alcance, medio
candid, (cándido)
candies, caramelos, golosinas
candlestick, palmatoria
capital letters, molde
car, automóvil, coche
cardboard, carta
card-index, ficha
care, to take, procurar
career, carrera
careful, to be, procurar
careful, you can't be too, poco
caretaker, conserje, portero
'carried forward', suma
carry out/through, to, realizar, verificar
carton, carta, cajetilla
case, caso
case, in any, caso, forma
case history, expediente
cash, efectivo
cash, to, cobrar
cassette-player, tocacintas
casual, (casual), eventual
casualty, accidentado
catch, to, coger, agarrar
catch up, to, alcance

cause, to, costar
caution, (caución)
cease to be, to, dejar
celebrate, festejar
cellar, bodega
cement, cemento
ceremony, to stand on, cumplir
certain, (cierto), seguro
certainly, caber, como, seguro
certificate, título
chamber-pot, vaso
chance, acaso, casual, chance
change, to, cambiar
change one's mind, to, mudarse, seguir, voluble
change (clothes), mudarse, cambiar
change (money), feria, sencillo, soltar
channel, canal
chaos, embrollo, follón
chap, tío, chico, cuate, sujeto, tipo
character, carácter, persona
charge, to, acusar
charge (prices), pedir, cobrar
charging off, to go, disparar
charming, precioso
charwoman, asistente, empleada
chase, to, perseguir
chat, chatter, charla, departir
chauffeur, chófer
cheat, to, (decepcionar), trampa
check up, to, revisar, controlar
check/bill, cuenta, vale
cheek(y), caradura, fresco, grosero
cherish the hope, to, ilusión
child, chaval, criatura, guagua
chimera, (ilusión)
chimney, chimenea
chit, vale
choice, elección, discreción
chore, tarea
chorus, (refrán)
Christ!, coño, (joder)
Christian name, apellido, pila
Christmas card, christmás
chunk, pedazo
church (Protestant), templo

cigar, cigarette, cigarro, puro
cigarette-lighter, yesquero
cistern, depósito
citizen, súbdito
city-planning, urbanización
claim, reclamación
'claret cup', chicha
clerk, dependiente
clever, abusar, listo, vivo
cliché, tópico
client, pensionista
climate (of opinion), ambiente
clipping, recortar
clock in/on, to, fichar
closet, armario, closet
cloth, paño
clue, not a, absoluto
coach (motor), bus
coarse, grosero
coast, costa
cock-crow, madrugar
cocktail (party), coctél, copa
coffee, café
coffee-cup, pocillo
coincidence, casualidad
'cold', a, constipado
collar, (collar)
collect, to, recoger, recolección
collide, to, chocar
Cologne, eau de, colonia
colossal, tamaño
coloured, colorado
come and get, to, buscar
come away from, to, quitar
come in!, adelante, pasar
come of it, to, resultar
come off, to, éxito
Come on!, andar
come out, to, salir
comfortable, cómodo
comma, coma
command, mandar
'commercials', anunciar
commitment, compromiso
'common', vulgar, ordinario
common sense, sentido
commonplace, tópico
commotion (conmoción)
competence, (competencia), preparación

cunt, coño, bizcocho
cupboard, armario, placard, closet
cure, cura
current, corriente, actual, curso
curse, to, injuriar
cushion, cojín
custodian, conserje
cut, cortado
cut (ignore), to, negar
cut away, to, recortar
cute, cuco (*C/A*)
cutlery, cubierto
cutlet, bife (*v.* also FOOD)
cutting/clipping, recortar

D

daily, diario
damage, perjuicio
dare, to, atreverse
dark-complexioned, (rubio)
data, dato
date, to fix a, concertar, estar, quedar
dawdle, to, demorarse, entretenerse
daydream, ilusión
D.C. (current), corriente
dead, muerto
dead centre, muerto
deal out, to, dar, repartir
deal with, to, tratar
Dear . . . (letters), querer
death-bed, agonía
death-duties, patrimonio
deceive, to, (decepción), mistificar, ilusionarse
decent, prudencial, decente
deception, (decepción)
decide, to, condicionar, determinar, quedar
decimal point, coma
decreasingly, vez
dedicate, to, dedicarse, misión
deep-freeze, congelador
default, falta
defraud, to, (defraudar)
degree, grado
deign, to, (condescender)

delay, to, demorarse, retrasar
deliberately, propósito
delicate, suave
delicious, (delicioso), rico
delightful, delicioso
deliver, repartir
deluded, ilusión
demand, to, exigir
demonstration, manifestación
denote, to, denunciar
deny, to, negar
depart, to, irse, marcharse
department store, almacén
department (govt.), secretaria
depends, it all, según
deplorable, funesto
deposit, abono, enganche, depósito
deprive, to, quitar
describe as, to, calificar
deserve, to, merecer, valer
deshabillé, salto, mañanita
desirable, conveniente
desire, to, desear
desist from, to, dejar
desk (school), carpeta
despatch, to, despedir
destination, destino
destitute, (destituir)
detach, to, aparte
detached, (destacar), margen
details, to fix, precisar
determine, to, (determinar), condicionar
detriment, perjuicio
devise, to, idear
devolve on, to, (devolver)
devote oneself to, to, dedicarse
dexterity, destreza
dial, cara, disco
dial, to, marcar
diary, (diario)
dictate, to, condicionar, dictar
difference, dar, poco
different, distinto
difficulty, problema, (convenir)
difficulties, to make, reparar
dig, to, remover
dilly-dally, to, entretenerse, demorarse

E

each one, quien
early hours, -bird, madrugar
earnestly request, to, solicitar
earn one's living, to, dedicar, ganar
Easter, fiesta
easy! Take it, disparar, calma, quieto, alterar, nervioso
easy, to make, (facilitar)
eaten away, agujero
eau-de-Cologne, colonia
eccentric, extravagante
edit, -or, editar
educated, culto, ilustrado, formación
education, enseñar, educación
effect, transcendencia
effect, in, efectivamente
egg, huevo, blanquillo
elastic, caucho, resorte, dar
elder, mayor
elevator, elevador
'elevenses', merienda
else, más
embarrass, to, acholarse, violento, (embarazada)
embezzle, to, (defraudar)
emergency (casual)
emit, to, echar
emotion, conmoción, emocionar
employee, empleado
'empty' (bottle), envase, bote (*Me*)
enclosed, incluso
encounter, to, encontrar
endure, to, soportar
engaged, novio, relación (*v.* also TELEPHONES)
engagement, compromiso
engraving, estampa
enjoy, to, apreciar
enormity, (disparar)
enough, bastar
enquire, to, preguntar
enrol, to, matricularse
entanglement, embrollo, lío
entertain, to, (entretener)
entertaining, divertido,

(entretener)
enthusiast, adicto
entirety, integrar
entrance, entrée, entrada
equivocate, to, (equivocar), vacilar
er . . . er . . ., este
erase, to, borrar
errand, misión
ersatz, sucedáneo
escape, escape
essential, imprescindible
estate (country), estancia
estate (housing), urbanización
even, hasta, incluso, así
even, not, ni
evening, tarde
event, suceso
events, at all, ser, modo
ever, cualquier, vez
everybody, quien
everybody else, demás
evidence, dato
evidently, parecer, como, ver
exact, to, exigir
exactly, (concretar)
exaggerate, to, exagerar, jalar (*Me*), abusar
example, copia
exchange, to, cambiar
exchange (telephone), central, conmutador
excitable, nervioso
excite, -ment, emocionar, excitarse, alterar, ilusión
exhaust (cars), escape
exhaust, to, extenuar, polvo
exhibit, to, exponer
expect, -ation, anticipación, esperar
expected, to be, lógico
expected, when least, pensar, mejor
expedite, to, (expedir), meter
expend, to, (desperdiciar)
expense, gastar
expertise, cancha
'experts', adicto
expiry, agonía
explain, to, explicar

explode, explotar
exploit, to, explotar, aprovechar
expose, expound, to, exponer
exquisite, precioso
extend, extension, extenso
extensive, extenso
extent, extenso, alcance, modo
extent, to a certain, modo
extenuate, to, (extenuar), atenuar
extra, reserva, accesorio, sobrar
extract, to, sacar, sustraer
extraneous, extraño
extraordinary, raro, casualidad, ocurrencia
extras (cars), acesorios
extravagant, (extravagante)
extreme, sumo
eye (needle), (agujero)
eye-glasses, anteojos

F

fabric, (fábrica)
'fabulous!', bárbaro, brutal, estupendo, chévere, máximo
facilities, comodidades, (facilitar)
fact, in, efectivamente, (actual)
fact that, by the, mismo
factory, fábrica
fail to, to, alcance, fracaso, explicar
fail, to (exam), suspender, (aprobar)
fail, without, falta
failure, fracaso
faint, to, desmayarse
faint, to feel, mareado
fair, -ly, bastante, (v. also notes on Diminutive, p. 22)
fair (so-so), regular, así, discreto
fair (industrial, etc.), feria
fair-haired, rubio
faithfully, q.e.s.m.
fall, to, caer
fallow, calma
family, familiar
family, of good, bien
famous, notorio

'fan' (enthusiast), adicto
fancy that!, fijar, parecer
far, not so, allá
far (along), how, altura, como
far from it!, menos
far-reaching, alcance, envergadura, trascendental
fashion, (modo)
fast, prisa
fast, to, ayunas
fasten, to, apretar, sujetar
'fatal', funesto
faucet, grifo
fault, culpa, faltar
fault, to find, reparar
favour of, to be in, partidario
fear, to, miedo
fearful, barbaridad, miedo
feather-duster, zorros
features, facción, señas
fed up, to be, disgusto, fastidiar, harto, (tener)
feel like, to, gana, venir
feeling, (afección)
fellow, chico, hombre, tío, tipo
fertilizer, abono
fetch, to, buscar
fever, calentura
few, poco
fewer, menos
financé(e), novio, pololo
'fiddle', to, trampa
fidgety, inquieto
field, campo
file, carpeta, expediente (v. also OFFICE MATTERS)
fill up, to, echar
fillet, bife (v. also FOOD)
filter (cigarette), boquilla
filth, -y, asco, mugre
find, to, buscar, encontrar, proporcionarse
find oneself, to, encontrarse
find one's way about, to, ubicarse, ambiente
find out, to, enterarse, determinar
fine (of a person), caracter, persona, tío
finger-print, huella

finish, to, acabar
finish off, to, apurar, resolución
fire, to (dismiss), destituir, (noticia)
fire, fuego
fire-place, chimenea
fire-wood, leña
firm (company), firma
firm, to hold, sujetar
first, at, pronto
first floor, piso
first of all, primordial, todo
fish, pescado
fishbones, espina
fish out, to, sacar
fit, to, convenir, corresponder, valer
fitting (suitable), adecuado, apto, corresponder
fix, to, arreglar, fijar
fix up, to, concretar, condicionar
flat/apartment, apartamento, piso
flatter, to, coba, engreír, suave
'flies' (trousers), (bragas)
flint (lighter), piedra
flirt, to, afilar (*Arg*)
floor, piso, suelo
'flop', fracaso
'flu', gripe
fly, to (hurry), correr
follow, to, seguir
follows that, it, luego
following (day), inmediato
'folly', a, disparate
fond of, to be, (afección), apreciar, cariño, partidario
font, pila
fool, bestia, imbécil, pendejo
fool of oneself, to make a, plancha
foolscap, ministro
foot-and-mouth disease, aftosa
foot in it, to put one's, pata, plancha
foot, to go on, andar, caminar
football, balón
footprint, huella
'for' (in favour of), adicto, partidario

for, to be (used), servir
forehead, frente
foreign, (extraño)
foresee, to, estar, ya
foreground, término
forget, to, cuenta
fork (roads), empalme
form, forma
formal, formal
formalities, gestiones, trámites
formidable, miedo
forthwith, ipso facto
fortunately, (desgracia)
forward, adelante
forward, to look, ilusión
forward, a great step, salto
found, is to be, caer
foundations, cimiento
frame, marco
franking (letters), franqueo
fraternity, (adicto)
fraud, (defraudar)
freakish, extravagante
free and easy, preocuparse
freeway, autopista
French fried, francesa
frequency, frecuencia
frequent, to, cursar
frequently, vez, frecuencia
Friday, 13th, martes
friend, cuate (*Me*)
fright, susto
frighten, to, meter
frightful, barbaridad, miedo
front of, in, frente
front, back to, revés
fuck, to, joder, fregar, coger, chingar (*Me*)
fulfil, to, cumplir
full up, completo
funerals, ardiente, velatorio
funny (peculiar), extraño, raro
funny (amusing), divertido, entretener
furious, echar, enchilarse (*Me*)
further on, allá, adelante
fuse, fundir
fuss, escándalo, follón
fuss, to kick up a, armar, follón

fuss of, to make a, engreír, mimar
fussy, difícil, particular, regodeón

G

gain, to, ganar
galore, granel
gamble, to, jugar
game, juego, partido
gap, hueco, (salvar)
garage, (coche), (v. also CARS)
garbage can, balde
garden, jardín
'gas', gasolina
gasp, last, agonía
gate, puerta
gather (speed), to, coger
gathering, concurrencia, tertulia
gauze, gasa
gazebo, mirador
gear(s), directa
General Delivery, (recomendado)
genial, (genial)
genius, genio
gentle, suave, (gentil)
'Gents', baño
genuine, regular, criollo
get, to (become), hacerse, ponerse, ir, llegar
get, to (fetch), buscar
get to (obtain), coger, conseguir, facilitar, procurarse
get, to (receive), llevar
get, to (understand), caer, ya
get as far as, to, alcance, llegar
get back, to, recuperar, cobrar, volver
get busy, to, apurar
get down to, to, dedicarse, liarse
get down to brass tacks, to, precisar
get hold of, to, coger, conseguir, agarrar (*R/P*), proporcionar, facilitar, sujetar
get into, to, meter
get on, to, andar, ir, seguir, cundir, éxito
get on well with, simpatizar,

get on with, to, cundir
get out, to, quitar, sacar
get (clean) over, salvar
get the money, to, cobrar
get through a lot of work, rendir
get to, to, llegar
get to know, to, conocer
'ghastly', funesto, cacharro
giddy, to feel, mareado
girl-friend, novio, pololo
give, to (stretch), dar
give (cause), to, costar
give back, to, devolver
give way, to, cedar
give up, to, dejar, abandonar
give, not to, restar
'given', determinado
gladly, gana, grado
glass, vaso
glasses (eye), anteojos
glue, cemento
gluttony, (golosinas)
'go', a, vez
go, let's, ir
go, to, ir, marcharse
go, to (fit in), caber
go, to have a, intentar, tratar
go ahead, adelante, allá
go as far as, to, alcance, llegar
go a long way, to, cundir
go-and-get/find, to, buscar
go back, to, volver, regreser
go charging off, to, disparar
go down well/badly, to, ver
go fast, to, correr
go first, to (cards), salir, mano
go of, to let, soltar
go off, to (guns), disparar
go on (doing), to, seguir
go out, to, egresar, salir
go over again, to, revisar
go too far, to, abusar, exagerar
go up, to, subir
go well, to, marchar, cundir
go without saying, to, preciso
goal, gol, tanto, motivo
goal-keeper, portero
good enough, valer
good, no, contraproducente, servir
good, not very, católico

help, daily, asistente, empleado
helpful, atento
'he-man', macho
hem in, to, apretar
hence, ahí
here, acá, ahí
Here he comes!, ya
hereby/with, presente
high, also
high-class, categoría
highest, the, sumo
high-gear, directa
highly strung, nervioso
high-ranking, categoría
high time, ya
highway, carrera, autopista
hill, costa
hire,to, alquilar, arrendar
hit, golpe, pegar
hitch-hike, autostop
hold of, to get, coger, sujetar, agarrar, facilitar, proporcionar
hold (firm), to, sujetar
hold out, to, extender
hold up, to demorar, retrasar
hold-up, (sujetar)
hole, agujero
holidays, feria, fiesta
hollow, agujero, hueco
home, hogar, nacional
homely, feo
home-produced, nacional, lugareño
home-work, tarea
honest, confianza, decente
honk/hoot, to, pitar
hope, esperar, ilusión, ojalá
hope to, to, pretender
horrible (weather), feo
host, -ess, anfitrión
hostess (air), azafata
'hot' (peppery), picante
hot water bottle, bolsa, (guaya)
hours, the 'small', madrugar
house, to move, mudarse
housing-estate, urbanización
how ...?, como, cuanto, más, tal, tan, altura, tamaño
how about ...?, qué, tal

however, cualquier
'howler', disparate
how old? (children), tiempo
How should I know?, saber
huge, tamaño
hunk, pedazo
hurry, to, correr, apurar, prisa
hurry, to (Trans.), meter
Hurry up!, andar, correr
hurt, to, doler
husband, (esposo)
hustle, to, apurar
hut, barraca, rancho

I

ice-compartment, congelador
ice-cream, mantecado
idea, concepto, hipótesis, ocurrencia
idea!, No, absoluto, ni
idea, not a bad, estar
ideas, to get wrong, ilusionarse
identity card, cédula
idiom, (idioma)
idiot, bestia, imbécil, pendejo
idle, holgar
ignition key, suiche (*Ve*)
ignore, to, caso, (ignorar), negar
ignorant, (educado), (culto)
ill-bred, (educación)
ill-mannered, feo, grosero, (formal)
ill-tempered, genio
illusion, (ilusión)
illustrious, (ilustrado)
imagine, to, suponer
imagine!, Just, fijar
imbroglio, embrollo, lío
imitate, to, remedar
immediate(ly), inmediato, ipso facto
impart, to, participar
impartial, preocuparse
impeccable, inobjetable
imply, suponer
importance, trascendencia
important, importar, significado
inactive, holgar

just so happens that, preciso
just too bad, paciencia, ni
justification, apología

K

keep, to, conservar, quedar
keeper, conserje
kettle, caldera
kick-off, to, sacar
kick up a row, to, armar
'kids' (children), chaval
kill, to, matar, muerto, ultimado
kind, atento (v. COURTESY)
kitchen, cocina
knife-grinder, afilador
knife-wound, -azo
knit, to, punto
knock into, to, chocar
knock, to, llamar
know, to, conocer, saber
know, as you, ya
know?, How should I, saber
know, not to, ignorar
know, to get to, concocer
know, to let (someone),
  participar
know what's going on, tanto
**'know' (wisdom before the
  event),** ya, estar

L

lack, to, falta
ladder (stocking), carrera, correr
'Ladies and Gentlemen', público
landlord, dueño
'lane' (highway), pista, canal
language, idioma
lantern-slide (v. LECTURES)
lanyap, ñapa
last, otro
last night, anoche
late, to be, llegar
lately, recién
later, luego
laudable, plausible
laughing, to burst out, echar
lavatory, baño
lawn, césped

layabout, vago
lazy, vago
lead (pencil), mina
lead (a life), to, llevar
leading note, sensible
leak, escape, fuga, salir,
  trascendencia
leak-proof, pila
leap, salto
learned, culto, ilustrado
lease, to, arrendar, alquilar
leave, to, abandonar, ir, marchar
leave off, to, dejar
leave go, to, soltar
leave (of absence), feria, permiso,
  licencia
lecture, conferencia, dictar (v.
  also LECTURES)
left, to be, quedar, sobrar
leg (furniture), pata
leg, to pull someone's, pelo
lend, to, dejar
lend a hand, to, echar
lesbian, torta
less, menos
less and less, vez
lessen, to, atenuar
let, to, dejar
let go of, to, soltar
let somebody down, to, defraudar
let somebody have, to, facilitar
let somebody know, to, participar
letter, carta
letter (of alphabet), letra, molde
library, (librería)
licence-plate, matrícula, placa,
  chapa
lid, tapa
lie, to, caer
lie down, to, echar
lieu, in, lugar
lift/elevator, elevador
lift, to give a, aventón
light, fuego, luz
light, to, fuego
light-blue, celeste
lighter, yesquero
like, así, como, estar, tal
like, more, mejor
like, to, apreciar, querer,

agradar, cariño
like, to be, parecer
like, to be just, ver
like, to feel, gana
like, to look, lucir, parecer, sonar
likely, indicado
likewise, igualmente
liking, cariño
line, raya
line (queue), cola
links (golf), cancha
liquor, trago
list, relación, ficha
Listen!, oír
little, chico, poco
living, to earn a, dedicarse
living-room, estancia, living
loaf, molde
loafer, vago
'local', the (pub), boliche
local, nacional, local, lugareño, tópico
location, ubicación, paradero
lock, chapa
lock, to, echar
lodger, huésped, pensionista, inquilino
long, largo
long and the short of, concretar, efectivamente
long as, so, tal
longer, no, dejar, ya
'loo', baño
look, to (appear), lucir, parecer, pinta, cara, ver, como
look after, to, atender
look as if, to, ver
look at, to have a, vistar, echar, ver
look for, to, buscar
look forward to, to, ilusión, perspectiva
look of things, by the, parecer, como
look-out point, mirador
loose (clothes), flojo
loose leaf, soltar
'loose' (liquids), granel, soltar
lose one's way, to, despistar
lot, a, cantidad

lot to do, to have a, falta
lottery, polla, jugar
loud, (alto), fuerte
lousy, asqueroso
lovable, amable
love, to, querer
lovely, precioso, lindo
loving, cariño
**luck, (desgracia), destino, ñapa
luck, with any, mejor
lump, pedazo
lump sum, suma
lunch, comida
lust, lujuria
**luxury, (lujuria)
lying-in-state, ardiente

M

machine, máquina, -dora
mad, loco
maddening, barbaridad
made up of, to be, integrar
maiden name, apellido
mail, to, echar
'make' (brand), marca
make, to (render), dar, poner
make out, to, extender
make the most of, to, aprovechar
make up for, to, recuperar
make up, to, integrar, confección
make use of, to, aprovechar, disponer
make widely known, to, divulgar
male nurse, practicante
malign, to, perjuicio
manage (to), to, alcance, conseguir, procurar, tirar, (manejar)
management, gerencia
mango, mango
manifest, notorio
manner(s), educación, formal, cursi
**mantelpiece, (estante)
manure, abono
many, not, poco
mark, to (take heed), advertir
mark (papers), to, calificar
marks (distinguishing), señas

occurrence, suceso, (ocurrencia)
odd, extraño, raro, extravagante
-odd, pico, tanto
odds, makes no, igual, mismo
odometer, odómetro
off, to head, aparte
offend, to, feo
offer, to, brindar
off-hand, (formal), (casual)
office, oficina
off-print, aparte
often, frecuencia, vez
oh!, oh!
oil, aceite
O.K., adelante, valer
O.K. thing, the, ver
old?, how, tiempo
old-fashioned, (modo)
older, mayor
omelette, (torta)
on purpose, propósito
once, vez
once, at, ahorita, tiro, antualito
   (*Co*)
one for the road, estribo
one-way, dirección, mano
only, más, sólo, faltar, único
only!, If, ojalá
open, to (parcel), deshacer
operate, to, manejar
opinion, concepto, decir,
   cambiar
opinion, in my, decir, parecer
opportunity, oportunidad,
   chance
opposite, frente
option, remedio
oration, (oración)
order, orden
order, first in, primordial
order, to, mandar
order to, in, motivo
order, to put in, condiciones
order, in working, condiciones
ordinary, corriente, regular,
   siempre, (ordinario)
organized, to get, gestionar,
   arreglar
other people, demás
out, -side, fuera

out of town, fuera
outing, paseo
outlook, perspectiva
outrageous, disparate, vergüenza
outskirts, afueras
outstanding, destacado
outstanding (bill), saldo
over there, allá
overdo, to, exagerar, abusar
overhaul, ajuste (*Me*)
overheads, gastos
overlook, to, cuenta
overriding, primordial
overtake, to, adelantar, rebasar
overtop, to, rebasar
overturn, derramar
owing to, motivo
own, very, mero (*Me*)
owner, dueño

P

pack, to, empacar, meter
pack/packet, cajetilla, bolsa
'pad', to, paja
pad (writing), block
paid, to get, cobrar
pail, balde
pain, dolor
paintbrush (brocha)
pal, cuate (*Me*)
panties, bragas
paper (exam), materia
paper (news), diario
paragraph, aparte
Pardon me!, *v.* COURTESY
parenthesis, paréntesis
parents, padre
parlour, living, sala
parson, (ministro)
part in, to take, intervenir,
   papel
partial to, partidario
particular, (particular),
   determinado
parting (hair), raya
part(s), (plieza), accesorio
party, fiesta, formal, juerga,
   partido
pass, to, rebasar, adelantar,

potato, papa, francesa
pot-hole, (agujero)
potter, to, entretenerse
pound, libra
pour out, to, echar, (derramar)
powder, polvo
powder-room, baño, excusado
practically, siquiera
praises, to sing the, celebrar
praiseworthy, plausible
prayer, oración
precise(ly), preciso, concreto
prefer, to, preferir
pregnant, embarazada
prejudice, (perjuicio)
premises, local
preoccupation, preocuparse
prescription, receta
present, actual, (presente), curso
present, for the, pronto
present, to be, asistir, estar
present, to give a, regalar
pretend, to, (pretender)
pretentious, cursi
pretty, bonito, guapo, lindo
pretty (fig.), bastante
previous, antes, otro
priest, cura
prime, primary, primordial
print (engraving), estampa
priority, top, primordial
private, particular
probably, mejor
problem, cuestión, problema
procedure, gestionar
proceed, to, seguir
process, to, procesar
procure, procurarse
produce, to, rendir, dar
professor, (profesor)
profit, provecho
progress, to make, cundir, adelantar
progress, in, curso
promise, to, comprometer
promote, to, adelantar
prompt, pronto
proprietor, dueño
prosecute, to, sancionar, procesar

prospect, esperanza, perspectiva
prospectus, prospecto
prove, to, resultar, verificar
proverb, refrán
provide, to, proporcionar
provoke, to, provocar, pulla
P.S. (postscript), dato
public, público
publish, to, editar
pudding, (budín)
pull, to, jalar
pull out, to, sacar, tirar
pull someone's leg, to, pelo
pump, bomba
punctual, punto, cumplir, (alrededor)
pupil, (pupilo)
pure, mero
purify, to, (apurar)
purpose, motivo, propósito
purpose, on, propósito
purser's office, comisaría
pursue, to, perseguir, dedicarse
push,   to   (fig.),   adelantar, preferirse
put in, to, meter
put in place, to, colocar
put on, to, poner
put one's foot in it, to, pata
put oneself forward, to, preferirse
put right, to, arreglar, condición
put through to, (v. TELEPHONES)
put together, to, armar
put up with, to, aguantar, soportar
puzzle (crossword), crucigrama

Q

qualifications, (calificaciones), colegiado
qualify, to, (calificar)
quarter (city), barrio, urbanización
quay, muelle
'queer', maricón, cajetilla (*R/P*)
quench, to, echar
question, cuestión

sanitary towel, paño, gasa
satiated, harto
satisfactory, adecuado
saucepan, olla
sausage, chorizo
say(s), según
say!, I, oír
say!, I'll, ya
say, that's to, decir, ser
say!, You don't, decir, ser
saying, refrán
saying, it goes without, preciso
scandal, escándalo, vergüenza
scare, to, susto
'scene', escándalo
schedule, cédula
school, escolar
scope, alcance, envergadura
scoundrel, vergüenza
scour, to (lit.), fregar
'scour', to (fig.), correr
'screw', to, fregar, chingar, polvo
screwdriver, desarmar
scribble, -pad, borrar
script (lettering), molde
scrub, to, fregar
seal (documents), sello
search, to, buscar, registrar
season-ticket, abono
seat, localidad
second-hand shop, bazar
secretary, secretaria
'see', to (like the blind man),
   caer, ya
see-if-one-can-get, to, buscar
see!, Let's, ver
seeing that, como
see off, to, despedir
see to, to, atender
see you, I'll (cards), querer
seem, to, parecer
segregate, to, aparte
seize, to, coger, agarrar
seldom, vez
self-, auto-
self-defeating, contraproducente
self-denial, (negar)
self-important, pedante
self-indulgent, regodeón
self-same, mismo

self-service, auto-
self-starter, arranque
semi-colon, punto
send, to (errand), mandar
send off, to, despedir, expedir
senior, mayor
sense, sentido
sensible, lógico, sensato
sensitive, sensible
sentence, oración, sentencia
separate, soltar, aparte
separately, aparte, soltar
serenade, mañanitas (*Me*)
serene, (calma)
servant, asistente, empleado
service (tennis), sacar
service (religious), culto
'set' (china, linen, etc.), juego
set out, to, exponer
setting, marco
settle, to, arreglar, echar, quedar
settle, to (details), precisar
settle for, to, quedar(se)
settle, to (in a place), ubicarse
settlement (account), liquidación
several, varios
shameful, desgracia, vergüenza
shame!, What a, pena, vergüenza
shanty, rancho, barraca
shanty-towns, suburbios
shape, forma
share (capital), inversión
share out, to, repartir
sharp (punctual), punto
sharpen, to, afilador
shatter, to, polvo
sheer, mero, puro
shelf, estante
shell, concha
sherry, jerez, manzanilla
shift (duty), turno
shine, to, lucir
shit, mierda, cagar, leche
shock, choque, impresión, susto
shoe-shine, limpiabotas, bolero
shoot, to, tirar, disparar
shop, almacén
shop assistant, dependiente
shopping, compras
shopping bag, bolsa, canasta

sound like, to, parecer, sonar
spacious, amplio
Spaniards, gringo, coño
spare, reserva, sobrar
speak, to, hablar (*v.* also
   TELEPHONES)
speech, discurso
spill, to, derramar
'spin', paseo
spine, espina
spit (skewer), brocha
splice, empalme
spoil, to, echar, estropear
spoil, to (children), mimar,
   engreír
spokesman, portavoz
sponge-cake, bizcocho
sponsor, to, auspiciar
sportsfield, campo, cancha
spot, to have a soft, partidario
spouse, esposo
spout, pico
spread, to, cundir, extender,
   trascendencia
spree, to go on, juerga
spring, muelle
springiness, resorte
spunk, leche
squeamish, to be, reparar
stamp (postage), sello, estampa
stand (e.g. bookstand), estante
stand, to, parar
stand (tolerate), aguantar,
   soportar
stand up, to, incorporarse, parar
stand a drink, to, brindar,
   convidar
stand still, to, parar
standard(s), norma
'start' (shock), susto, repente
start . . ., to, echar
start again, to, volver, resumir
start up, to (cars), arrancar
state, lying in, ardiente
station waggon, rural
stature, complexión
stay, estancia
stay, to, quedar
steal, to, sustraer
steep, brusco

steering-wheel, dirección,
   volante
stein (mug), chop, tarro
stencil, cliché
step forward, a great, salto
steps, to take, gestionar,
   procurar, medidas, trámite
sterile, calma
stewardess, azafata
stick, to, pegar
still (do/have/etc.), to, seguir
stimulants, excitar(se)
stint (of duty), turno
stir, revolver
stockings, medias
stomach, empty, ayunas
stone (fruit), hueso
stool, banqueta
stool, to go to, (cagar)
stop, parada
stop, to, dejar
stopper, tapa
storeroom, almacén, depósito
storey, piso
storm, tormenta
stove, cocina
straight, derecho
strange, extraño, raro
straw, paja
straw, the last, falta
streetcar, tren
street-corner, esquina, bocacalle
stretch, alcanzar, dar
strike a chord, to, sonar
strike (industrial), holgar
string, cuerda
stroke, golpe
stroke (on typewriter), barra
stroll, paseo
strong-minded, carácter
strung, highly, nervioso
stuck-up, sobrar, engreír
stud (road), tope (*Me*)
study, to, cursar
stupendous, estupendo
stupid, tontería, imbécil, simple
suave, (suave)
subject, argumento, cuestión,
   materia, sujeto
submit, to, condescender, sujetar

tease, to, meterse, vacilar, pelo, pulla (*Me*)
teeny-weeny, chico
telephone exchange, central, conmutador
tell, to, que, determinar
temper, -ament, genio
temperature, calentura
tempt, to, provocar
tenant, inquilino
tent, carpa
terrible, barbaridad
'terrific', barbaridad, brutal, estupendo, chévere (*C/A*), máximo (*Me*), mecate (*Me*), hacha (*Sp*)
textile, (fábrica)
Thank goodness!, menos
thanks to, intermedio
that, (este)
That's right!, eso, andar
then, luego
theory, hipótesis
there, allá, ahí
there?, Is anyone (oír)
there is/are, hay
thereabouts, alrededor, así
therefore, luego, así, total
'they', quien
thin, flaco
thing, a good, cuenta, convenir
thing, to do the right, cumplir, ver
thing!, What a . . . (adj.) . . ., más
thingummybob, chisme
think, to, pensar
think, I, decir
think so, I, parecer
think up, to, idear
this/that, este
thou, tú, vos
thoughtful, atento, solicitar
thrilling, emocionar
through, incluso
through, to go, traspasar
through (agency of), intermedio
throw, to, echar, arrojar
throw away, to, arrojar, botar, tirar

throw a party, to, festejar (*L/A*)
thumb-tack, chinche
thunderstorm, tormenta
thus, así, modo
ticket, billete, boleto, entrada
ticket-collector, guarda, controlador
ticket-office/window, boleto
tie down, to, sujetar
tie up, to, amarrar, apretar
tight, to hold, sujetar
tighten, to, apretar
tight-rope, flojo
tiles, to go on the, juerga
'time', a, vez
time (telling the), (para)
tin/can, bote, lata
tiny, menudo
tip (gratuity), ñapa
tire/tyre, cubierta
tired, descanso
title, título
toady, barba (*Me*), coba (*Me*), engreír
toast, to (health), brindar
together (with), como, junto
toil, tarea, laburo (*R/P*)
'toilet', baño
tolerate, to, aguantar, soportar
toll (on motorway), cuota
Tom, Dick and Harry, Fulano
tomato, jitomate
tone down, to, atenuar, (calificar)
tongue, (idioma)
tongue, to hold one's, callarse
tonight, (anoche)
'tons', montón, granel, sobrar
too bad, paciencia (*R/P*), ni (*Me*)
too much/many, abusar, exagerar, sobrar, demasiado
toothbrush, brocha
top, to, rebasar
top, on, encima
top gear, directa
topical, (tópico)
torment, (tormenta)
toss up, to, echar
total, suma
totality, integridad

touch, to, tocar
tough guy, guapo
town-planning, urbanización
town square, zócalo
toyshop, bazar
track, pista, canal, huella
track, off the, despistar
track down, to, ubicar
trade (skill), (oficina)
trade-name, marca
traffic, circulación, tránsito
train, tren
training, formación
tram, tren
transfer, to, trasladar, traspasar
trash-can, balde, desperdiciar
travel widely, to, recorrer
treat, to, convidar
treat of, to, tratar
tremendous, tamaño
trespass, to, (traspasar)
trestle table, tabla
trick, not to miss a, estar
trifle, pudín
trim, to, recortar
triplets, (cuate)
triumphantly, (realizar)
trouble, molestar, pena, problema
true, cierto, verdad, verificar, caso
trumps, (pinta)
trustworthy, confianza
try, a, tentativa
try, to, intentar, tratar, procurar, pretender
try, to (law), procesar
try-and-find, to, buscar
try, doesn't, rendir
try out, to, probar
'tumble' to, to, caer, ya
tumbler, vaso
turn, to, volver
turn into, to, convertirse
turn out, to, resultar, salir, llegar
turn out badly, to, cebarse
turn (things) over, to, remover
turn round, to, dar, retorno, revolver

turn, to be one's, corresponder, tocar, turno
turning (street), bocacalle, esquina
turnpike, autopista, cuota
twins, cuate
twirp, bestia, imbécil, pendejo
type, to, pasar
type, tipo
typewriter, máquina
tyre, caucho, cubierta

U

ugly, feo
um . . ., este
umpire, árbitro
umpteen, pico, tanto
un-, poco
unabashed, alterar
unassailable, inobjetable
unaware, ignorar
uncertain, precario, voluble
under- (done, etc.), poco
underdeveloped, retrasar
understand, to, caer, enterarse, explicarse
understanding (adj.), comprensivo
understate, -ment, atenuar
undertake, to, comprometer
undistinguished, discreto
undo, to, deshacer, desarmar
undoubtedly, caber, seguro
uneasy, inquieto, (excitarse)
unfortunate, -ly, desgracia, lamentar
unhealthy, insano
unimpeachable, inobjetable
uninterested, preocuparse
unique, único
unlucky, desgracia
unmoved, alterar
unpopular, ver
unpredictable, precario
unreliable, (formal)
unscrupulous, caradura
untrue, (cierto)
unusual, extraño, raro
unwillingly, grado

unwise, contraproducente
unworried, preocuparse
up-and-about, alto
up-and-down (roads), accidentado
up to, hasta
up to him/her, etc., allá
up-side-down, revés
upbringing, educación
upheaval, jaleo
uphill, costa
uproar, jaleo
upset, disgustar, alterar
upstage, término
urinal, baño
usage, acepción
use, to, aprovechar, gastar, usar
used for, to be, servir
use of, to make, aprovechar, (usar), disponer
useless, (servir)
useless, worse than, contraproducente
usual, siempre, corriente, regular
usually, soler
utmost, sumo

V

vacation, feria, licencia (*R/P*), permiso, puente
vacillating, voluble
vague, (vago)
valid, valer
valuable, apreciable, (precioso)
vanilla ice-cream, mantecado
various, (varios)
vase, (vaso)
vast, extenso
vent, to give, curso
verdict, sentencia
verify, to, (verificar)
very (adj.), mero, mismo, preciso
very, not, poco
vice versa, revés
view, (prospecto), mirador
villa, quinta
villager, (lugareño)
violent, (violento)
V.I.P., categoría

virtually, siquiera
visit, to, conocer
vital, imprescindible, trascendencia
voluble, (voluble)
vomit, to, arrojar, trasbocar
vulgar, (vulgar)

W

wages, sueldo, gajes
waiter, -tress, camerero, garzón
wait for, to, esperar
'wake', velatorio
walk, to, andar, caminar, estar, paseo
walk up, to, subir
wallet, cartera
wander-plug, banana
wangle, trampa
want, to, querer, falta
ward, pupilo
warden, conserje
warehouse, almacén
warn, to, advertir, avisar, prevenir
warning, without, pronto
warrant, cédula, título, merecer
wash up, to, fregar
wash-basin, pila
wash-out, fracaso
waste, to, desperdiciar, (gastar), (perder)
waste away, to, extenuar
waste(paper) basket, papel
waste time, to, perder, gastar
watch (shift), turno
watchman, guachimán, guarda
waterfall, salto
waver, to, vacilar
way, acá, mano, dirección, sentido
way (fig.), forma, modo, así, plan
way, by the, propósito
way, in the, sobrar (*v.* also COURTESY)
way, on his, estar
way, to find one's, ubicar
way, to give, ceder